CW00410841

INSIGHT

Tuscany

APA PUBLICATIONS

Part of the Langenscheidt Publishing Group

L

ABOUT THIS BOOK

Editorial
Project Editor
Barbara Balletto
Managing Editor
Emily Hatchwell
Editorial Director
Brian Bell

Distribution
UK & Ireland
GeoCenter International Ltd
The Viables Centre
Harrow Way
Basingstoke
Hants RG22 4BJ
Fax: (44) 1256-817988

United States
Langenscheidt Publishers, Inc.
46–35 54th Road
Maspeth, NY 11378
Fax: (718) 784-0640

Worldwide
APA Publications GmbH & Co.
Verlag KG (Singapore branch)
38 Joo Koon Road
Singapore 628990
Tel: (65) 865-1600
Fax: (65) 861-6438

Printing
Insight Print Services (Pte) Ltd
38 Joo Koon Road
Singapore 628990
Tel: (65) 865-1600
Fax: (65) 861-6438

© 1998 APA Publications GmbH & Co.
Verlag KG (Singapore branch)
All Rights Reserved
First Edition 1991
Third Edition 1998

CONTACTING THE EDITORS
Although every effort is made to
provide accurate information in
this publication, we live in a
fast-changing world and would
appreciate it if readers would
call our attention to any errors or
outdated information that may
occur by writing to us at:
Insight Guides, P.O. Box 7910,
London SE1 8ZB, England.
Fax: (44 171) 620-1074.
e-mail:
insight@apaguide.demon.co.uk

The Stendhal syndrome – with
its peculiar symptoms of
fainting and ectasy at the sight
of overwhelming beauty – are
hazards for anyone writing about
Tuscany. The authors of *Insight
Guide: Tuscany* have produced a
book which may allow visitors to
share a similar experience.

How to use this book

Insight Guides have a well-proven
formula of informative and well-
written text paired with a fresh
photojournalistic approach. The
books are carefully structured,
both to convey a better understanding of each place and its
culture, and to guide readers
through its myriad attractions:
◆ The first section, with a yellow
colour bar, covers the region's
rich **history** and lively modern
culture in authoritative **features**
written by experts.
◆ The main **Places** section, with
a blue bar, provides a run-down
of all the places worth seeing.
Places of major interest are
cross-referenced by numbers or

An alluring Tuscan panorama

letters to specially commissioned full-colour maps.

◆ The **Travel Tips** section at the back of the book offers recommendations on travel, hotels and restaurants, as well as an Italian phrasebook. Information may be located quickly by using the index printed on the back cover flap, which can also serve as a bookmark.

◆ Photographs are chosen not only to illustrate the geography of Tuscany and the beauty of its towns and villages, but also to convey the atmosphere.

The Contributors

Building on previous editions edited by **Rosemary Bailey**, this brand new edition was edited by **Barbara Balletto**, an Italophile who gave birth to a new son, Luca, just as the book was going to press. **Lisa Gerard-Sharp**, who is very knowledgeable about all things Tuscan, from Etruscan grave-robbing to the social habits of the modern populace, contributed to the original book and wrote new sections on *Wild Tuscany*, *Tuscan Architecture* and *Crafts*. **Christopher Catling** helped expand the historical chapters, enhancing the fine section devoted to the Renaissance by **Russell Chamberlin**. **Valentina Harris** and **Maureen Ashley** describe the very considerable pleasures of Tuscan food and wine respectively.

Nicky Swallow, who lives in Florence, checked the facts on the ground, helping to bring up to date the provincial chapters written by a team including Gerard-Sharp, Bailey and Chamberlin, plus **Marco de Stefani Paul Duncan**, **Lorella Grossi**, **Susan Zucker** and **Yvonne Newman**. The Travel Tips section, originally compiled by **Gabriella Ferranti**, was also expanded.

The principal photographers were **George Taylor**, **Guglielmo Galvin**, **Patrizia Giancotti** and **Albano Guatti**.

Thanks go to **Mary Morton** for proofreading and indexing the book and also to **Jeff Evans** for putting Travel Tips in order, while **Sylvia Suddes** and **Tanvir Virdee** in the Insight Guides office pulled the whole lot into shape.

Map Legend

— ·· —	International Boundary
— —	Regional Boundary
– – –	Province Boundary
·•·	National Park/Reserve
– – –	Ferry Route
✈	Airport International / Regional
🚌	Bus Station
P	Parking
❶	Tourist Information
✉	Post Office
♰	Church / Ruins
†	Monastery
☪	Mosque
✡	Synagogue
♜	Castle / Ruins
∴	Archaeological Site
∩	Cave
★	Statue / Monument
1	Place of Interest

The main places of interest in the Places section are coordinated by number with a full-colour map (e.g. ❶), and a symbol at the top of every right-hand page tells you where to find the map.

CONTENTS

Carrara girls
enjoying the
summer
holidays

Travel Tips

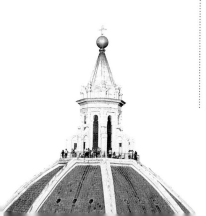

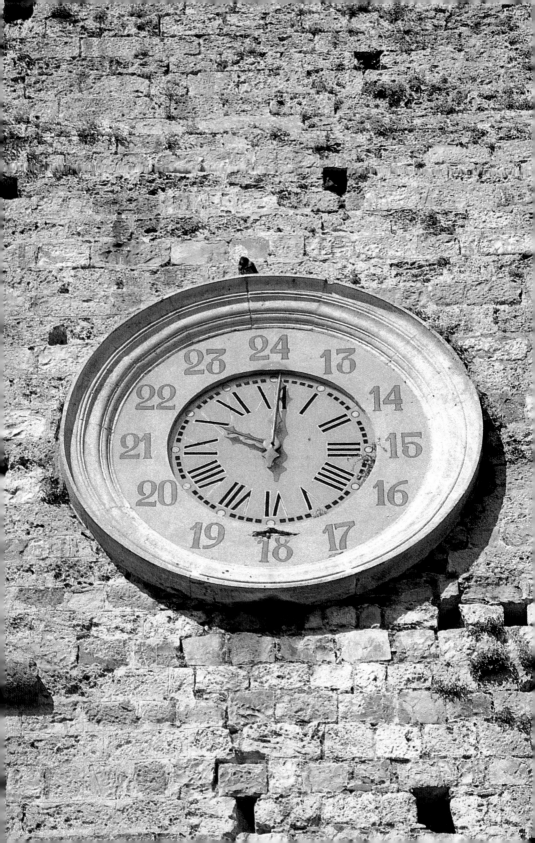

THE TUSCAN MIRACLE

Birthplace of the Renaissance, a strong tradition of village life, a picturesque countryside: these factors and more contribute to the enigma that is Tuscany

From the top of a village tower the Tuscan landscape lies below: the most civilised rural scene on Earth. Yet driving through southern Tuscany at night there is little sense of civilisation, still less of domesticity – even farm animals are kept indoors.

In the distance, a succession of small lights trail across the black countryside: tenuous links with separate, inward-looking communities. The spaces in between are remote, uncivilised. The blackness and emptiness of the countryside go back to medieval times and beyond; the "Tuscan miracle" only illuminates the cities.

The novelist D.H. Lawrence described Tuscany as where "men had been at their intensest, most naked pitch, here at the end of the old world and the beginning of the new". To Florentines, Michelangelo's *David* is the symbol of the ancient republic and the epitome of their own character. *David* is not just a study in naked intensity, but an awkward new spirit, struggling to be born out of marble. Emilio Pucci, the aristocratic fashion designer, used to visit *David* for inspiration.

In giving birth to the Renaissance, Tuscany designed the modern world. In his painting, Giotto projected Tuscany into space. Brunelleschi crowned space with his Florentine dome, the greatest feat of Renaissance engineering.

Naked beauty

In the Carmine frescoes, Masaccio peopled space with recognisably human figures. His *Expulsion from Paradise* reveals Adam and Eve in all their naked beauty. Gone is the medieval coyness; present is the palpable suffering of a couple who have lost everything. Even Michelangelo's version in Rome's Sistine Chapel does not plumb such tragic depths.

The Tuscan miracle, however, is not a frozen

PRECEDING PAGES: bullfighters in Siena's Campo; spiralling hysteria at the *Palio*; the band takes a break; Chianti grape harvest. LEFT: timeless timepiece. RIGHT: the anguish of Adam and Eve in Masaccio's *Expulsion from Paradise*.

Renaissance portrait but a living procession of Tuscans at ease with their artistic setting and identity. Tuscans do have an innate aesthetic sense but the Tuscan tapestry is a rich weave which has been created by many different threads. Literary Tuscany is a strand which can be clearly traced through Boccaccio and Pet-

rarch. Dante's verses adorn many Florentine walls and Tuscan squares. Republican Tuscany is best glimpsed through its fortified town halls while humanist Tuscany is enshrined in poetry, sculpture and art, the fruits of patronage and craftsmanship.

Aristocratic Tuscany still lingers in Medici palaces, villas and sculptured gardens, as well as the ancestral homes of the Rucellai, Corsini and Frescobaldi. Bourgeois Tuscany parades along Florence's Via Tornabuoni, patronises the arts and restores family farms.

Peasant Tuscany traditionally takes a little of everything from the land: game, beans, chestnut flour, unsalted bread, olive oil, and, of course, the grapes needed to make Chianti and Brunello. Tuscan cuisine combines proportion and variety. Like the Tuscans themselves, it is of good peasant stock. Variety is also the secret of Tuscany's townscapes: from medieval hilltop towns to Etruscan villages; from *fin de siècle* spa towns to sophisticated mountain resorts; from the splendour of a Renaissance cathedral to a stark Romanesque church.

Architecturally, the cities are microcosms of all periods. Etruscan Maremma fades to Romanesque Pisa; Gothic Siena to medieval San Gimignano; and Renaissance Florence to Grand Ducal Chianti.

McCarthy noted: "The peculiar beauty of the Tuscan landscape is the combination of husbandry with an awesome and elemental majesty and silence; the olives' silver and the various greens of the growing crops appear an embroidered veil on a wilderness of bare geology."

With few exceptions, it is foreign poets who dwell on the cultivated tranquillity of corn, olives and vines. Tuscans are historically wary of space, preferring a safe, tribal existence in small towns to an alien, romantic notion of the countryside.

Ambrogio Lorenzetti's *Città sul mare*, the first known European landscape painting,

Nature tamed

The natural landscape is powerful, stretching from Carrara marble quarries to Maremma wilderness; from Livorno's rugged coastline to the mountainous Casentino. Much of the land appears tamed: the Chianti hills, the Mugello valley and "the Arno swirling past with its usual coffee-coloured foam" (Virginia Woolf).

Wooded Monte Amiata and the Sienese moon craters reveal another truth. Etruscans cultivated the land, Tuscans have tried to civilise it and foreigners romanticise it. A deep relationship with the land has always been present but it does not imply an ease with the land, still less a mastery. As the American writer Mary

depicts an elaborate walled city against an austere backdrop. *Good Government*, the Sienese masterpiece, is idealistic in its portrayal of a cheerful, busy countryside. The pillaging and looting in *Bad Government* look infinitely more convincing. The "Tuscan miracle" therefore is, surprisingly, urban.

Given an urban heritage going back over two and a half millennia, Tuscany, even by Italian standards, is highly civilised. Tuscans prefer living in large villages or small towns today, echoing the Etruscan ideal, which was confirmed by the rural perils of medieval Europe.

Etruscan cities were conceived of as entities, settlements carved out of the countryside, never mere urban sprawl. When the civilisation disappeared, its imprint remained strong enough for D.H. Lawrence to record: "Because a fool kills a nightingale with a stone, is he therefore greater than the nightingale? Not he! Rome fell, and the Roman phenomenon with it. Italy today is far more Etruscan in its bones than Roman, and always will be."

This elegy is borne out by modern and medieval "Etruscans". Tuscans apparently feel no guilt about acquiring Etruscan treasures from local tombs. A family's ill-

Each town was a small state with its own land, local government and traditions.

In claiming an urban identity, even small villages still feel like towns today and consider themselves as such. *Città* is a perception of status, not size. Battles for independence have reinforced but not forged this cultural identity: it was always there.

The secret of Tuscan identity lies in each town's sense of completeness. Tuscan towns go against the current of modern homogeneity and internationalism; Florence

gotten Etruscan urns are treasured ancestral relics, valued above Roman coins. And it was Etruscan settlements, not Roman grids, that provided the framework for the Tuscan townscape and identity.

In medieval Lucca and Florence, nobles were often obliged to spend part of the year in town in order to instil a sense of belonging to something bigger than a war-mongering tribe. The ideal of *civiltà*, or urban identity, extended from the largest city-state to the smallest town.

LEFT: Tuscans prefer a safe, tribal existence in small towns, like Cortona.
ABOVE: cultivated tranquillity of corn, olives and vines.

is becoming more Florentine and Siena more Sienese. The town opens inwards to its inhabitants; everybody shares in its traditions and is regenerated. In the large cities this identity is maintained against enormous odds. Great passion and pride is attached to local traditions: to a Sienese bank manager, his role in the annual *Palio* may be more important than his career. *Campanilismo* (provincialism: literally, loyalty to one's own bell-tower) is a longer-held, deeper faith and guarantees a future to local saints.

The Tuscan miracle is rooted in the Tuscans' sense of place, family and craftsmanship. Olive Hamilton, speaking of a Lucchese, said: "It does not surprise a Tuscan that a chemist in our small town has written a two-volume work on the region from early Etruscan times." In this sense, particularly, Tuscans are highly cultured.

Dante and Petrarch excluded, Tuscany is steeped in visual rather than in literary traditions; art is the natural expression of identity. The full power and disturbing truthfulness of the art is the mystery of the miracle. The "Tuscan miracle" is more than the sum of its artistic parts. Even the notion of the "Tuscan artist" is a geographical expression, an outsider's label for Florentine, Pisan, Pistoian or Sienese artists. It is meaningless to compare Giotto's early

Renaissance belltower in Florence with the Romanesque leaning tower of Pisa.

As for art, Ambrogio Lorenzetti's wall frescoes show medieval Sienese chivalry while the *Macchiaioli* Impressionists paint a coherent picture of 19th-century Livorno. Even within Renaissance art, diversity is the norm. Piero della Francesca's mystical frescoes in Arezzo echo Masaccio's naturalistic Florentine frescoes: yet the alternative approaches of mysticism and realism represent the yin and yang of Renaissance art.

In Tuscany, the gap between an artist and an artisan is smaller than elsewhere in the world.

A TUSCAN HALL OF FAME

From medieval times right through to the modern age, Tuscans have made a significant impact on the world as we know it today. Familiar to many are the names from the world of art, including Giotto, Leonardo da Vinci, Michelangelo, Donatello, Masaccio and Cellini – all of whom were born either in or near Florence.

Arezzo-born Giorgio Vasari was also a painter, but he became better known as an art historian and author of the much-read *Lives of the Artists*. The realm of Tuscan literature also includes Italy's three most famous writers: Dante, Petrarch and Boccaccio (who was born in Paris but actually raised in Florence).

Tuscany was home to astronomer Galileo, the philosopher Machiavelli, architect Brunelleschi and Amerigo Vespucci, the merchant-turned-explorer after whom the American continent is named.

The operatic composer Puccini hailed from Lucca, while opera itself was born in Florence in the late 16th century. Even the familiar piano has its roots here, invented by a Florentine in 1710.

In modern times, the most famous names associated with Tuscany tend to come from the world of fashion: Emilio Pucci, Guccio Gucci and Salvatore Ferragamo – the latter actually a transplanted Neopolitan.

To a picture restorer in Arezzo or to a weaver in Prato, the distinction is irrelevant. Adamo, the chief wine taster with Contessa Contucci's family firm, considers that after 30 years of drinking Vino Nobile he is both a master craftsman and an unsurpassed artist. Tuscan virtues are many, but they do not include modesty.

Questi primitivi is a term often applied to foreigners, southerners and Sardinians, in increasing order of scorn. During World War II, the American art historian Bernard Berenson was rebuked by a Florentine manicurist whose help he was seeking: "*O Signore, per noi tutti gli stranieri sono ugualmente odiosi*" ("Oh, Sir, for us all foreigners are equally hateful").

Chauvinism aside, Tuscans are polite, expect politeness in return and often criticise another Tuscan for being *mal educato*. If in doubt about what to say, such blandishments as "*è un posto meraviglioso*" ("it's a wonderful place") can be used indiscriminately, even in Livorno's mosquito-infested swamps, industrial Poggibonsi or in the aptly-named Scrufiano.

A direct appeal to local pride can lead to unexpected gifts: the chance to meet Signor Parenti's "unique" donkey, "the only one within Florence's city walls", or to visit an abbey normally closed to the public.

"*Fare bella figura*", literally "looking good" or "making a good impression", stresses the importance of "face", which is a Tuscan's image in the community. Appearances are a touchstone of civilised behaviour. Indigenous Etruscan looks can be found in the streets of Chiusi or Volterra, "the full dark eyes, the pointed beard, long inquisitive nose and the Mona Lisa smile of a terracotta tomb figure" in the words of the English travel writer H.V. Morton. Tuscan looks are the product of perfect genetic engineering. classic Medici; luminous Sienese; austere Masaccio.

Linguistic rivals

The "pure" Tuscan dialect has helped in giving disparate towns a regional identity and national status. Modern Italian is the Tuscan dialect. Florence and Siena rival each other in claims for linguistic "purity", thus proving that city-state superiority is thriving.

LEFT: picking olives, as pictured by a 15th-century artist. **RIGHT:** shepherd near Chiusi: peasant Tuscany takes a little of everything from the land.

Tuscans reveal themselves in their language. The Florentine proverb "*Uomo senza roba è una pecora senza lana*" ("A man without clothes is like a sheep without wool") indicates both the importance of appearance and medieval Tuscany's original source of wealth. Tuscan includes colourful oaths such as "*porca miseria*" ("holy pork") and "*per cortesia*", an expression of great civility.

An old saying confirms innate Tuscan wariness: "Keep away from sick doctors, dogs that don't bark, men that don't speak, people who go to mass twice a day and quarrels with those who are bigger than you are."

Certain images of the Tuscan miracle remain. *Città sul mare*, the city as bastion against the darkness; and, in Pienza, the *civiltà* that led a Tuscan Pope to construct a palace around a view, the first time the concept of a view entered European architecture. Two images of people interlock: the modern Tuscan holding her jewellery like a religious relic and the ancient Etruscans, echoing through the centuries like the names of their own lost gods. While watching oxen slowly pulling a plough through olive groves and vineyards, the art scholar Bernard Berenson recorded "a feeling that I was looking at what has been going on ever since civilisation began". ❏

FOREIGN WRITERS IN TUSCANY

Authors and poets have long been fascinated with Tuscany, and it is partly from their words that the world's vision of the region has been formed

In the words of Dr Johnson, "a man who has not been to Italy is always conscious of inferiority." But many English writers had already beaten Dr Johnson to Florence. In 1737, Sir Horace Mann, Minister to the Grand Ducal Court, announced: "If I could afford it, I really would take a villa near Florence but I am afraid of it becoming a cheesecake house for all the English."

A century later, *Inglese* was a generic term for all foreigners. A hotel porter might say: "Some *Inglesi* have arrived but I don't yet know whether they are Russian or German." Given the hordes of foreign writers in Tuscany, the manager might have welcomed Dickens, Dostoyevsky, Goethe or Heine – all of whom, at one time or another, were inspired by their travels through the region.

The poet Shelley pronounced Tuscany a "paradise of exiles" tempted by art, adventure and escape from persecution. But the exiles' motives were as varied as their prose styles. Henry James preferred real Tuscans to "one's detested fellow-pilgrims", while Leigh Hunt expressed the accepted Romantic view: "Florence has more convenience for us, more books, more fine art, more illustrious memories, and a great concourse of Englishmen." A healthy climate, picturesque peasants, cheap villas and an abundance of servants decided the issue.

Gloomy view

In the 18th century, travellers tended to be leisured aristocrats or eccentric dilettantes. Tobias Smollett, the misanthropic English writer, found nothing to admire in Tuscany. He failed to appreciate the entrepreneurial nature of the Tuscan aristocracy, finding it undignified for "a noble to sell a pound of figs or to take money for a glass of sour wine".

He abhorred the Tuscan practice of *cicisbei* (18th-century "toy boys") and generally con-

PRECEDING PAGES: the elemental majesty of the Tuscan landscape. LEFT: Henri Stendhal.
RIGHT: John Ruskin, "a bishop of aesthetic taste".

sidered the Tuscans immoral and treacherous. Little of Tuscany finds its way into his novels, while his *Travels Through France And Italy* are tales of unmitigated gloom.

The Romantic poets brought a much-needed enthusiasm to Tuscany. But even the Romantics thought of material comforts: the exiled Lord

Byron travelled "lightly" with seven servants, five carriages and additional furniture carts. Once in Florence, the patrician republican identified with Dante's exile, later alluded to in *Childe Harold's Pilgrimage*. Byron threw himself into Renaissance art and was "dazzled, drunk with Beauty" in Santa Croce.

His affair with Contessa Teresa Guiccoli gave him an entrée into Tuscan provincial society and enabled him to boast that he had not "Florenced and Romed and Galleried and Conversationed" but had "been amongst all classes, from the *conte* to the *contadino*".

His friend Shelley devoured Pisan landscapes and Livornese seascapes but had little interest in the natives. As his wife Mary said after his death, "We lived in utter solitude." In Bagni di Lucca, Shelley washed away his remaining inhibitions: "My custom is to undress and sit on the rocks, read Herodotus until the perspiration has subsided, and then to leap from the edge of the rock into the fountain." When Shelley drowned near La Spezia, Byron and Leigh Hunt cremated him on the beach with offerings of wine, oil and frankincense.

Tuscany soon became a pilgrimage for the later Romantic poets such as Tennyson and Wordsworth. "Emotion recollected in tranquillity" was the keynote: neither poet particularly

an opinionated but sensitive portrait of the region in the 1870s.

Thin disguises

If Tuscany only appears indirectly in his novels, it is because James succeeded in transforming his experiences into real literature; he did not want to be identified with the dilettante scribblers of "Little Tuscany". In *The Aspern Papers*, James included the Shelley Circle – in disguise, of course.

Dostoyevsky, exiled in a delightful spot beside the Pitti Palace, found little Tuscan inspiration for *The Idiot*. He complained that

enjoyed Tuscany at the time, yet both later idealised their experiences.

The Stendhal Syndrome

Although officially a diplomat in Florence, Stendhal spent most of his time absorbing Renaissance frescoes and planning his novel, *Le Rouge et le Noir*. As with Byron, the Santa Croce Effect sent Stendhal reeling: once outside, "I walked in constant fear of falling to the ground." This aesthetic sickness is now known as the Stendhal Syndrome.

Henry James was one of the few foreign writers able to see through Tuscany's literary and artistic veil. His *Portrait of Places* gives

"the population of Florence spends the whole night on its feet, and there's a terrible deal of singing".

The most romantic mid-Victorian couple was undoubtedly the poets Elizabeth Barrett Browning and Robert Browning. Robert brought his wife to their Florentine *palazzo* because of her poor health. There he cunningly used local Chianti to wean Elizabeth off her long addiction to laudanum. According to Virginia Woolf, Elizabeth "tossed off a tumbler and slept the sounder".

Elizabeth attributed her improved health to the spiritual powers of the Tuscan climate rather than the wine and her husband's lively erudition was stirred by Tuscan architecture, Mannerist painting and botany.

Elizabeth tolerated her husband's mild liberalism, but she herself was a fervent believer in Italian Unification. In essence, Browning loved the Florence of the past and Elizabeth loved the Florence of the future. Apart from their relationship, work and the house, neither lived much in the present nor had a burning desire to meet the natives. Both were inspired by a mythologised Florence, "When Galileo stood at night to take

> **LORD BYRON'S VIEW**
>
> The Medici Chapels, proclaimed Byron, are "fine frippery in great slabs of various expensive stones, to commemorate fifty nobles and forgotten carcasses."

the vision of the stars." Their 15th-century *palazzo*, redecorated in Victorian style, is a literary museum and a haunt of writers.

The 20th century brought E.M. Forster, with his ironic analysis of the resident English community at play. Forster's *A Room With a View* is justly famous for its portrayal of the heroine's encounter with alien culture and passions. Lost in Santa Croce without a *Baedeker*, Lucy panics and mistakes a Machiavelli monument for a saint. But gradually "the pernicious charm of

FAR LEFT: Johann Wolfgang von Goethe.
LEFT: Dostoyevsky found "a terrible deal of singing" in Florence. **ABOVE:** Virginia Woolf saw "loneliness".

Italy worked on her, and, instead of acquiring information, she began to be happy".

In her *Diaries*, Virginia Woolf looked at the Tuscan people with a cool appraising eye: "They seem stunted, dried up; like the grasshopper and with the manners of impoverished gentle people; sad, wise, tolerant, humorous." Along with many other writers on Tuscany, she sees her own image reflected in the landscape, "infinite emptiness, loneliness, silence…"

D.H. Lawrence, living in his "grave old Tuscan villa" in Scandicci, thought he was communing with the original Etruscans rather than with his farmer neighbours. "The curious, fine-nosed Tuscan face, with the half-sardonic, amber cold eyes. Their curious individuality with their clothes worn so easy and so reckless." His philosophy dominated the landscape. In *Aaron's Rod*, his most Tuscan novel, he wrote: "I reckon here men for a moment were themselves, as a plant in flower is for the moment completely itself. Then it goes off. As Florence has gone off."

War story

World War II prevented further literary flowering, but in *War In Val D'Orcia*, Iris Origo, an Anglo-Florentine, painted a dramatic picture of the Tuscan battlefield. As a young woman, Origo was part of Lawrence's artistic circle but her understanding of the Tuscans set her apart.

Soon after the war, the Welsh poet Dylan Thomas came to Tuscany for the first time and was entranced: "The pine hills are endless, the cypresses at the hilltop tell one all about the length of death, the woods are deep as love and full of goats." He apparently enjoyed a hedonistic lifestyle, vegetating in the sun and devouring asparagus, strawberries and wine at only 20 lire a glass.

Tuscany continues to befuddle the minds of visiting writers. While inspiring the writer's life, the region often has a disturbing or numbing effect on literary output. The portrayal of Tuscany in contemporary foreign novels too often lacks credibility. Although Tuscans are no longer portrayed as peasants or forces of nature, there is still "no foundation in natives" in literary Chiantishire. ❑

Ioan. Stradanus inuent.

Phls Galle excud.

Decisive Dates

ETRUSCANS AND ROMANS

800–500BC: Etruscan civilisation flourished. Etruria Propria, a confederation of 12 states, included Arezzo, Cortona, Chiusi, Fiesole, Populonia, Roselle, Vetulonia, Volterra.

480–290BC: Romans in power; they annexed Etruria and founded colonies at Ansedonia, Roselle, Volterra, Luni and Lucca.

91BC: Roman citizenship was extended to Etruscans.

80BC: Faesulae (now Fiesole) becomes a Roman military colony.

59BC: A colony of Roman army veterans found Florentia (Florence) on the banks of the River Arno.

AD200–600: Region invaded by Lombards, Goth and Franks.

AD306: Constantinople becomes capital of Roman Empire; the Byzantine period follows.

AD476: The Fall of Rome.

MEDIEVAL TUSCANY

1000–1300: German emperors conquer Italy, followed by constant warring between Guelfs (supporters of the papacy) and Ghibellines (supporters of the Holy Roman Empire).

1062: Pisan navy wins an overwhelming victory over the Saracens of Sicily in a battle off Palermo.

1115: Florence is granted the status of a *comune* – an independent city governed by a council drawn from the mercantile class.

1118: The consecration of Pisa cathedral.

1125: Florence begins its expansion with the takeover of Fiesole.

1173: Bonnano Pisano begins work on Pisa cathedral's campanile, now known as the Leaning Tower.

1246: Work on Florence's Santa Maria Novella begins.

1250: Florence's Bargello built.

1260: Sienese defeat the Florentines in battle of Montaperti.

1289: Florence crushes Arezzo.

1294: Arnolfo di Cambio begins work on Florence's Santa Croce church.

1296: Di Cambio begins work on Florence's Duomo, which – excepting the dome – was completed in 1369.

1302–11: Giovanni Pisano sculpts the pulpit in Pisa cathedral.

1310: Siena's Palazzo Pubblico is built.

1314: Dante Alighieri begins work on *The Divine Comedy*.

1330: Andrea Pisano is commissioned to design and cast bronze doors for Florence bapistry.

1334: Giotto di Bondone begins work on the Florentine campanile.

1338: Pietro Lorenzetti paints the *Good and Bad Government* fresco in Siena's Palazzo Pubblico.

1348: Black death strikes Florence, killing a third of the population.

1350: Boccaccio starts work on *The Decameron*.

ca. 1360: Florence's Ponte Vecchio is erected by Taddeo Gaddi.

1384: Arezzo is conquered by Florence.

1390: John Hawkwood, *condottiero*, becomes Captain General of Florence; inter-city wars fought.

DAWN OF THE RENAISSANCE

1406: Pisa is defeated and becomes part of the Florentine state.

1420: Papacy returns to Rome from Avignon.

1421: Florentines pay the Genoese 100,000 florins for Livorno.

1425: Masaccio paints *The Life of St Peter* frescoes in Santa Maria del Carmine.

THE MEDICI

1434–64: Cosimo de' Medici rules Florence.

1436: Brunelleschi's dome for Florence Duomo is completed.

1452: Alberti's *Ten Books on Architecture* is published.

1469–92: Lorenzo de' Medici is ruler of Florence.

1478: Sandro Botticelli paints *La Primavera*.

REPUBLICAN TUSCANY

1497: "Mad monk" Savonarola is hanged for heresy in Florence's Piazza Signoria.

1504: Michelangelo completes his statue of *David*.

1513: Niccolò Machiavelli writes *The Prince*.

1527: The Sack of Rome.

1529: The Republic of Florence comes to an end as armies of Pope Clement VII and Emperor Charles V besiege the city.

1537: Alessandro de' Medici is murdered by his cousin.

1545: Cosimo I has one of the world's first botanical gardens designed for medicinal purposes.

1550: Giorgio Vasari's *Lives of the Most Excellent Architects, Painters and Sculptors* first published.

1555: Florence defeats Siena and incorporates its rival into the Florentine state.

1558: Benvenuto Cellini's *Autobiography* is published.

1564–1642: The Pisan Galileo Galilei discovers the principles of dynamics.

GRAND DUCHY TUSCANY

1716: Decree issued by the Grand Duke of Tuscany defines boundaries of Chianti and establishes laws governing production and sale of wine.

1737: Gian Gastone, the last male Medici, dies; Tuscany falls to the House of Lorraine.

1796: Napoleon's first Italian campaign.

1815: The Grand Duchy is absorbed into the Austrian Empire.

WARTIME TUSCANY

1848: The War of Independence.

1861: The proclamation of the Kingdom of Italy.

1865–1870: Florence is briefly capital of Italy; the Piazza della Repubblica is built in 1865 to celebrate.

1896: Puccini's *La Bohème* is performed for the first time.

1915: Italy enters World War I on the Allies' side.

1922: Benito Mussolini comes to power.

1940: Italy forms pact with Germany and Japan, and enters World War II against Britain and France.

1943: The fall of the Fascists. Mussolini is executed at the end of the war, in 1945.

1946: Italy becomes a republic.

PRECEDING PAGES: a 16th-century illustration of the cycle of olive oil production.
LEFT: Francesco Petrarch: to his contemporaries a living representative of antiquity.
RIGHT: Giacomo Puccini, the composer of *La Bohème*.

MODERN TUSCANY

1957: The Treaty of Rome; Italy is a founder member of EEC (now the European Union).

1966: Massive flooding in Italy: the Arno overflows in Florence and many works of art are damaged or destroyed.

1970: The first regional elections held.

1985: A great frost destroys between 50 and 75 percent of Tuscany's olive trees.

1987: Year of the *sorpasso*, the "overtaking": Italy's economy outstrips that of the UK and France.

1989: The Leaning Tower of Pisa is closed in response to its increasing tilt.

1993: A terrorist bomb in Florence kills five people

and damages the Uffizi. Prato is elevated to provincial status, becoming Tuscany's 10th province.

1994: Italy exchanges Proportional Representation for a first-past-the-post system. A right-wing government ushers in the Second Republic. Giorgio Vasari's frescoed interior of Brunelleschi's Florence cathedral dome is revealed after a five-year restoration programme.

1996: Most Tuscans celebrate as the electorate does an about-turn and elects Romano Prodi's left-wing Ulivo Party, marking the first time such a government has held power in Italy.

1996–97: Freak fires and floods ravage much of the region, destroying property, roads, homes and nature reserves and killing at least 14 people. ❑

THE ETRUSCANS

Although their origins remain mysterious, Tuscany's highly civilised early
inhabitants have had a profound influence on the region and its people

Modern Tuscans are proud of their Etruscan heritage and they feel no shame about stealing their own heirlooms; sadly, the ransacking of newly discovered tombs is rife. There are stories of farmers pretending to grow vegetables under cover while furtively digging up some ancient treasures. Most middle-class Tuscans have at least one item and a few conceal collections worthy of a museum. Many a wealthy dinner party ends with a showing of Etruscan treasures. A gold brooch is readily available for the price of a small Fiat. Pots are caressed with love. Jewellery is examined under a magnifying glass, its minute images of deities and animals admired and enjoyed. This orgy of sensual indulgence is something the Etruscans would have loved.

As the freshest face in the ancient world, the Etruscans are often seen as a mythical people out of time. The Etruscans were "rediscovered" in the Romantic era and since then a "scholarly" Etruria and a "poetic" Etruria have been at variance. While Etruscologists have pieced together a picture of a complex urban civilisation with robust art forms, Tuscans see a myth shrouded in ritual sacrifice, an indecipherable language and delicate eroticism. Mystery aside, the colour and life of Etruscan art contrast with the cold marble perfectionism of the Greeks and Romans. This alone encourages Tuscans to speculate on racial continuity and to recognise themselves in the Etruscan rather than in the Roman civilisation.

Early immigrants

Etruscan origins are hotly disputed. The Romantics and latter-day writers believed that the Etruscans sailed from Asia Minor. However, Dionysius, writing as the Etruscan civilisation neared its end, held that the Etruscans were natives with an indigenous culture too deeply

engrained to be Oriental. Most modern scholars believe that the Etruscans migrated from Eastern Europe over the Alps and represent the flowering of the early Italic tribes. What is clear is that between the 8th and 4th centuries BC "Etruria Propria" flourished as a confederation of 12 city-states in central Italy. Northern

Etruria, roughly equivalent to modern Tuscany, included Arezzo, Chiusi, Cortona, Populonia, Vetulonia and Volterra.

Etruscan seafarers and merchants first settled on the coast and began smelting iron ore from Elba and importing Oriental ceramics, glass and silverware. Greek naval supremacy meant an opening to Hellenistic culture: ships sailed to Corinth with honey, gold and bronze figurines and returned to Vetulonia and Populonia with perfume and painted wine jars. The inland cities such as Chiusi and Volterra thrived on hunting, farming and internal trade.

Over the next two centuries, the Etruscans allied themselves to the developing Roman

LEFT: Etruscan tomb painting.
RIGHT: part of the fortification wall at Chiusi, one of Tuscany's major Etruscan sites.

power and by the first century BC all the Etruscan territory was annexed. Although Etruscan and Latin coexisted, Etruscan culture was crushed; their role degenerated into the provision of soothsayers, musicians, dancers and fighters for Rome.

The original confederation had a complex urban and social structure: each city was originally run by a king, later by local aristocrats and finally by a priestly oligarchy. The lords owned large landholdings or navies and were served by serfs and slaves. Whereas

SEXUAL STEREOTYPE

The Greek Theopompus observed that Etruscan women "often strip off in the presence of men" and that they "do easily give in to anybody".

The women were depicted as pale while the men were uniformly reddish brown, either sun-tanned or ritually painted. Friezes of serene married couples, tender lovers, absorbed wrestlers, erotic dancers, or grieving warriors reflect the fullness of Etruscan life.

Aristocratic Etruscan women had freedom, social status and influence. They are frequently depicted attending banquets without their husbands, riding covered wagons to their landholdings and playing flutes or lyres at funerals.

the serfs were rewarded with agricultural plots, the slaves danced and sang for their supper. With urbanisation, an independent class of artisans and merchants emerged. The granting of the same Roman citizenship to the middle classes as to the aristocratic priests and magistrates was a blow to the Etruscan princely tradition.

Since there is no extant Etruscan literature, our knowledge of the living Etruscans is oddly dependent on a reading of their funerary art for clues. We know them as they would like to be known, these idealised aristocrats elevated by Greek myths. In looks, they are certainly the Lawrentian "long-nosed, sensitive-footed, subtly-smiling Etruscans".

Restless race

In art, the men are rarely still: they charge through games, boar-hunts, processions, journeys, dances, banquets and diving competitions. Even on the sarcophagi, they look ready to fight the underworld single-handed. The "ordinary" Etruscan is only glimpsed in passing: a prized blonde courtesan flits past dancing slaves; a serf mourns his dead master.

The Etruscans were called founders of cities by the Romans, expert at building cities of the living as well as cities of the dead. The *Libri rituales* prescribed the rites involved in selecting a sacred city site. The cities followed the contours of the land and sited the necropolis below the city walls and the living city above. If cities of the dead predominate today it is by accident and not by design. Public buildings, built of wood and clay, did not survive. The remains of a rare stone temple in Fiesole only hint at the vitality of the original building, once enlivened by friezes of dancers and mythical animals.

Pre-Roman stones

From what remains of the cities, there was enough to impress Roman and Renaissance architects. Volterra's Porta all'Arco is a deep gateway inspired by Mesopotamian architec-

But it is the tombs that remain as a cultural testimony to the power, wealth and beliefs of their owners. Death reflected life: the poor were often buried in shallow graves or their ashes put in small urns; the rich were buried in chamber tombs and stone sarcophagi decorated with pottery. Tombs, in every shape and form, can be seen in the Etruscan necropoli: "temple" tombs at Saturnia; melon-shaped tombs at Cortona; Oriental "trench" tombs at Vetulonia. At Sovana, "pigeon-hole" tombs are niches cut into the rock, while at Chiusi a mysterious labyrinth reputedly conceals the sarcophagus of Lars Porsenna, mythical king of the Etruscans. Chiusi

ture: its three faceless stone heads, perhaps deities, add gravity and protection to the city. The huge dry-stone walls at Saturnia, rebuilt to defend the city against Roman incursions, are still standing. Pitigliano is an Etruscan inland town with medieval finishing touches. Sovana also keeps the original town plan, complete with ancient sunken streets, *vie cave*, and a drainage system dug into the volcanic rock. Roselle neatly compartmentalises its sacred, industrial and residential areas.

LEFT: the Mistress of the Tomb: myth shrouded in ritual sacrifice.
ABOVE: the delicate eroticism of Tuscan dancers.

also contains early "well" tombs, those in which the ashes were placed in a shallow dish and then in a small round grave. The tombs and mode of burial varied according to the local custom and period.

At the height of the Etruscan civilisation, large "chamber" tombs emerged, often containing frescoes. Although most of the tomb painting lies just outside modern Tuscany, some can still be seen in its natural setting at Chiusi. Painted by skilled craftsmen, the frescoes portray domestic scenes and outdoor pursuits as well as the sacred journey.

The Etruscans were as vital in death as they were in life but underneath the liveliness lay a deep fatalism, underscored by the hopelessness of predicting the unknown will of the gods. Locked into an unequal relationship, the Etruscans were bound to a treadmill of fear and appeasement. In keeping with primitive religions, natural forces were personified as gods of the sea, earth and rising sun. The Etruscans also reinvented Greek gods in their own image: Zeus, Hera and Athena were Tinia, Uni and Minerva. Oriental and Greek motifs coexisted: Egyptian sphynxes watched Etruscan winged demons pursue menacing Greek Furies.

Divination, human and animal sacrifice were used to stave off divine retribution. The Books

beliefs. This revelation, derived from the Greeks' experience, transformed the after-life into a shadowy, demonic world without hope or human joy. As scepticism flooded in, the age of religious innocence gave way to the age of experience and Etruscan religion began to die.

In Etruscan funerary art, the man is often shown wearing his chains of office over his bare chest. He may hold an egg, container of the soul, or clutch the *patera*, a circular dish arguably symbolising the continuity of life. The bejewelled woman is surrounded by a mixture of feminine and sacred symbols: perfume boxes and earrings to beautify; a pomegranate or pine

of the Dead prescribe rules for interpreting thunder and lightning, animal entrails, and the flight of birds. But the central vision was one of a painful leavetaking or "death journey" to the underworld, hounded by demons. From there, if the gods had been appeased by sacrifice, the dead had the potential to become divine. In this painful leavetaking, some see a lingering memory of the original journey from the Orient or Eastern Europe.

But from 4 BC onwards, the Etruscans became convinced that the dead person passed into the realm of the afterworld rather than surviving in the tomb itself. Until then, Greek myths had bolstered Etruscan legends and

cone to symbolise either sexuality or death; a mirror to reflect her physical and spiritual perfection. In effect, these were portraits which were commissioned to show to the gods the noble patrons at their best.

Etruscan art is essentially regional; Arezzo had a reputation for *Arretino*, fine red pottery and for its metalwork. The famous bronze *Chimera* remains a magical illusion: a goat's head springs from a lion's back and is seized by the lion's tail, suddenly transformed into a serpent's mouth. Chiusi boasts canopic urns, cinerary urns with an idealised effigy of the deceased on the lid, while Cortona's bronze figurines represent Etruscan deities. Volterra runs the gamut of Etruscan demonology and Greek mythology. The "cinerary urns" are in fact small alabaster sarcophagi featuring sea monsters, beaked griffins and sirens in addition to Ulysses, Iphigenia and Oedipus.

Mystery language

The Etruscan language is as mysterious as the Etruscan origins. Although the alphabet is borrowed from Greek, the language, read from left to right, is part of no known linguistic group and defies interpretation. Many claim to have

DIFFICULT DECIPHERING

The University of Perugia has created a database of more than 100,000 Etruscan words in a sustained attempt to break their perplexing code.

most of the 10,000 shorter texts can be read accurately. These texts are mostly funerary inscriptions and religious dedications. The one known book, a priest's manual discovered wrapped around an Egyptian mummy, has still only been partially deciphered.

The art critic John Ruskin saw an unbroken line of tradition from the tomb paintings of the Etruscans to Giotto and Fra Angelico. Certainly, the Etruscan influence on the Romans was considerable. Apart from introducing

found a key text equivalent to the Rosetta Stone. In Marsiliana a writing tablet was found engraved with the Greek Euboic alphabet used as a model for Etruscan.

Despite considerable progress, the unintelligibility of Etruscan is part of a glamorous myth. True, there are no external keys such as dictionaries or bilingual texts but even by the 18th century, the sounds of most letters, names and gods had been identified and simple texts translated. Today, the core grammatical and phonetic structure is known and, by deduction,

LEFT: 5th-century Tomb of the Monkey, Chiusi.
ABOVE: ruins of the Etruscan city of Vetulonia.

to Rome the purple toga, an abundance of gods and soothsayers who were competent, the Etruscans also added a set of religious, humanistic and regional values which far outlived the Roman empire.

The Etruscans exerted a dynamic influence on Roman art before the original creativity was stifled by Classicism. Today, the Etruscan influence still emerges in modern art: Massimo Campigli's ochres and burnt browns are modelled on Etruscan landscapes, as are Paolo Busato's photographs. Tuscans still see the land as Etruria, untouched by the succession of Roman and Catholic empires imposed on it through the centuries. ❑

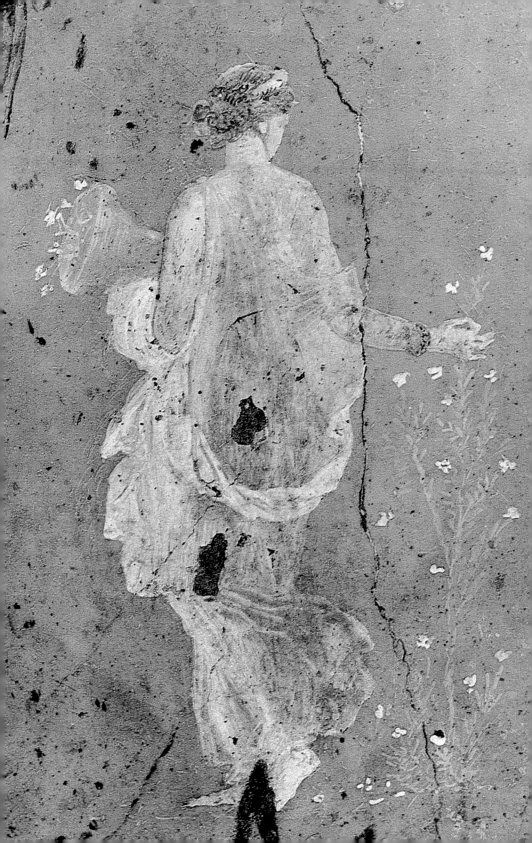

THE ROMAN LEGACY

As the Roman empire increased its might, great roads and new colonies sprang up across what is now Tuscany, leaving a permanent imprint on the landscape

Drivers in Pisa are all too familiar with the traffic-clogged Via Aurelia, the main coast road between Rome and the north. A few feet below the honking motorists lie the smooth stone slabs of the original Roman road, headed with military precision for the harbour of Pisae, which was once on the coast. Pisa is now 8 km (5 miles) inland, but the roads of Tuscany, as in so many other places, remain where the Romans put them.

Not all remaining roads are busy. There is a surviving stretch of the Via Clodia, the Roman road from Rome to Saturnia; a straight march, a footpath between fields and overgrown hedgerows, leading from the baths at Terme di Saturnia up the steep hillside to Saturnia itself.

Halfway town

Saturnia is a quiet little town, no more than a village, drowsing under the immense weight of its past. It was the Etruscan Aurinia, the main town of the Ager Caletranus, the intermediate zone between the great centres of northern and southern Etruria, which was under the control of Vulci just before the Roman conquest.

It came under Roman control as a *praefectura* in 280 BC and in 183 BC a Roman colony was founded there, attributed to the Sabatina tribe. The Romans renamed the town Saturnia after Jupiter's father.

Roman towns in Tuscany were either built upon the foundations of Etruscan cities as part of a continuous development, or else they were established as new Roman *coloniae* on the ruins of Etruscan towns, or as new settlements. In the 2nd century AD Appian described the colonies in his *Bellum Civile*: "As the Romans subjugated the people of Italy successively, it was their habit to confiscate a portion of land and establish towns upon it, and to enrol colonists of their own in the towns already on it.

They intended these for strongholds ... either to hold the earlier inhabitants in subjection or to repel enemy inroads."

Rome annexed Etruria in 351 BC and from the 3rd until the 2nd century BC, as part of the massive road building programme which was to transform Italy, four great Roman roads were

built across the territory: the Via Aurelia, which ran up the western seaboard to Pisae and the naval base at Genua in Liguria; the Via Clodia, which stopped at Saturnia; the Via Cassia, built in 154 BC to connect Rome with Florentia; and the Via Flaminia, built in 220 BC to connect Rome to Umbria and the Adriatic.

It's hard to imagine the impact these giant engineering projects must have had on the local inhabitants as surveyors and workmen spanned rivers with elegant stone bridges, built drains to prevent their new roads from flooding and at times even cut through the hills themselves.

Etruscan roads were all designed to connect the interior with the coast, whereas Roman

---

LEFT: *Primavera*, a fresco from ancient Roman times, anticipates the later style of Botticelli.

ABOVE: mosaic floor at Roselle, Grosseto.

roads all led to Rome, thus the axis was turned 90°, from east-west to north-south. The new Roman roads purposely avoided the great Etruscan cities which slowly fell into decline, whereas the new Roman cities such as Pistoriae (Pistoia) grew in importance.

New colonies were founded at Ansedonia, Fiesole, Roselle, Populonia, Volterra, Luni and Lucca. The cultural identity of the Etruscans was gradually absorbed into that of the Romans, a process which accelerated in 91 BC when Roman citizenship was extended to the Etruscans. The Romans learned many things from the Etruscans – principally the Tuscan

Santo Stefano; and particularly on the Isola di Giannutri, near Grosseto. Most Tuscan cities have something to show, though sometimes a little detective work is required.

Roman colony

Ansedonia, the Roman Cosa, was founded as a Roman colony in 273 BC on the hilltop site of an earlier settlement. The Roman city has been excavated and the site contains a main street, remains of a forum, a walled acropolis and, dominating the city, the ruined capitolium – a tripartite sanctuary for the triad of Jupiter, Juno and Minerva.

arch which they developed as a central element in their extraordinary aqueducts, bridges and buildings, relegating the classical columns of ancient Greece to a more decorative role.

It was from the Etruscan kings that the Roman monarchy, and later the Republican magistrates, took their symbol of power: the *fasces*, an axe surrounded by a bundle of rods, an eloquent symbol of the right to execute or scourge. (Sculpture depicting the *fasces* dating from 500 BC has been found at the Etruscan city of Vatluna, the Roman Vetulonia.)

The most complete remains in Tuscany are at Fiesole, Roselle and Cosa (Ansedonia); the best villas are near the coast, on Elba; near Porto

The city's 1.5 km (1 mile) of wall is virtually intact, as are many of its 18 guard towers. The site is overgrown and many of the ruins are covered in brambles, giving it a melancholy atmosphere. Saplings are sprouting in the forum, returning the dead city to the earth.

Below the promontory is the silted up Roman port, and nearby, the Tagliata Etrusca (Etruscan Cut), which is not Etruscan at all but a drainage canal cut by the Romans to connect the port with the lake of Burano, to stop the lake and the harbour from silting up. The cleft in the rocks, the so-called Bagno della Regina (Queen's Bath), is not, as is sometimes claimed, a rock sanctuary, but part of the drainage works.

Fiesole, which possibly dates from the 8th century BC, is an Etruscan settlement overlooking the valleys of the Arno and the Mugnone. As Faesulae, it was a Roman military colony from 80 BC and later became the capital of Roman Etruria. The Piazza Mino da Fiesole is built on the site of the Roman forum.

The archaeological site, set on a hillside near the Duomo, features a remarkably well-preserved 3,000-seat Roman amphitheatre dating from 80 BC, which is still used for performances. Nearby

FIRST LANDOWNERS

The prosperous city of Luni was originally settled by 2,000 colonists, each of whom received a gift of a total of 1.6 hectares (3.8 acres) of land.

are Roman baths and on the other side the ruins of a Roman temple, both from the 1st century BC, as well as a 3rd-century BC Etruscan temple, set against the Etruscan city walls.

Detective work is necessary in Florence, the Roman Florentia; the Roman grid-iron street plan is clearly visible in maps, with the Piazza della Repubblica following the outline of the old *castrum*. The perimeter of the amphitheatre, outside the city walls to the southwest, is still described by the little streets surrounding the Piazza S. Croce: the Via Torta, Via Bentac-

cord and the north side of the Piazza Peruzzi.

In Lucca, the original street plan is also still evident. Luca, as the Romans named it, began as a military colony in 178 BC and featured a 10,000-seat amphitheatre that was originally to the north of the city, outside the walls. In time, it was largely dismantled, and most of its remains are below street level.

During the Middle Ages, however, houses were built using the remaining walls of the amphitheatre, thus fossilising its outline and four main entrances. Fragments of it are still visible from the surrounding lanes, incorporated in the outer walls of the houses.

Luni, called Luna by the Romans, was founded in 177 BC and was the springboard for the conquest of the Ligurian tribes in 15 BC. The Roman city, its forum, a number of houses, and its amphitheatre have been excavated and today it is regarded as an important site for archaeologists.

Near-complete remains

Another extensive excavated site is at Roselle, the Roman Rusellae. The Etruscan city was taken by Rome early in the 3rd century BC. It was originally an island, dominating the waters of the gulf. The ruins are satisfyingly complete, with a nearly intact circuit of Romano-Etruscan walls, a Roman forum, paved streets, basilicas, villas, amphitheatre and baths.

Volterra was the Etruscan city state of Velathri. It became the important Roman municipality of Volterrae in the 4th century BC but was on the wrong side during the civil war and fell to Sulla in 80 BC. The Arco Etrusco has a Roman arched vault on massive Etruscan bases with three Etruscan basalt heads incorporated into the arch.

The ruins of the 1st-century BC Roman amphitheatre are outside the city walls to the west of the Porta Fiorentina. They are best seen by looking down on them from the city walls.

By creating the roads and major cities of Tuscany, the Romans left a permanent imprint on the landscape. A millennium later, the ruins of their great bridges, amphitheatres and city walls were the inspiration for the next great blossoming of Italian culture: Tuscany's coming of age, the Renaissance. ❑

LEFT: the Teatro Romano at Fiesole, outside Florence.
ABOVE: the remaining city walls at Cosa, Grosseto.

FEUDS OF THE CITY-STATES

For many centuries, Tuscany was the scene of fiercely battling city-states,
with first citizen soldiers and later the mercenary condottieri *at the front line*

A t the beginning of the 15th century, Florentine writer Leonardo Bruni described his city: "The City stands in the centre of the State like a guardian and a master. Towns surround her, just as the moon is surrounded by stars. The Florentine State might be compared to a round shield, with a series of rings surrounding a central knob. The central knob is the City itself, dominated by the Palazzo Vecchio, a mighty castle, the centre of the whole shield. The rings around it are formed first by the walls and suburbs, then by a belt of country houses, and finally by a distant circle of towns. Between the towns are castles and towers reaching the sky."

Florence was then at the height of its power, with many other cities and towns subject to it. Bruni's pride and love are obvious; what he does not say is that all the other towns and cities in the state are held down by brute force. But Bruni probably thought that hardly worth mentioning: after all, that was what all other Italian cities were striving to achieve.

Power bases

Between the ending of the Roman Empire, in the 4th century AD, and the beginning of the foreign invasions in the 16th century, the story of Italy is a catalogue of conflict between its cities, each of which was a sovereign state. Gradually, the larger absorbed the smaller. In the far south, Naples dominated the area from Rome to Sicily In and around Rome, the Popes built up a power base. In the north, Milan swallowed up all its neighbours on the Lombard plain. And in Tuscany, a three-way battle was conducted between Florence, Pisa and Siena.

In the early stages the battles between the city-states were conducted by the citizens themselves, all able-bodied men between the ages of 15 and 50 sallying forth beyond their city's walls to fight the men of the neighbouring city. When Florence crushed Arezzo in 1289 at

Campaldino, the blood-letting was so great that thereafter the cities began to fight out their differences with mercenaries, the *condottieri*.

Throughout the 14th century, the *condottieri* held the balance of power. Commanding companies numbering thousands of men, they sold their services to the highest bidder. The city

that could afford them – and control them – dominated its neighbours. Few could control them, however, and that is why the *condottieri* system got such a bad name. The *condottieri* had a vested interest in conflict, and if there were no battles to fight then trouble was created. From being paid to fight on behalf of a city, it was a short step to blackmailing that same city into paying you not to attack them.

Some *condottieri* were bought off – Sir John Hawkwood, the infamous and piratical leader of the much feared White Company, was given a palatial villa and a substantial estate as his reward for retiring gracefully from the fray. Hawkwood craved immortality

LEFT: Florence in the 15th century.
ABOVE: Lorenzetti's *Bad Government* (1337–39).

and wanted an equestrian statue to be erected in Florence – instead the miserly Florentines opted for the less expensive solution of an illusionistic fresco, painted by Paolo Uccello to look like a statue, in the cathedral in Florence. Other *condottieri* were better served – Donatello, the Florentine sculptor, was employed to create the bronze statue of Erasmo di Narnithat that stands beside the cathedral in Padua, and Andrea Verrocchio, another Florentine, made the powerful bronze of Bartolomeo Colleoni

WRITER AND FIGHTER

Even Dante took part in the city-state conflicts, fighting to the last bloody battle between citizen-soldiers at Campaldino in 1289, when Florence crushed Arezzo.

---

that stands in front of Venice's Scuolo Grande di San Marco.

Siena employed Guidoriccio da Fogliano as its *condottiero*, and his portrait, depicting him in ceremonial battle dress, can be seen on the walls of the Palazzo Pubblico. In the adjoining room of the palace, Lorenzetti's great fresco, *Good and Bad Government*, served as a constant reminder to the medieval rulers of Siena of the consequences of their decisions. Under the heading of *Bad Government*, the fresco depicts a countryside ravaged by bandits, fields left uncultivated, churches and other public buildings in ruin, and women being robbed and raped in broad daylight.

By contrast, *Good Government* results in a city full of happy, well-dressed people, schoolchildren listening attentively to their lessons, and merchants prospering.

It was these same merchants on whom the burden of paying the *condottieri* fell. They were caught on the horns of a dilemma, desiring domination over their trade rivals, and yet aware of the high cost of war, in terms both of taxes and economic instability. When they waged war on neighbouring cities, they often did so in the name of "Guelf" or "Ghibelline" partisanship.

The Guelfs were broadly made up of the rising middle class of merchants, bankers and members of the trades guilds, who nominally supported the Papacy in its long battle against the Holy Roman Emperor, and who wanted a greater role in city government. Conversely, the Ghibellines, the old feudal aristocracy, supported the Emperor, because he seemed the best guarantor of their virtual autocracy. Since the Emperor was often German or Spanish, and an absentee ruler, paying nominal allegiance to such a distant figurehead was far preferable to the threat of the Pope exercising real and temporal power closer to home.

That at least was the theory. In reality, Guelf and Ghibelline were often little more than badges and battle slogans. When one party defeated its rivals in any city, it would often fragment. In Florence, for example, when the Guelf triumphed, it split into factions, known as the *Neri* and the *Bianci*, the Blacks and the Whites. Dante was one of those who, though a Guelf, was a Black, and so he was forced into exile, falsely accused of corruption during his term of office as a city counsellor, when the Whites came to power.

Outside Tuscany, many city-states fell under the dominion of a single ruler – some of them former *condottieri* who ended up rulers of the cities they once protected, founding dynasties. The Tuscan city-states and republics maintained their independence far longer, but eventually even they fell to a dynastic power as the Medici transformed themselves from private citizens to Grand Dukes. ❑

LEFT: Florentine nobles. **RIGHT:** Giorgio Vasari's *Foundation of Florence* (1563–65) in the Palazzo Vecchio.

THE MEDICI

One family dominated the politics of Tuscany for 300 years,
from 1434 to 1737: the gifted but determined Medici

Ruefully reflecting on the mistakes that had led him to be imprisoned and tortured before being cast from office, Niccolò Machiavelli, former Chancellor of Florence, wrote his masterpiece *The Prince*, in which he admiringly recounted the ruthless methods used by the Medici to claw their way to absolute power in Tuscany, admitting that they had the gift of ruthless single-mindedness that he lacked. Even more remarkable is the way that this family threw up gifted individuals, generation after generation, and, whilst being masters of realpolitik and military strategy, also performed such an important catalytic role, through their sponsorship of the arts, that Florence and Tuscany become the engine of European cultural regeneration that we know as the Renaissance.

The man who laid down the foundations for the family's meteoric rise was Giovanni de' Medici (1360–1429), founder of the Medici bank. This was just one of 100 or so financial institutions flourishing in Florence in the 15th century, but Giovanni's master-stroke was to develop a special relationship with the Church, eventually securing a monopoly over the collection of the Papal revenues.

Giovanni's son, Cosimo, developed this relationship still further: one of his great coups was to attract the prestigious General Council of the Greek Orthodox and the Roman Catholic churches to Florence – the equivalent, in today's terms, of being chosen as the headquarters of the European Union, or the headquarters of a worldwide body such as the United Nations. These two great Christian churches had been at loggerheads for six centuries. Their assemblies in Florence were intended to find ways of burying their differences and creating a unified Christian church. This they failed to do, but the meetings had a lasting impact on Florence. Not only did they create a stimulating climate of theological and

intellectual debate, out of which the Renaissance was to grow, but also the gorgeous dress and ceremony of the Papal entourage – and the even more flamboyant and exotic manners and dress of their Greek counterparts – provided artists with a rich source of exotic subjects – the inspiration, for example, behind Benozzo

Gozzoli's richly detailed fresco of the *Journey of the Magi* in the Palazzo Medici-Riccardi.

Cosimo himself eschewed such riches. He was a man who took pride in simplicity, ordering Brunelleschi, the temperamental but gifted architect of the Florence cathedral dome, to modify his designs for the Medici palace on the grounds that they were too ostentatious. More to his taste was the work of the architect Michelozzo, who designed the marvellously airy library in San Marco, Florence, as a repository for the Medici book collection, and as the world's first ever public library. Such generosity was typical of Cosimo, who spent a fortune in endowing Florence with public buildings.

LEFT: Lorenzo de' Medici had a gift for diplomacy.
ABOVE: Cosimo de' Medici took pride in simplicity.

Among his friends he counted many of the greatest minds of the era: humanists who shared his thirst for knowledge, especially classical knowledge, for this was an era in which the lost classics of Greece and Rome – Plato, Cicero, and the like – were being rediscovered and translated.

Though a devout Christian, who regularly spent time in retreat in his private cell at San Marco, he believed strongly that God's grace was best leavened by a healthy dose of human intellect and reason. This made him an effective and humane ruler of the city – for that is what he was in all but name: following his father's

PATRONS OF THE ARTS

Because they combined a genuine aesthetic sense (which enabled them to detect new trends in culture) with great commercial acumen and ruthless political skill, the Medici were the most outstanding art patrons in European history. This patronage began with Giovanni, continued with his son, Cosimo, and was particularly evident during the reign of Lorenzo "Il Magnifico", who encouraged some of the greatest artists of the early Renaissance. Botticelli shared Lorenzo's childhood home; Leonardo da Vinci owed him his appointment to the Milanese court; and the 15-year-old Michelangelo was given a home in his palace.

advice to "keep always out of the public eye", Cosimo never sought public office. Instead, he wielded immense influence behind the scenes, so that no major decision was taken in the city without his being consulted. After his death in 1464, his fellow citizens voted to dignify him with the same title once bestowed on Cicero: Pater Patriae – Father of his Country – and these are the words carved on his simple tomb in San Lorenzo church.

Lorenzo de' Medici inherited his father's love of the classical philosophers, and his gift for diplomacy. An outstanding poet in his own right, he promoted the study of Dante's works in Tuscan universities, elevating the Tuscan dialect to equal status with Latin. His greatest gift to the Italy of his day was peace. By using his diplomatic gifts to hold the great rival powers of the Papacy and the Holy Roman Empire apart, Tuscany and the whole of northern Italy enjoyed a period of relative prosperity in which merchants prospered and great fortunes were made. With the countryside no longer ravaged by war or held to ransom by lawless mercenaries, wealthy individuals began to build the villas that are still such a characteristic feature of the Tuscan countryside. Lorenzo himself led the way, retreating regularly to his rural retreats at Fiesole and Poggio a Caiano where he enjoyed breeding racehorses and ornamental hens.

Prophetically, Pope Innocent VIII declared that "the peace of Italy is at an end" on learning of Lorenzo's death in 1492. From that moment on, the sounds of battle were heard again and again at the gates of northern Italian cities, during a period in which the aspirations of small city-states to remain independent were dashed by powerful imperial or papal armies. Lacking the wisdom, intelligence and political acumen of earlier generations of the Medici, Lorenzo's successors were expelled from the city as Savonarola, the firebrand Dominican preacher, filled his fellow Florentines with anti-Medici zeal – shrewdly claiming that their love of pagan philosophers and their fondness for the depiction of pagan gods in painting and sculpture would bring God's wrath upon the city.

Erotic art, fine clothing, secular poetry, mirrors, bronzes, sculptures of all sorts were collected and smashed, or burned in what Savonarola termed "Bonfires of Vanity". Botticelli supported the movement, recanting of his past fondness for neo-Platonic ideas, turning from such mesmerising paintings as the *Birth of Venus* and the *Primavera* to equally complex Christian allegories, such as the *Mystic Nativity*. Michelangelo carved his *David*, the boy hero standing up to the bullying giant Goliath, as a symbol for the city's desire to rid themselves of the Medici. He also helped to design and build new defences for the city, but when the combined forces of the Medici and Holy Roman Emperor held the city to siege in 1530, he took himself off to hide – irony of ironies – in the Medici mortuary chapel, attached to San Lorenzo church. Vasari attributes his cowardice to the artistic temperament, and whilst he was in hiding he worked the masterly reclining figures of *Day* and *Night*, *Dawn* and *Dusk*, which now adorn the tombs of two minor members of the Medici family.

Alessandro de' Medici, who led the victorious siege of the city, rubbed salt in the wounds of his fellow citizens by having himself crowned Duke of Florence, claiming absolute power for himself where his predecessors had been content with influence. When he was murdered in 1537 by his own cousin, with whom he had been having a homosexual affair, the city was relieved of one burden but faced with another – that of choosing a successor, since Alessandro had no natural heir. Various candidates were canvassed and it was Cosimo, descended from Giovanni de' Medici via the female line, who emerged victor, partly by persuading his fellow citizens that he would appoint counsellors and consult widely before making decisions.

Once in power, Cosimo revealed his true colours as he systematically set about destroying all opposition. Not only was he unrelenting in his pursuit of the republican leaders who had opposed his election, tracking them down in their exile and bringing them back to be tried and executed in Florence, he also set about conquering old enemies – Pisa, Siena, Massa Marittima, Montepulciano – with a ruthlessness and brutality that is still remembered and resented to this day. The whole story is told on the ceiling of the Palazzo Vecchio council chamber in a series of bloody frescoes painted by Vasari to honour Cosimo I in 1563–65.

LEFT: Palazzo Medici-Riccardi in Florence.
RIGHT: the Medici coat of arms.

To his credit, Cosimo not only forced Tuscany into political unity and established security in the region, he also set up an effective civil service to administer the dukedom, based in the Uffizi (literally "the Offices") in Florence, which proved effective right up to the point when Tuscany joined the United Kingdom of Italy in 1860. So effective was this civil service that Tuscany continued to be ruled effectively even when, as so often happened, Cosimo's successors proved to be corrupt, incompetent, self-indulgent or mad. Few made their mark on the city in quite the same way as the earlier generation, though Cosimo II did the

world a great favour by patronising Galileo, making him court mathematician to the Medici and providing him with a home after his trial and excommunication by the Inquisition.

The family also amassed an astonishing collection of art, which Princess Anna Maria Lodovica, the last of the Medici line, bequeathed to the city of Florence at her death in 1743, along with all the Medici palaces and gardens, ensuring that many of the greatest works of the Renaissance were not sold off or dispersed, but would remain in the city that gave them birth. Today, these priceless works form the backbone of Florence's three main galleries: the Uffizi, the Pitti and the Bargello. ❑

DEFINING THE RENAISSANCE

*Exactly when and why it began is subject to debate, but the roots of the Renaissance
are undoubtedly in Tuscany, where history and art are inextricably intertwined*

One of the great myths of history provides a kind of Hollywood scenario for the "birth of the Renaissance", linking it to the fall of Constantinople in 1453, when scholars were supposed to have escaped, clutching their precious Greek manuscripts, to Italy. There, these manuscripts became a kind of magical seed, taking root, growing and bearing fruit almost immediately as "the Renaissance".

Of course, this is nonsense; like any other human phenomenon, the Renaissance had roots deep in history. Today, we know quite a lot about *how* the Renaissance happened, but we still do not know *why* it occurred at that particular time and in that particular place.

Contemporaries were equally puzzled. Writing in the 1430s, the scholar Lorenzo Valla said: "I do not know why the arts most closely approximating to the liberal arts had been in so long and deep decline and almost died out, nor why they have come to be aroused and come to life in this age."

Valla might also have added: "Why did it happen in Florence?" It was, of course, the political fragmentation of Italy which created the Renaissance, each little city-state contributing something unique to the whole. But the process certainly started in Florence, and the city dominated the cultural scene until the early 16th century.

The best book on Renaissance statecraft is by the Florentine writer Machiavelli and the best book on commerce by the Florentine Pegolotti. Art history owes everything to the Tuscan Giorgio Vasari, and the whole course of art was changed most obviously by the Tuscans Giotto, Botticelli, Michelangelo and Leonardo da Vinci.

Mystery to muse

Again and again over the centuries, attempts have been made to analyse the causes of the

LEFT: Sandro Botticelli's *St Augustine in his Study* (*circa* 1480), Church of the Ognissanti, Florence.
RIGHT: grain merchants in Florence.

Florentine flowering, with reasons ranging from the poverty of the soil to the quality of the light. But it is no more possible to "explain" this than any other mystery of the human spirit.

The very word "renaissance" is a Florentine invention. In his book *Lives of the Most Excellent Architects, Painters and Sculptors*, first

published in 1550, Vasari, first of the art historians, remarks that the reader "will now be able to recognise more easily the progress of [art's] rebirth (*il progresso della sua rinascita*)".

But what, exactly, did Vasari mean by *rinascita*? What was being "reborn"? Vasari was referring to a rebirth of the art and architecture of classical times, that is, before Emperor Constantine transferred the seat of Empire to Constantinople at the beginning of the 4th century AD, causing Byzantium to become the centre of art and culture. A distinctive architecture, based on Roman models, using bricks and featuring domes and cupolas, was developed. Byzantine artists covered the interiors with mosaics, a Roman decorative form which they developed into a sumptuous art form; the thousands of glazed stone fragments catching the light in a way no fresco ever could. The best examples in Italy are in Ravenna, made in the 5th and 6th centuries, but the style prevailed in the 11th century in San Marco, Venice, and even in the 13th century in the magnificent Baptistry in Florence. It was the stiff formalised work of the Byzantine artists that Vasari, who dismissed them as "a certain residue of Greeks", was attacking, and which was completely overthrown by the new naturalism of the Renaissance artists.

Architects drew and measured the ruins of the Roman cities, rediscovering their building techniques and their rules of proportion: the "classical orders". Vitruvius's *Ten Books on Architecture*, the only surviving manual from classical times, was studied anew and became the basis, in the 15th century, for Alberti's treatise of the same name.

Reality in nature

Painting, which of all the arts is pre-eminently *the* art of the Renaissance, owed little to antiquity, partly because no Roman examples survived to be used as models. Renaissance artists broke new ground discovering perspective and observing the natural world which surrounded them. The 14th-century Florentine artist Cennino Cennini gave good advice to his fellow artists. "If you wish to draw mountains well, so that they appear natural," he wrote, "procure some large stones, rocky, not polished, and draw from these." The idea of a handful of stones standing in for the Alps or the Apennines might seem ludicrous, but it was a pointer to the new road the artist was taking, the road to reality in nature.

The classical world provided the inspiration for the artist to rise above the narrow medieval world, with its emphasis on theological studies. But, once started, he went his own way. What was reborn was an artistic sensibility but a re-cycled past.

Art historians divide the great period of transition into three sub-periods, using the logical Italian terms Trecento (1300s), Quattrocento (1400s) and Cinquecento (1500s). ❑

RIGHT: Leonardo da Vinci's *Adoration of the Magi* (1481), Uffizi Gallery.

THE TRECENTO:
THE ARTISTS' WORKSHOPS

This was an era of transition and co-operation, of the workshop and the fresco –
and of Giotto and the Pisani, who were perhaps ahead of their time

Until the Quattrocento, the term "artist" had no particular significance, being virtually interchangeable with "artisan" or "craftsman". All were members of guilds, or *arti*: there was an *arte* for the shoemaker, no more and no less valid than the *arte* for the goldsmith, itself a sub-division of the immensely powerful Silk Guild.

The guilds extended their control, as a matter of course, over the decorative as well as the useful arts. Sculptors and architects were enrolled, logically enough, with the masons, and painters formed a sub-division of the apothecaries on the general principle that they had to have some acquaintance with chemistry to prepare their colours.

Far from resenting the obligation to join associations, painters and sculptors formed their own groups, or *compagnie*, created both within and across the boundaries of the larger guilds. The reasons were both social and technical. Socially, members could help each other, the group as a whole sharing both profits and losses. Technically, an increasing amount of work was done in co-operation, either on a kind of conveyor-belt system (two or three men might be engaged at successive stages in the shaping of a pillar, from rough hewing to final carving) or working side by side.

The growing popularity of the process known as *buon fresco* demanded this co-operative approach. The medium of fresco painting had been introduced about a century earlier, and time had shown that it was the most permanent of all forms of mural art since the colouring became an intrinsic part of the plaster itself. (Michelangelo was to use the technique in the greatest – and probably the most famous – of all works carried out using the process, the Sistine Chapel in Rome.)

In addition to these large, set tasks, the workshop (or *bottega*) would produce a variety of smaller articles for sale, either on speculation or on commission, ranging from painted scabbards and armorial bearings to holy pictures

and statues. There was widespread demand for religious art, which provided the bread and butter for hundreds of small *botteghe*. A peasant may have scraped together a few lire for a picture; a parish priest might have a large sum at his disposal and commission a mural or even an altar piece, or a merchant who had made his fortune might be anxious to propitiate fate and show appropriate piety.

The potential client had little interest in the identity of the craftsmen producing his order. But, if expensive colours were used (gold, silver, or blue made from the semi-precious lapis lazuli), then the fact was clearly stated in the contract, along with the date of delivery of the

---

LEFT: Giotto's *Madonna and Child* (*circa* 1320–30).
RIGHT: *Madonna Enthroned* (*circa* 1280–85) by Cimabue, who discovered Giotto.

finished piece. Commissioned work was almost invariably done on these written contracts which, in addition, usually specified how many figures were to appear in the finished painting, their activities and attributes. Religious paintings touched on the delicate area of religious orthodoxy and the wise craftsman ensured that his client stated exactly what he wanted.

Dour patron

A typical patron was Francesco Datini, a wool merchant of the little town of Prato, 16 km (10 miles) from Florence, whose story is told in Iris Origo's book *The Merchant of Prato*. After making his fortune, social and religious pressure prevailed upon him to decorate his house with religious paintings. He was superstitious rather than religious, indifferent to aesthetics, and he went about the business of commissioning holy pictures with the same dour eye for a bargain which made his fortune in wool.

In 1375 he was ordering from a *bottega* in Florence "a panel of Our Lady on a background of fine gold and a pedestal with ornament and leaves, handsome and the wood well carved, making a fine show with some figures by the best painter, with many figures. Let there be in the centre Our Lord on the Cross or Our Lady – whomsoever you find, I care not so that the figures be handsome and large, and the best and finest you can purvey and the cost no more than 5 or 6 florins."

Members of a *bottega* were usually contracted for three years, renewing or disbanding their company but always either reforming it or joining another. The practice began to die out at the beginning of the Quattrocento under new pressures – in particular, the dominance by a number of great painters who could afford to regard members of the *bottega* virtually as their employees, and by the emergence of grand patrons such as the Medici.

The vast majority of the workers in these art shops are virtually anonymous. They were conscientious and skilled, rather than brilliant, but they formed the sub-soil from which the genius of the Quattrocento could flourish. The actual working pattern of the *bottega*, whereby a group of lesser men would paint the main body of a picture, leaving it to the identified master to

RIGHT: fresco in Palazzo Vecchio, from the workshop of Giorgio Vasari (1567–72).

put the finishing touches to it, would continue into the so-called High Renaissance of the Cinquecento, making it difficult and at times impossible for the most skilled art critic to say that such a painting is, beyond a doubt, the work of a particular famous artist.

First impressions

Comparing Trecento (or Gothic) paintings in any Tuscan art gallery with the work of Quattrocento (or early Renaissance) artists reveals a compelling difference: whereas Gothic paintings are iconographic, revelling in the use of celestial gold and presenting a spiritual

Madonna and Child for worship and contemplation, the same subject in the hands of Renaissance painters becomes a study in living flesh, the figures of mother and child endowed with attitudes, character, emotions and pyschological motivation. Scholars argue endlessly about why this great change occurred, but there is near-universal agreement on who started it: Giotto di Bondone (1267–1337), who, according to Vasari, "restored art to the better path followed in modern times".

Tradition has it that Giotto was working as a shepherd boy until Cimabue, himself a pioneer of greater naturalism in art, discovered that Giotto could draw a perfect circle freehand, and

offered to train him as an artist. Pupil soon surpassed master, and Giotto went on to create the great St Francis fresco cycle in the Upper Basilica in Assisi and the Life of Christ fresco series in the Scrovegni Chapel in Padua. In Florence his main masterpiece is in the Franciscan church of Santa Croce, where his work (and, of course, that of the *bottega* that assisted him) covers the walls of the two chapels to the right of the choir. Here, a series of quite vivid, though damaged, vignettes tells the story of the Finding of the True Cross and the Life of St Francis.

Despite his supposedly rural experience, even in Giotto's work nature is formalised and in the background. It is the humans who occupy the foreground, vibrantly alive.

Giotto, who died in 1337, was ahead of his time in introducing character and individuality to his art. He was not, however, entirely alone in these endeavours. Nicola (1223–84) and Giovanni (1245–1314) Pisano, the father and son team, were achieving similar advances in sculpture at the same time as Giotto was breakling new ground in art.

At the time when the Pisani were living and working in Pisa, it was the fashion for Pisan merchants to ship home Roman sarcophagi from the Holy Land or North Africa for eventual reuse as their own tombs. Scores of them still line the cloister surrounding Pisa's Campo Santo cemetery. Inspired by the realistic battle scenes carved on these antique marble tombs, the Pisani created their own versions: great pulpits sculpted with crowded and dramatic scenes from the Life of Christ, which can be seen in Pisa's cathedral and baptistry, and in Sant'Andrea church in Pistoia.

In architecture, the classical inspiration that helps to define the Renaissance had never disappeared to quite the same degree as it had in art. The very name Romanesque – meaning derived from or in the Roman style – indicates the essential continuity between the architecture of Rome and that of Tuscany in the 1300s. Churches were still built to the same basilican plan as those of the late Roman period and, though the façades of many Tuscan churches look quite unclassical, they are still based on

LEFT: Florentine woodcut of banking scene.
RIGHT: *Maestà* by Duccio di Buoninsegna, a Trecento artist who gave Byzantine art a more human feel.

the geometry of the Roman hemispherical arch, as distinct from the four-centred arches of Venice or the pointed arches of French Gothic. What distinguishes Tuscan Romanesque from Lombardic or Piedmontese is the exuberant use of polychrome marble to create complex geometrical patterns. Pisa was the seminal influence here – trade links with Spain and North Africa led to the adoption of arabic numerals in place of Roman, and to the fondness for surface patterning in architecture, copying Moorish tilework and textiles.

From Pisa the oriental influence spread to Lucca, Prato, Pistoia and even to Florence, where it was to pave the way for the great polychrome campanile built by Giotto during his time as cathedral architect. Straddling two ages, Giotto has been claimed by rival art historians both as a Gothic artist and as the pioneer of the Renaissance. Perhaps if war, compounded by the ravages of the Black Death, had not ravaged Europe from the 1340s, dampening artistic endeavour and depressing artistic patronage, the Renaissance might well have blossomed sooner than it did. As it was, another 60 years were to pass before the naturalism pioneered by Giotto and the Pisani was to re-emerge, this time as a mass artistic movement. ❑

THE ART OF THE FRESCO

The technique of fresco is an ancient one, used in the Minoan palace at Knossos and by the Romans, most notably at Pompeii. It was the Renaissance masters, however, who truly perfected the art, which involves painting on damp, fresh lime plaster. The binder is in the lime, which, when it dries, forms a calcium carbonate that actually incorporates the pigment into the material of the wall, producing very strong, vivid colours.

It was a painstaking process. The master would first make a rough outline drawing in charcoal, known as a "cartoon", on the roughly plastered wall. Over this was laid a layer of fine, smooth plaster, the *intonaco*. The outlines of the cartoon were punched through with a series of pinholes. Charcoal was then rubbed through the holes, leaving the outline on the wet plaster as a series of dots, a technique called "pouncing". For backgrounds, or when the master himself was doing the painting, the work was done from memory, with the original cartoon placed nearby. Only the amount of plaster that could be covered in one day's work was laid and, provided there was room, any number of men could work side by side from the top of the wall downwards. It was a system which placed a premium on the skill of the individual at absorbing the style of the master.

THE QUATTROCENTO: THE ARTIST EMERGES

The 15th century marked a formal farewell to the spiritual Gothic style of art and welcomed a new Realism featuring perspective – and emotion

A great breakthrough took place in Florence at the beginning of the 15th century, a moment so important that it can be dated to within a few years, and a new philosophy of life flowed through the city.

It was such a marked transformation that, in 1453, the scholar and polymath Leon Battista Alberti returned from many years in exile and marvelled at the changes that had been wrought in his city. The dedication in his book *Treatise on Painting* is a tribute both to those who were making the change and to the spell which Florence cast over its children. Movingly he describes how he came back to his city "beloved above all for its beauty" and singled out a small band of artists for especial praise – "you, Filippo (Brunelleschi); our dear friend Donatello and the sculptor Nanni (Ghiberti) and Masaccio" – all, he declared, worthy of comparison with any of the masters of antiquity.

Thus, until the 1740s, Florence became a kind of dynamo, providing light and energy for the entire peninsula. The city retained its dominance in art for barely a lifespan, however, because it exported so much of its native talent – which ensured the spread of Renaissance values but, with it, Florence's own relative eclipse.

The breakthrough began when the Florentine *Signoria*, or government, decided to refurbish the ceremonial centre of Florence: the group of buildings consisting of the cathedral, the campanile – begun by Giotto in 1334 and finished after his death but to his design in 1359 – and the octagonal baptistry.

This little black-and-white building had a special place in Florentine affections and when, in 1401, it was decided to offer a thanksgiving for the city's escape from plague, the baptistry was chosen to benefit. The wealthy Wool Guild

announced that they would finance the design and casting of a second set of bronze doors for the baptistry that would be even grander than those of Pisano. The design for it was thrown open to competition.

Out of the many entrants, seven were chosen each to execute a panel on the same subject: the sacrifice of Isaac. Two of the entrants, the 23-year-old Brunelleschi, later credited as the creator of the "Renaissance style" in architecture, and the 20-year-old Lorenzo Ghiberti, produced work which caused considerable difficulty to the judges.

Both the panels exist today, one preserved in the Museo dell' Opera del Duomo, the other in the Bargello Museum. Comparing the two, posterity finds it impossible to say which is "better". The *Syndics*, at a loss to choose, came up with a compromise, suggesting that the artists should share the work. Brunelleschi declined

---

LEFT: Brunelleschi's revolutionary cathedral dome.
RIGHT: Madonna and Child from Masaccio's *San Giovenale Triptych* (1422), in the Uffizi.

and took himself off to Rome, while Ghiberti began work on the doors, completing them 22 years later.

He was offered the commission to produce a second pair: these took him 27 years. During the almost half-century that he worked on the project, it is possible to see in his contracts the changing status of the artist. In the first contract he is treated essentially as an artisan, expected to put in a full day's work "like any journeyman".

In the later contracts, he is treated far more as a free agent, permitted to undertake other commissions. Ghiberti, too, made explicit the

Born Tommaso Cassai in San Giovanni Valdarno in 1401, Masaccio journeyed to nearby Florence at the young age of 21 and joined the painters' guild. His brilliance was already known.

Although he often teamed up with the older Masolino da Panicale, it was on his own where Masaccio's genius became evident. He took up where Giotto left off, particularly with the human figure – adding to it the mysterious, potent ingredient of perspective; using light and shadow to give great depth and intensity to his work. By 1428 Masaccio was dead, but the mark he made on the Renaissance during his brief life was indelible.

change by boldly including his own self-portrait among the sculptures of the door.

Learning from the ancients

Meanwhile, in Rome with his friend Donatello, Brunelleschi was discovering how the ancients had built their enormous structures. In an entirely new approach to the past, he examined originals rather than copies of copies. One of his findings – or possibly, inventions – was the *ulivella*. Intrigued and puzzled by the existence of regular-shaped holes in the huge stone blocks of the ancient buildings, he assumed that they had been made to allow the block to be gripped by some device, and designed a kind of grappling iron to fit. Whether or not the Romans had actually used such a device, it was very useful – and a demonstration of the benefits to be gained by studying the past.

Brunelleschi returned to Florence at about the time that the *Syndics* of the Wool Guild, who also had the responsibility for the cathedral, were puzzling over the problem of completing it. Arnolfo di Cambio had begun it in 1296, and it had been completed, all except for the dome, by 1369. Nobody knew how to bridge this immense gap which, for half a century, had been covered by a temporary roof.

In 1417 a special meeting was called to debate the problem and consider suggestions, and Brunelleschi put forward his solution. He was mocked for it because it dispensed with the wooden centering, over which architects traditionally built their arches and vaults, supporting their weight until the key stone was in place. But, in desperation, the *Syndics* offered him the job. Brunelleschi solved the problem by building a dome that was pointed in sections, supported by ribs with the lightest possible in-filling between them. He built two shells, an outer skin and an inner one: one way in which the crushing weight of the dome, the problem which had prevented its construction, was considerably reduced.

The work took 16 years, and was completed on 31 August 1436. This was the first Renaissance dome in Italy, the largest unsupported dome in Europe, bigger than the Pantheon in Rome which Brunelleschi had studied, bigger even than the great dome which Michelangelo raised a century later over St Peter's in Rome.

It was Brunelleschi's successor, the scholar Alberti, who first applied the classical orders to domestic architecture and created what we now think of as the Renaissance *palazzo*. Whereas Brunelleschi introduced the columns, pediments and cornices he copied from Roman ruins into his churches, there were no surviving examples of Roman domestic architecture for the 15th-century Florentines to copy. When Rucellai, a wealthy Florentine merchant, asked Alberti to design a palace for him, Alberti took as a model the Colosseum in Rome and applied its tiers of arches to the façade of a three-storey *palazzo*. Though it was the only *palazzo* he built, and though Brunelleschi's design for the Medici palace never got beyond the model

to *Herod*. The observer is looking at a banquet where the diners are recoiling in horror from the offering. Beyond the banqueting rooms can be seen a succession of two more rooms, giving a remarkable and, for contemporaries, almost eerie sense of depth.

A new perspective

Like the difference between Giotto's mobile, dramatic figures and their static, formal predecessors, perspective gave a new vista to civilisation. Its most dramatic form was that employed by the young Masaccio.

His great painting of the *Trinity*, in the church

stage, these two architects developed a new type of building, a system of proportion and an elegance of line which is still in use today.

Brunelleschi's other major breakthrough was his use of perspective. Alberti described its effect to a generation for whom it appeared almost a magical technique: "I describe a rectangle of whatever size I wish which I imagine to be an open window through which I view whatever is to be depicted there." Donatello (1386–1466) eagerly used the technique in his bas-relief of *Salome offering John's head*

LEFT: Donatello's *St George* shows a new realism.
ABOVE: Ghirlandaio's *Birth of the Baptist.*

of Santa Maria Novella, is an intellectual exercise in the use of perspective that is also infused with religious awe. Beneath a *trompe l'oeil* classical arch stands the immense figure of God the Father, half supporting a cross on which there is an equally immense figure of Christ; below them are various saints and donors and a *memento mori* of a skeleton in a sarcophagus revealing an ancient warning: "I am what you are, and what I am, you shall be."

The huge figures stand out from the background and appear to loom over the observer. As a young man, Michelangelo used to stand before these, copying them again and again to fix the style in his mind. Eventually, therefore, some essence of this experimental period of the Renaissance found its way into the Sistine Chapel, that shrine of the High Renaissance dominated by Michelangelo's work.

The classical arch in Masaccio's painting is a pointer to a curious development which took place during the Quattrocento – the clothing of Biblical figures in a totally anachronistic way, either in classical Roman attire or in contemporary Florentine dress.

The frescoes which Domenico Ghirlandaio

(1449–94) painted in the Sasseti Chapel in the church of Santa Trinità supposedly concern the prophecies of Christ's birth and the location should be Augustan Rome. But it is an Augustan Rome which bears a remarkably close resemblance to 15th-century Florence and the people standing round waiting for the awesome news are all citizens of Florence wearing their normal clothes. Lorenzo de' Medici is there, as is his mother, his children, friends and various colleagues.

In this odd approach to the past, ancient Hebrews, Egyptians or Romans appear in costumes that would not have seemed out of place in contemporary life. Apollo is usually depicted as a young dandy, Jesus Christ in the robes of a 15th-century scholar.

Mythological elements

Early Renaissance painters were preoccupied with technique. Their subject matter remained largely unchanged: religion was still the most important concern. But in the second half of the Quattrocento a new, exciting and somewhat disturbing element began to appear: the mythological and the allegorical.

The supreme practitioner in this field was Sandro Botticelli, who worked with Leonardo da Vinci in Verrocchio's workshop but developed in a totally different direction. His most famous painting – certainly the most mysterious of the early Renaissance – is *La Primavera*, painted in 1478 and hung in the Uffizi.

Nine supernatural creatures are placed in an exquisite natural setting. On the left, a young man is aiming at, or pointing at, something. Next to him a group of beautiful, grave-faced women are performing a solemn ritual dance. On the right is the only figure who seems to be aware of the observer: Botticelli's stunningly beautiful "mystery" woman with a provocative half-smile. Beside her what appears to be an act of violence adds a discordant note: a bluish figure is leaning out of the trees and clutching at a startled girl.

In the background, but dominating the whole, is the most enigmatic figure: a pale woman whose expression has been variously described as frowning, smiling, gay, melancholy; whose stance has also been described in conflicting ways as dancing; as that of a consumptive; as pregnant; as offering a blessing. The figure itself has been "firmly identified" as both Venus and the Virgin Mary.

What Botticelli was trying to do was to restate classical mythology in Christian terms while remaining true to the original – and true to his own quirky self. However, he was later influenced by the gloomy, savage friar Savonarola – who turned Florence into a Puritan reformatory in the 1490s – and, almost overnight, ceased his joyous mythological paintings, concentrating instead on orthodox religious subjects. ❑

LEFT: the city of Florence in the 15th century.
RIGHT: Masaccio's *Trinity* (*circa* 1425).

THE CINQUECENTO:
THE HIGH RENAISSANCE

*A peak – and then a plummet. Economic and political decay
in the region eventually took its toll on Renaissance art*

Even to the untutored eye, there is a profound difference between the work produced before and after the 1520s in Tuscany and elsewhere, most noticeably in Florence. Partly this was the result of an immense political crisis. Italy had become a battleground invaded again and again by warring foreigners. In 1527, a savage army, composed partly of mercenaries, sacked Rome and held the Pope to ransom. Italy was never to recover from that experience, which was the curtain-raiser for a period of foreign domination that would not end until the 1800s.

The peak phase of the Renaissance – in Florence, at least – was entered with the advent of Leonardo da Vinci and Michelangelo, but the decline came very soon afterwards, particularly when Michelangelo left for Rome with Raphael to work for Pope Julius II. Other artists followed suit: the major Florentine families – other than the Medicis – could no longer afford to make commissions, so there was no longer any kind of independent art scene.

Florence's glory fades

Shortly after the Sack of Rome, the Medici Pope Clement VII clamped down on his native city of Florence, ending republicanism and preparing the way for the first dukedom. Meanwhile, in the world of art, the glory was departing from Florence as the impetus of the Renaissance shifted to Rome and Venice. From the middle of the 16th century, Florentine artists tended to be court artists, dancing attendance on the Medici dukes. Among them was the artist-cum-historian Giorgio Vasari.

Until recently, Vasari's work as an artist was dismissed almost as contemptuously as his work as art historian was received enthusiastically. However, posterity owes him a debt of thanks, both as architect and as painter. Not

only did he build the Uffizi for Duke Cosimo I, but in his paintings in the great Salone dei Cinquecento, the parliamentary chamber of the Palazzo Vecchio, he created outstanding contemporary representations of the city and its

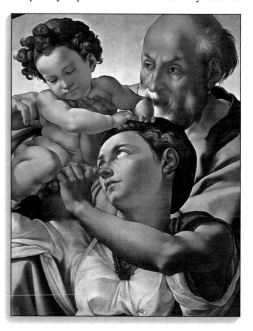

surrounding countryside. Equally fine is his frescoed interior of Brunelleschi's dome, revealed in 1994 after a five-year restoration programme.

The genius of Leonardo

Although the glory was departing from Florence, the sunset was stupendous. It could scarcely be otherwise with two such giants as Michelangelo and da Vinci still working in the city. Leonardo, born in 1452, trained in the *bottega* of Verrocchio, thus carrying the medieval systems on into the new era. One of Vasari's anecdotes claims that Verrocchio, on seeing his young apprentice's work, laid down

---

LEFT: Renaissance zenith: Michelangelo's *David*.
RIGHT: *The Holy Family*, also by Michelangelo.

his brush and never painted again. Unlikely though the incident is, the anecdote shows that Leonardo was recognised as being almost a freakish genius in his own lifetime.

An illustration of his restless, endlessly enquiring mind is shown by an incident on 28 December 1478 when, passing the Bargello, he noticed a body hanging from a window – one of the Pazzi conspirators. Taking out the notebook he always carried, he sketched the corpse, then meticulously noted in his mirror-writing: "Small cap tan coloured: doublet of black satin, black-lined jerkin, blue coat lined with black and white stripes of velvet. Bernardo di

Bandino Baroncelli. Black hose." He gave no indication whatsoever of any emotion, whether pity or satisfaction.

Leonardo left Florence for Milan at the age of 30, shortly after that incident. He came back again in 1502 when he was commissioned by the *Signoria* to create the great mural, the *Battle of Anghiari* in the Council Chamber, returned to Milan in 1506 then finally crossed the Alps and became court painter to François I of France. His contribution to the history of ideas is incalculable but his physical contribution to Tuscan art history is relatively small. Typically, both the *Battle of Anghiari* and the *Adoration of the Kings* in the Uffizi are unfinished. And his two

most famous paintings, the *Mona Lisa* (a portrait of a virtuous but otherwise undistinguished Florentine housewife) and the *Virgin of the Rocks*, are in Paris and London respectively.

Michelangelo Buonarroti is very different. His greatest work, the Sistine Chapel frescoes, is also outside Florence, but he did leave an enduring imprint upon his home city, in the form of the walls that gird it and the sculptures that grace it.

The next generation

Michelangelo was nearly a generation younger than Leonardo, born in 1475 when the Renaissance was approaching its apogée. His father was a poor but proud country gentleman who thoroughly disapproved of the idea of his son becoming an artisan or artist; in his mind there was no clear distinction. Michelangelo, too, was apt to be a little touchy on the subject. Although he served his apprenticeship in a *bottega*, he later rejected the idea that he touted for trade, "I was never a painter or a sculptor like those who set up shop for the purpose."

A Vasari anecdote describes how the young Michelangelo, then around 13 years old, made a drawing of the various tools in the workshop. His master, Ghirlandaio, was so impressed that he drew Lorenzo de' Medici's attention to the talented boy. As a result Michelangelo entered the princely Medici household, eating at the same table and studying with the same scholars as Lorenzo's own children.

Another story relates that once, during a quarrel, a bigger youth called Torrigiani (who later was to design the funerary monument of Henry VII in London's Westminster Abbey) broke Michelangelo's nose with a mallet.

Michelangelo was just 18 when Lorenzo de' Medici died in 1492. Florence was plunged into chaos because Lorenzo's son, Piero, was extravagant and unpopular and the Florentines chased him out of the city. Michelangelo's ties with the Medici were no longer so advantageous, and he took the road to Rome.

There he undertook the work by which he is best remembered. He also worked for the next 40 years on a task he never completed: the great tomb for his patron and taskmaster, Pope Julius II. The unfinished statues for this tomb, the famous *Slaves*, are now in Florence's Accademia gallery. In them it is possible to see, five centuries later, the sculptor's technique.

As in a *bottega*, the roughing out of the figures was done by apprentices, the master giving the finishing touches. It is profoundly moving to see in some of them the shallow depressions surrounding the figure, made by the rounded head of a chisel, which seems to be "freeing" the figure, as though it already existed and was simply trapped in the stone.

Florence has many statues by Michelangelo; although often unfinished, they always reveal the chisel strokes of a master. They include the famous *David*, and the statues of *Dawn*, *Evening*, *Day* and *Night* in the Medici chapel.

In the Casa Buonarroti in Via Ghibellina are displayed some of the sculptor's working drawings and a few of his earliest works. Although Michelangelo is remembered as a painter and sculptor, he was also an engineer of very considerable skill and a poet of sensitivity and insight.

Man of many talents

Michelangelo was just 25 when Benvenuto Cellini was born in 1500. Cellini admired his great compatriot so much that, when Torrigiani invited him to go to England, he turned down the offer, claiming he could not associate with a man who had so disfigured his hero. Or so he wrote in his remarkable autobiography, and it is probably true enough for, despite his many and manifest faults, Benvenuto Cellini had a warm and generous nature.

Like so many of the artists of his time, he was skilled in a number of crafts – he was, improbably enough, a gunner. He played a role in the tragic Sack of Rome which, in effect, brought the Renaissance to an end. Acting as gunner in defence of the Vatican, he assured his supporters that the Pope promised him absolution "for all the murders that I should commit".

In Florence, his most famous work is that beautiful but curiously heartless statue of *Perseus slaying the Gorgon*. The statue used to grace the Loggia dei Lanzi on Piazza della Signoria but, once it has been restored, it will be protected in a museum. But it is indicative both of Cellini and of the phase into which

---

LEFT: *Saint Ambrose* by Ghirlandaio.
ABOVE: portrait of Benvenuto Cellini.

A SCULPTOR FIRST

It was as a sculptor rather than a painter that Michelangelo saw himself, and he would touchingly sign his letters *"Michelangelo scultore"*.

the art of the Renaissance was moving that his best known work would be the elaborate golden salt-cellar which he made for François I of France.

The road to Rome

Raphael was a gentle, handsome young man who seemed to have no enemies. He was not a Tuscan; he was born in Umbria in 1483 and received his basic training in the workshop of Perugino, working on frescoes in Perugia. In 1500, however, at the impressionable age of 17, he came to Florence,

where he absorbed the works of Leonardo da Vinci and Michelangelo.

He left Florence in 1508, attracted to Rome by the fiery Pope Julius II, who was planning a series of architectural embellishments to the Vatican. There the young Raphael easily proved himself. He painted the series of rooms known as the Stanze della Segnatura and, under the Medici Pope Leo X, was placed in charge of archaeological excavations in Rome itself.

Thus, the last true artist of the Renaissance introduced into the mother city of Europe that passionate search for the past which triggered off the Renaissance in Florence nearly two centuries earlier. ❑

DANTES DI ALEGIERIS FLORETINI

TUSCAN LITERARY CLASSICS

Tuscany's artists were not alone in their creativity. The region produced many great writers whose innovative works made their own unmistakable mark on history

In a crowded field, three towering figures provide some orientation to Tuscan literature. Dante, Petrarch and Machiavelli follow each other chronologically and, because each caused, as well as recorded, great changes, it is possible to plot the course of the region's history — particularly the Renaissance period — through them.

Dante made the bold decision to write his epic *The Divine Comedy* in Italian, the language of the market-place, instead of the dead language, Latin. The Latin works upon which Petrarch prided himself have long been forgotten, and it is his lively letters, so modern in their description of everyday life and people, which are prized today. And poor Machiavelli – the Florentine bureaucrat whose name was to enter most European languages as a synonym for all that was deceitful and devious, as though he were responsible for what he described – laid down the blueprint for modern politics.

Cast into exile

Born in 1265, Dante was an exact contemporary of Giotto, whose work he admired. But where Giotto sensibly kept out of politics, Dante involved himself wholeheartedly and was exiled for his pains during one of Florence's upheavals. He never returned to Florence, and eventually died in Ravenna in 1321.

The Divine Comedy (*La Divina Commedia*), which deals with the great mysteries of religion, had a profound effect on Italian thought. Most people know at least one line, in translation, from the inscription over the gate to Hell: *Lasciate ogni speranza voi ch'entrate* : "Abandon all hope you who enter".

Today historians ransack the *Comedy* to identify historical figures (most of them in Hell, where Dante tended to consign his enemies). It is a vivid story with a meticulous chronology and philosophers and theologians still debate its significance.

LEFT: Dante painted by Andrea del Castagno.
RIGHT: Boccaccio, also by del Castagno.

Francesco Petrarch, though a Florentine, was born in Arezzo, where his parents had been exiled during the same feuds that caused Dante's expulsion. He met Dante, and was a lifelong disciple, but his own interests lay in the classical past. Petrarch was one of the first to hunt down and discover the lost classical literature without

which the Renaissance – the "re-birth" – could not even have begun. He travelled widely, had an enormous circle of friends and kept in regular contact with them through his letters.

It was as much through these letters as through any formal work that the "new learning" was disseminated. But Petrarch also shared, with his English contemporary Chaucer, the awareness that the humble and the humdrum were just as legitimate literary subjects as the noble and the extraordinary. In poetry, he devised the sonnet form which took his name – Petrarchan – which was to greatly influence the poets of Elizabethan England.

The dogged, disappointed and courageous

Niccolò Machiavelli was born in 1469, nearly a century after Petrarch's death. Viewed from almost any angle, his life looks like a failure. As a career diplomat, rising to be Secretary of the Republic, he never wielded real authority. As a convinced republican, he was obliged to spend his later years currying favour with the now openly despotic Medici.

His appearance and habits were totally at variance with the personality that comes across in his political writings. There he is ice-cold, logical, in total command. In real life

he was shabby, lecherous and adulterous. Something of that dual character comes through in his portraits: his expression is almost hangdog, furtive, yet with an inner, self-mocking integrity.

He was, despite all appearances to the contrary, an idealist. His notorious book *The Prince* was only one of a large output, including a delightful comedy, *Mandragola*, which is still staged today. There are few writers who have been so misjudged as this republican who wrote the classic textbook on the practice of tyranny.

Town chroniclers

One great class of Italian literature of which there is virtually no equivalent in any other countries is that of the urban chronicles. Almost every city had some devoted citizen carefully recording history as it happened, some achieving the status of true literature. In Florence the outstanding chroniclers were the Villani brothers, writing in the first half of the 14th century.

In Siena, at about the same time, Donato di Neri and his son were compiling the Cronaca Senese, while in Pisa Giovanni Sarcambi not only made a most lively literary record but also illustrated it with exquisite line drawings that serve to bring the times to life.

Although innovations in literature were less spectacular than in art and architecture, there are a number of outstanding "firsts". Francesco Guicciardini wrote the first true History of Italy, and Giovanni Boccaccio (1313–75) produced Europe's first novel. *The Decameron*, which Boccaccio, the son of a Florentine merchant, began writing in 1350, is a collection of tales told by 10 young aristocrats who retreat from the plague which struck Florence in 1458. Staying in a country house, they spend the time telling erotic stories and reciting poems, and poking fun at the wily ways of the clergy.

The Decameron opens with a detailed and grisly description of the plague which has become a classic in its own right; many of the stories themselves are so vulgar that they are often toned down considerably in translation. All demonstrate Boccaccio's well-honed skills as a storyteller. He also wrote *Filostrato and Teseide*, used by Chaucer in his *Troilus and Criseyde* and *Knight's Tale*.

Finally, there were the truly Renaissance figures who expressed themselves in all the arts, including literature – as exemplified in Michelangelo's poetry and Cellini's swashbuckling *Autobiography*. Cellini, a brilliant sculptor, part-time soldier and, by his own account, murderer, was also a superb writer. He wrote a heart-stopping account of the problem of casting the exquisite *Perseus*, a bronze sculpture destined for the Loggia dei Lanzi. Cellini records that, at a crucial moment, he ran out of metal and had to throw in the family pewter in order to complete the statue. ❏

LEFT: Boccaccio and Petrarch, in a 15th-century French manuscript. **RIGHT:** Niccolò Machiavelli.

A TIME OF WAR

*Unification in the latter part of the 19th century and the two world wars
in the 20th century forced a somewhat scarred Tuscany into the modern world*

Since the glories of Rome and the Renaissance, Italy has written little history. The head of Italy's Bureau of Statistics likens modern Italian history to a muddle, "a happy antheap where everyone is running about and no one is in control". The alternative is the "strong man" view of recent history, as expressed in the Florentine saying, "whose bread and cheese I eat, to his tune I dance". But, while Rome danced to martial music, Tuscany sometimes starved or burned.

Tuscany has been buffeted rather than enriched by its recent past. Well-kept war memorials in shabby towns attest to the loss of two generations, one abroad and one at home. Look at Asciano, a village dwarfed by its Carabinieri stronghold, built by Benito Mussolini and still used to this day to maintain law and order. Visit Montisi where, for the price of a drink, locals will describe the German bombing of the village tower, a story complete with sound effects, gestures and genuine sorrow. Ask proud Florentines why the medieval houses on the south side of the Arno are lost forever.

Bold flourish

The welding of Tuscans into Italians started promisingly enough, but the end-result is still only to be seen abroad or at international football matches. Piazza della Repubblica, built in 1865 to celebrate Florence's brief spell as Italian capital, remains a bold flourish of nationhood. But when the capital was transferred to Rome, Tuscan allegiance unquestionably remained in Tuscany.

Unification, under the leadership of Count Camillo Benso Cavour, a French-speaking Piedmontese, was seen as a foreign threat to the *de facto* sovereignty of Florence and the smaller city states. Defenders of the Risorgimento, the Movement for Italian Unification, appealed to nascent patriotism. Critics of uni-

fication cited Dante's pleas to Tuscan liberty before both sides settled down to start subverting the power of the new rulers.

Unification represented a missed chance for Italy. By failing to help shape a national identity, Tuscans also fell victim to the clearer vision of a "strong man". Even before World

War I, Mussolini was making inflammatory speeches while a weak parliament practised the art of "timely resignation", a ploy used ever since to stage-manage a new coalition.

Although the pre-war Tuscan economy thrived under weak government, it was no match for growing social pressures and a deepening gulf between society and state. With few real policies, one of the last liberal governments blundered into World War I. Italy's unpopular late entry cost Tuscan lives and support. The pyrrhic victory was exacerbated by a power vacuum, economic problems and a revolutionary working class. Benito Mussolini, from neighbouring Emilia, wasted no opportunity in

LEFT: Italian troops in 1939 waiting to join the ever-growing Italian army in East Africa.
RIGHT: convent schoolgirls of a former age.

proclaiming, "Governing Italy is not only impossible, it is useless", before proceeding to govern it impossibly but fairly usefully for 20 years.

By 1922, the corporate state was literally under construction. The economic benefits lasted until 1929 but the aesthetic effects linger on in functionally "improved" cities all over Tuscany. Florence Station, from which trains presumably ran on time, was the first Functionalist station in Italy. At the outbreak of World War II, most Tuscans were cautiously neutral. Mussolini, despite having signed the Pact of Steel with Germany, only entered the

Institute was a known fascist sympathiser, the German consul risked his life to protect Florentines who had been denounced. After the liberation he was granted the freedom of the city.

Florence was liberated in August 1943 but Mussolini and the German forces survived the winter behind the so-called "Gothic Line" in the Apennines. Apart from Florence, the partisans were very active in the Monte Amiata area; also in the Val d'Orcia where the writer Iris Origo, an Englishwoman married to an Italian *marchese*, sheltered many refugees and prisoners of war in her villa, La Foce.

Bagni di Montecatini - Piazza Umberto I

war in 1940, after the fall of France. By 1943 the north was under German control but the Allies were progressing northwards from Sicily. Allied bombing, German entrenchment and an emerging Tuscan Resistance transformed Tuscany into a battleground.

Anti-fascist cells had been secretly set up by the communists and Catholics in key towns under German and neo-Fascist control. Florence was split: while it was the intellectual centre of the Resistance it also harboured strong fascist sympathisers. Even after the city was captured by the Allies, individual fascists held out, firing from the rooftops. Surprising loyalties emerged: while the director of the British

Writing about it at the time, she grimly observed, "In the last few days I have seen Radicofani and Cortignano destroyed, the countryside and farms studded with shell holes, girls raped, and human beings and cattle killed. Otherwise the events of the last week have had little effect upon either side; it is the civilians who have suffered."

Nor were the Allies completely blameless. The modernity of Grosseto, Livorno and Pisa today owes much to Allied bombing in 1943. The British War Office reports naturally exon-

ABOVE: Calm before the storm: Montecatini in the early 1900s. **RIGHT:** "strong man" Benito Mussolini.

erated the Allies: "No damage of any signi-ficance is attributable to Allied action [in Florence]." The Allies issued their troops with booklets listing various buildings to be pro-tected, but baulked at the prospect of safe-guarding the "living museum" of Florence: "The whole city of Florence must rank as a work of art of the first importance." According to one report: "The great monuments, nearly all of which lie north of the river, escaped practically undamaged because, though the enemy held the northern bank against an advance, our troops deliberately refrained from firing upon them."

Commendable feats of Allied bravery included the penetration of enemy lines via the Pitti Palace-Uffizi passageway, a secret route used by the Medici in similar crises. Despite Allied concern and care, Florence nevertheless lost innumerable bridges, streets, libraries, churches, *palazzi*, paintings, and Tuscan lives. But in contrast to the "mutilated victory" of 1919, Italy lost the war but won the peace.

Massimo Salvadore, a supporter of the par-tisans in Florence, saw the war as a character-building exercise: "Without it [we] would surely have sunk into a morass of low politics and intrigues." That was still to come. ❑

THE GROWTH OF THE GRAND TOUR

Tuscany – particularly Florence – has been a magnet to foreign visitors since the 17th century, when a few adventurous eccentrics ventured forth into this strange land. By the 1700s, rich aristocrats were attracted to the region's alien psyche, perfect climate, low cost of living and undervalued works of art. Florence became an essential stop on any European tour.

But it was only in the 18th century that the middle classes joined the aristocratic dilettanti and literati on the road to Tuscany. Art was well and truly on the agenda, with foreign visitors flocking to see the Uffizi sculptures and Botticelli's *Medici Venus*. By the 1850s, escapees from

mid-Victorian England had made Florence *"une ville anglaise"*, according to the Goncourt brothers.

At the turn of the 20th century, the Anglo-Florentine community was well established, although World War I chased away many. The "Grand Tour" resumed in the 1920s and 1930s, but mainly for society figures and intellectuals rather than for leisured young aristocrats. The tradition continues to this day, with sons and daughters of "the establishment" coming to attend language and Renaissance art courses – with the less inspired lounging around in Hermès scarves and Gucci moccasins, rather than looking at "boring" paintings.

TUSCANY TODAY

The challenges facing modern Tuscans are many, and include achieving a successful blend of the old and the new

Tuscans today often compare their political system to the Leaning Tower of Pisa, an object of curiosity precisely because it defies appearances and does not fall down. The belltower is also an apt symbol of *Campanilismo*, attachment to one's region.

True Tuscans are provincial, conservative and independent. Since World War II, they have tended to vote for right-wing governments nationally but for left-wing councils locally. Until recently, this meant Christian Democracy at national level and communism at regional level. On the surface, this appeared a rather curious recipe for success.

Given the level of national opposition to communists, the Communist Party evolved an aggressively pro-regionalist stance. The reward was the "red belt" across central Italy, run by left-wing coalitions since the first regional elections in 1970. Red Tuscany formed the central strand between Emilia Romagna's model economy and rural Umbria. Despite the transformations in the "new Italy", the "red" regions survive under broad left labels as some of the most efficient of regional governments.

The Tuscan Left believes in a broad but increasingly secular church. Civic culture, regional pride and fierce individualism form the real faith. The power of the Left is as much a reflection of regional hostility to Roman centralisation as an espousal of social-democratic principles. Even in "red belt" Tuscany, the region's most popular newspaper is the right-wing but regional *La Nazione*, not the left-wing but national *La Repubblica*. How could a Roman product possibly compete with a Florentine/Sienese masterpiece?

Crisis? What crisis?

By the early 1990s, over 50 post-war governments had come and gone and "ungovernability" was again a common cry. To many observers, the crisis lay not in Italy's flawed institutions but in its flawed administrations and moral torpor. Senior party leaders tended to die in office; governments suffered from predictability, not instability; from opportunism, not lack of opportunity.

Partitocrazia, the party system, supplanted democracy. The long arm of the party stretched

from government to public corporations, industry, banking, the judiciary and the media. The reality of party power was genuinely subversive: the fostering of an "old boy network" based on *clientelismo*, political patronage. However, the public were slow to realise that a system they tacitly condoned concealed far greater evils. *Tangentopoli*, or "Bribesville", was the name given to the political corruption scandals that erupted in the early 1990s, which was followed by a resurgence in terrorism.

Florence literally exploded in May 1993, after a terrorist bomb attack beside the Uffizi killed five people and damaged priceless paintings. The atrocity was seen as a challenge to

LEFT: *Fare bella figura*: young bloods pose in front of Arezzo cathedral. **RIGHT:** classic Tuscan profile.

the state, and blamed on collusion between the Sicilian Mafia, the secret services and the political old guard. Florentines responded in anger and generosity, with the Uffizi staff working without pay to reopen the gallery. Most of the building and the paintings damaged in the attack were restored by 1995.

Mani Pulite, the "Clean Hands" campaign, ushered in *glasnost* and the attempted reform of a discredited political system. A network was uncovered through which shares of public funds were misappropriated by administrators and politicians, resulting in a third of *deputati* (MPs) being investigated for corruption and assailed by accusations – still being investigated – relating to the *Mani Pulite*.

In the April 1996 elections, Italy did an about-turn towards what is essentially a Labour government, electing Romano Prodi's Ulivo Party – a coalition of PDS, Verdi (the Greens) and various other left-wing parties. This marked the first time such a government has held power in Italy. Tuscany has always been heavily left-wing, so the election result brought great jubilation throughout the region.

Tuscans still balance their love of liberty against fears of political instability. The continuing preference for left-wing councils can

two former prime ministers – the socialist Craxi and the democrat Andreotti – being imprisoned. The 1994 general elections saw the switch from proportional representation to a largely first-past-the-post system, modelled on British lines. This change was so momentous that Italians refer to it as the "Second Republic".

These elections were won by an alliance spearheaded by media magnate Silvio Berlusconi. The right-wing government was elected on an anti-corruption ticket, with promises of privatisation, business competence, new jobs, new faces and an end to the old regime. It didn't last long. Berlusconi only governed for seven months, and during that time was now be seen as a sign of conservatism rather than radicalism. In Tuscany, the former communists (now the PDS) may have changed their name but not their spots. This hedging of bets is in keeping with the Tuscans' desire for regional independence. Moreover, if threatened by a central government that is out of touch with local concerns, Tuscans will instantly retreat into regionalism. In the end, provincialism rides roughshod over national politics.

Economic realities

The quality of life in historic town centres is excellent and Tuscans are not prepared to jeopardise it for more heavy industry. Topography also helps preserve the past: hilltop towns cannot expand, so development is restricted to the plains or, in Florence's case, to new suburbs or satellite cities.

In recent times, the Italian economy has moved slowly but finished fast. Tuscany followed this pattern with a late Industrial Revolution in the 1880s and a slow post-war recovery in the "long boom" of 1958–63. High labour costs then hampered progress; strikes, housing crises and terrorism did the rest. But in 1987 came the much-publicised

MEDIEVAL EXPORTS

Now, as well as in past centuries, the most thriving industries in Tuscany include Volterra's alabaster, Arezzo's gold and Empoli's glassware.

ployment, Tuscany appears to have recovered faster than many regions in Italy, but still faces the daunting countrywide problems of restructuring the economy to meet the Maastricht treaty's criteria for inclusion in the European Monetary Union, refurbishing a seriously crumbling communications system, controlling industrial pollution and adjusting to EU and global competition.

Luckily, Tuscany's traditional industries show no signs of fading. Prato is living proof: the cloth trade of the 12th century has become

Sorpasso, or "overtaking", when the Italian economy outstripped its British and French rivals. Tuscany's contribution was to slip smoothly from a rural to an industrialised society.

Since then, the recession has taken its toll, reinforced by public spending cuts and the loss of public confidence. In the early 1990s most public sector work came to a halt: the new moral climate meant that few civil servants dared sign contracts in case they were accused of taking bribes. Recently, despite high unem-

a highly skilled industry while remaining a collection of family businesses.

Nor did the great Renaissance families all die out. Strozzi is still an important name in Florentine banking and business circles, as are Frescobaldi and Antinori in the wine and food trade. Florentine design genius emerges in the styling of Ferragamo, Gucci and Pucci.

Many popular medieval industries are still minor classics: Siena's *panforte*, Carrara's marble. Tuscany also exports terracotta vases, della Robbia style ceramics, antiques and leather goods.

Such small- and medium-sized firms are in the dynamic private sector of the Tuscan

LEFT: Pitigliano street shows the narrowness and depth of urban life. **ABOVE:** *carabinieri* at play.

economy. By contrast, the public sector has a high profile but low prestige. Until recently, IRI, the Institute for Industrial Recovery, and ENI, the state energy company, ran the region without either energy or industry. However, privatisation programmes for state umbrella companies including banking, telecommunications, service and investment sectors have been launched.

It is easy to see Tuscan agriculture as a victim rather than a beneficiary of economic growth: a mass exodus from the land occurred between 1951 and 1971. Although large-scale wheat and cattle farming have drawn many

farmers back to the fertile Val d'Arno and Val di Chiana, traditional Tuscan farming is labour-intensive and relatively unmechanised.

But four decades of industrial development have not erased three millennia of rural settlement. The Romans perfected the mix of grain and tree crops and this *coltura promiscua* is still characteristic of Tuscan farmscapes. The olive groves at Lucca date back to Roman times and Elban wine was linked to Etruscan bacchic rites. Contrary to popular belief, most wine-growing is small-scale, with vineyards set on terraced slopes unsuitable for other crops.

For this continuity of land use, Tuscans have to thank their medieval system of *mezzadria*,

or sharecropping, which brought security of tenure to the peasants. Although *mezzadria* contracts were officially banned in 1978, the old patron-client relationship continues to exert a significant pull. Meanwhile the "exodus from the land" is giving way to the "flight from the city" as urban Tuscans appreciate the attractions of old farmhouses in tranquil upland settings. Part-time farming, property inheritance, gentrification and the increase in second-home ownership are winning a new population.

Tourism or traffic

Tuscans protest the influx of rich German and British residents, but the foreigners argue that they have restored entire villages such as Sovicille, near Siena, or Bugnano, near Lucca, for future generations. In turn, Tuscan land-owners have become more astute about tourism: *Agriturismo* (farm stays) are increasingly popular, both as a way of making the farm pay and as an opportunity to reinvest profits in the restoration or conversion of family property.

The government is now promoting the countryside, medium-sized towns and the revival of the historic town centre. The region's harmonious blend of craft, service and manufacturing industries makes Tuscany a model economy. Its cultural heritage and natural beauties also make it a highly desirable tourist destination.

Tuscans have mixed feelings about the influx of visitors. In 1994, following the controversial example of Venice, Tuscany's historic towns first raised the issue of restricting the number of visitors or imposing a tourist tax. Tourists are guilty of not staying long enough or spending enough, particularly "East European day-trippers". While towns like Siena, San Gimignano, Pisa, Arezzo and Cortona may be grateful for contributions to their coffers, many within their local councils regard the move as counter-productive.

For residents and visitors alike, traffic is a blot on the horizon, particularly in Florence. The *Vigili Urbani* complain that their 600-strong force was designed to police 400,000 residents, not the summer population of 7–8 million. Noise and air pollution harm major buildings and modern sensibilities. In the historic centre, pollution has been reduced by a

LEFT: the older generations enjoy companionship and a quiet life. **RIGHT:** the vintage Chiantishire hills.

traffic ban, but some residents complain that restrictions on traffic in the centre merely lead to the clogging of the *viali*, Florence's arteries.

Work in progress

According to UNESCO, Italy possesses over half of the world's cultural treasures, so it is fair to assume that in Tuscany, the holder of the lion's share, a number should be undergoing restoration at any one time. In Italy, 90 per cent of restoration work is funded by the private sector. In Florence, the Masaccio frescoes in the Carmine Church were restored by Olivetti, while Cassa di Risparmio, the Tuscan bank, re-stored the Gozzoli frescoes in the Palazzo Medici-Riccardi, as well as works in the Uffizi.

The most impressive recent restorations include the Simone Martini *Maestà* in Siena and the Piero della Francesca fresco cycle in Arezzo. In Florence's Duomo, the magnificent restoration of the frescoes inside Brunelleschi's dome was completed in 1994, with work on the south and central façade finished in 1995. The Leaning Tower of Pisa has been closed since 1989 in attempts to halt its downfall; if Tuscans can set their political house in order, there might be salvation for more than a mere toppling tower. ❏

CHIANTISHIRE: AN ENGLISH AFFAIR

The doyen of Anglo-Florentine society, Sir Harold Acton (1904–94), called his adopted home "a sunny place for shady people". It is not by chance that Tuscany is twinned with Kent, the Garden of England and the guardian of Englishness. Every year in Florence alone, up to 10,000 British (and 15,000 Americans) try to complete the transformation from foreigner to Anglo-Florentine. It usually takes 10 years for an incomer to achieve this "citizenship", but it can take only a month if one is famous, rich, beautiful or related to Harold Acton.

For the incomer – who usually takes up residence in one of Tuscany's 200,000 isolated farms – there are three golden rules: to eulogise the countryside, to be self-sufficient and to interact well with the natives.

"Chiantishire" residents of recent years include Lord Lambton (of 1973 call girl scandal fame), Lord Gilmour (former UK defence secretary), the Powells (family of a former adviser to Lady Thatcher) and millionaire and Labour MP Geoffrey Robinson (whose villa near San Gimignano is used by the family of Tony Blair). From the creative set come writers Harold Pinter, Muriel Spark and John Mortimer, sculptor Matthew Spender (whose family and late father, Stephen, were portrayed in Bertolucci's *Stealing Beauty*) and fashion designer Paul Smith.

WILD TUSCANY

Sated by the art treasures of the region, nature-lovers

are seeking quieter places in which to rest or roam

Elizabeth Jennings is one of many gifted modern poets to fall under the Tuscan spell. "Take one bowl, one valley/Assisted by hills to peace/And then set cypresses up/So dark that they seem to contain their repeated shadows/In a straight and upward leap."

The Welsh poet Dylan Thomas praised the Florentine countryside: "The pine hills are endless, the cypresses at the hilltop tell one all about the length of death, the woods are deep as love and full of goats." It's a seductive rural image, nicely in tune with the sensibilities of contemporary visitors.

Classic Tuscany is a civilised scene of silvergrey olive groves, vine-clad hills, sunflowers shimmering in the heat, and dark silhouettes of cypresses, arranged in double file along a timeless avenue. This infinitely civilised landscape was shaped by the *mezzadria* sharecropping system, which encouraged farmer and peasant to work in unison for mutual profit.

Utility only serves to enhance its remarkable beauty, from the cherry trees in blossom to the geometry of ploughed fields worked by plodding oxen.

Into the wild

Given the civilisation of the landscape, "wild Tuscany" might seem a misnomer. However, beyond the classic chessboard of vineyards, a rugged wilderness awaits, matched by semi-tamed terrain with enough romance for the distinction to be immaterial. In northwest Tuscany, there are woods as thick as rainforests, while the south has the primeval emptiness of the Sienese moonscape. On the west coast, the Maremma marshlands remain the emptiest and ecologically purest stretch of Italian coastline. The great Lorenzo de' Medici (1449–92) invites us to "assuage our restlessness" by exploring a wilderness of "leafy woods, rocks, high hills, dark caves, wild animals in flight".

PRECEDING PAGES: the cloudy heights of Monte Senario. **LEFT:** negotiating a suspension bridge near Pistoia. **RIGHT:** poppies brighten the fields in spring.

The animals are indeed in flight, given Italian hunters' fondness for the chase. The power of the hunting lobby means that, with the exception of wild boar, large animals are scarce in many parts. Outside designated reserves, birdwatchers and animal-lovers fare less well than botanists and general nature-lovers. Although

birdsong can be a rarity in semi-cultivated terrain, bird-watchers are rewarded with several of the best Italian sanctuaries, notably Bolgheri in Livorno province, Burano in the Maremma, and Bottaccio in Lucca province. Elsewhere, hawks and golden eagles enjoy the majesty of the mountains but life is no pastoral idyll for roebucks and other deer, ravaged by hunting. Against the odds, the Apennine wolf has made a recent comeback in mountainous regions, encouraged by the profusion of small mammals and even shaggy mouflons (mountain sheep).

The scorpion and the diamond-headed viper pose a faint threat to hikers, so local advice should be sought before setting out. Far more likely is a chance encounter with a Sunday hunter: to avoid being mistaken for a beast, bright clothes are advisable during the shooting season. Lone ramblers should not argue with huntsmen, especially those disturbed in areas where hunting is forbidden.

Rural pursuits

Away from the cultural crowds, nature-lovers can indulge in trekking and skiing, horse riding and mountain biking, climbing and caving, gliding and paragliding, sailing and surfing. In the versatile Mugello alone, outdoor enthusiasts can enjoy riding and hiking, fishing and

Trekking and Apuane Trekking are key paths in the Apuan Alps, while the Grande Escursione Apenninica (GEA) is a 25-day trek to Emilia and Umbria along the ridges of the Apennines. However, even in the Alps, gentler rambles are available, from nature trails to pony-trekking along bridle paths. Those in search of rewarding but less strenuous walks should choose a well-known resort such as Abetone or book walking tours with a specialist travel agent.

The majestic Apuan Alps

This mountain chain, with its awe-inspiring landscape, runs parallel with the coastline and

canoeing, or swimming in waterfalls and forest pools. In winter, climbing frozen waterfalls is an alternative to cross-country skiing. Riding is practised throughout Tuscany, with more riding stables and well-worn mule tracks than anywhere else in Italy. Cycling is increasingly popular, with provisions for transporting bicycles by rail on most northern branch lines.

Although hiking is less well-organised than in Britain or France, Tuscany is a ramblers' paradise in Italian terms. Better mapped than most regions, Tuscany provides the greatest variety of trails, from relaxing to rigorous. Serious hikers can follow the long-distance trails run by the Italian Alpine Club (CAI). Garfagnana

the Apennine ridge. Behind the well-groomed beaches of Versilia, on the western side of the chain, lurks the rugged hinterland of marble quarries and mountain ridges, narrow gorges and thermal springs. This desolate landscape was devastated by floods in 1996 but has recovered. Lago di Vaglia, in the heart of the mountains, is a reservoir containing a drowned medieval village that can be seen periodically.

In the Apuan Alps, the underground landscape is equally inspiring, with caves often as deep as mountains are high. The caves are also notoriously long and labyrinthine. In Fornovolasco, east of Forte dei Marmi, the Grotta del Vento represents the region's most fascinating caverns, complete with echoing chambers and crystal pools. The caves are riddled with steep gorges and secret passages, slowly revealing stalagmites and stalactites, fossils and alabaster formations.

Lunigiana and Garfagnana

Lunigiana, the mountainous area north of Carrara, is wedged between Emilia and Liguria. The region is criss-crossed by streams, with canoeing carried out in the clear waters of the river Magra. From Aulla, a convenient base, there

are organised tours of glacial moraines, karst gorges, caves and botanical gardens. Garfagnana lies on the borders of Emilia Romagna and northern Tuscany, between the Apuan Alps and the Apennines.

Parco dell'Orecchiella, north of Castelnuovo, is the region's most spectacular park. While closely resembling the Apuan Alps, it is higher and wilder, with a mixture of woodland and pasture, picturesque clearings and mountain streams. As well as pools rich in freshwater shrimps, salamanders and newts, the wildlife

LEFT: fishing at a Garfagnana lake. ABOVE: enjoying the rewards of hiking up Monte Capanne, in Elba.

> **THROUGH THE LENS**
>
> The renowned photographer Antonio Barletti has described Tuscany as "a harmonious composition, a collage of man and nature".

includes deer, roebuck, wild boar, mouflons, badgers, otters, weasels, stone martens and wolves. The wolves' satisfaction with the habitat is explained by the profusion of hares and alpine marmots.

The Apennines

While the Apuan Alps are more varied, the Apennines have not been ravaged by quarrying. They include the range on the Emilian border, the loftiest in the northern Apennines, as well as those in the Casentino and Mugello. Centred on the resort of Abetone, the rugged northern range is ideal hiking country.

Abetone, commanding the mountain pass separating Tuscany and Emilia, rightly calls itself the balcony over Tuscany. As the most important winter sports centre in central Italy, the resort offers cable cars, chair lifts and even artificial snow. Fortunately, the mountain air also makes Abetone invigorating in the most stifling Tuscan summer, when the cable car takes walkers up to the leafy heights. Despite the ravages of hunting, the forest is home to roe-deer, mouflons and marmots, with golden eagles swooping over the crags.

One of the most rewarding stretches of the rugged long-distance path (GEA) lies between Abetone and Cisa. Yet Abetone is also suitable for less energetic walkers, who can stroll along well-marked paths in the woods.

The Casentino, north of Arezzo, forms a series of razor-like crests and deep woods which straddle Emilia and northeast Tuscany. Centred on Bibbiena in the Upper Arno, these ancient forests are the region's finest. While the Emilian side is characterised by steep bluffs and stratified outcrops, the Tuscan side is softer, with picturesque waterfalls and streams. In the undergrowth, eager locals hunt for the fruits of the forest, from strawberries to mushrooms.

Hikers and pony-trekkers can follow the long-distance trail (GEA) but should bear in mind that the rescue services are often required in these treacherous forests. Fallow deer and mouflon were introduced in 1870 for hunting purposes, and again in the 1960s after local depredations. Today, sightings of the shaggy sheep, badger or porcupine are more frequent than glimpses of the eagle owl, deer, weasel, wildcat or wolf.

The Mugello, the hilly region north of Florence, resembles a landscape painted by Giotto, whose homeland this was. The Mugello can be explored on horseback, by following the old bridle paths between Bologna and Florence. The valleys along the Sieve, the main tributary of the Arno, are dotted with villages, olive groves and vineyards. The transition from valley to mountains means that olive groves give way to chestnut and oak forests before culminating in beech woods and waterfalls. Upper Mugello is a harsh, wild landscape of mountain peaks and passes, with ridges and ravines carved by rivers over the years. The challenging crests and mule tracks make for rugged trekking country.

Classic Chianti

While the Florentine Chianti is devoted to wine, the Sienese side is wilder, with vineyards gradually giving way to slopes covered in holm oaks, chestnuts and juniper. A tour of the vineyards may reveal wine cellars with great oak casks, matched by olive presses with massive granite grindstones. A 15-km (9-mile) hilly hike from Greve in Chianti to Panzano covers the Via Chiantigiana and its offshoots, passing farms, cypresses and chestnut groves.

AGRITURISMO: A TASTE OF COUNTRY LIFE

The most charming way of appreciating the countryside is to sample *agriturismo* – the term used to describe rural farm stays. Traditional accommodation might present itself as an *azienda agricola* (working wine estate or farm), a *tenuta* (an estate, whether working or not), a *villa padronale* (gracious villa), *casa colonica* (a farmhouse) or a *podere* (farm). Some of the grandest places are in the Chianti area (which spans both Florence and Siena provinces), with simpler farmhouses set in mountainous Lunigiana and Garfagnana.

During peak season, it is best to book in advance. Official accommodation tends to be booked for a minimum of a week but individual arrangements are possible. Given the disparity in style and price, visitors should request a photograph or detailed description of the property or book through a recognised agent. Every local tourist authority produces farm-stay booklets.

If you need any other good reasons to sample the rural lifestyle, think food. An *azienda agricola*, the most common *agriturismo* option, possibly produces its own honey, *pecorino* cheese, salami, fruit and vegetables, even *grappa*, olive oil, chestnuts, walnuts or truffles. A *degustazione*, or tasting of the estate wines and farm produce, is truly the best first bite of rural life.

In subtle Siena province, much is classic Tuscany, with olive groves, gently rolling hills, and dark cypresses standing sentinel. However, stretching from Siena to Montepulciano is a singular moonscape known as the *crete senesi*, the strange hillocks marking the Sienese badlands. Barren or virtually treeless, this is beguiling territory nonetheless, with solitary farmhouses marooned on the crests of hills. Organised spring tours trail the valleys of the rivers Abria, Ombrone and Asso, calling at farms selling *pecorino* cheese or wine. This seemingly empty terrain is home to foxes, badgers and wild boar. Monte Amiata, the site of an and steep cliffs, linking sea lilies and Mediterranean scrub (*macchia*). This unique sanctuary for waterfowl is also the preserve of wild boar, foxes and porcupines. On La Spergolaia ranch nearby, the legendary *butteri*, the last of the Maremman cowboys, break in sturdy wild horses. The Maremma sustains around 600 beasts, a mixture of semi-wild ponies and white longhorn cattle. The park can be explored on horseback, on foot or by bus from Alberese, a one-horse hamlet with a cowboy's soul.

Tuscany is a landscape for the senses, appreciated by the urban cowboy or the rugged explorer, the armchair traveller or the commit-

extinct volcano further south, presents the province's wilder face, with a profusion of thermal springs bubbling amidst the beech and chestnut groves. With its mossy banks and majestic grandeur, the mountainous setting is suitable for hiking, horse riding and skiing.

Marshy Maremma, the southern coastal strip, is a composite of natural Tuscany. The Parco Naturale della Maremma, with its soft whale-backed hills parallel to the coast, is dotted with Spanish watchtowers, parasol pines and coastal dunes. Waymarked paths connect the shoreline

LEFT: horses can be hired in many locations.
ABOVE: cypress copse after the harvest.

ted conservationist. Despite the mechanisation of farming, conservationists are winning the battle between pastoralism and progress. The poignant scene described by novelist Virginia Woolf (1882–1941) survives: "The poplars and the streams and the nightingales singing and sudden gusts of orange blossom, and the white alabaster oxen with swinging chins; and infinite emptiness, loneliness, silence… only the vineyards and the olive trees, where they have always been." Equally present is the dark-hued wilderness cultivated by Iris Origo, the Anglo-Florentine writer: "the faint eeriness, faint dread, without which the sunny hillside might have seemed a little tame". ❑

A TASTE OF TUSCANY

Purity and simplicity: Tuscan cooking makes full use of bountiful local products to create dishes that are as much a joy to prepare as they are to taste

Tuscany has everything to offer the visitor in terms of food. There is a rich selection of fruit and vegetables from the prolific countryside, and a fantastic bounty from the sea – everything from red mullet to mussels, tender beef and pork, excellent oil with which to cook and dress it and superb wines with which to wash it down. To finish off there are hearty cheeses and divine cakes and desserts.

What is immediately striking about Tuscan food is that, no matter what you are eating or where you are eating it, it is always very rustic, very simple, designed to nourish the soul and the spirit as much as the body. Tuscan cooking is never elaborate or excessive; there are no fussy decorations, complicated reductions of sauces or subtly blended flavours. But there is a basic, honest simplicity about their dishes which have made them popular for centuries the world over.

Tuscany produces its own inimitable versions of Italian staples: pasta dishes with gamey sauces of hare, wild boar, even porcupine; *polenta* with fresh *funghi*; rabbit or roast baby goat. But along with a particular attitude to food, Tuscany also has many dishes and delicacies unique to the region; most available the year round, others – such as chestnuts, truffles and wild mushrooms – more seasonal.

Hearty stews

Legumes are used widely throughout Italy, but are a particular mainstay in Tuscany, where *cannellini*, or white kidney beans, are favoured. Tuscans, in fact, are known as *Toscani Mangiafagioli* – bean eaters, because the pulse is used so much in local specialities, adding a smooth texture as only well-cooked beans can. Thick soups and hearty bean stews are served in terracotta pots – even in the most elegant of restaurants – often enhanced by a trickle of olive oil which is added at the table.

PRECEDING PAGES: a parade of Tuscan cooks.
LEFT: Pistoian *prosciutto* vendor. **RIGHT:** on offer: *cinghiale* (wild boar), hams, salami… and wine.

Tuscan cooks favour methods that can be carried out on a large scale and preferably out of doors – a grill over an open wood fire is something you will come across behind chic Florentine restaurants or in the garden of rural *trattorie*. Fresh herbs like sage, rosemary and basil are used, as they grow, in abundance.

The most important Tuscan meat dish is the excellent *bistecca alla Fiorentina*, a vast, tender, juicy and succulent beef steak – preferably from cattle raised in Val di Chiana. It is brushed with a drop of the purest virgin olive oil and grilled over a scented wood fire of oak or olive branches, then seasoned with salt and pepper before serving. In good Florentine and Tuscan restaurants in general, you will be able to see the meat raw before you order.

Another famous Tuscan meat dish is *arista alla Fiorentina*, consisting of a pork loin highly seasoned with chopped rosemary and ground pepper. The origin of this dish goes back to the 15th century. At the Ecumenical Council of

1430 in Florence, the Greek bishops were served this dish at a banquet and pronounced it "*aristos*", which in Greek means very good. The name stuck and it has become a feature of Tuscan cuisine ever since. It is a particularly useful dish because it keeps very well for several days and is even better cold than hot.

Local ham can include wild boar meat, and there is a salami flavoured with fennel called *finocchiona*. Soups are made of the ubiquitous beans, and include *acquacotta*, a vegetable soup with an egg added before serving, and *pappa al pomodoro*, a thick soup of bread and tomatoes. Also well known in this category is the Florentine speciality *ribollita*, meaning "boiled again": a second boiling of the soup increases the density and improves the flavour.

Although beef- rather than bean-based, a special stew is *peposo*, a fiery blend of meat and vegetables from Impruneta, a town near Florence that is famous for its terracotta. Legend has it that the dish once provoked a general strike. While Brunelleschi was in the town hunting for tilemakers to assist him with the roof of Florence's Duomo, he tried *peposo* and liked it so much that he brought a cook back with him to Florence – along with an agile young boy who, the architect thought, could

EATING ITALIAN-STYLE

Italians love their food, and Tuscans are no exception. But there are "rules" to be followed if you want to "eat as the Italians do". Cappuccino in the afternoon? You'll be branded a tourist. Salad *before* the main course? Never.

Usually, breakfast consists of just an espresso or cappuccino, drunk on the hoof in a local bar if not at home, perhaps with a *panino* (filled bread roll) if you are really hungry. Dinner, too, is generally a fairly minor event, with perhaps a light soup or *frittata*, sometimes eaten as late as 10 or 11pm. Lunch, however, is a different story. This is a truly gastronomic event, to be shared and savoured with friends and family at leisure – which is why for several hours in the middle of the day you'll find churches locked, museums shut, shops closed and streets empty. All attention is on the table.

Traditionally, a full-blown, no-holds-barred Italian meal will begin with an *antipasto* – a bit of salami, some roasted peppers, for example. Then follows the first course, *il primo*, usually a pasta, risotto or soup. *Il secondo* is next, consisting of meat or fish accompanied by vegetables. Salad is always served after this, effectively cleansing the palate in preparation for *i formaggi* (cheese) and *i dolci* (dessert), the last often being fruit-based. Top it off with an espresso. *Buon appetito!*

take bowls of the stew to his workers on the scaffolding, thus eliminating the need for them to have a lengthy midday break to get food. But the workers would have none of it – they went on strike to get their lunch hour back. Perhaps a good reason why the dish has remained a speciality of Impruneta – and not Florence.

The coastal province of Livorno produces the delicious *cacciucco*, an immense seafood and fish soup claimed to be the original *bouillabaisse*. The story goes that the soup originated in the port after a tremendous storm that left a widowed fisherman's wife desperately trying to feed her many children.

During the Renaissance, food had its place among the arts along with painting, sculpture, poetry and music. Many extraordinary dishes were created around that time; menus at Florentine banquets abounded with dishes such as pasta cooked in rose water and flavoured with sugar, incredible candied fruit and almond confectionery, the famous hare stew called *lepre in dolce e forte*, and many more.

Frozen delights

Caterina de' Medici was responsible for much of the renewed interest in the creation of original dishes. A keen gourmet, she encouraged

The children were sent begging for something to eat. As the fishermen had nothing else to give, the children came home with handfuls of mussels, a few shrimps, half a fish and some fish heads. The clever mother put them all in a pot, added herbs and tomatoes from her garden and created the glorious *cacciucco*. While *zuppa di pesce* can be eaten all over Italy, *cacciucco* can be eaten only in Livorno and surrounding areas. It is ladled over a thick slice of toasted bread flavoured with garlic.

LEFT: *The Fruit Vendor*, a 16th-century still-life by Vincenzo Campi, shows the region's rich harvest.
ABOVE: a typical market scene, in Pisa.

her cooks to experiment and was responsible for the introduction of ice-cream to the northern regions from Sicily, where it had been eaten for decades thanks to the Arabs who brought it over from North Africa.

When she left Florence to marry Francis I of France, she took many of her recipes and ideas with her. There are many Italians who claim that it was largely through her efforts that the French learnt to cook at all! To this day, the origin of *lepre in dolce e forte*, the hare stew made with candied lemon, lime and orange peel, cocoa, rosemary, garlic, vegetables and red wine, is contested by both Italian and French cooks. It is still called *dolce forte* in French.

The cheeses available in Tuscany are plentiful and varied. There is a delightful overspill of cheeses from neighbouring Emilia Romagna including, of course, the King of Cheeses, *parmigiano reggiano*. It is used extensively to complement Tuscany's marvellous pasta dishes and soups.

Other cheeses made locally include *marzolino*, a ewe's milk cheese made in March when milk is most plentiful in the Chianti valley; *mucchino*, cow's milk cheese made in and around Lucca by the same procedure as *pecorino*; *Brancolino* from the town of Brancoli; the delectable *formaggette di Zeri*, made with half ewe's and half cow's milk in Massa Carrara; and all the local rustic *cacciotte* and *ricotta* made with cow, goat and ewe's milk. Hunting is a popular local sport (though tourist participation is discouraged) resulting in plentiful supplies of *cinghiale* (wild boar) and numerous small birds, from sparrows to quail.

Mountain harvest

Chestnuts are a staple of the region, particularly in mountain areas, where they are made into flour, pancakes, soups and sweet cakes like *castagnaccio*, flavoured with rosemary and pine nuts. The season peaks around mid-

FABULOUS FUNGHI

There are many different varieties of wild mushrooms growing in abundance amongst the trees in the Tuscan hills – although the type of mushroom found will depend very much upon the type of tree it is growing next to or under – but the most sought after is the perfect *porcine* (*boletus edulis*), which grows to enormous size and thickness.

If you want to try your hand at picking them yourself, make sure you go with someone who knows what they are doing, as many types are poisonous. If you don't want to take the risk, just purchase some from a roadside market during the August–October season.

Fresh wild mushrooms can be prepared in a number of ways, but perhaps the best is to grill the large *porcini* in the Tuscan way, like a steak: rub each with a slice of lemon, stick them with slivers of garlic and sprigs of nipitella (a variety of thyme) – or, even simpler, just brush them with olive oil and salt.

Dried *porcini* are even more versatile and tasty than the fresh version, as the dehydration concentrates the flavour. When regenerated by soaking in lukewarm water, they are ideal for use in risottos or pasta sauces. If there is one food purchase you make during your visit, it should be a bag of high-quality dried *porcini*.

October, when chestnut – and steam train – lovers can travel on a restored 1920s steam train from Florence's Santa Maria Novella station to Marradi's *Sagra delle Castagne*, or chestnut festival, to partake in the celebrations.

In the autumn, when the rains fall, the hills become a target for family outings. Long lines of cars park along the side of the mountain roads – particularly in the Maremma, Garfagnana and Mugello areas, where little groups of people don stout shoes and arm themselves with baskets and hooked knives, searching for the delectable harvest of *funghi*. The wild mushroom season is awaited impatiently, as the

Yet, despite the restrictions imposed by the licence, the dangers of picking the wrong thing, and the shortness of the season, wild mushrooms are widely available at restaurants, in the markets and at roadside stalls from late August to early October.

If there is any one food item that causes more excitement in Italians than wild mushrooms, it is the *tartufo*, or truffle – particularly the white truffle, which begins to form in early summer and matures by the end of September, with a season lasting until approximately the middle of January. Truffles are "underground fungi", developing close to the roots of oaks, poplars,

spoils are highly prized both for their pungent flavour and the handsome price they will fetch in the market.

You need to be an expert, however, if you decide to go mushroom picking. Each year during the season the newspapers are filled with horror stories about families poisoning themselves with their own hand-picked mushrooms, and it is easy to make a dreadful mistake. Some local authorities have passed laws preventing people from picking the mushrooms unless they have paid for and been issued with a licence.

LEFT: mushroom vendors in Lucca. **ABOVE:** locally made pasta is a great gift and is easy to transport.

hazelnut trees and certain pines. But the exact location of a "truffle trove" is a well-guarded secret, with truffle hunters regarding their talented dogs, who unearth the strong-smelling delicacy, as highly important members of their families.

Truffles are sold by the gram and handled as carefully as if they were gold nuggets – and expect to pay as if they *were* gold, for these are precious commodities. Although it is nearly impossible to describe the taste, true Italian food connoisseurs will tell you that there is nothing on earth like a plate of plain, buttered *tagliatelle*, with a sprinkling of parmesan and liberal shavings of white truffle on top.

While the most highly prized (and strongest smelling) white truffles are to be found in the Piedmont region, Tuscany also has its share, mainly centred around the town of San Miniato, which produces 25 per cent of Italy's crop and hosts a variety of truffle-related activities during the month of November. There are stands of all kinds in the squares, plays in the deconsecrated church of San Martino, demonstrations of traditional handicrafts and restaurants featuring special

truffle-based menus throughout the festival.

Other truffle-related activities and fairs are held in the San Miniato area in October: the *Sagra del Tartufo Bianco* at Corazzano and, at Balconivisi, *Il Palio del Papero* (a parade culminating in a goose race) and the *Sagra del Tartufo di Balconivisi*.

Sweetmeats

Siena is famous for the *Palio*, for its Gothic beauty, and for its incredibly wide selection of sweetmeats. *Cavallucci* are delicious little hard biscuits which are usually served at the end of a meal and dipped into glasses of Vin Santo.

Panforte, an Italian Christmas speciality, is unmistakable in its brightly coloured octagonal cardboard box. It is a rich, sweet cake of candied fruit, nuts, spices, honey and sugar, sandwiched between sheets of rice paper.

Ricciarelli are delightful, diamond-shaped almond cakes, also saved for the Christmas celebrations, along with the delicious, golden rich rice cake called *torta di riso*. The local *pasticcerie* are filled with these and many other delectable varieties.

In other areas of the region, different specialities appear. At Castelnuovo della Garfagnana they make a wonderfully simple cake of chestnuts called *torta garfagnina*; on the borders with Emilia Romagna they bake a delicious apple cake, the *torta di mele*.

Pistoia produces the pretty *corona di San Bartolomeo* for the feast of St Bartholomew on 24 August, when mothers lead their children to church wearing this cake "necklace" to receive a blessing from the saint. Prato has *biscottini di Prato* made from almonds, eggs, flour and sugar, delicious dipped into the local Vin Santo. In Livorno they make gorgeous, light, golden buns called *bolli*. A speciality of Lucca is a ring-shaped plain cake known as *buccellato*, and an unusual sweet tart of spinach and chard with pine nuts. Finally, in Florence, around carnival time, you find *schiacciata alla Fiorentina*, a simple, light sponge cake.

The incredible *zuccotto*

But the pride of place amongst all Tuscany's sweet specialities is the incredible *zuccotto*, a sponge cake mould with a filling of almonds, hazelnuts, chocolate and cream. Once eaten, it is never forgotten. There is no general agreement, however, as to the origins of its name. Literally translated as "small pumpkin" (an obvious reference to its rounded shape), *zuccotto*, being a dome-shaped Florentine speciality, is thought by some to affectionately refer to the Duomo — or is perhaps a slightly irreverent allusion to the clergy. In the Tuscan dialect, a cardinal's skullcap is also called a *zuccotto*.

Tuscany is truly a food-lover's paradise. But remember, this is not the region to seek out complicated or intricate dishes. The food of Tuscany is a pure and simple art. ❑

Liquid Gold

Tuscany's olive oil has long been famous for its quality and excellent flavour and texture. The humid, temperate climate of the Tuscan hills is especially suitable for growing olives and the trees, hung with white nets before harvest, are as characteristic a sight as vines or cypresses.

The oil produced is so good that *bruschetta*, a quintessential Tuscan dish, consists simply of a slice of bread, toasted, rubbed with garlic and trickled with thick, green olive oil of the best possible quality. Tuscans are passionate about olive oil; they believe it is the most important cooking ingredient, and that its flavour and strength fundamentally affect the final dish.

They are immensely proud of their oil, too; wherever you go locals will claim that their olive oil is the very best available. There is a restaurant in Grosseto, *Enoteca Ombrone*, which has over 40 varieties of olive oils, and you can sample and compare them all at the table. The oils can vary enormously in sweetness, fruitiness, flavour and colour. An olive oil from Siena or Florence may appear quite different from the produce of Lucca or Grosseto.

In Tuscany the harvest begins in November or December and the olives are picked and processed during the following weeks. Some are picked while green, but usually they have turned almost black before they are picked for oil. Olives should always be picked by hand if possible. To make sure that not a single one is lost, the ground underneath the trees is covered in nets so that the olives fall down into them and can be gathered up more easily.

The technique of picking olives is a long and laborious task: the end of each small branch is held firmly in one hand while the other hand pulls downwards and strips off olives, leaves and twigs to let them fall on to the ground. A machine has yet to be invented which can accomplish the job so well.

After the olives are picked, they are taken to a local mill where they are pressed, traditionally by stone, nowadays more commonly using steel rollers. The initial "cold pressing" produces the very best and most expensive oils; thereafter the mash is pressed using heat which produces a greater yield but inferior oil. Quality is measured by acid content, the finest oil being *Extra Vergine* with an acid level no higher than one percent, followed by *Soprafino*, *Fino* and *Vergine*.

Olive oil, like wine, has different characteristics depending on the year it is made and the area where the olives are grown. It goes rancid quickly and should be used within a year of its pressing. Also, it absorbs smells and flavours very easily, which means it must be stored with some care.

Tuscan cooks use olive oil all the time: to brush on to meat for grilling and roasting, to dress salads, to pour over warm vegetables or potatoes, to trickle into soups and stews before serving, to deep fry sweet cakes and fritters. The quality of oil chosen depends on what it is to be used for;

richer oils are more suitable when the flavour is likely to dominate the dish.

A few excellent oils worth seeking out are Extra Vergine di Scansano, Extra Vergine di Macchiascandona, Extra Vergine di Montalcino, Extra Vergine di Seggiano cru Querciole, Extra Vergine del Chianti, Extra Vergine di San Gimignano cru Montenidoli, and Extra Vergine Badia a Coltibuono.

Although Tuscany was only the sixth largest producer of Italian olive oil in 1994, the quality of Tuscan oil is known to be outstanding. In recognition of its superiority, Tuscan oil is accorded DOC status, as if it were a wine. Unfortunately, the costs of superior Tuscan oil are also often comparable with those of superior wines. ❑

LEFT: there's nothing like an Italian *gelato*.
RIGHT: freshly picked green olives.

NECTAR OF THE GODS

To many, Tuscany is Chianti, known the world over as the quintessential Italian red wine. But don't overlook the region's other equally commendable libations

As the fossilised vines to be found at San Miniato attest, there have been grapes in Tuscany since long before man arrived on the scene. The region's early inhabitants, the Etruscans, were certainly enamoured with the fruits of the vine, as is evidenced by the wine cup found in an Etruscan tomb at Castellina-in-Chianti and surviving Etruscan frescoes that depict scenes relating to Bacchus, the Roman god of wine.

The vine – along with olives and grain – became an integral part of Tuscany's agriculture very early in the region's history, but it was some time before the area became known as Chianti. There was a reference to some land situated "in clanti" in a document dated 790, but it is not known for sure if the scribe meant to write "chianti". In the 13th century, however, the area was defined by name in several instances – and was first found describing a wine at the end of the 14th century.

Not surprisingly, monasteries played a large part in establishing a successful viticulture in the area – as they did through much of medieval Europe. Several old monastic sites – such as Badia a Coltibuono and Badia a Passignano – are still important wine estates today.

A struggle for stature

The wicker-covered Chianti flask, called a *fiascho*, is rarer these days in Italian restaurants than red-and-white check tablecloths. This emblem of the early days of Tuscan vine culture – now considered impractical, expensive to produce and a bit too "rustic" – has been superseded by an elegant square-shouldered bottle, reflecting the upgrading in quality of one of Italy's best-known wines.

If you order wine in a bar or restaurant in Tuscany, you will almost certainly be served the local *vino da tavola* (table wine) in an unlabelled jug or bottle. It is always drinkable and

PRECEDING PAGES: earthly pursuits – grape-picking in the Chianti vineyards. **LEFT:** the Sangiovese grape in full bloom. **RIGHT:** sampling the fruits of the vine.

often very good. Now, however, Tuscany is much more conscious of its standing as a producer of higher quality DOC (*Denominazione di Origine Controllata*) wines and increasingly you will find a sophisticated list of superior Tuscan vintages.

Nevertheless Tuscany *is* still Chianti – to

the chagrin of producers of the region's other fine wines. But Chianti passed through a stormy period in the late 1970s and 1980s which caused many to despair of its ever being able to live up to its traditional image. The problems stemmed from the laudable attempts to control standards of wine production in this extensive area.

The heart of the Chianti district stretches in a large oval between Florence and Siena, with branches extending west towards Lucca and Pisa, south to Montalcino, southeast to Montepulciano, east to Arezzo and past Pontassieve, and north past Pistoia (*see pages 174–5*). The heartland is called **Chianti Classico**, and it is over this territory that concern for the quality of the wine has longest been evident.

The first move, in the 1800s, was to lay down a strict formula for making the wine and reaffirm the traditional practice of *governo*, which involves keeping some grapes back during the harvest and leaving them to dry gently so that, when the main body of the wine has finished its fermentation, the reserved grapes can be added to the vat. This provokes a second fermentation, said to make the wine softer and rounder, but which mainly makes it livelier and ready to drink sooner.

Quality control continued with the founda-tion of the *Consorzio Chianti Classico* in 1924, and later with the "DOC" designation when Italy joined the European Union. (See "A Designation of Quality", below.) By the 1970s, Chianti producers were hemmed in by tradition, national law and *consorzio* rules to making wines in one specific way.

The problem was that this approach did not produce the quality or style of wine that they wanted. The best quality grape of Tuscany is Sangiovese, but producers were restricted to using between 50 and 80 percent of it; white grapes and *governo* make for a light wine for early drinking, but they were after a fuller wine

WHAT THE DESIGNATIONS MEAN

The concern for the quality of wine has been evident in the Chianti Classico area since the 1700s, when grapes and wines began to be classified and recommended methods of production were developed. The real mover in this area, however, was Barone Bettino Ricasoli, who, in the mid-19th century, conducted experiments that led to a specific formula for making the wine.

In 1924 a consortium, the *Consorzio Chianti Classico*, was founded to control production. To signify that a bottle was "Consorzio approved" – contained the Ricasoli blend of grapes, minimum alcohol content, minimum ageing and so on – a special sticker was placed around its neck

carrying the symbol of the Consorzio, a black cockerel (*gallo nero*). Three years later, the satellite Chianti zones banded together to form their own *consorzio*, Chianti Putto, which took as its symbol a *putto*, or cherub.

Once in the European Union, Italy had to develop a country-wide wine law. In line with EU regulations, "quality" wines were designated *Denominazione di Origine Controllata* (DOC), distinguishing them from their "lesser" brethren, called just *vino da tavola*. In 1984 Chianti joined the élite (including Brunello di Montalcino and Vino Nobile di Montepulciano) that were entitled to call their wines DOCG, the G standing for *e garantita*, "and guaranteed".

which would age well. The solution was found in typical Italian fashion. There were those who perpetuated the image of quality while lowering standards, cutting corners and engaging in a sales war that resulted in the price of Chianti dropping so low that its production was either fraudulent or loss-making. And there were others who decided to ignore the law and made high-quality Chianti as they believed it should be made, with whatever grapes they reckoned worthwhile. There were those who made much less Chianti and put their efforts into producing fine wine untrammelled by legal constraints; they gave each a *nome di fantasia* (invented name) and sold it as *vino da tavola*, but at a suitably high price. There were also just a few who soldiered on trying to produce the best Chianti they could within the law.

Salvation came in 1984 when Chianti achieved DOCG status. This change presented an opportunity for the revamp of the regulations that was so needed and it was willingly, if somewhat argumentatively, embraced.

There remains an argument in the making of Chianti as to whether or not *governo* should still be practised. Tuscany is the only region of Italy to utilise this method of winemaking, and although it has long been considered an intrinsic part of producing youthful, fruity wine, its use is now being questioned because of the demand for more long-lived wines.

Supertuscans

Despite the remaining arguments, Chianti has been improving beyond recognition since 1984. In the meantime, however, a plethora of individually named, costly *vini da tavola*, dubbed "supertuscans" became firmly established. The wine list of any restaurant in central Tuscany will certainly include Chianti. It will probably also contain one or more names like Coltassala, Flaccianello, Mormoreto, Tavernelle, Tignanello or Le Pergole Torte.

These are often wines made solely with Sangiovese, or Sangioveto, a superior clone. Sometimes they are a blend of Sangiovese and Cabernet Sauvignon, the French grape which gives excellent results in Tuscany. They are occasionally made solely with Cabernet. The only way to divine their constituents is to care-

LEFT: the traditional Chianti bottle, the *fiascho*.
RIGHT: making *Vin Santo* in the Chianti heartland.

fully scan the back label (which may not reveal all) or to ask.

To add a little spice to the quest for good drinking, a single name on a wine list will not necessarily signify a "supertuscan". Numerous estates have a particular vineyard whose wine, when kept separate, is always better than the rest. Each is labelled with its vineyard name as well as its official designation: Chianti or Chianti Classico. Tuscans are expected to know that Montesodi, for example, is a particular *cru* (single vineyard wine) of Chianti Rufina from the Frescobaldi estate. So the one word is often all that is put on the list in a restaurant. In shops,

where the label can be scanned, life is easier.

The general, but not infallible, rule of thumb is that Classico is better than non-Classico. A good non-Classico producer can always outclass an average Classico estate. On the better, more matured, wines the label will state *Riserva*, which indicates the wine has been aged at least three years, mainly in traditional oak barrels. For easy drinking, the lively Chianti non-*Riserva*, informally called simply *normale*, comes into its own.

One would have thought that the harvest of a wine of such renown would be commemorated by great celebrations, but this is rarely the case. The vintage is a nerve-racking period and nail biting is seen more often than singing and dancing. In late September and October the weather can be erratic and a sudden rainy squall can turn perfectly ripe bunches of grapes into a rotting mass.

Even when the harvest is successfully completed, there is little time to relax. A year's livelihood and several years' reputation is tied up in the large vats of bubbling grape juice, and they require constant attention and careful monitoring. Producers with rings round their eyes are far more likely to have been up all night attending to their wine than carousing. A regional celebration is in any case impossible because the vintage, which can last three weeks or so, starts and finishes at different times in different zones.

Then there are the **Vin Santo** grapes to guard. Vin Santo ("holy wine") is a dessert wine made all over Tuscany from white Trebbiano and Malvasia grapes. Once picked, they are dried slowly, weather permitting, either hanging up, lying on straw mats, or in shallow stacked crates. Six weeks to four months later, raisin-like, they are pressed and the small amount of concentrated, sweet juice that results is put into small barrels. There it slowly ferments and matures, untouched, for a number of years.

Most Vin Santo is sweet, but some is dry. Nearly all of it is rare, expensive and often a real treat. It is served at the end of a meal with *cantuccini* or *biscotti di Prato*, hard almond biscuits which are usually dunked in the sweet golden wine.

Many more wines of note

Red wine in Tuscany is still inextricably linked with Chianti, but it shouldn't be. It really ought to be linked with the Sangiovese grape. Chianti, although well diffused, is not Tuscany's only red wine; Sangiovese is far and away the predominant grape of the entire region, despite occasional outcrops of Cabernet Sauvignon. There are several clones of the grape planted: Sangioveto, Sangiovese Grosso, Sangiovese Piccolo, Prugnolo, Brunello and so on. A fierce debate rages constantly about which are superior and which are similar.

Brunello is found around the town of Montalcino, south of Siena. The wine, Brunello di Montalcino, is one of Italy's best, though it only dates back to 1870. It was the result of a firm conviction of Ferrucio Biondi-Santi, then only 20 years old, who put his beliefs into action, and his descendants have kept the name Biondi-Santi in the forefront of the wine's reputation. Lack of tradition can be a disadvantage – but there are advantages too. One of Brunello di Montalcino's prescribed characteristics is a long minimum ageing period (four years, three and a half of them in oak).

This was felt by some to be too long for all but the grandest wines, which then need to mature longer in the bottle. So a younger wine, **Rosso di Montalcino**, was swiftly created in the same style. The two co-exist comfortably and the risk of discontented producers "bend-

ing" the law has been avoided. Chianti's traditions could never have accommodated such flexibility.

The Prugnolo clone of Sangiovese predominates further east and produces **Vino Nobile di Montepulciano** around the town of the same name. Vino Nobile may be best described as a halfway house between Brunello di Montalcino and Chianti Classico. Like both these wines it has been decreed DOCG, giving Tuscany three of the first five wines in Italy that have been elevated to that stature.

ABOVE: new vintages sampled at a wine festival.
RIGHT: local products of the vine on display.

Whites very much take second place in Tuscany. They are light, simple and pleasant but generally, despite continual improvements, could not be described as "great". Most are based on Trebbiano and Malvasia grapes and are named after the locality of their origin.

The main exception is the dry, elegant, but quite full-bodied **Vernaccia di San Gimignano**, of which Michelangelo apparently said: "It kisses, licks, bites, thrusts and stings." The grape name Vernaccia crops up in a few parts of Italy but each bears no relation to the others: Vernaccia seems to imply no more than a "local" grape.

The other exception was the great fashion of the 1980s: the French variety Chardonnay. More and more producers turned over one or more plots to the grape, many invested in small, new oak barrels from France, called *barriques*, to mature the wines, and whoops of delight could be heard all over Tuscany as the results started appearing.

Traditionalists who believe that all good things in Tuscany should be Tuscan in origin either had to let the excitement pass them by – unthinkable – or else retire to the libraries to try to prove that Chardonnay was planted in Tuscany long ago after all. ❑

TUSCAN WINES: A BRIEF BUYER'S GUIDE

There are a few basics to keep in mind when shopping for wine in Tuscany. First read the label. Make sure the wine has the "DOC" designation; try to understand who produced the wine, avoiding acronyms (such as CA.VI.T.) and go for the wines with family names and/or farms; and look for the *gallo nero* (black cockerel) on the bottleneck if you want a good Chianti.

In general, 1971, 1983, 1985, 1988, 1990 and 1997 are said to be outstanding Tuscan vintages (although anything prior to 1985 will need to have been well stored). The 1997 vintage, in fact, is said to be extremely good – but expect it to be in short supply and expensive. "Excellent" vintages

are thought to be 1978, 1982, 1986, 1994 and 1995 – but again check that older wines have been stored properly. Vintages to avoid at all costs: 1972, 1976, 1984, 1989, 1991 and 1992. Specifically, 1990 was a good year for Vino Nobile di Montepulciano; both 1990 and 1993 were notable for Chianti; and 1988, 1990 and 1993 were exceptional years for Brunello di Montalcino.

As for prices, 5000–6000L will buy a basic "plonk" and the cheapest possible *gallo nero* goes for around 8,000L. You can get a very good wine for between 12,000 and 15,000L, while the really excellent bottles will set you back 20,000L or more.

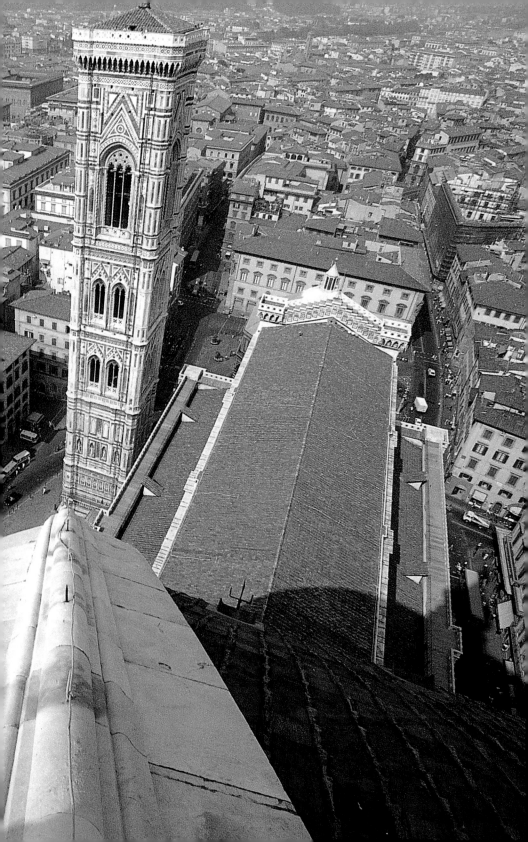

ARCHITECTURAL TREASURES

*Tuscany combines rich urban heritage with a delightful rural
legacy to create a unique architectural tableau*

Many visitors share the wistful sentiments of Henry James: "The more I look at the Florentine domestic architecture, the more I like it; and if I am ever to build myself a lordly pleasure-house, I don't see how in conscience I can build it differently from these." Tuscany makes prospective purchasers of us all, as we view a succession of Chianti villas and rustic farmhouses, medieval tower-houses and palatial *palazzi*.

The Tuscan town square is often one's lasting visual memory of the rich cityscape. Tellingly, the writer Enrico Guidoni calls the piazza "the definitive image of what the modern city has lost". Set at the heart of a community, it offers a chequerboard of medieval or Renaissance buildings. The arena can be the evocative amphitheatre of Siena's Campo, the civic stage set of Florence's Piazza della Signoria, or the tiny but perfectly formed piazza at Pienza, a memorial to papal power. At once functional and decorative, the square remains the social and commercial heart. The symbol of both the square and Tuscan provincialism is the belltower, or campanile.

The piazza has had multiple functions, acting as the civic, religious, ceremonial or commercial centre. The square was also home to medieval guilds and merchants, nobles and prelates, with more modest houses concealed behind. Yet the classic piazza is the civic and religious heart of town, with a town hall (*palazzo del comune*), belltower, cathedral (*duomo*) and baptistry (*battistero*). Familiar features are a gracefully carved well-head, an arcaded courtyard, and a cluster of patrician palaces with severe façades and overhanging roofs. The square was originally paved in herringbone brick or marble, but some were replaced by flint flagstones in the 18th century. Despite its harmony, this perfect piazza is often the result of piecemeal development, demolition

and rebuilding. The seductive spell of Tuscan harmony often flies in the face of the architectural facts.

Architectural highlights

Curiously, Tuscan architecture is characterised as much by diversity as it is by harmony: harmony in its aesthetic sweetness; diversity in its range of buildings, from Romanesque cathedrals to Renaissance palaces, town halls to tower-houses. The region is equally rich in religious and secular architecture (*see page 114*), with the bustling urban heritage complementing the tranquil, sunny rural landscape of villas and farmhouses.

Civic architecture is particularly rich. The Tuscan town hall, with accompanying belltower, encapsulates a civic ideal. In the past, it promised a degree of democracy to the merchant guilds, the nobility and the people. The Palazzo del Comune, known by different local names, has been the seat of local government

---

PRECEDING PAGES: Montepulciano. **LEFT:** campanile and rooftops of Florence. **RIGHT:** Pienza's perfectly formed piazza, featuring a *cisterna* and town hall.

since medieval times. This imposing, fortified building dominates the square today, as surely as it has always dominated the lives of local citizens. The best-known is the fortress-like Palazzo Vecchio, Florence, its austerity belied by a palatial interior. However, even the smallest commune has a grand town hall. In the Mugello, Palazzo Vicari in Scarperia resembles Palazzo Vecchio, with its impressive 14th-century merlons and corbels. Such public palazzi are often studded with stemmae, stone-carved

coats of arms belonging to prominent citizens or noble clans.

In numerous cities, including San Gimignano, there is also an adjoining balcony known as the *arengo*, from which politicians would harangue the crowd. Nearby is usually a loggia, providing shelter from the sun or rain, as well as a meeting place, today often used as a small market. Thus, Tuscany's grandest buildings serve much the same purpose today as they have always done.

Urbanisation

Visually, urban Tuscany is the product of medieval and Renaissance builders, even if Roman and Etruscan stones were recycled. Dismissing the Middle Ages as a period of decadence and decay does an injustice to the region's prosperity and architectural heritage. In Tuscany, the period represented a marked social rebirth, with the flowering of independent city-states in the 11th century. By 1200 most towns had become burgeoning centres with distinctive identities and a civic pride evident in the grandiose town halls and tower-houses. The medieval cathedrals and civic buildings were a testament to the citizens' refined taste, just as the ordered country estates later became a Renaissance symbol of peace and prosperity.

The medieval skyscrapers of San Gimignano signified the civilising effect of urban living, with the *signori* (feudal lords) encouraged to relinquish their castles for city life. The *borgo*, or fortified city, was also home to landowners and merchants, particularly with the rise of the *popolo grasso*, the wealthy middle class in the 14th century. The medieval city became a symbol of safety during the city-state conflicts.

Tuscan Romanesque

This style is less solemn, less philosophical than French, English or German Romanesque. Its hallmarks are surface decoration and space rather than sobriety and solidity, with simple bricks transformed by a marble veneer.

The style, centred on Florence, favours contrasting patterns of dark and light marble as well as striking geometric designs. The form was first realised in the city baptistry, with its round-headed arches, classical proportions and a striving for weightlessness. The Florentine model retains a certain simplicity of form, contrasting the austerity of Romanesque with the traditional Tuscan love of polychrome marble patterns.

Given city rivalries, Tuscan Romanesque delights in distinctive regional variations, as in the differentiated stripes and arcading in Lucca. In San Michele, a city masterpiece, the chiselled style of the delicate colonnades emphasises the height and exuberance of the façade.

Pisan Romanesque

The maritime republic of Pisa was an 11th-century power, trading with northern Europe and the Muslim world. As a result, the Pisan style is

---

REALISTIC VIEW?

"I am afraid," commented the author Henry James, "that behind these so gravely harmonious fronts is a good deal of dusky discomfort."

a glorious hybrid: austere Norman Romanesque inspired by a Moorish Sicilian aesthetic and the Tuscan taste for marble. While the severe colonnaded galleries owe much to Norman models, Sicily inspires the seductive decorative elements such as exuberant arabesques.

Yet the colourful geometry of the multi-coloured marble is essentially Tuscan. The palette contrasts white marble from Carrara, rosy pink from Maremma and dark green from Prato. A hallmark of the style was its talent for selecting a theatrical space: in Pisa the main buildings present a unified whole, placed on the lawn like prisms on a baize cloth. The Pisan

balancing height with breadth. In great churches such as Santa Croce in Florence, naves and aisles are not vaulted but use the open trusses favoured by Romanesque architecture.

However, Gothic details adorn Romanesque designs, as in the triangular pediments on the baptistry at Pisa. In the absence of pure Gothic, it is best to refer to Romanesque dressed in Gothic clothes. For instance, Case dei Guinigi in Lucca, the final flowering of Tuscan tower-houses, contain Gothic mullioned windows but also Romanesque round-arched arcading. Nonetheless, the Cistercian abbey of San Galgano echoes French Gothic while the gabled Gothic

Duomo was the prototype, with its contrasting bands of colour, blind arcading, colonnaded gallery and the geometry of inlaid marble. Inspired by Pisa, the cathedrals of Siena, San Miniato, Prato and Lucca use zebra-like stripes and an interplay of light and shade.

Medieval cityscape

Given the rich Roman heritage, Tuscans did not take to the Gothic form, with its pointed arches and sheer verticality, but preferred symmetry,

LEFT: Pisan Romanesque style, seen in the Duomo's blind arches, colonnades and inset square diamonds.
ABOVE: Franciscan church of Santa Croce in Florence.

church of Santa Maria della Spina in Pisa feels more French than Tuscan.

Not that Gothic gables are a guide to a medieval atmosphere. Many Tuscan towns are authentically medieval, as is the case with Cortona, Lucca, San Gimignano and Volterra. As the largest medieval city in Europe, Siena is arguably the most authentic, with strict building regulations in place since the 13th century. Certainly, its Gothic spirit is intact, from red-brick palaces to herringbone alleys, all moulded to a mystical Sienese sensibility.

Without question, fortifications played an important role in medieval Tuscany. Walled towns, often known as *borghi* and built on hilltops, are emblematic of the Tuscan city-scape. Anghiari, Buonconvento, Monteriggioni and Montepulciano all provide proof that preserving walls helps preserve a distinct identity. While a *castello* was either a fortified village or a castle, a *rocca* was usually a defended garrison post and a *fortezza* was a fortress of strategic importance.

The region abounds in ruined or restored examples, including castles at Poppi and Prato, and the pair of fortresses in Florence. Siena province alone boasts San Gimignano's rocca and watchtowers as well as the massive *fortezze* in Siena and Montalcino, which have

both been converted into wine-tasting centres.

Tower-houses were castle-residences serving as both warehouses and fortresses, self-sufficient enclaves symbolising the wealth of the feudal nobles or prosperous merchants, and their scorn for civil authority. Key features included a well for a constant water supply, an inner courtyard to provide light and ventilation, and an external staircase to the *piano nobile*, the grand residential first floor. As the great Tuscan families grew wealthy on banking and the cloth trade, their homes became more palatial and domesticated. In time, decorative details were added, notably graceful courtyards

SACRED SITES

Religious architecture represents one of the highlights of Tuscany. Any tour would certainly include the cathedrals of Florence, Lucca, Pisa and Siena. Lesser-known gems include Barga's Romanesque cathedral, Montepulciano's Renaissance San Biagio and the Romanesque San Miniato al Monte in the Florentine hills. In many cases, the architecture is inextricably bound up with the artistic wealth on the walls. This is true of the Gothic church of Santa Maria Novella in Florence or Arezzo's San Francesco, with its poignant fresco cycle by della Francesca. By contrast, exteriors can be austere or even unfinished, a sign that patrons squabbled or ran out of funds.

The siting is also significant, with cathedrals usually constructed on sacred spots hallowed since Roman or Etruscan times. Mendicant churches tended to be built outside the city walls, with the surrounding square often becoming a major city market. Abbeys and monasteries, which could be as large as medieval towns, were built on virgin sites, and blended civic and Christian concerns.

Some of the most intriguing architecturally are the Romanesque abbey of Sant'Antimo, the Baroque Certosa di Pisa, the Carthusian foundation of Camaldoli, the hilltop monastery of La Verna, and Monte Oliveto Maggiore, a Benedictine foundation in the woods south of Siena.

complete with sculpted wells, coats of arms, ornate arches and a loggia on the first or top floors. Despite 16th-century modifications, the Florentine Palazzo Davanzati preserves much of its medieval atmosphere. The palace is impressive, from its iron-bolted doors and formidable façade pierced by numerous small windows to an internal courtyard boasting a well with a pulley system designed to supply water to each floor. The interior presents a charming portrait of domestic life, from 15th-century frescoes and tapestries to the *cassoni*, Tuscan wedding chests, and even a privileged child's bathroom.

Riccardi, the Medici home and banking head-quarters, a massive mansion with an arcaded inner courtyard. He also designed Palazzo Pitti (1444), the prototype of a patrician palace, boasting strict classical proportions and a rus-ticated façade. Yet there are lingering traces of feudal times in the Gothic windows and heavy cornices. Built for Cosimo de' Medici, Palazzo Pitti clearly symbolises the power and prestige of the owner.

However, some nobles simply modernised their feudal seats. Palazzo Spini-Ferroni, a crenellated three-tiered fortress close to the Arno, was a 13th-century watchtower before

Renaissance palaces

The Florentine palazzo was a direct descendant of the tower-house but without an outmoded defensive function. In keeping with the new humanist spirit, architects designed gracious private palaces as proof of their revivalist skills, not simply as symbols of patrician pride. Fore-most amongst the trailblazers was Michelozzi (1396–1472), who pursued the architectural principles of Alberti and Brunelleschi. Miche-lozzo designed the Florentine Palazzo Medici-

becoming a palatial home. Just around the cor-ner looms the grandiose Palazzo Strozzi, a rus-ticated stone cube of mammoth proportions built for the greatest banking dynasty. Rustica-tion was intended to underline the Strozzi's power. The writer Mary McCarthy rightly felt that the palace evoked "the giganticism of the human ego". Whereas Palazzo Strozzi empha-sises strength and stability, homes such as Palazzo Rucellai were more harmonious, em-bellished with elegant loggias, classical motifs and decorative friezes.

Florence may be the most innovative Renais-sance city, but Pienza is the best preserved. Pienza was built by Pius II as a papal city, offer-

LEFT: rose-coloured rooftops of Siena surrounding the Campo. **ABOVE:** the Palazzo Pitti, prototype of a patrician palace, designed by Michelozzo.

ing both an echo of imperial patronage and a humanist memorial to his papacy. In 1462, the architect, Rossellino, grafted a monumental Renaissance core onto medieval grandiosity. All the elements of civic life were set on one tiny square, its geometric shape giving tension to the whole. Using a well-head as the lynch-pin, the piazza embraces an episcopal palace, a dignified town hall with an open loggia, and a tower embodying Tuscan pride. In his private palace here, the Pope delighted in hanging gardens,

> ### LASTING IMPRESSIONS
>
> A century after the architect Filippo Brunelleschi completed his dome, Michelangelo commented: "Similar to you I will not build, better than you I cannot."

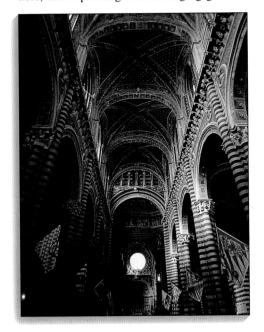

delicate loggias and rooms for every season. His bedchamber, panelled in spruce to mask the damp odour of a new house, enjoyed views on all four sides, from an inner courtyard to the hilly countryside.

Renaissance architects

As the cradle of the Renaissance, Tuscany is where the profession of architect first came into its own. Imbued with a new humanist spirit, architects of the stature of Brunelleschi, Alberti, Michelozzi, Rossellino and Sangallo made their mark on churches, palaces and villas. Florence, which saw itself as the inheritor of Roman grandeur, is naturally the city with the greatest concentration of Renaissance monuments. Strongly influenced by Tuscan Romanesque, the buildings were models of visual restraint, dedicated to proportion, perspective and classical motifs.

Brunelleschi (1377–1446), the father of Renaissance architecture, left his masterpiece on the Duomo in Florence. His dome was the fulfilment of the Renaissance ideal, a feat of Florentine engineering. For Brunelleschi, steeped in Classical lore and well-versed in Tuscan Romanesque, the Roman Pantheon acted as a model. After the shell of the cathedral was complete, an ultra-light dome was required to cover the octagonal void. Given the vast dimensions of the void, his innovative solution used two concentric shells, with eight marble ribs defining its octagonal shape. The dome was erected by labourers working without a safety net, using a system of cantilevered brickwork in herringbone design.

Alberti (1404–72) is considered the archetypal Renaissance man, a patrician playwright, humanist and philosopher, composer and lawyer, athlete and architect. He rivalled Brunelleschi in his gift for geometry and desire to revive "the immutable laws of architecture", yet also sought to respect the Tuscan taste for decoration. As an architectural historian, he revived Vitruvius' theories and put them into practice in Florence. The laws of proportion, perspective and the use of the classical orders all came into play in the Duomo and in the Florentine Palazzo Rucellai (1446). This landmark palace was inspired by the Colosseum and the buildings of classical Rome. Alberti emphasised the verticality of the facade by introducing pilasters in the three classical orders: Doric surmounted by Ionic and Corinthian. The Roman influence is present in the porches and panelled doors as well as in the frieze, which bears the crests of the Medici and Rucellai families.

The magnificent Rucellai loggia was the last to be built in 15th-century Florence, such was the profligacy it engendered. Weddings and festivities in the loggia may be no more but the family remains ensconced in part of the palace.

Rural retreats

Tuscany's rich urban heritage risks overshadowing the delightful rural legacy of sunny villas and picturesque hilltop farmhouses. In medieval Tuscany, the traditional manor or fortified seat was bound by solid walls or battlements. This country refuge evolved into the gracious patrician villa-residence of Renaissance times. In the 13th century, there were two forms of rural retreat, the feudal domain – the grand preserve of the landed nobility – and the *casa da signore*, the busy hub of a country estate. This was a crenellated property with a watch-tower, surrounded by a variety of farm buildings and cottages, and owned by the gentry or bourgeoisie.

The villa as a country retreat was a Renais-

try and a rationalisation of form and function. Embellished by porticoes, the villa was built on a square plan around an inner courtyard, with a loggia on the first floor.

Set in ornamental gardens and encircled by walls, the villa enjoyed superb views, often from a hilltop. At a time when peace reigned in the Tuscan countryside, the gardens were regarded as a bucolic retreat, an essential part of the architectural composition. The grounds consist of a *giardino segreto*, a geometrical walled garden, with formal parterres and topiary, kitchen and herb gardens, lined by avenues of cypresses or lemon trees. The design, enlivened

sance concept, reflecting the gracious rural lifestyle cultivated by the Tuscan nobility. The villas were generally elegant but not ostentatious, in keeping with the cultural conservatism of the Florentine nobility. However, the grandest Medici villas, such as Cafaggiolo, designed by Michelozzi, were sumptuous princely estates. Poggio a Caiano (*see "Villas and Gardens", page 213*) is the model Renaissance villa, with its harmonious design and colonnaded loggia harking back to the grandeur of classical times. The rural design reflected a desire for symme-

by water gardens, was set in the 16th century when the Mannerist style acquired colonnades and statuary, grottoes and follies. By the 17th century, the crisp geometry of the gardens was matched by formal terraces, virtuoso waterworks, and sculptures of sea monsters cavorting with mythological figures. In their ease and openness, the gardens were in harmony with the house and the patrician owner.

As the Renaissance architect Alberti declared, "Only the house of a tyrant can look like a fortress: an ideal home should be open to the world outside, beautifully adorned, delicate and finely proportioned rather than proud and stately". ❐

LEFT: interior of Santa Maria dei Servi, Siena.
ABOVE: church and farmhouse, Monte Amiata.

TUSCAN CRAFTSMANSHIP

Tuscany is a treasure trove of everything from gilded cherubs, marble busts and bas-reliefs to carved olive wood sculptures and hand-dyed silks

Medieval Tuscany was devoted to the wool, silk, cloth and marble industries. Moreover, the Medici dynasty were patrons of the minor arts, not just the major ones. Tuscan craftsmen were willing pawns in a game of city-state rivalry and mercantile one-upmanship. As a result, the region teemed with specialised artisans.

The Tuscan craft tradition thrives today, drawing inspiration from medieval and Renaissance masters. Florentine sculpture and statuary harks back to Cellini's bronzes; the decorative style of the della Robbia family survives in ceramics. Expert craftsmen work in furniture and ceramics, stone and marble, bronze, gold and silver, silk and fine fabrics. Sienese gold-making dates back to Etruscan times, as does the alabaster-carving tradition in Volterra. Prato has been the centre of the textile trade since medieval times, while Empoli has been associated with glass-making since the end of the 14th century, and Lucca has been renowned for its silk-weaving since the 17th century. With a tradition dating back to 1425, Tuscany is, after Faenza in Emilia-Romagna, the oldest Italian centre for *maioliche*; majolica is the Italian version of French faience or English fine porcelain. The centre, Montelupo, near Florence, makes *maioliche* inspired by the work of the della Robbia workshops. Genuine craftsmen continue to work in Scarperia in the Mugello, the centre of Italy's cutlery industry.

Florence has long been known for its gold and silver smiths, exotic dyes, marbled paper and marquetry. Florentine crafts are not fossilised but constantly evolving, building on a rich past, such as *intarsio*, the ancient craft of inlaying semi-precious stones in intricate mosaics, whether wall panels or table tops. Local workshops also specialise in the restoration of works encrusted with semi-precious stones.

▷ **SILKEN PROMISE**
The *Antico Setificio Fiorentino* was founded by fashion designer Emilio Pucci, who made his reputation with dyed silks. This workshop is a romantic revival of Renaissance dyeing skills and designs.

△ **MARBLE MADNESS**
Selling a marble workshop's wares. The craftsmen's children seem to treat the workshops as a playground. As adults, some will study marble-working at school in Lucca or Carrara.

▽ **CRAFTY CRAFT**
Scagliola is a Florentine craft which creates the effect of inlaying. The technique (used for table tops or trays) uses pulverised marble, gesso and tints rather than inlaid marble.

▽ BAGS OF STYLE

An elegant display of Florentine leatherware. In Florence, good quality leather goods are on sale in the Mercato Centrale (San Lorenzo market) and in the leather workshops around Santa Croce.

▽ ON A PLATE

Contemporary ceramics in Cortona, a sophisticated medieval hill-top town. Colourful Tuscan porcelain and medieval ceramics can be seen in the local *Museo dell'Accademia Etrusca*.

◁ RAW HIDES

A traditional leather-worker in Pienza. Tuscany is noted for its thick, supple leather-ware, both hand-made or mass-produced. Shops and markets all over Tuscany sell shoes, wallets, belts, bags and so on. There are good bargains to be had, but check carefully for quality before buying.

◁ GOLD STANDARD

Jewellers are clustered on Florence's Ponte Vecchio, as they have been for years. There is a long tradition of gold-making in the city, even if the gold and jewellery centre has now moved to Arezzo. The Renaissance masters Cellini, Ghiberti, Brunelleschi and Verrocchio all trained as goldsmiths.

▽ TUSCAN TERRACOTTA

Putting the final touches to a terracotta figure before the final firing. These craftsmen specialise in reproductions of ancient pieces, and use the same techniques practised in Renaissance times.

MOULDING CARRARA MARBLE

The Carrara quarries in the Apuan Alps of northern Tuscany are the finest in Italy, and the local Carrara marble-workers are always in great demand.

The workshops of Pietrasanta are coated in white marble dust, and littered with marble torsos of nudes and horses, angels and saints. The "model-maker" takes the block of marble and hews the rough shape using a hammer and chisel. Then the sculptor goes to work. Finally, the "decorator" adds finishing touches. Unlike bronze-workers who sign their work, the masterpieces of most marble-workers remain anonymous. It is a labour of love.

The marble for Michelangelo's *David*, the sculpture that made his reputation, was quarried in Carrara. In 1504, it took 40 men four days to move the marble giant into position on Florence's Piazza della Signoria. Times change – but not too much. When the local Carrara masons were commissioned to make monumental busts of Saddam Hussein, the Iraqi president, the job still required a vast team. As one marble-worker put it: "Even Michelangelo had his slaves. He could not have done it alone".

FESTIVALS

Tuscany's festivals aren't staged to attract tourists – they're an authentic and flamboyant expression of local traditions and rivalries

Festivals are Tuscany's richest theatre, ranging from the simple *sagra* (feast) to the most complex Italian festival of all, the *Palio*. In a sophisticated festival, scenes of high drama or contemporary relevance can recall a pagan or medieval past, succumb to Bacchic indulgence or soar to mysticism and magic.

Even the most ordinary festival reveals an unbroken tradition, a curious competition or a rustic delicacy. There are *feste* in honour of fire and water, *ravioli* and wine, historic football jousts, saints and witches. Every conceivable animal is celebrated, from thrushs to crickets. Even the Virgin's Holy Girdle is worshipped.

It is difficult to avoid such small festivals in Tuscany. Any of the following signs suggest the unfolding of a secret rite: a parish church decorated with banners and snapshots of horses; huddles of town dignitaries plotting in corners; agile boys tossing flags; and a trestle table set for 200. Inevitably, the table is piled high with stodgy chestnut *polenta*; wizened old men are "helping" uncork the local wine.

Just for fun

Don't let initial appearances deceive: in the background, yesterday's motorbike daredevil is today's Renaissance courtier in harlequin tights. Somewhere, a mechanical donkey fails to start but the fireworks explode anyway. Ask anyone what the festival is "about" and the innocuous reply will be *allegria*, "fun".

But *allegria* belics the seriousness of intent. Festivals are a distorting mirror to Tuscan life, projecting the rawness and romanticism of civic pride onto a citizen's individualism. Even if there is no overt competition, each participant expects the finest horse, the most lavish costume, the biggest bonfire or the longest *contrada* procession.

This expectation usually crystallizes around the *contrade*, little cities within a city. These

emerged in the 12th-century "communes" when a particular square, church and fountain became associated with a local area and character. The *contrada* spirit, particularly marked in Siena, Arezzo and Lucca provinces, inspires most of Tuscany's festivals. Without such passion, many would have degenerated into tourist

displays. With it, the survival of *palio* and *glostra* rivalries is ensured.

In Siena, the archetypal *contrade* city, each of the 17 *contrade* has its own organisation, church and even museums housing the *Palio* memorabilia. These announce births, marriages and deaths: marriage is celebrated with a flag-waving display and funerals are attended by a *contrada* page. Children are enrolled at birth and membership is for life.

Children learn *senesità*, the city's proclaimed values of freedom, friendship and altruism. They are also gently indoctrinated in *contrada* folklore, *Palio* triumphs and disasters. The boys practise the noble arts of flag waving, drum-

---

PRECEDING PAGES: watching the *Palio* from a prime location. **LEFT:** in full traditional rig for Siena's *Palio*. **RIGHT:** winner in a Maremma horse race.

ming and nobbling the enemy *contrada*'s horse, while girls learn how to cook *risotto* for 100 *contradaioli* on feast days. Both sexes absorb *contrada* values: stealth, diplomacy and single-minded victory. At its highest, the *contrade* spirit fosters individual excellence and a striving towards collective perfectionism. Even the humblest *palio* races reflect local *contrade* traditions and are not a mere parody of the Sienese model. Asciano and Querceta always race donkeys rather than horses. Likewise, Livorno's *palio marinaro*, a regatta along the canals, is a natural choice for a seafaring city. Jousts or *giostre* are a rougher variant on the *palio* theme.

stand packed with local dignitaries. The segregated members of the five opposing *contrade* explode in a riot of drumming and banner waving. In turn, the knights try to hit and carry off the ring on the Saracen's shield. As each knight gallops up to the Saracen, supporters are quiet while rival fans stamp, whistle, scream and wave. The guiding spirit is completely anti-Olympiad: winning, not taking part, is definitely what counts.

Arezzo runs an elaborate *giostra* with a more complex scoring system and greater rewards and punishments. The winner receives a gold lance, adulation from one *contrada* and hatred

Belligerent beginnings

The origins lie in medieval fist fights and the jousts are still a safe way of reliving and relieving ancient rivalries. There are moments when the *giostre* have the fervour of a war ceremony, or the finality of a farewell service for crusaders. Although the buffalo races and bullfights have now died out, real or mechanical falcons, bears, donkeys and horses still "joust" regularly.

Two dramatic jousts at Arezzo and Sarteano re-enact local feuds, disguised as the ritual savagery of medieval crusaders. The jousts centre on charges at a dummy representing the "Saracen". In Sarteano, a cortege circles into the medieval square and bows to the *notabili*, the

from the three losers. A knight missing the target can be knocked off his horse by a savage "cat-of-three-tails".

Each *contrada*, ensconced on its own side of the Piazza Grande, is engrossed in the accompanying procession which is a contradictory mix of medieval costume and modern sentiment. As Archibald Lyall wrote of Arezzo, "Beautiful ladies ride in the procession, their make-up by Elizabeth Arden and their costumes out of the Duc de Berry's *Book of Hours*." The religious festivals range from simple homage to obscure saints, to Grassina's elaborate "Way of the Cross", a re-enactment of the ascent to Calvary and the crucifixion. Prato's

"Display of the Virgin's Holy Girdle" is certainly the oddest.

According to legend, Doubting Thomas could not accept either the resurrection or Mary's assumption until he found roses in Jesus's empty tomb and then saw the Virgin in heaven removing her girdle for him. The girdle eventually reached Prato Cathedral in the 12th century via Thomas and the Holy Land crusades. *Pratese* merchants, conscious of their priceless relic, display it five times a year to incredulous crowds.

> ### GOOD OMEN
>
> To many Tuscans, having a successful firework display during *Scoppio del Carro* means that their harvest for that year will be a good one.

Flaming dove

The fullest religious festival is Florence's "Exploding Carriage", *Lo Scoppio del Carro*, celebrating the resurrection and the success of the First Crusade. On Easter Day, citizens excitedly squeeze into the Piazza del Duomo to catch a glimpse of a mechanical dove or a miracle. The essential elements are: a tense wait for an uncertain fire, intense children who believe in magic, and a suspension of adult disbelief that a firework dove is the Holy Spirit.

The ritual began when Pazzino de' Pazzi returned from the First Crusade to Florence in 1305. Legend has it that he was the first to scale the walls of Jerusalem and seize a piece of the Holy Sepulchre. Every year, these precious chips are taken from San Miniato to the baptistry where a spark from the stones lights the holy fire. The fire, carried in procession to the Duomo, is later used to ignite the dove.

Six white oxen drag the creaking, gilded carriage into the square. De Pazzi had the first simple *carro* built to bring the holy fire to the city and successive popes made more opulent carriages. The present one, dating from 1700, resembles a Japanese palanquin on wheels. In a moment of inspiration, Leo X added the dove to the ritual.

As High Mass in the Duomo comes to an end, children outside eye the magic box of flowers and fireworks and will it to explode. Inside the Duomo, children gaze at the firework dove suspended on a wire above the high altar. At the intoning of the *Gloria*, the dove, fizzing

with sacred fire, swoops through the open doors and ignites the triumphal carriage. Amid the chiming of bells, shrieks and fireworks, the dove fizzles out, its mechanical miracle accomplished.

Although today's participants are more likely to be shopkeepers than peasants, the sense of relief is just as great. The liberated crowds spill over the Ponte Vecchio, wander to lunch near the Boboli Gardens or watch the foolhardy dive into the river. The atmosphere is one of exhilaration. A successful ritual repre-

sents a joyous release of tension for all.

The simplest and most dramatic festival is held in Monte Amiata. Here, Abbadia di San Salvatore's traditional *Fiaccole di Natale* or "Christmas Torches" is a mountain festival built around towering, conical bonfires. Originally a pagan mid-winter festival, its medieval roots lie in the vigil kept by villagers and shepherds as they waited for Midnight Mass on Christmas Eve. Carols, storytelling, feasting and fires helped to drive away the cold. In the gathering of shepherds, the long wait, the ritual worship, the cold of the mountains, there are echoes of Bethlehem.

Today, pyramids of fire are still used to re-

LEFT: spectators at Livorno's *palio marinaro*, the seafaring city's famous regatta.

RIGHT: a band prepares for its role in a local festival.

kindle memory and collective faith. The fire making is a male art and village boys compete in building the most graceful fire to adorn their local piazza. The surrounding forests, in common ownership since 1300, symbolise local pride and the fires are a seasonal thanksgiving. The bonfires of chestnut wood from Monte Amiata illuminate the town hall, squares and alleyways. Torchlit processions and dancing to mandolins die out only with the fires at dawn. The dying embers signal the explosion of the winter sports season: skiing, nature trails and New Year balls.

Pork and beans

Despite their pagan, religious or seasonal labels, many festivals are really a pretext for gastronomic delights. One tiny village near Florence holds a festival to celebrate the broad bean harvest in early May. Radicofani unashamedly holds a *Ravioli Festa* while Montale and Montalcino ennoble and eat the thrush in *Sagra del Tordo*. The celebrations are not limited to locals: casual visitors are also welcome to enjoy a dip in the pot. If the beans, thrush or white truffles do not appeal, *porchetta* (roast pig) is usually on sale.

But for uninhibited merrymaking there is nothing to equal *Carnevale*, a pagan spring carnival with a Christian veneer. Arezzo, San Gimignano and Piombino compete with allegorical or *Commedia dell'Arte* floats followed by processions of harlequins, courtiers, jesters and popes.

Viareggio's pre-Lenten carnival offers an unequalled display of political satire and burlesque, most visibly portrayed on the imaginative floats, which, after being in the *Carnevale* itself, remain on display all year – a tribute to the talented designers. Combining ancient pagan rituals and Christian values, *Carnevale* is the time to discover the masked desires of close friends and colleagues.

The last word belongs to Horace Walpole, writing in Florence in 1740, "The end of carnival is frantic bacchanalia; all the morn one makes parties in masque to the shops and coffee houses and all the evening to the operas and balls. Then I have danced, good gods! How I have danced!" ❑

RIGHT: triumph and unbearable happiness at the end of the Siena *Palio.*

PLACES

*A detailed guide to the entire region, with principal sites
cross-referenced by number to the maps*

Sometimes the delights of Tuscany all become too much, and a curious disease afflicts visitors, known as the Stendhal Syndrome. It manifests itself in sensitive visitors so overcome that they sometimes faint away completely. Stendhal recorded his own experience: "The tide of emotion which overwhelmed me flowed so deep that it scarce was to be distinguished from religious awe. As I emerged from the port of Santa Croce, I was seized with a fierce palpitation of the heart; I walked in constant fear of falling to the ground." Wagner was similarly affected, bursting into tears at the sight of the Duomo in Siena.

Tuscany has always been a favourite destination for travellers and pilgrims. But there is a risk of becoming so surfeited by the richness of the artistic inheritance of Tuscany that you may find yourself exclaiming with Mark Twain: "Enough! Say no more! Lump the whole thing! Say that the creator made Italy from designs by Michelangelo!"

The English poet Laurie Lee fled to the hills after a visit to Florence. "I'd had my fill of Florence," he wrote, "lovely but indigestible city. My eyes were choked with pictures and frescoes, all stamped one on top of the other, blurred, their colours running. I began to long for those cool uplands, that country air, for the dateless wild olive and the uncatalogued cuckoo."

The truly wonderful thing about Tuscany is that its artistic riches are fully matched by the radiance of nature, and the grace of the people who live there. As the novelist E.M. Forster observed: "The traveller who has gone to Italy to study the tactile values of Giotto, or the corruption of the papacy, may return remembering nothing but the blue sky and the men and women who live under it." And there's nothing wrong with that.   ❑

PRECEDING PAGES: vineyards in Badia a Passignano, Chianti; view over the rooftops of Lucca; town and harbour of Porto San Stefano.
LEFT: a leafy Roman road.

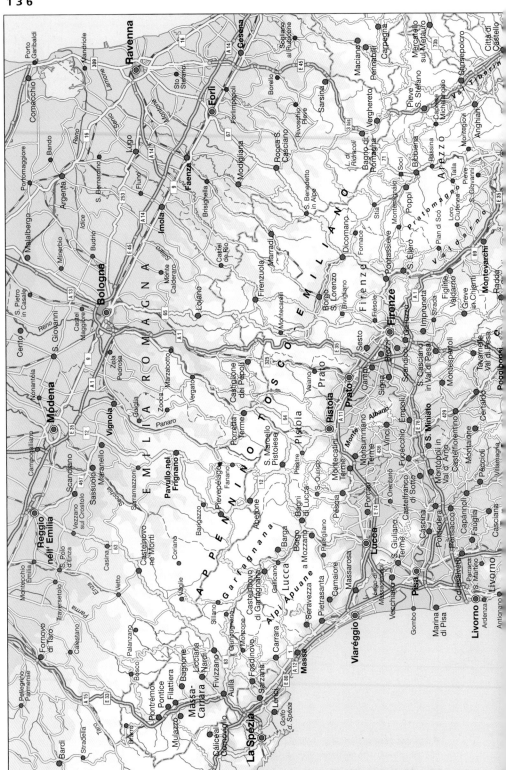

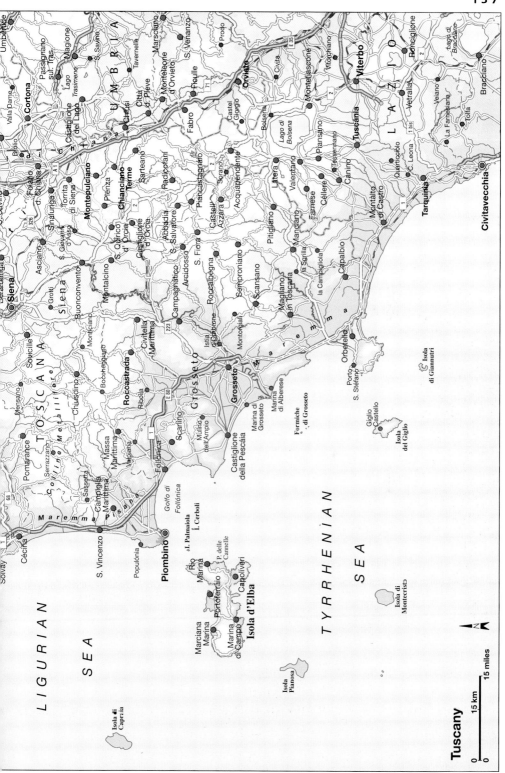

Tuscany

0   15 km
0   15 miles

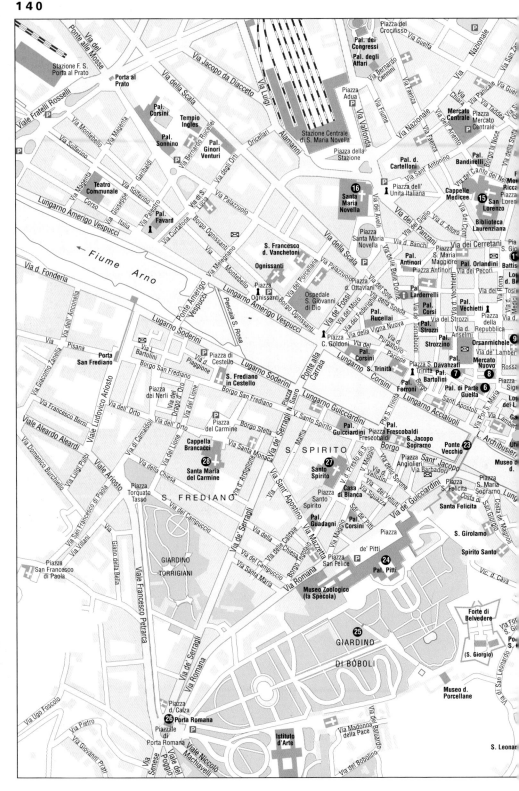

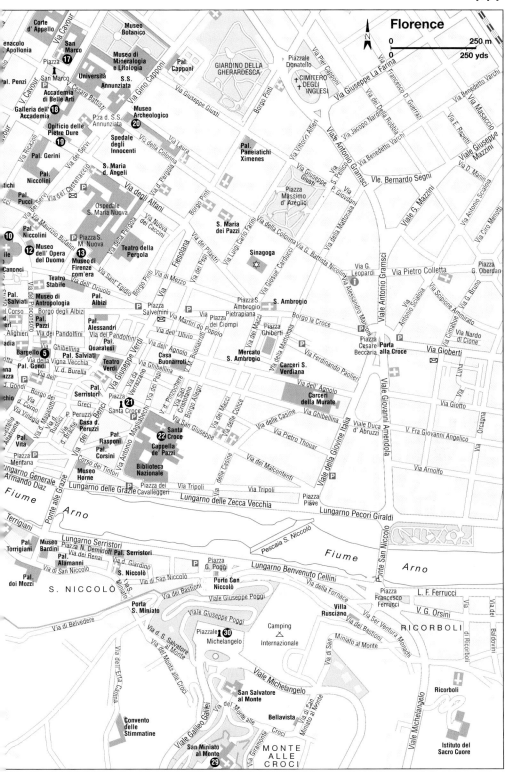

THE CITY OF FLORENCE

*The throbbing heart of Tuscany and the cradle of
the Renaissance, Florence is a truly outstanding city – in
a country full to bursting with spectacular sites*

Viewed from the surrounding hills, Florence seems to be floating in a bowl which, at dusk, is tinged violet. The honey-coloured walls and myriad, rose-coloured roofs of the city combine to make a unity which is dominated by a single, vast building, the cathedral, or Duomo. It is by far the biggest building for miles around, with its roof and dome in the same subtle colour-range as the surrounding smaller buildings above which it seems to float like a great liner among tugs.

There are few towers or spires. Giotto's multi-coloured campanile next to the Duomo, plain in outline but intricate in detail, and the thrusting tower of the Palazzo Vecchio, elegant and sombre, soar above a generally low profile. The overall impression is not that of a city, composed of tens of thousands of units, but of one single, vast building, a majestic palace.

This is symbolic of Florentine history: unity in diversity, a mansion occupied by a single family. Frequently there are family quarrels: members are even prepared to make common cause with foreigners to get the better of a neighbour, but they are still one family in one abode.

Close contact with the city can be at first disconcerting, even disappointing and claustrophobic. The streets are narrow, hemmed in by towering, plain buildings. There is no delicate filigree, as in Venice, or cheerful baroque, as in Rome, to tempt the eye.

Some of the buildings resemble 19th-century warehouses – grim structures that were erected at a time of social unrest and so discharging the primary function of fortresses. In any case, Florentine taste runs to the understated, the restrained, the prudent, as befits a race of farmers.

But gradually, the visitor comes to terms with a city which, though sharing basic characteristics with the larger family of Italian cities, is a unique mixture. The no-traffic laws in the historic centre– while often abused – has, for the most part, given Florence back to pedestrians. The streets are again part of the city's fabric, simultaneously discharging the role of stage-set and communication link. It's a liberating atmosphere: the visitor is free to wander, stop, and wander again, absorbing all the city has to offer.

PRECEDING PAGES:
pausing to reflect
at the Bargello
Museum.
LEFT: the Duomo.
BELOW: hazy day on
the River Arno.

Overwhelming riches

For the visitor to attempt a comprehensive survey of Florence on one single visit will simply invite fatigue, then boredom. The monuments and localities which figure in the following bird's-eye view are chosen on a necessarily arbitrary basis. Some, of course, select themselves; others have been included because they can stand as an example for their class as a whole, or illustrate some particular point of the Florentine story.

The rich ochre colours of Florence's terracotta tiles is enhanced after rain.

BELOW: street performer with an impressive backdrop: the Palazzo Vecchio.

The city has been grouped into four sections: starting with the area around the Palazzo Vecchio; followed by the area around the Duomo; and then by three important religious foundations (which, for reasons which will be explained, have been grouped together in the narrative though physically scattered around the city). The final section is the River Arno and beyond. Nearly all the places are within easy walking distance of one another.

As Florence is a small town, it is possible to walk its entire width, from the Porta Romana in the south to the Porta San Gallo in the north, in half an hour or so. During World War II, an aircraft dropped three or four bombs to the west of the town on a line running roughly north-south. Had the pilot corrected his course by a fraction to take him over the centre, then those bombs would have taken out almost everything we imagine when we think of Florence.

The civic heart

Of all the great Italian city squares, Florence's is the most perversely irregular. There is nothing in the **Piazza della Signoria ❶** to compete with the harmony that makes Venice's San Marco a vast, unroofed hall. There's nothing here of the grace of Siena's curved Campo, or the simple majesty of Rome's Capitol. Instead, the buildings follow each other around the perimeter of the Piazza in no particular order.

Tucked uncomfortably on one side is the **Palazzo Vecchio ❷** (open Fri–Wed; closed Sun pm and pub. hols; entrance fee), the seat of government for the past six centuries. Next to it is the elegant **Loggia dei Lanzi ❸** (open Fri–Wed; closed 1pm Sunday; entrance fee), crammed with statues, which doesn't seem to relate to anything in particular. The huge fountain in the centre is the subject

of amiable mockery by the residents of Florence themselves, and no two buildings in the Piazza seem to have the same façade.

With a despot's love of order, Duke Cosimo I tried to impose an artificial unity on the square, and Michelangelo even came up with a scheme to continue the shape of the Loggia all the way round. Such schemes came to nothing, leaving the Piazza as a perfect illustration of Florentine "unity in diversity".

Despite the absence of an overall plan and the bristling individuality of the buildings, the Piazza as a whole does come together. In general, it has changed little over the centuries, as can be seen by comparing the contemporary painting of the execution of Savonarola in the Piazza in 1498 with the square today. The narrow platform in front of the Palazzo Vecchio sums up the function of the Piazza della Signoria: it is all that remains of the original *Ringheria* – literally, the "haranguing place", where orators could address the assembled citizenry.

The **Marzocco**, the lion symbol of the city which prisoners were forced to kiss, can be found here, as well as a copy of Michelangelo's immense statue of David, commissioned in 1501 to mark an important change in the constitution.

Nearby is the statue of the first Medici duke – and the first Medici to so aggrandise himself – Cosimo I. The Loggia dei Lanzi (named after the *landsknechts* or mercenaries employed by Cosimo) used to have a statue of Perseus holding the head of the Gorgon (*see page 67*). Cosimo commissioned Cellini to do this work, which is being restored prior to its move to a museum.

The interior of the Palazzo Vecchio itself, begun in 1299 and finished in 1314, belies its grim exterior. The courtyard, with its copy of an enchanting fountain by Verrochio, is a delight. The portentous **Salone dei Cinquecento** was built for the Republican *Council of 500* introduced by Savonarola in 1496. It was transformed into a throne room for Cosimo I by Vasari, who produced vast, rather tasteless but historically fascinating frescoes lauding the exploits of the Medici. Finally it served as the first parliament of a united Italy when Florence briefly became the Italian capital in 1863.

Although the Palazzo still functions as Florence's town hall – you might even catch the incongruous sight of a wedding party, as it is very much a working building – most of the historic rooms, including the Medici suite and the grim little cell where Savonarola was held before his execution in the Piazza below, are usually open to the public.

Adjoining the Piazza are the immense galleries (*see page 147*) of the **Galleria degli Uffizi ❹** (open Tues–Sun 9am–10pm; for advance booking tel: 055-234 7941; entrance fee). The gallery's name reflects the fact that it was originally a building where the city's administration offices (*uffici*) were housed.

As a result of the terrorist explosion nearby in 1993, some works are still being restored and portions of the gallery remain closed. The famous but long-closed Vasari Corridor, however, reopened in 1997, but it is still subject to periodic and unpredictable closure because of staffing problems.

Chronologically, the Palazzo Vecchio is the second city hall of Florence. Its predecessor, the **Bargello ❺** (Via del Proconsolo; open daily till 1.50pm; closed

Map,
pages
140–41

TIP

For a meal with great views over the Piazza Signoria, try the new café at the Uffizi Gallery, on top of the Loggia dei Lanzi.

BELOW: Bartolomeo Ammannati's Neptune Fountain in the Piazza della Signoria.

alternate Sun and Mon; entrance fee), was built 50 years earlier in 1250 as the seat of the chief magistrate, the *Podestà*. The Bargello was, in effect, police headquarters – reflected in its forbidding exterior. The building is now a museum specialising in sculptures; it has a rich collection of works by artists like Brunelleschi, Michelangelo, Cellini, Donatello and many others – and is not nearly as bewildering as the Uffizi.

Completed in 1255, the Bargello is the oldest public building in Florence. Its elegant but grim courtyard was frequently the scene of public executions.

Four centuries of history

Just west of the Piazza della Signoria is a loosely associated group of three buildings which takes you across some four centuries of Florentine history, from the embattled Middle Ages to the era of ducal control. The **Palazzo di Parte Guelfa** ❻ (just off the Via del Terme) was the headquarters of the all-powerful Guelf Party which, after the defeat and expulsion of the Ghibellines, completely ruled the city. The Palazzo was built in the 13th century, but was subsequently enlarged on a number of occasions – an indication of its expanding status in Florence.

Also referred to as the Museo dell'Antica Casa Fiorentina, the **Palazzo Davanzati** ❼ (closed for restoration, due to reopen early 2000) is the earliest example of a patrician's home adapting to a more comfortable and safer age. Built about 1330, its painted walls and ceilings are excellent examples of Trecento work serving to soften and brighten domestic architecture, turning a fort into a home.

BELOW: *Madonna and Child with Angels* (1455–66) by Fra Filippo Lippi, part of the Uffizi collection.

Nearby, the lively **Mercato Nuovo** ❽ – also known as the "Straw Market" – belongs to another world. "Nuovo" is only relative, for the elegant covered market was built around 1550. It is still a popular shopping place, particularly

for visitors looking for high quality leather goods, although it does contain a certain amount of tourist "tat". Here is the **Porcellino**, the amiable bronze boar, whose snout is polished to gleaming gold by the rubbing of visitors who touch it as a means of ensuring a return to the city on the Arno.

Map, pages 140–41

The religious centre

It is characteristic of the Florentines that the main artery of their city, the street which links the two great monuments of the Palazzo Vecchio and the Duomo, does not bear some grand impressive name. It is still known as the Street of the Hosiers – Via Calzaiuoli – after the trade of the stocking-knitters who were concentrated here. It still specialises in footwear. The guilds were concentrated in this area: on the left of the street is **Orsanmichele** ❾ (open daily; closed 12–3pm), the guild church, built on the site of the 9th-century San Michele ad hortum. Its exterior is in effect an open-air sculpture gallery, with various statues displayed in individual niches set into the wall of the building.

Holding up to 20,000 people, the enormous size of the **Duomo** ❿ (open daily) is emphasised by the smallness of the square in which it is placed, and the narrowness of the streets which enter it. At no point can one take in the whole.

Despite the Duomo's dominating presence, the little **Battistero (Baptistry)** ⓫ (open daily 1.30–6.30pm; closed Sun pm; entrance fee) in front of it easily holds its own. The Florentines particularly revered the baptistry, the oldest building in the city. It was built on, or reconstructed from, a 7th-century building sometime between the years 1060 and 1120 and served as the cathedral of Florence until 1228 when it was relegated to the role of baptistry.

Dante was among the eminent Florentines baptised there (he nearly drowned

There is a floorplan of the Uffizi on the last page of this book.

ABOVE: exterior of the Bargello.
BELOW: detail of Botticelli's *Primavera*, another Uffizi treasure.

UNDERSTANDING THE UFFIZI

Mental indigestion is an inevitable hazard in any Italian tour. It achieves acute form in Florence, acutest of all in the Uffizi – the oldest gallery, and one of the greatest art collections, in the world. The only possible cure is avoidance, to fight down the temptation to look at every picture. Walk around first, enjoy some superb views, get your bearings. It is essentially a U-shaped gallery, with most famous works – such as Botticelli's *The Birth of Venus* and Piero della Francesca's *The Duke and Duchess of Urbino* – grouped along the East Corridor in rooms 7–18.

Rooms 25–33, where the South and West corridors meet, also house some well-known works, such as Michelangelo's *The Holy Family* (Room 25) and *The Venus of Urbino* by Titian (Room 28). In this section is the entrance to the Vasari Corridor, an aerial walkway along the east side of the Ponte Vecchio hung with the self-portraits of many great artists.

Remember that the overall scheme of the Uffizi is chronological, thus making it possible to pick out groups or periods. Which to choose comes down to personal taste. The Uffizi does present an unrivalled opportunity to follow the development of Renaissance art from Cimabue onward through to the mannered works of the late Cinquecento.

Saint Luke *by*
Giambologna, one of
14 niche statues in
Orsanmichele, which
was originally a
grain market before
it became the guild
church in 1367. Each
guild was allowed to
decorate a niche.

BELOW: view of
Florence from the
Piazzale
Michelangelo.

in the great font) and the wealthy Wool Guild (*Calimala*) lavished vast sums on its interior. In particular, they commissioned the superb Venetian mosaics which decorate the interior of the cupola.

The *Calimala* then turned their attention to the three great doors, first commissioning a Pisan to create bronze doors for the south entrance, then initiating a competition for the other two doors, which was won by Lorenzo Ghiberti. There is no mistaking the second pair (the east doors, facing the Duomo) – which took Ghiberti 27 years to create and which Michelangelo described as the "Gates of Paradise" – for there is always a little knot of people standing staring at them. But the present panels are newly installed copies. The original panels are in the **Museo dell'Opera del Duomo** ⑫ (open Mon–Sat; entrance fee), while the competiton panels are in the Bargello.

The two doors are divided into 10 panels, each representing a scene from the Old Testament. Round the panels are heads representing the Sibyls and the Prophets. To get an idea of the incredible detail, and the precision to which Ghiberti worked, look for his self-portrait. It is halfway down on the right-hand side of the left-hand door and, though only a few inches high, is a perfect portrait – a little, balding man peering knowingly out.

It took the Florentines over 400 years to decide just what kind of façade they wanted for the west front of the Duomo – the side immediately facing the baptistry. Again and again both artists and the city fathers came up with some scheme which satisfied nobody (when the first Medici pope, Leo X, visited his native city in 1515 they even erected a cardboard front for it). The present front was designed in 1887 and has inevitably come in for criticism.

After the multi-coloured splendour of the freshly restored exterior, the inte-

rior of **Santa Maria del Fiore** (the Duomo's official name) comes at first as a disappointment. Many of the treasures have been removed and are now in the Museo dell'Opera del Duomo (on the eastern side of the Piazza). The overall colour scheme of the interior is muted, coming to life only at the time of religious festivals when immense crimson banners are hung on the walls and pillars.

But the relative lack of architectural detail allows the eye to pick out the remaining treasures which highlight the city's history. High on the wall immediately to the left of the entrance are two large murals of soldiers. The right-hand one is of an Englishman, John Hawkwood, a mercenary soldier or *condottiero* who first attacked Florence for his paymasters and then became the city's Captain-General in 1375. It was intended to erect a monument to him, but thriftily the Signoria settled for this clever *chiaroscuro* imitation, which gives the impression of a three-dimensional monument, painted by Uccello in 1436.

Further along the same aisle is the painting *Dante Declaiming the Divine Comedy* by Michelino. On Dante's right in the painting are Hell and Purgatory, while on his left is a contemporary view of the city's major monuments. For years readings from the *Comedy* used to be given in the Duomo during Lent, a fact which would doubtless have given Dante wry amusement, and in 1465 this painting was commissioned to mark the second anniversary of his death.

The Duomo's greatest treasure is the *Pietà* by Michelangelo, which is now in the museum. He sculpted it for his own tomb in 1550, though it was never finished. It is entirely different from his earlier, and perhaps more famous *Pietà* in St Peter's in Rome; where that is all calm, resigned acceptance, this is simply the utter defeat of death.

Lorenzo the Magnificent took refuge in the nearby **New Sacristy** on Easter Sunday morning in 1478 when the Pazzi Conspirators wounded him and murdered his brother Giuliano during High Mass. Although you can't actually walk in the New Sacristy, you can observe the artwork (including a Lucca della Robbia terracotta relief) through glass doors.

If you have a head for heights, ascend to the gallery of the **dome** (open Mon–Sat; closed pub. hols; entrance fee). It is not for vertigo sufferers: the gallery is narrow and the balustrade low, but only here can Brunelleschi's stupendous achievement be fully appreciated. It was originally intended to cover the interior of the dome with mosaic, which would have emphasised its soaring majesty; instead Vasari was commissioned to cover it with bold allegories, which were restored in 1994.

East of the Duomo, on the Via dell'Oriuolo, is the interesting **Museo di Firenze com'era ⓭** (open Fri–Wed till 2pm, Sun till 1pm; closed pub. hols; entrance fee). One of the most fascinating exhibits here is a 19th-century copy of the huge and famous woodcut *Pianta della Catena* made around 1470, which shows an early view of the city.

Memories of the Medici

A few streets to the northwest of the Duomo is the heartland of Medicean Florence: the **Medici Palace** and the church of **San Lorenzo**. The main façade of

Map, pages 140–41

There is a floorplan of the Duomo on the last page of this book.

ABOVE: Michelangelo's famous *Pietà*. **BELOW:** the gilded east door of the Baptistry.

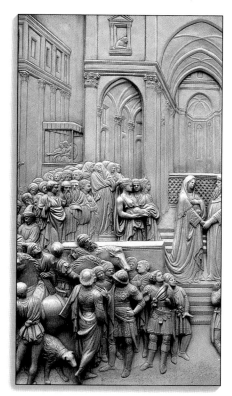

BELOW: Benozzo Gozzoli's *Journey of the Magi* fresco in the Palazzo Medici-Riccardi.

the palace is on the Via Cavour, one of the few streets in Florence to have changed its name – it was known as the Via Larga at the time of the Medici.

The palace – now known as the **Palazzo Medici-Riccardi** ⓮ (open Thur–Tues; closed 1–3pm; Sat and Sun open till 12 noon) from the name of the family to whom the Grand Duke Ferdinand sold it in the 17th century – is dignified but not ostentatious. It still has the look of a fortress about it, particularly in the façade of the ground floor with its massive blocks of "rustic" masonry. It is today the Prefecture of Florence, but the **Cappella dei Magi** (open Thur–Tues; closed 1–3pm and Sun pm) and the Medici Museum are both open to the public.

The museum contains various mementoes of the family, including the poignant death-mask of Lorenzo, but it is the Capella which contains one of the brightest jewels in the Medici crown, the newly restored *Procession of the Magi* by Benozzo Gozzoli, painted in 1459. This painting has been reproduced again and again, for it breathes the spirit of the Florentine Renaissance in its mixture of real figures of identifiable people, historical re-creation and delight in colour.

The immense procession, winding its way through a delightfully improbable landscape, is led by a handsome, richly dressed youth on horseback – the young Lorenzo. Behind him comes his grandfather, Cosimo, soberly dressed, attended by a black servant. Other members of the family are in the group – which includes the painter himself, with his name inscribed on his hat. In the distance is the Medici country Villa Cafaggiolo – and a couple of camels to remind the observer that the picture is set in the Middle East!

San Lorenzo ⓯ (open daily; closed 12–3.30pm), although consecrated in 393, had its present structure commissioned by the Medici from 1420 onwards,

according to designs by Brunelleschi. After the latter died, the work was continued by Antonio Manetti and then by Michelangelo, who added on two sacristies as well as the Cappelle Medicee and the Biblioteca Medicea-Laurenziana.

Of particular note in the basilica are Donatello's pulpits with bronze relief of the Passion, and the Old Sacristy with sculptures by Donatello. The cloister leads to the **Biblioteca Medicea-Laurenziana** (open weekdays 10am–1pm), commissioned by Cosimo de' Medici, housing 10,000 volumes of the Medici library and featuring an innovative staircase designed by Michelangelo.

The entrance to the **Capelle Medicee** (open daily till 1.50pm; closed alternate Sun and Mon; entrance fee) is actually outside the church, in the Piazza della Madonna degli Aldobrandini. Here are the **Capella dei Principi** (the mausoleum of the Medici grand dukes) and the **New Sacristy** (the Medici Tombs), the latter Michelangelo's first architectural commission.

The two New Sacristy tombs of Giuliano and Lorenzo de' Medici are graced with the symbolic figures of *Dawn*, *Dusk*, *Night* and *Day*, conveying to the observer an unforgettable feeling of uneasiness, of sadness, of loss.

Black and white friars

The three great buildings of Santa Maria Novella, San Marco and Santa Croce are widely separated in the city – the first near the Statione Centrale, the second on the far eastern side of the city, a little beyond the Palazzo Vecchio; and the latter in the north. They are grouped together here because they illustrate a truth about Florence, in the absence of which even the most splendid buildings lose something of their significance. The truth is that religion was a driving force – probably even stronger than commerce or the desire for self-aggrandisement – a force that on more than one occasion nearly drove the city to destruction.

The church of **Santa Maria Novella** ⑯, begun in 1246, was designed by Dominican monks. Though dignified and indeed majestic, it reflects their gloomy preoccupations: striped like a tiger, the family chapels are sombre and overwhelming, their murals little more than illustrations of sermons. The **Spanish Chapel** carries this to extremes, with its murals dedicated to the 13th-century theologian, Thomas Aquinas, who was, of course, a Dominican.

The Spanish Chapel now lies within the **cloister museum** (open Sat–Thur till 2pm; entrance fee) adjoining the church, as do Uccello's frescoes. In the church itself are Masaccio's *Trinity* and the chapel is frescoed by Fra Filippino Lippi and Ghirlandaio.

Decorations in the church were carried out well into the Renaissance, with work by Brunelleschi, among others, so there is a lightening of the spirit. But the overall impression is a somewhat gloomy one, with a rather threatening air. It was in Santa Maria, incidentally, that Boccaccio's seven young maidens met in the spring of 1348, where they were joined by three young men and launched the comedy of *The Decameron*.

Bonfire of the vanities

Ironically, the convent of **San Marco** ⑰ was almost entirely rebuilt with money provided by Cosimo de'

Map, pages 140–41

A plan of San Lorenzo church is found on the last page of this book.

ABOVE: Santa Maria Novella, a fine example of Italian Gothic architecture. **BELOW:** statuary in the Palazzo Medici-Riccardi garden.

Medici; the irony lies in the fact that San Marco became the headquarters of the friar Girolamo Savonarola, who was the greatest and most determined enemy of Cosimo's grandson, Lorenzo. Cosimo engaged his own favourite architect, Michelozzo, who had designed the Palazzo Medici, to build San Marco and spent more than 50,000 florins upon it, as well as presenting it with a magnificent library.

Savonarola was Prior of San Marco from 1491 until his execution in 1498. During those years he totally dominated Florence, nearly succeeded in overthrowing the Medici and even presented a challenge to the papacy. The vivid portrait of him by Fra Bartolomeo, which can be seen in San Marco, shows a man with a forceful but ugly face, a great beaked nose and burning eyes.

Contemporary reports of his sermons show that they were only average in content and delivery. It was their burning sincerity which moved his audience, coupled with the fact that his prophecies of damnation seemed to come true with the French invasion of Italy, and occupation of Florence in 1494. The people of Florence – ever responsive to novelty – reacted positively to this harsh, austere retainer. When he ordered them to cleanse their bodies and homes of the Devil's frivolities, they proceeded to burn their precious ornaments on a bonfire in the Piazza della Signoria.

There was, naturally, a strong reaction. Just a year later, Savonarola's power crumbled. The people abandoned him to the powerful enemies who had been waiting for this moment. He confessed that he had been deluded and his visions false. They hanged him, with two of his disciples, in the Piazza della Signoria and burnt the bodies afterwards. There is a plaque in the pavement commemorating the spot.

A Venetian merchant who happened to witness the burning of the valuable art and other treasures by Savonarola's followers offered 22,000 florins cash for the objects. The Florentines replied by throwing his own portrait onto the bonfire before lighting it.

BELOW:
souvenir stall.

The Convent of San Marco is now a **museum** (open daily till 1.50pm; closed alternate Sun and Mon; entrance fee). The prize exhibits are, perhaps, the murals of Fra Angelico, himself a Dominican but one who brought a delicacy to his work quite at variance with the austere tenets of that order. Each of the friars' cells is graced by one of his murals, and at the head of the stairs is the most famous of them all, the *Annunciation*, where he almost achieves the impossible in showing how a young girl receives the news that she is to be the Mother of God. Savonarola's cell is laid out as he knew it, complete with desk and elegant, but decidedly uncomfortable-looking chair.

Map, pages 140–41

In the immediate vicinity of San Marco are several sites of note, the first and foremost being the **Galleria dell'Accademia** ⓲ (just across the Piazza San Marco on Via Ricasoli, open Tues–Sun 9am–10pm; entrance fee). Often identified by the enormous queues outside (at times even longer than those at the Uffizi), it was founded in 1784 by Grand Duke Pietro Leopoldo as an exhibition space for art of every period. Its star attraction – and the focal point of the entire museum – is the colossal statue of *David*, which was carved from a single piece of marble and established Michelangelo as the foremost sculptor of his time before the age of 30. Now shielded by glass (it has been the target of several acts of vandalism, the most recent resulting in the loss of a big toe in 1991), the impressive work stood in front of the Palazzo Vecchio, when it was replaced by a copy. Also in L'Accademia are Michelangelo's unfinished but powerful *Slaves* (also known as *Prisoners*), carved for the tomb of Pope Julius II.

ABOVE: *motorini* are easier to park than cars. **BELOW:** Savonarola by Fra Bartolomeo.

Near to L'Accademia, with its entrance on the Via Alfani, is the museum **Opificio delle Pietre Dure** ⓳ (open Mon–Sat till 2pm; closed pub. hols; subject to variation; entrance fee), where major restoration of artistic treasures takes place. Exhibits include inlaid semi-precious stones used in pietra-dura, as well as workbenches and instruments once used by the craftsmen.

The **Museo Archeologico** ⓴ (open Tues–Sat until 2pm, Sun and public holidays until 1pm; entrance fee) is also nearby, on the Via della Colonna. It features an important collection of Greek, Egyptian, Etruscan and Roman art.

A place for celebration

The great **Piazza Santa Croce** ㉑ was a particularly favoured place for such large-scale activities as horse races and tournaments. *Calcio in Costume*, a historic football match, continues to be played in the Piazza, as it has for centuries.

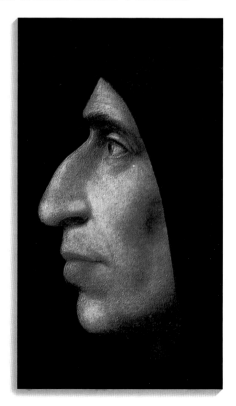

It was here that Lorenzo de' Medici held the most sumptuous tournament of all on the occasion of his marriage. "To follow the custom, and do like others, I gave a tournament on the Piazza Santa Croce at great cost," he recorded complacently. "I find that about 10,000 ducats was spent upon it." Featuring many souvenir and leather shops, the square is now dominated by a statue of Dante.

Although the façade of **Santa Croce** ㉒ dates from the mid-19th century, Arnolfo di Cambio began work on the church in 1294. With the lightness and elegance associated with Franciscan churches, it is the pantheon of Florence – and, indeed, of Italy, since this

A detail from one of the doors of Santa Croce church, whose wealth of art treasures and sheer architectural magnificence makes it a popular sight in Florence.

is where so many of the country's illustrious dead were laid to rest. The tomb of Michelangelo, designed by Vasari, is here and invariably has a little bunch of flowers laid upon it. Here also are the graves of Ghiberti and Galileo; and of Machiavelli, who died in 1527. Among these great Italians is a solitary Englishman, John Catrick, Bishop of Exeter, who came on an embassy from King Henry V in 1419 and died in the city. And crowning all are the frescoes of Giotto. Santa Croce's 500th anniversary in 1994–95 was designed to coincide with the conclusion of a major restoration programme.

This area, which is the lowest in the city, recorded water levels in the piazza itself as high as 6.2 metres (20 feet) in the 1966 flood. The watermarks are still visible today on some buildings. The cloisters, designed by Brunelleschi, lead to the highly original **Pazzi Chapel** (open Thur–Tues; closed 12.30–3pm; entrance fee), which contains 12 terracotta Apostles by Luca della Robbia.

The **Museo dell'Opera di Santa Croce** (open Thur–Tues; closed 12.30–2.30pm; entrance fee) houses Cimabue's world-famous 13th-century *Crucifix*, which was badly damaged (along with many other art works in the museum) in the flood.

Across the river

The Florentines look upon their river with decidedly mixed feelings. It has brought wealth but it has also brought danger for it is entirely unpredictable.

In summer it can shrink to nothing more than a trickle along a dried-up bed. In winter, however, the Arno becomes a raging brown torrent. As recently as 1966 it flooded the city, causing great damage—probably the worst flood since the great inundation of 1330 destroyed the ancient Roman bridge.

BELOW:
Santa Croce, rising above the rooftops.

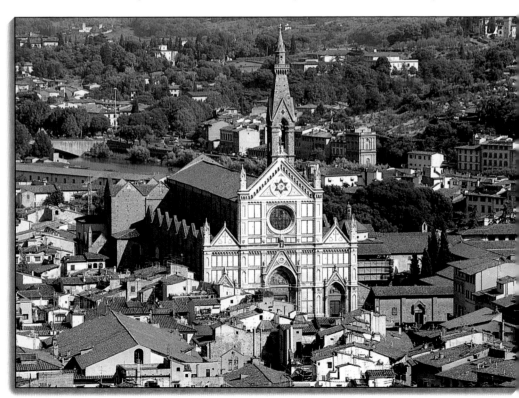

The present bridge, the **Ponte Vecchio** , was erected by Taddeo Gaddi some time after 1345 and has become virtually a symbol of Florence itself. Fortunately, the Germans spared it when they blew up every other Florentine bridge in their retreat to the north during World War II. It bears, therefore, the same appearance that it has borne for six centuries. Even the goldsmiths and jewellers who throng it today were first established there in the mid-16th century. Before the goldsmiths, the shops on the bridge were occupied by butchers and tanners, who commonly used the river as a dumping ground until they were evicted in 1593.

It was for Ferdinando's father, Cosimo I, that Vasari built the extraordinary **Vasari Corridor** (open by appointment; enquiries at the Uffizi) in 1565. Running from the Uffizi to the Pitti across the Ponte Vecchio, the private walkway made a physical as well as symbolic link between the two centres of Medicean power. In his film, *Paisà*, Roberto Rossellini shot an unforgettable sequence of the fighting that took place along this gallery during the German retreat, which caused damage so severe that the gallery has been closed until recent years.

Opposition to the Medici

The part of Florence beyond the river, the **Oltrarno**, has a character all of its own. It was not even a part of the city until an expansion of the walls in the 12th century encompassed it. Here the nobles gathered in the 14th century to make their last stand against the victorious populace who would henceforth run the city until the Medici grip tightened.

In the 15th century, this area was the centre of opposition to the Medici, spearheaded by the Pitti family. It was they who built the **Palazzo Pitti** , the

Map, pages 140–41

"It would be a very plausible river if they would pump some water into it. They all call it a river, and they honestly think it is a river, do these dark and bloody Florentines. They even help out the delusion by building bridges over it. I do not see why they are too good to wade."
– MARK TWAIN

BELOW:
symbol of Florence:
the Ponte Vecchio.

TIP

Florence's best
markets include Borgo
San Lorenzo, the
Mercato delle Pulci
(Piazza di Ciompi) and
that of Sant'Ambrogio
(Piazza Ghiberti).

most grandiloquent of all Florentine buildings which, by the irony of history, eventually became the seat of government for the Medici dukes themselves.

The Palazzo Pitti flaunts itself, a vast cliff of golden-brown stone enclosing on three sides an equally vast *cortile*, the whole being the antithesis of Florentine restraint. The visitor, crossing that arrogant, shadeless approach on an Italian summer's day, might well feel that there is a lot to be said for Florentine restraint. Legend has it that this *cortile* was built of such dimensions as to incorporate the entire Palazzo Strozzi: the Pittis and the Strozzis were bitter rivals and this was a great snub to the latter.

The Pitti was built after 1440 to the design of the Medicean architects Brunelleschi and Michelozzo, but it was specifically planned to eclipse Medicean grandeur. According to Machiavelli, Luca Pitti had no scruples about laying his hands on public funds to build his palace, and even offered asylum to criminals who could either pay or work.

The Medici, however, triumphed over Luca Pitti; he was pardoned, but ruined, and the palace was still unfinished when his descendants sold it to the Medici in 1549. It was then completed to an immense design and in due course became one of the royal palaces of the kings of Italy.

Today it is home to museums and art galleries on probably an even greater scale than the Uffizi, the foremost of which is the **Galleria Palatina** (open Tues–Sun 9am-10pm; entrance fee). Here, in an opulent setting, are hung some masterpieces by artists such as Raphael, Rubens, Van Dyck and Titian; adjoining the gallery (and included in the admission) are the recently renovated and reopened **Appartamenti Monumentali** or Reali (State Apartments), also lavishly decorated with impressive works of art. The palace also contains the **Gal-**

BELOW: view of
Palazzo Pitti as it
was in 1599.

BELVEDER CON PITTI

leria dei Costume (enter via Boboli Gardens; open Tues–Sun till 1.50pm; closed alternate Sun and Mon; entrance fee); the **Galleria d'Arte Moderna** (open as the latter); and the **Museo degli Argenti** (open Tues–Sat and alternate Sun and Mon till 1.50pm; entrance fee). Despite its name, the latter contains an exceptional collection of not only silver plate, but ivory, glassware and priceless works of art made with precious stones (*pietre dure*).

An excellent antidote to the overwhelming splendours of the Pitti are the enchanting Boboli Gardens or **Giardino di Boboli** Ⓧ (open daily until 1 hour before sunset; closed 1st and 4th Mon of the month; entrance fee), attached to them. Begun by Duke Cosimo in 1549, they are not only an attraction themselves with their fountains and grottoes and shady walks, but provide exquisite views of Florence from gradually rising ground.

Within the gardens are the **Museo delle Porcellane**, or Porcelain Museum (open daily till 1.30pm, closed alternate Sun and Mon; entrance fee), and the 16th-century **Forte di Belvedere**, originally a fortified villa built for the Medici but now a venue for exhibitions and cultural events.

The **Via Romana**, which begins just past the Palazzo Pitti in Piazza San Felice, goes to the **Porta Romana** Ⓧ, providing an artery from the centre of the city, via the Ponte Vecchio, to the outside world. The gates of Florence were more than a means of entry and exit. The larger ones, like the great Porta Romana, built in 1328, were both a garrison and a customs post, collecting dues on all the goods that came into the city. You can now walk a section of the ramparts near Porta Romana.

Three churches of note are also situated on this south side of the city, each remarkable in its own way. The first, not far from the Ponte di Santa Trinità, is

Map, pages 140–41

This Italian Empire chair (dating from around 1810) sits among some fine works of art in the Galleria Palatina.

BELOW: Palazzo Pitti as seen from Boboli Gardens.

Map, pages 140–41

ABOVE AND RIGHT:
San Miniato al
Monte, one of the
oldest churches in
Florence.
BELOW: pottery is
for sale everywhere.

Santo Spirito ⑦, its modest 18th-century façade masking the beautiful and harmonious interior. Filippo Brunelleschi was commissioned to build a church here in 1444 by the Augustinians. Although he died two years later, his design was finally realised in 1487. The numerous paintings inside provide an insight into the work of some of the lesser-known masters of the Renaissance period.

To the west of Santo Spirito is the church of **Santa Maria del Carmine** ㉘, which contains one of the greatest treasures of Italian painting – the **Brancacci Chapel** frescoes (open Wed–Mon, closed Sun am; entrance fee). Considered by many to rival even Michelangelo's Sistine Chapel in Rome, the work of Masolino (including *Temptation of Adam and Eve*), Masaccio (including *The Expulsion from Paradise* and *The Tribute Money*) and Filippino Lippi is truly magnificent. Unfortunately, due to the popularity of the frescoes, visitors are only allowed 15 minutes to see them.

Farther to the east, dominating a hilltop (and battling a subsidence crisis), is **San Miniato al Monte** ㉙. A building stood on this site as early as the 4th century; the present structure was started in 1018 and is a fine example of Florentine Romanesque architecture. Of particular interest inside are the Capella del Crocifisso, a tiny vaulted temple with pillars, terracotta and paintings; and the 11th-century crypt, which houses the relics of St Minias. You can hear the monks chanting each afternoon at 4.30pm.

San Miniato towers above the **Piazzale Michelangelo** ㉚, which is most easily reached from the Porta Romana along the enchanting Viale dei Colli, constructed in the 19th century, or else by climbing up from the river, past the Porta San Niccolò, taking the winding paths through the gardens to the Piazzale. Another 19th-century construction, adorned with bronze copies of Michelangelo's statues, the Piazzale is one place that no visitor should miss. From it is visible the entire panorama of the city, which manages to look much as it would have done in the time of the Medici – despite the vast convulsions of the intervening centuries.

On the edge of the city

This southern section of Florence outside the remainder of the city wall is doubly poignant; it was here that the republic of Florence came to an end in 1529 when the combined armies of Pope Clement VII and the Emperor Charles V besieged the city. The area is a reminder, though a rapidly fading one, that Florence is a country town: a brisk walk along Via di San Leonardo will take you from the very heart of the city out into vineyards, olive groves and maize fields.

The area to the north of Florence is also slowly succombing to "urban sprawl". Fiesole (*see page 165*) is a prime example. In its heyday it was one of the chief towns of the Etruria Propria and could claim to be the mother of Florence itself; now it is little more than a highly refined and slightly subdued suburb of the spreading city it overlooks from its steep hilltop vantage point.

To get to Fiesole from Florence, take bus No. 7 via Stazione-Duomo-San Marco or, if you are driving, leave the city centre at the Piazza della Libertà and travel along the Via Don Giovanni Minzoni. ❑

A DAY IN THE LIFE OF FLORENCE

Colourful, eccentric, exciting – the city never stops moving

Restless Florence wakes up to the whirring of the Pulizia Stradale water machines and the street cleaners in the Piazza del Duomo. The bars gradually fill with a democratic mix of Florentines enjoying a coffee, brioche and a glance at *La Nazione*. Just before 8am, students gather around Piazza San Marco in the hope of squeezing into an inadequately small lecture hall.

In fine weather, Florentines weave into work on *motorini*, far easier to park than cars. Thanks to a partial ban on city centre traffic, Florence is becoming a pedestrian's paradise and a driver's nightmare, at least during the day.

As the early cool turns humid, the air-conditioned shops near Via Tornabuoni open their elegant doors for business. Even for those who choose to patronise home-bred designers, the choice is dazzling: Raspini, Coveri, Ferragamo, Pucci, Gucci. By 11am, the smart morning coffee crowd surges into Giacosa.

Those with *tanto da fare* (lots of work to do) opt for repeated trips to more plebeian establishments where local or international affairs can be picked to pieces over an espresso or four. Over in Via Cavour, the *funzionari* (civil servants) may be swapping insults over more *espressi*. Outside the post office, the senior citizens are gathering to while away the morning in idle but impassioned debate.

The peckish sneak into nearby Cantinetta Antinori for an early rustic lunch in palatial surroundings. Florentines with more than an hour to spare head home for pasta and *riposo*, the latter variously interpreted as anything from watching TV to simply sleeping. At the end of the rush come hordes of starving school children: no packed lunches here: the school day finishes at 1.30pm.

ABOVE: Ceramic flowers to tempt the gift hunter.
BELOW: Florence: a shopper's paradise.

Break for lunch

For those who are stuck in town, lunch is a *pasta primo* at the counter or a *crostone ai carciofi* eaten in a *birreria*. In Giubbe Rosse in Piazza della Repubblica, employees, entrepreneurs and local politicians grab a quick ravioli in a restaurant which was once the haunt of Risorgimento revolutionaries and later became a salon for Futurist painters. Although many of the bigger shops are now open through the lunch hour, around two o'clock the centre by now is semi-deserted.

Not all culture stops in the afternoon: colourful street banners advertise the latest exhibitions. Art lovers visit the magnificent sculptures of nudes and horses at the Marino Marini museum or to the latest photographic exhibition at the Rucellai's frescoed palazzo.

The third rush hour gets under way. In sleepy Oltrarno, gallery attendants and shopkeepers wake up over a coffee and a conversation about the next Florence-Juventus football clash. If business is slack, Santa Croce leather workers and San Frediano silversmiths abandon shop and head for the nearest bar.

By early evening, people watchers are already sipping *aperitivi* in Rivoire on Piazza della Signoria.

After seven o'clock, the Piazza della Repubblica is the first stop on the youth circuit of *pizzerie*, *gelaterie* and noisy video bars. Workers head home to Campo di Marte or Sesto, bank managers and retailers to Bagno a Ripoli, while the wealthy return to Bellosguardo or the slopes of Fiesole. Around nine, the streets empty as Florentines disappear into *trattorie* or elegant *ristoranti*. After dinner, bustling Via Calzaiuoli attracts mime artists, puppeteers and comedians.

Hot tickets

Natural culture vultures, Florentines of all classes buy season tickets to the theatre, opera and music seasons. Florentine theatre combines foreign classics and Florentine favourites in the Teatro Verdi and Teatro della Compagnia as well as in the grander Teatro Comunale. As for opera and ballet, Florence is no longer considered a "cold piazza". In Fiesole, summer crowds gather to see international opera and ballet companies perform in the atmospheric Teatro Romano. In the city below, students flock to Forte di Belvedere's open-air film festival.

Film fans and inveterate clubbers scan *Firenze Spettacolo* to see what's on. Less "cultural" but equally active are the Viali, the streets which replaced Florence's town walls. Driving along them at night, try to avoid the inside lane or you may find yourself in a queue for a transvestite rather than the traffic lights.

By this time the *giovanotti* (young men) are watching a light show or eyeing the American students at a disco; Florentines drink a final Fernet Branca *digestivo*, the *borghesi* at home and the yuppies at a jazz club. Arty eccentrics linger on at a *trattoria*, creating poems and paintings late into the night. ❑

Map, page 140–41

BELOW: *aperitivi* in the Piazza della Repubblica.

FLORENCE AND PRATO PROVINCES

This region was the most advanced in Europe throughout the Middle Ages and the Renaissance, resulting in an important agricultural, historical and artistic heritage for its people

Map, page 166

The province of Florence is full of towns and villages perched on steep, cypress-covered hills. Below them, straggling down to the bottom of the valleys, are the vineyards that have been producing some of the most famous wines in Italy since the Renaissance – red Chianti and Carmignano and white Malvasia and Trebbiano.

The best place from which to observe the mountains of the Mugello is a seat in the Roman amphitheatre at **Fiesole ❶**. These mountains to the north of Florence once provided hideouts for ruthless medieval barons who occasionally descended into the valleys from their fortified lairs to sack and pillage. At first Fiesole could fend for itself. But in 1125 it was the Florentines who attacked the city and destroyed it, leaving only the Duomo and the bishop's palace.

From Florence the Via Bolognese, the SS65, runs west of Fiesole past villas built on sites which are desirable for their magnificent views down into the valley to Florence. The main route from the centre of town is the Via San Domenico, which changes name several times before reaching Fiesole.

On the Via Vecchia Fiesolana is the **Villa Medici**, which was built by Michelozzo between 1458 and 1461 for Cosimo il Vecchio's youngest son, Giovanni.

Today the interior of the villa no longer retains its original decoration; much of it was swept away in 1772 and replaced with the English Chinoiserie style by Robert Walpole, Earl of Oxford. The villa is not generally open to the public, but if you ring the bell (the entrance is on Via Giovanni Angelico 2), somebody will usually be willing to show you round the terraced gardens, which retain their original lines.

Archaeological treasures

The road climbs on up to Fiesole's centre, the lively main piazza, named after Mino da Fiesole, a Quattrocento sculptor and a native of the town. Bars and *pizzerie* surround the Duomo, which contains some of the best examples of Mino da Fiesole's works – the tomb of the Bishop Salutati and an altar-front in the Capella Salutati. The **Duomo** itself dates from 1024 to 1028 and contains frescoes and sculpture by lesser known, though excellent, artists.

On the west side of Piazza Mino da Fiesole is the 11th-century bishop's palace and the Seminary, both with fragments of the Etruscan acropolis wall in their garden, and to the east is the Palazzo Pretorio. The piazza itself was once the site of the Roman Forum and a road leads from it to the **Teatro Romano**, which was excavated in 1911 and is used during the sum-

PRECEDING PAGES: Florence viewed from Fiesole. **LEFT:** Franciscan monk, Fiesole. **BELOW:** stained-glass intricacy.

mer for concerts and other performances. In early 1997, three of Fiesole's archaeological attractions – the **Museo Archeologico**, **Museo Bandini** and **Antiquarium Costantani** – were combined into a **Zona Archeologico** (open daily; closed first Tues of the month; one entrance fee for all sites).

The extensively restored archaeological museum contains interesting Bronze Age and Etruscan finds and is now linked by an underground corridor beneath the road to the Costantini collection of Greek and Etruscan objects. The third part of the complex is the tiny Bandini, in Via Duprè, containing an art gallery with a fairly wide and representative selection of paintings from the early and middle Renaissance, as well as some School of della Robbia terracottas.

The route to Fiesole passes through the village of **San Domenico ❷**. Apart from its magnificent view of Florence, it is well-known for its monastery and church of San Domenico di Fiesole. Both contain important remains of an art collection much vandalised during World War II. In the first chapel on the north side of the church is *Madonna with Angels and Saints* by Fra Angelico, who lived in the monastery; in the chapter house is his *Crucifixion*.

Erected in the 1st century BC, the Teatro Romano *in Fiesole is one of the oldest Roman theatres. The structure could hold around 25,000 spectators.*

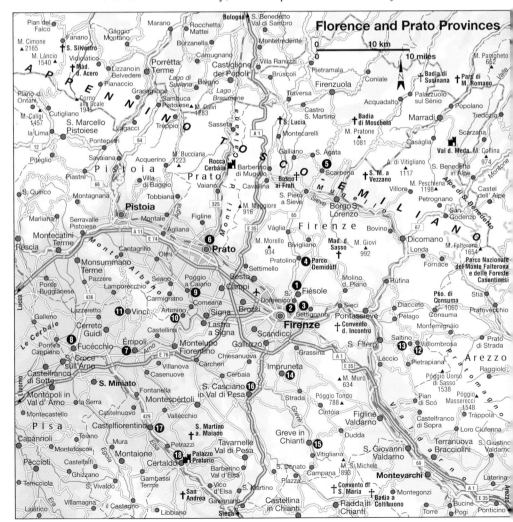

The Via Badia leads to the **Badia Fiesolana** (open Mon–Fri), which was the cathedral of Fiesole until 1028. The present building was left unfinished in 1464 and it incorporates the façade of a smaller Romanesque church. This earlier façade is an excellent example of the Florentine Romanesque style, which uses as surface decoration layers of green and white marble. There is a tiny open piazza in front of the church where you can sit for a while and admire the view of Florence.

Map, page 166

On the northern side of Fiesole, on the road that winds through the olive groves to Olmo, is a turning on the right to **Settignano ❸**, which has been home to many illustrious people. Michelangelo spent his youth at the Villa Buonarroti. At the **Villa I Tatti** (open Mon–Fri) lived Bernard Berenson (1865–1959), the American art historian who restored the villa to house a large collection of Renaissance paintings eventually inherited by Harvard University. Other well-known residents of Settignano included Desiderio da Settignano, an important Renaissance sculptor, Tommaseo, D'Annunzio and Eleanora Duse.

A fine Renaissance villa which survives here with most of its original garden intact is the 15th-century **Villa Gamberaia** (open daily; closed 12–1pm; booking is necessary Sat, Sun and pub. hols; tel: 055-697205; entrance fee).

The tiers of stone seats at Fiesole's Teatro Romano seem to dwarf visitors.

Settignano is also richly endowed with ecclesiastical treasures: **Santa Maria** has a 16th-century pulpit by Buontalenti and a white terracotta *Madonna with the Child and two Angels* by Andrea della Robbia; **San Martino a Mensola** contains a triptych by Taddeo Gaddi.

The Via Bolognese from Fiesole climbs northwards to Pratolino and to the **Parco Demidoff ❹** (open Mar–Sept, Thur–Sun; entrance fee). At one time the park (in fact, a vast garden) contained the Villa Pratolino, later named the Villa Demidoff, which was built in 1569 and demolished in 1820 as a misguided economy measure. Practically nothing of the gardens of the former Medicean villa survive except for Giambologna's massive statue, *L'Appennino*. Today, although the garden is wild and unkempt, it's a lovely cool place to seek refuge on a hot afternoon. Be warned, though: the custodian here keeps strange hours, so check the opening times in advance of a visit.

BELOW: remnants of the demolished Villa Demidoff, Pratolino.

The Mugello Valley

The **Mugello** has great associations with the Medici; it is the region from which they originated and it is one of the regions on which they lavished a lot of attention. In 1451 Cosimo il Vecchio had Michelozzo alter the old fortress of **Cafaggiolo** in **Val de Sieve**, creating a country retreat. He did the same at the old Castello del Trebbio, slightly further to the south.

The run-down appearance of the exterior of **Villa Cafaggiolo** (only open for group visits; tel: 055-845 8793 for information), which has lost one of its towers, hides a magnificent interior, most of which is used for the storage of hay – strange for such an important building. It also suffers today because of the siting of a sliproad to the Bologna–Florence motorway just in front of the building. How the mighty have fallen.

Castello del Trebbio (open Easter–Nov, Mon–Fri by appointment only; tel: 055-8458793), by contrast,

Painting inside Prato's Palazzo Datini, once the home of Francesco Datini– a man immortalised by Iris Origo in The Merchant of Prato *(1957).*

BELOW: local hunters after *cinghiale* (wild boar) and birds.

has a much more satisfactory existence. It has been extensively restored and, more than any other 15th-century Tuscan villa, retains the feudal atmosphere of a Medici villa.

Facing Villa Cafaggiolo, high on a thickly wooded outcrop, is the Medici fortress of **San Martino**, built in 1569 by Lanci and Buontalenti to enable Cosimo I to defend the Florentine state. Today this massive pentagon-shaped castle is completely derelict and has been closed for restoration.

Just north of San Piero da Sieve is **Scarperia ❺**. Its spotless monuments are rarely visited, yet there is much to see. **Palazzo Pretorio** in the main street is one of the finest examples of 13th-century civil architecture in Tuscany.

The outer façade, decorated with the coats-of-arms of local notables, carved in stone or worked in della Robbia terracotta, faces the **Oratorio della Madonna della Piazza** in the small square. The Oratorio is a tiny, darkened room in which, over the altar, is a *Madonna and Child* by Taddeo Gaddi.

At the bottom of the main street, near the entrance to the town, is the **Oratorio dei Terremoti**, which contains another fresco of the *Madonna and Child*, said to be by Filippo Lippi.

Scarperia is famous as a centre of knife-making, and in the local workshops traditional methods are still used to craft knives by hand. In September there is an international knife exhibition in the town. The newly installed **Museo dei Ferri Taglienti** (Museum of Cutting Tools) is in the Palazzo dei Vicari (open Sat and Sun pm; entrance fee).

A turning on the left of the southern approach to Scarperia wends its way through dense woodlands to the remote **Bosco ai Frati** convent (open daily; ring the bell and a helpful monk will usually be happy to let you in). This Francis-

can retreat retains the peace and solitude of the Franciscan ideal that places like Assisi lack; no touring hordes, no postcard sellers, only the peace and quiet offered by a church and its convent in a clearing in the woods.

These buildings were restructured by Michelozzo around 1440 for Cosimo il Vecchio. They house a little-known, large wooden crucifix, gessoed and painted by one of the greatest masters of the Italian Renaissance, Donatello.

Map, page 166

West of Florence

Prato ❻, to the northwest of Florence, has recently been promoted to provincial status, a fitting tribute to the third largest city in Tuscany and long-time rival of Florence. The city possesses an extraordinary relic: in the **Duomo** is what is believed to be the girdle of the Virgin Mary. The legends surrounding this relic have been celebrated by Agnolo Gaddi, whose frescoes cover the walls of the Chapel of the Holy Girdle, and there is a sculpture by Giovanni Pisano with a statue of the *Madonna and Child* on the altar.

Outside the Duomo is the Pulpit of the Holy Girdle, designed by Donatello and Michelozzo, where on Christmas Day and several other holy days in the year the girdle is exhibited to the faithful (*see page 125*). The **Museo dell' Opera del Duomo** (open Wed–Mon; entrance fee), on the Piazza del Duomo, contains paintings, sculptures and reliefs by Donatello.

Today Prato is renowned for its textile manufacturing industries; its factory outlets sell fine fabrics, cashmere and designer clothes. Although the trade has made contemporary Prato a rich city, it was already an important centre for textiles in the 12th century and its magnificent monuments are evidence of its former great wealth.

ABOVE: fountain in Prato's Piazza del Comune. **BELOW:** Prato's Duomo.

The small, ancient centre of the city, enclosed within its medieval walls, contains – apart from the Duomo – the **Church of Santa Maria delle Carceri** behind the **Castello dell'Imperatore**. It was begun by Giuliano da Sangallo in 1485 in a Brunelleschian style. The Castello was built by Frederick II Hohenstaufen in the first half of the 13th century and is unique in Tuscany, taking as its model the Norman castles of Apulia (Puglia).

In the Via Rinaldesca is the mid-14th century **Palazzo Datini** (open Wed–Mon; closed 12–3.30pm), former home of the man who invented the promissory note and founder of the city's riches in the wool trade. Further north in the Piazza Commune is the **Palazzo Pretorio**, once Prato's seat of government, now housing the Galleria Comunale.

To the west of Florence, the first major stop along the superstrada is **Empoli ❼**. The main piazza in this country town is named after Farinata degli Uberti, who made a speech to the Ghibelline Parliament in 1260, saving the town from destruction after the Battle of Montaperti. As a result, the centre of Empoli – around the church of Sant'Andrea – retains its earliest buildings, some dating back to the 12th century.

Like other Tuscan towns it has many religious paintings, now housed in the **Museo della Collegiata** (open Tues–Sun; closed 12–4pm; entrance fee). The collection ranges from Masolino to Pontormo.

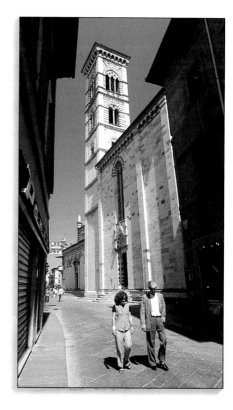

The Padule di Fucecchio is private property, but you can call the research centre in Larciano (tel: 0573-84540) for guided tours.

BELOW AND ABOVE: different aspects of the Villa Poggio a Caiano.

A few miles west of Empoli is **Fucecchio ❽**, the ancient core of which is surrounded by more modern outskirts. A variety of its buildings, including Castruccio's Tower, are worth visiting. It is also famous for being the home of Gianni Schicchi, the protagonist in Puccini's opera of the same name.

The **Padule di Fucecchio**, to the north of the town, is the largest inland marshland in Italy. The area was a Medicean fishing ground here in the 16th century, and Cosimo I had a bridge and weirs built to facilitate the sport. It is now home to rare birds and a variety of flora.

From Empoli, it is fairly easy to visit two important Medici residences, the **Villa Poggio a Caiano** in the town of **Poggio a Caiano ❾** and the **Villa Artimino** just outside the hilltop village of Artimino.

Poggio a Caiano (open Tues–Sun till 1.30pm; entrance fee) is one of the most magnificent buildings of the 15th century. It was converted by Giuliano da Sangallo for Lorenzo de' Medici between 1480 and 1485, and from its position above the town it dominates the surrounding flat countryside, which of course was Lorenzo's intention. The entire building sits on a continuous loggia that surrounds the house and supports the *piano nobile*. Lorenzo's son, Giovanni, who eventually became Pope Leo X, continued the building work, commissioning from the della Robbia family a frieze for the entrance pediment.

Some internal decoration is proof that the Florentine leader was very conscious of modelling himself on the ancients. Two of the main rooms have scenes from Roman history painted by Andrea del Sarto and Pontormo, into which have been injected matching scenes from the history of the Medici family.

In the 19th century the gardens were converted according to the fashionable English style. They were given romantic temples, an aviary, fountains and a

mock-Gothic ruin. Most recently, the villa was used as a country residence by King Umberto of Italy, and the few remaining furnishings date from then.

The villa was also the scene of the ghastly double murder of the Grand Duke Francesco and his wife in 1587. Now the huge bare rooms are sad and desolate and the building has been converted into a somewhat tawdry museum.

The walled village of **Artimino** is about 11 km (7 miles) from Poggio a Caiano. Its huge villa (open by appointment only; tel: 055-8792030) was built by Bernardo Buontalenti as a hunting lodge for Ferdinand I in 1594. Inside is a small Etruscan museum (open Thur–Tues am; entrance fee). One architectural curiosity of the Villa Artimino is the number of tall chimneys it has on the roof. The stables have been beautifully converted into a distinguished hotel, and there is also a restaurant specialising in dishes with Medici origins.

Half a mile down the hill on the other side of Artimino is an Etruscan cemetery from whose stones the nearby 7th-century church of Pian di Rosello was built.

Was Leonardo born here?

From Artimino a tortuous road leads via Carmignano to **Vinci** on the southern slopes of Monte Albano and to the village of Anchiano, the latter the alleged birthplace of Leonardo da Vinci. The medieval castle of the **Conti Guidi** in Vinci houses the **Museo Leonardiano** (open daily; entrance fee), a museum which exhibits a vast selection of mechanical models built to the exact measurements of Leonardo's drawings. There is also the **Biblioteca Leonardiana** (open Tues–Fri 3–7pm; entrance fee), devoted to the documentation of the man's life and work. In **Anchiano**, near his rustic birthplace, is another museum featuring the more prosaic mementoes of his life.

Map, page 166

ABOVE: urn in the Museo Archeologico Etrusco, in the basement of the Villa Artimino.
BELOW: the view from Villa Artimino.

Valdarno

To the east of Florence, off the SS70 which goes to Consuma, is a narrow pass which climbs tortuously up the western slope of the Pratomagno hills to the monastery of **Vallombrosa** ⑫. This, the first house of the Vallombrosan Order, was founded by San Giovanni Gualberto in the 11th century. By the time Gualberto died in 1073, the Order, part of the Benedictine Rule, was spreading all over Italy. Its power became so great that in 1866 it was suppressed, and today only four monks remain to say the offices of the church.

In the vicinity of Vallombrosa are Romanesque churches worth visiting – **San Pietro** in **Cascia**, **Sant'Agata** in **Arfoli**. There is also the tiny village of **Saltino** ⑬, handy in the winter for the ski runs of nearby **Monte Secchieta**.

The Chianti

In 1716 a decree issued by the Grand Duke of Tuscany defined the boundaries of the area known as Chianti and established the laws governing the production and sale of wine. Today this region is the world's oldest wine-producing league. The Chianti Classico area includes the communes of **Barberino Val D'Elsa**, **Impruneta**, **Greve**, **San Casciano** and **Tavernelle Val D'Elsa**.

Closest to Florence in this area is the town of **Impruneta** ⑭, an important sanctuary in the early medieval period when a shrine was erected here to house an image of the Virgin Mary, which was supposed to have been the work of St Luke and believed to be capable of performing miracles. This shrine, the **Basilica di Santa Maria**, with its terracotta tabernacle by Luca della Robbia in Michelozzo's Chapel of the Cross, underwent numerous alterations throughout the centuries, until finally it was badly damaged by a bomb in World War II.

For more information on the Chianti region, refer also to Nectar of the Gods *(page 103),* The Chianti Wine Trail *(page 174) and the* Chianti *section of the* Siena Province *chapter (page 274).*

BELOW:
coaxing a new-born lamb to its feet.

Subsequent restoration and repair to this and to other pre-17th century buildings have meant that Impruneta has retained a great deal of its early character, though without the patina of age. Brunelleschi insisted that the tiles for the roof of the Duomo in Florence be supplied by Impruneta, which is still important as a centre for terracotta production.

South of Impruneta, in the centre of the Chianti area, is **Greve** ⑮, whose annual September Mostra Mercato del Chianti (Chianti Classico Fair) in Piazza Matteotti attracts much attention. Fairs have been held in the marketplace since the Middle Ages and today the market also does an excellent trade in the Chianti's other main products – extra virgin olive oil, traditional boar sausage and a variety of local handicrafts.

An oft-missed jewel just five minutes' drive from Greve is the ancient, tiny medieval walled town of **Montefioralle**, which was built as a feudal castle. Its narrow streets, stone houses and underpassages are beautifully preserved, and splendid views are to be had from the various *trattorie* in the town.

San Casciano ⑯ in Val di Pesa, another quiet old Chianti town, is enlivened every February by a carnival. The town's reputation today rests solely on the great quantity of art held by the Collegiata Church, the Convent, the Church of St Francis and the Church of the Misericordia – paintings by Simone Martini, Ugolino di Neri, Taddeo Gaddi and Fra Bartolomeo.

The Val d'Elsa

Because the town of **Castelfiorentino** ⑰ in the Val d'Elsa is split between two sites, it has two centres. The older of the two has its origins in the Middle Ages and is located around the Piazza del Popolo.

But now the town's former beauty is somewhat lost among the sprawling modern outskirts, while the hill town of **Certaldo** ⑱, further to the south, has been saved from being swallowed whole because its upper part, **Certaldo Alto**, is fairly inaccessible. It straddles the summit of a steep hill and is reached by a winding road. Consequently the integrity of the medieval townscape has survived virtually intact. It consists of a central street, off which are a series of alleyways.

It is built predominantly of red brick and its claim to fame is that Boccaccio, author of *The Decameron*, came here towards the end of his life and died here in 1375. What is thought to have been his home was restored in 1823, bombed during World War II, and has now been rebuilt and can be visited.

The differences between Certaldo Alto and Certaldo Basso are marked by the silence of the former where, on summer afternoons, the only sounds are footsteps and the distant music of a radio. The town is crowned by the 15th-century **Palazzo Pretorio**, the front façade of which is studded with terracotta coats of arms. Exploration around the back of the town will reveal the early gateways, the portals of which are still intact and which lead down to steep, narrow approach lanes. The frescoed rooms of the **Palazzo del Vicario** (open daily; entrance fee) are worth visiting. The Palazzo also houses a delightful hotel and a renowned restaurant. ❑

Map, page 166

BELOW: view of the medieval town of Certaldo.

THE CHIANTI WINE TRAIL

A trip to Tuscany, home of the famous Chianti Classico and other fine Italian wines, is not complete without exploring some wine estates.

What has become known as the Chianti area of Tuscany covers an enormous region, spanning seven different wine "zones". At its heart, in the hills between Florence and Siena (the area shown on the map), is Chianti Classico, while the remainder – the Colli Fiorentini, Colli Senesi, Colline Pisane, Colli Aretini, Rufina and Montalbano – spread out over central Tuscany.

The main centres in Chianti Classico are Greve, Panzano, Castellina, Gaiole, Fonterutoli and Radda – the official seat of the vintners' association known as the Consorzio dello Gallo Nero. Scattered in and among these towns, many of them accessible off the picturesque route N222, are innumerable vineyards and estates. Most of the estates welcome visitors. Treasure troves of art and history as well as wine, they are well worth exploring. *Chianti News*, available at local hotels and restaurants, lists estates open for wine-tasting.

Estates owners are usually proud to show off their wines and explain their particular methods of wine-making. They will discuss the astounding number of factors, from soil conditions to pruning and grafting, which come into play in order to produce the region's distinctive wines, as well as the science behind processes such as fermentation to ageing. Experimentation is constant, and the different schools of thought encountered along the way are fascinating. Any given winemaker could discuss for hours the pros and cons of various types of wood used in the barrels and casks for ageing and storage.

But the best reason for visiting the vineyards is without question… the tasting. Sip, savour and enjoy.

△ **ROLL OUT THE BARRELS**
Although chestnut was the traditional wood of the region, Chianti *normale* is now usually kept in large oak barrels for several months. The smaller barrels are known as *barriques*; the larger are *botti*.

△ **KEEP IT PURE**
Modern wine-makers are keen to protect fermenting wine from the air. Barrels may have special fittings containing sulphur, which is added to the wine to prevent the spread of bacteria.

▷ **A FINE HARVEST**
A picker shows off his basket of Canaiolo grapes at Isole e Olena.

Map of the Chianti region showing:

Rufina, Firenze, Pontassieve, Sieve, Arno, Grassina, Impruneta, Strada in Chianti, Inoioa, Castollo di Gabbiano, Le Bolle, Figline, Santa Cristina, Greve in Chianti, S. Giovanni, Panzano, Vignamaggio, Montagliari, Fontodi, Montevertine, Monte-varchi, Radda in Chianti, Badia a Coltibuono, Isole e Olena, Campanelle, Castellina in Chianti, Gaiole in Chianti, Castello di Fonterutoli, Castello di Brolio, Villa Cerna, Querce-grossa, Felsina Berardenga, San Felice, Castelnuovo Berardenga, Pianella, Siena, Asciano, Arbia, Ombrone

▲ Wine Estates

THE GREAT ESTATES

The Chianti Classico region reeks of history, with its many ancient castles and monasteries dotting the landscape, once the battleground of the Guelphs and Ghibellines. Many of the wine estates are hundreds of years old, have been passed down from generation to generation, and have themselves played an important role in the region's history.

A perfect example of such a wine dynasty is the name of Antinori, which has become synonymous with Tuscany and fine wines. The family's involvement in the wine industry dates back more than 600 years. The driving force behind the family business today is Marchese Piero Antinori (above), who is justifiably proud of his company's reputation for both tradition and innovation – particularly with regard to grape varieties and ageing.

The several Antinori estates range from the imposing Badia a Passignano in Chianti Classico to the new Ornellaia estate in Bolgheri, started by Ludovico Antinori, Piero's brother.

◁ **HOLY WINE**
Trebbiani and Malvasia grapes hang up to dry for *vin santo*, made in Chianti and other parts of Tuscany. The wine is fermented and aged for up to six years in small barrels or *caratelli*. This strong dessert wine is comparable to a good medium sherry.

△ **LABEL OF DISTINCTION**
Hard-earned DOCG labels on bottles of Chianti Classico at Riecine estate near Gaiole. The wine here is made using both meticulous and classic methods.

CONSORZIO DEL MARCHIO STORICO
CHIANTI CLASSICO

PISTOIA

Maps:
City 180
Area 182

The smallest Tuscan province, Pistoia is sandwiched between Lucca and Florence and was fought over for centuries by both. Today it enjoys a more peaceful existence

Pistoia province is part fertile plain and part mountains, bordered in the north by the Apennines where Abetone, a popular ski resort, is little more than an hour's drive from the city of Pistoia. The other major town in the province is Pescia, cradled in the plain of the Valdinievole and famous for its flower production. The province is also important for railway construction, embroidery, furniture making and shoe manufacture. Here too is Montecatini Terme, an elegant international spa town.

Pistoia ❶ (pop. 94,500) is only 37km (22 miles) from Florence and rather unfairly neglected as a result. Its historic heart is a delight and it has enough good hotels tucked away in the medieval streets, as well as excellent restaurants and elegant shops, to make it an attractive alternative base.

The citizens of Pistoia take great pride in their many historic monuments and churches. There are shops as glamorous as in Florence or Lucca and the traffic could compete with any town in Italy; but when dusk falls, the lamp-lit shadowy streets of Pistoia still have an authentic medieval atmosphere. Church bells peal, Franciscan monks stride along in their unmistakable brown habits and rope belts, and the stone slabs outside the shops are laid out with goods for sale just as they were in the Middle Ages.

PRECEDING PAGES:
Villa Garzoni and gardens at Collodi.
LEFT: 12th-century façade of cathedral of San Zeno, Pistoia.
BELOW: campanile soaring high above Pistoia's Piazza del Duomo.

A rich history

Pistoia was originally a Roman town, founded as a staging post on the Via Cassia, but it was razed to the ground in AD 400 by the invading Longobards. It flourished as a banking centre during the Middle Ages when most of its important buildings were constructed, but it suffered during the wars between Florence and Lucca, eventually falling under the dominion of Florence.

The impressive trapeze-shaped walls with bastions and four gates that still encompass the centre of the city were built by the Medici during the 15th century. Happily, the central **Piazza del Duomo ❹** is traffic-free and, when not full of bustling market stalls (Saturdays and Wednesdays), it is a good place to quietly take stock of Pistoia's riches.

The **Cattedrale di San Zeno ❸** is originally 5th-century but was rebuilt in the Romanesque style in the 12th century with a splendid façade of green and white marble stripes. A marble porch was added later and decorated with an exquisite blue and white Andrea della Robbia bas-relief.

Inside are many medieval frescoes and Renaissance paintings, the tomb of the poet Cino da Pistoia, and – most glorious of all – the massive silver altar in the chapel of San Jacopo (Saint James), decorated with bas-reliefs and statues over a period of two centuries by many different artists, including Brunelleschi. It

is a priceless work and usually the chapel is kept locked, so ask the sacristan if you want to take a closer look. Next door, above the tourist office, is the **Museo della Cattedrale**  (open Tues, Thur and Fri; closed 1–3.30pm; subject to variation, tel: 0573-369272 for further information).

Beside the Duomo is the soaring campanile, originally a watchtower, to which have been added three tiers of green and white Pisan arches reflecting the Duomo façade. Opposite is the 14th-century octagonal **baptistry** of San Giovanni in Corte, designed by Andrea Pisano. It has the most wonderful high brick ceiling and a huge font of many different coloured marbles.

The Piazza is completed by a number of fine Renaissance palaces, including the **Palazzo del Podestà**, which is still the city's law court. Opposite is the **Palazzo del Comune** (Town Hall), built in the 13th and 14th century with a harmonious façade of arches and delicately pointed windows, decorated with the ubiquitous Medici crest and a grim black marble head.

Majolica plaque on the Ospedale del Ceppo, which was named after the offering boxes in which alms for the poor were collected.

Inside is a courtyard and sweeping stairway and sculptures by celebrated modern artist Marino Marini, many of them based on his favourite theme of riders and horses. At the foot of the stairs is his *Rider Miracle* from 1953. Upstairs in the first and second floor rooms is the impressive art collection of the new **Museo Civico** 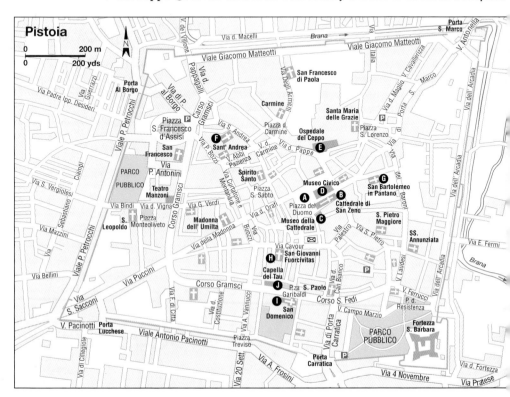 (open Tues–Sat; closed Sun pm; entrance fee), which includes a rare 13th-century painting of St Francis, a number of 15th-century altarpieces from churches in Pistoia and many delightful polychrome wooden sculptures, such as the 15th-century *Angel* by Francesco di Valdambrino and an exquisite 16th-century *Madonna and Child*, as well as works by many more recent artists.

To the north of the Piazza del Duomo in Piazza Giovanni XII is the **Ospedale del Ceppo** 🄴. It was built in the 14th century and still functions as a hospital.

Above the portico is a brilliantly coloured majolica frieze by Giovanni della Robbia which is well worth observing in detail. In rich blues, greens, yellows and browns it depicts the *Seven Acts of Mercy*: worthy citizens handing out food to the poor, comforting prisoners and the sick, washing the feet of dusty travellers and ministering to the dying. The figures are realistic, and sometimes even humorous, despite the gravity of their occupations.

A congregation of churches

Pistoia has a large number of churches, many of great architectural interest, some with notable art works – in particular the Pisano pulpits, which are the great pride of the town. A few of the churches are neglected or under restoration, some are closed, some so badly-lit it is impossible to see anything, and some have been so altered and embellished that their interest lies mainly in the way they reveal the different styles that have emerged over the centuries. Most are within easy walking distance of each other and a rewarding selection could be visited in a morning's tour, bearing in mind that most will close at midday until 3 or 4pm.

Sant'Andrea ⒡, in the Via Sant'Andrea, has an arcaded façade and reliefs above the central door. Inside is a richly painted wooden ceiling and narrow nave well-lit from the upper clerestory. Here is one of the famous pulpits by Giovanni Pisano, created in 1298 and modelled on the Nicola Pisano pulpit in the Pisa Duomo. The sharply carved marble reliefs border on the melodramatic in their depiction of the life of Jesus and the Last Judgement. In the right of the nave hangs a wooden crucifix, also by Giovanni.

San Bartolemeo in Pantano ⒢, in the Piazza San Bartolomeo, is one of Pistoia's oldest churches, built in the 12th century with a five-bay façade and

Map, page 180

TIP

If you stay in the centre of Pistoia, be sure to get a sticker which entitles you to park; cars are otherwise banned, so leave your's near Fortezza di Santa Barbara and walk 10 minutes or so to the centre.

BELOW: majolica frieze of *Seven Acts of Mercy* by Giovanni della Robbia, Ospedale del Ceppo.

Just one of the many works of art inside the church of San Bartolomeo in Pantano.

BELOW: piazza in central Pistoia.

rich in marble carvings and reliefs; those above the door are based on Roman sarcophagi. Inside there is a reconstructed pulpit by Guido da Como (1250) with marble reliefs showing Christ's nativity, the whole massive construction resting on the backs of men and lions carved out of marble.

In the Via Cavour is the 12th-century church of **San Giovanni Fuorcivitas** , thus named because it was built outside the city walls. It has an elaborate green-and-white striped marble façade and walls in the Pisan style. The fine works of art inside include the pulpit created in 1270 by Fra Guglielmo da Pisa, a water stoup by Giovanni Pisano and a touchingly beautiful white glazed terracotta of the *Visitation,* by Luca della Robbia.

The church and monastery of **San Domenico** , in the Piazza Garibaldi, is an example of 13th-century Gothic style and a good illustration of what not to do to a church. Its original windows have been filled in and new ones inserted, and huge paintings have been chopped about. But inside are a number of colourful original frescoes and works claimed to be by Rossellino and Bernini.

Opposite San Domenico is **Cappella del Tau** (Mon–Sat till 2pm; entrance fee). This former chapel is now an artistic monument, with darkly dramatic Gothic frescoes on its walls and vaulted ceilings, including a fine fresco of *The Fall.*

Other churches worth including in a visit to Pistoia are Santa Maria del Grazie, San Francesco, San Paolo and Spirito Santa. But at almost every turn there is *some* architectural find which will enrich a meander through the narrow streets, from a fine *palazzo* to a simple carving over a doorway.

The main shopping streets, with excellent clothes, shoes, leather and jewellery stores, are the Via Cavour, Via Cino, Via Ateo Vannucci and Via Orafi, and it is here that the evening *passeggiata* takes place. On 25 July the *Giostra*

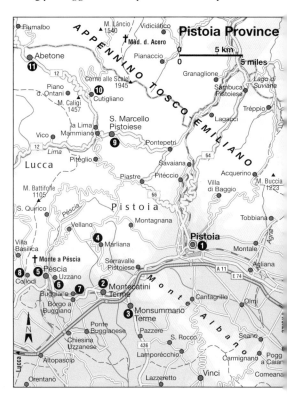

dell'Orso (Bear Joust) is held in the Piazza del Duomo, a colourful costumed display of a joust between 12 knights and a bear, though the bear is now a wooden model. About 5 km (3 miles) outside the town, in Via Pieve a Celle, is Pistoia's famous zoo (open daily; entrance fee), set in a large pine forest.

**Maps:
City 180
Area 182**

The spa towns

West of Pistoia, and most easily accessible via the A11 autostrada are the spa towns, the grandest of which is **Montecatini Terme ②**, famed throughout Europe for its elegance and luxury. It was rebuilt by the Grand Duke Leopold of Tuscany in the 18th century and has since become a company town with whole avenues of huge spa buildings dispensing waters to drink and treatments ranging from baths and inhalation to the famous mudbaths. You can stroll through the magnificent parks, or sip the waters in marble pavilions – or, of course, you could commit yourself to a complete cure (*see page 187*).

The word "pistol" apparently derives from Pistoia, named after the daggers known as pistolese *which were worn by the local soldiers.*

Montecatini Alto is the original medieval fortified town above the thermal springs, and can be reached by funicular railway or by road. Although full of wealthy tourists in high season, it is still a charming and restful place to visit, with a shady walk of chestnut trees around the lower terrace of the village and panoramic views over the plain of the Valdinievole.

The main square, **Piazza Giuseppe Giusti**, has large open cafés. Little remains of the original fortress, although its walls and towers are being restored. The adjacent church of St Peter has Romanesque origins, but has been hideously restored with its columns and exquisitely carved capitals barely visible.

Monsummano Terme ③ is the birthplace of the poet Giuseppe Giusti (1809–50) and the site of a particularly extraordinary spa, a thermal grotto,

BELOW: the *funiculare*, or cable car, leading from Montecatini Terme to Montecatini Alto.

Grotta Giusti (open daily mid-Mar–mid-Nov; entrance fee), where the steam treatments are actually taken deep in underground caves.

Driving north of Montecatini along the N633, you arrive at **Marliana** ❹ via a stunning mountain road. Marliana has the remains of a castle, and a campanile from which there are magnificent views.

A little further on is **Vellano,** a hilltop fortified village, which is well worth exploring. It is still a working village, little changed since medieval times. It's a handy place to break for lunch as Vellano has a number of good family restaurants with windows overlooking the valley slopes and olive terraces.

Pescia ❺ itself is best known for its flowers, with the largest flower market outside Holland. The market itself can be visited but it is necessary to get there early because it is all over by 8am. Pescia is a prosperous town, surrounded by nurseries, greenhouses and olive groves as well as acres of flower gardens.

Elegant villas, sheltered by cypresses, are visible in the hills beyond Pescia, many of which can now be visited or even rented. The town itself, most of which is 13th-century in origin, is divided by the River Pescia, and at its centre is the Piazza Mazzini, dominated at one end by the Oratory of the Madonna di Pie di Piazza, which dates from the 17th century. It has a finely carved wooden ceiling, embellished with gold leaf, by Giovanni Zeti, and there is a delightful little painting beneath the altar illustrating 17th-century Pescia.

At the opposite end of the Piazza is the Palazzo Comunale with its fortified tower, still used as the town hall. On the other side of the river is the 17th-century baroque cathedral, which still retains its 14th-century bell tower.

Pescia's most prized works of art are the earliest known paintings of St Francis, in the church of San Francesco in the Via Battisti. In the church of Sant'Antonio

ABOVE: peaches from Pescia.
BELOW: the approach to Buggiano.

are frescoes by Bicci di Lorenzo. In the hills above Pescia is the Convento di Colleviti, a peaceful Renaissance monastery, accessible by footpath from Pescia.

Map, page 182

Contrasting villages

Just south of Pescia are two villages worth visiting, though they are in dramatically different states of repair. **Uzzano** ❻ is a pretty hill village with winding streets, but it is not in good shape and many of the houses are in danger of collapse. However, it has an interesting gateway and a curious church right at the crest of the hill which has a rose window and an elaborate Pisan doorway.

Buggiano ❼, by contrast, has been carefully restored. If you head towards the church and campanile you will find a very fine *palazzo* where a proud caretaker will appear and show you round for a small consideration. The building has massive oak beams and lovingly preserved frescoes on the walls, and houses a store of documents from the town which date back to 1377.

The village of **Collodi** ❽, once part of Lucca province, was the scene of fierce fighting during the wars between Lucca and Florence. Today it is a peaceful place, straggling up the hill behind the famous Villa Garzoni, with only a few ruins of its original fortifications remaining. It is worth climbing up the winding stone steps of the pretty streets to be rewarded with wide-ranging views of the plain below. In the church of San Bartolomeo are wooden sculptures, 15th-century frescoes and terracotta statues.

The **Villa Garzoni** (open daily Jun–Sept; Sat, Sun and pub. hols Oct–May; entrance fee) can be visited; access is through the 17th-century baroque gardens, which are enchanting. Fountains and flower beds are laid out in an elaborate formal pattern with parterres and pools, behind which is a complicated series of

ABOVE AND BELOW LEFT: the gardens of Villa Garzoni. **BELOW:** Collodi's Pinocchio Park, a children's favourite.

Map,
page 182

TIP

If you're a skier who doesn't like to queue, avoid Abetone on winter weekends, when the wait for ski-lifts can be eternal.

BELOW: the grand Palazzo Pretorio in Cutigliano.

interconnecting stairs and terraces leading to waterfalls, hidden statues, grottoes and a maze. Within the 17th-century villa are grand reception rooms, bedrooms and galleries decorated with flowery frescoes, polished terracotta floors and charming, if faded, furnishings.

But the most appealing room in the house is undoubtedly the kitchen with its huge fireplace, cast-iron cooking utensils and well-scrubbed pine table, where Carlo Lorenzini wrote *Pinocchio,* using the pen name of Collodi. The local people are very proud of their little wooden hero and find it irksome that so many people believe that the famous puppet was created by Walt Disney.

Proper tribute is paid in the nearby **Pinocchio Park** (open daily till sunset; entrance fee), which is full of bronze monuments of *Pinocchio* characters and a square of mosaics by Venturino Venturi depicting familiar episodes from the story. There is also a good restaurant on the site, the Gambero Rosso.

Mountain pursuits

The drive up into the mountains to the north of Pistoia is stunningly beautiful, especially in autumn when the colours of the trees rival those of New England. But winter sports enthusiasts will prefer it with a good covering of crisp snow.

The main town here is **San Marcello Pistoiese ❾**. It is traditionally known for the *Mongolfiera*, or hot-air balloon, which is launched every year on 8 September to mark the end of the summer. According to local legend, if the balloon rises higher than the bell tower, there will be a good harvest. Near to San Marcello, at Mammiano, is a spectacular foot suspension bridge, 220 metres (720 ft) long, connecting the village with the road across the River Lima.

Cutigliano ❿, further down the valley, is a typical mountain village, surrounded by fir trees. Limited skiing and a cable car service is available, but the more dedicated will probably prefer Abetone. Cutigliano has a surprisingly grand 14th-century Palazzo Pretorio with numerous shields emblazoned on the façade, including the ubiquitous Medici coat of arms. Opposite is a quiet village loggia, with arcading and stone seats.

Abetone ⓫, about 90 minutes' drive from Pistoia, is 1,400 metres (4,660 ft) above sea level and is the most important ski resort in central Italy, with ski lifts, cable cars and chair lifts to a wide range of *pistes*, catering for intermediate and advanced skiers. It has two ski schools and a wide variety of accommodation, as well as cinemas, clubs, discos, swimming pools and ice rinks. It is a centre for international skiing with competitions including "Pinocchio on skis", a mini-Olympics for children, every April.

In the summer this is a good centre for climbing and walking expeditions in the surrounding forests of pine and chestnut trees. *Rifugi*, or mountain shelters, are dotted around the area, supplying basic shelter and sometimes restaurants as well (*see also page 87*).

Abetone is also well supplied with mountain restaurants which command wonderful views of the dramatic landscape and supply hearty food and restorative drinks. A local speciality that can be warmly recommended is the *Grappa di mirtilli*, a strong spirit made from mountain bilberries. ❏

Taking the Waters

Spa treatment in Italy is available on the country's National Health Service, and many Italians are firm believers in the benefits of taking the waters. The spa cure has remained virtually unchanged for hundreds of years, since Papal couriers used to carry the waters to Rome, and Ugolini di Montecatini wrote his treatise on mineral waters in the 14th century.

Tuscany is the location of a large number of different spas, ranging from open-air hot springs used by local people to luxuriously equipped and medically regulated residential establishments. Most can be visited for a few hours or a day and make a very pleasant diversion during a holiday; but less dilettante practitioners would recommend taking a full cure, which can last for a week or 10 days. The most appealing aspect of it is that you don't really need to have anything wrong with you to take a cure, and it is an excellent restorative way to spend a vacation.

There is plenty of medical evidence for the physical benefits of mineral waters taken externally and internally, but it is the concept of the complete cure that is so attractive. All the spas are in the middle of beautiful countryside, surrounded by mountains and lakes.

At Saturnia, near Grosseto, is a newly developed spa on an original Roman site. Now modern Romans come over from the Italian capital for the day to take the waters. In summer it can be an enervating experience since the water here is very warm; perhaps the best time to go to Saturnia is in winter when it is quieter and the pools steam gently in the frosty air.

Montecatini Terme is by far the most splendid of all the spas, famed throughout Europe and frequented since the 18th century by the grand and leisured. It comprises whole avenues of huge spa buildings dispensing waters to drink and treatments from baths and inhalation to the famous mudbaths.

The Leopoldina pavilion is the most magnificent, a baroque 1920s edifice of rose marble, with fountains gushing the healing waters and an orchestra playing. Glamorous women sip coffee and eat pastries served by formally attired waiters.

The different waters, prescribed for varying ailments, are dispensed with great formality from elaborate brass taps over marble basins worn smooth with use. It is recommended to drink the waters in the morning on a empty stomach, preferably while walking.

The strangest spa treatment of all is at the Grotta Giusti, near Monsummano Terme. This spa offers a complete range of treatments from thermal baths to hydro-massage, but the hot thermal springs themselves are deep underground, fed by an eerie green thermal lake. White hooded figures shuffle down a rocky, winding passage of stalagmites and stalactites into a dimly-lit cave where rows of chairs and shrouded, sweating wraiths look like a scene from a Fellini movie. The further you descend, the hotter it gets: the levels are appropriately named Purgatorio and Inferno.

No wonder the composer Giuseppe Verdi called this place the eighth wonder of the world when it was discovered in 1849. ❏

RIGHT: Sunday bathers enjoy the natural hot springs at Saturnia.

MASSA-CARRARA

*To many, Tuscany's northernmost province means just
one thing – marble – but it is also home to some picturesque
medieval villages, castles, resorts and breathtaking vistas*

Map,
page 192

Firenze

Massa-Carrara, bordering on Liguria, has been part of Tuscany only since the middle of the 19th century and is very different from the archetypal image of the Tuscan landscape.

Inland, Lunigiana is a little-known region of pine-covered mountains, craggy ravines and remote castellated villages. The coast is a predictable, over-developed continuation of the Versilian Riviera, but overshadowed by the marble industry. The beaches are dominated by the majestic marble peaks of the Apuan Alps glittering deceptively like snow in bright sunshine.

The towns of Massa and Carrara have both prospered as a result of the still-thriving marble trade, although the resulting industrial development has blighted great swathes of the surrounding area. **Marina di Massa ❶** is a popular resort with fine wide sandy beaches interspersed with groves of pine trees and a promenade of pretty pastel-shaded holiday villas.

The ribbon of development extends up to and beyond **Marina di Carrara ❷**, where the beach is divided by the sight and sound of the mighty port out of which ships carry marble all over the world.

Massa ❸ is a busy modern town but has a well-preserved medieval centre, built by the Dukes of Malaspina who ruled Massa for three centuries, holding sway over the entire region. The core is the Piazza degli Aranci, edged with orange trees and presided over by the elegant 17th-century Palazzo Cybo Malaspina, with airy courtyard loggias where cultural events are staged in summer.

Beyond a cluster of narrow winding streets stands the Duomo at the top of a wide flight of steps. It was begun in the 13th century but now has a baroque interior and a modern marble façade. The crypt, where the Malaspinas were entombed, is a museum.

Massa's fortress

Massa is dominated by its magnificent Renaissance **Castello**. Beyond the narrow old streets of the town, walk on up through leafy lanes past decaying villas dotted over the mountainside.

The walls of the old fortress provide marvellous views and welded onto it is a graceful Renaissance palace, its delicate marble pillars and frescoes providing a powerful contrast to the grim towers of the original castle. After World War II it was used as a prison but is now slowly being restored as a cultural centre, and is therefore closed to the public.

The main evidence of the marble quarries in **Carrara ❹** is the river of white mud that flows through the town, which has a dusty, disaffected air about it. It is very much a working town, not a monument to marble; there are few fine marble statues to be seen. Even

PRECEDING PAGES:
Carrara marble
caves.
LEFT: cutting giant
blocks of the
famous stone.
BELOW: Massa
matron.

the **Duomo** – with distinctive features like its 14th-century rose window, Pisan-style façade and, inside, the 14th-century statue of the *Annunciation* – is in serious need of cleaning.

The interesting sights are within a few streets of one other and are adequately signposted. Worth visiting is the **Accademia delle Belle Arti**, a 16th-century Malaspina residence built around an older medieval castle. To view the galleries you need permission from the director, but a brief reconnoitre will reveal splendid marble bas-reliefs on the walls, and sculptures from the Roman site of Luni as well as a Roman altar found in the marble quarries.

In nearby Piazza Alberica are two imposing 17th-century *palazzi,* and here every July there is a massive symposium of work in marble. Carrara also holds a biennial sculpture exhibition and an annual International Marble and Machinery Fair.

Marble workers

Of particular interest in Carrara are the marble ateliers, of which there are a number in the Piazza XXVII Aprile. Atelier Niccoli is full of marble craftworkers and sculptors, hair protected from dust with newspaper hats, all intently carving and drilling to produce a huge range of marble statues, friezes and ornaments. Many of these workshops welcome visitors.

The quarried marble was originally dragged down to this square by oxen, "pulling as though to break their hearts under the tyranny of the stone", as Edward Hutton described it. Later the huge blocks were brought by train and truck from the nearby quarries. The marble caves are fascinating to visit; you can either take a guided tour or, better still, drive up there yourself and just wander

Almost all the 300 or so quarries in and around Carrara date from Roman times, making it the world's oldest continuously used industrial site.

BELOW: scenic beauty of Carrara's "marble mountain".

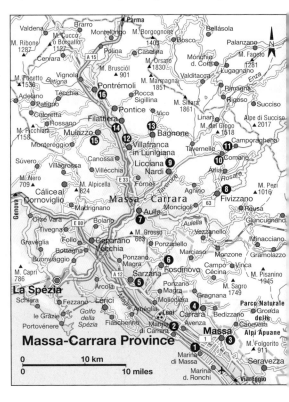

around, following signs for **Cave di Marmo**, and taking the obvious safety precautions. The quarries of Colonnata and Fantiscritti are open for visitors on weekday mornings, and souvenir shops are located on site. Tours can be organised by the Cararra Tourist Office (tel: 0585-240046).

The fine-grained, pure white marble for which Carrara is renowned has been quarried here since Roman times. Italian medieval churches are decorated with marble from Carrara, and it has supplied artists from Michelangelo to Henry Moore – who both came here personally to select sculpture blocks – with raw material. It is still the world's most important source of marble.

There are 300 quarries scattered throughout three steep valleys, the **Colonnata**, **Fantiscritti** and **Ravaccione**. Here the villages cling on to sides of mountains which have been sliced away like chunks of cheese. Dusty little houses have washing flapping from the windows, tomatoes and beans lovingly planted in any available crevice, and little marble exhibits carved by the quarry workers themselves.

An interesting "cottage industry" is associated with the tiny village of Colonnata: the production of *lardo* (lard), which is preserved in marble vats. All over Italy *lardo di Colonnata* is to be found on restaurant menus.

Hutton, writing earlier this century, captures the drama of the marble caves, describing them as "glens of marble that lead you into the heart of the mountains, valleys without shade, full of a brutal coldness, an intolerable heat, a dazzling light, a darkness that may be felt."

There are extraordinary views down into the quarries where the marble has been excavated deep into the ground. Precarious-looking staircases are strung across the sides, and massive trucks look like dinky toys as they trundle across

ABOVE: marble isn't *everyone's* business in Carrara: a local butcher takes a break.
BELOW: marble polishing in Carrara.

Map, page 192

the smooth marble surface far below. Modern equipment such as wire saws and compressed-air drills substitute for a time when marble blocks of 25 tons were transported manually on rollers lubricated with soap, and two men took an hour to saw through one centimetre of marble.

There is a marble museum, the **Museo del Marmo** (open daily; closed 1–2pm in winter, 1–4pm in summer), on Viale XX Septembre between Marina di Carrara and Carrara. Displays include many varieties of marble and granite and geographical and historical exhibits, but no information is available in English.

Just on the border of Tuscany before heading inland is **Sarzana** ❺, a bustling market town which has been colonised by artists and is being carefully restored. There is a large market in the Piazza Matteotti which is surrounded by arcades of Romanesque arches sheltering smart little cafés.

Finally, in a scruffy area off the Via Aurelia north of Carrara, there is **Luni**, the original Roman settlement from which marble was shipped. There is an amphitheatre and museum, and excavations have revealed columns, capitals, mosaic floors and tomb fragments.

Land of a hundred castles

Luni gave its name to **Lunigiana**, "the land of the moon", an almost undiscovered part of Tuscany which sees few tourists and makes little provision for them. It has always been a main trading route, however, and its many castles were built to extract tolls from pilgrims and merchants by the powerful Malaspina family who controlled the region.

Lunigiana was in the front line of fighting at the end of World War II, and this has left its mark. Since then there has been inevitable rural depopulation with

Lunigiana became known as the "land of the moon" because of the moon-like luminescence of the marble shipped from the port of Luni in Roman times.

BELOW: the hills of Lunigiana.

many people emigrating to the United States. Now an enlightened attitude to tourism promises new hope for the area, villages and castles are being restored and the roads are in good repair. There are enough hotels, pensions and local restaurants to make a visit comfortable but its attractions are unlikely ever to generate mass tourism. This means that its inhabitants will not grow rich, but it will probably help preserve the charm of the area.

It is a mountainous region of steep winding roads, deep wooded valleys and unpolluted, rushing streams. On the lower slopes of the hills vines and olives grow. Higher up are forests of oak and the chestnut trees which have provided a staple of the local diet for centuries, and there are deer and wild boar (*cinghiale*) in abundance. The terrain ranges from the busy, productive flat valley of the River Magra to the profound silence of deep river gorges. Narrow valleys are dotted with tiny villages, quiet except for the sound of cowbells, dogs barking and the occasional gunshot.

The region is famous for its Romanesque churches and intact medieval villages as well as its castles, many of which are in the process of restoration through government grants. A number have been taken over by artists and sculptors and are used both as private homes and cultural centres.

The inhabitants of Lunigiana are proud and insular, in rural areas still growing most of their own food and wine and olives and regarding all other produce with some suspicion. They will buy in grapes from Chianti, making the wine themselves rather than buy an unknown finished product from foreigners.

Lunigiana is becoming a popular area for property hunters, although the locals still find it hard to understand the fascination of a ruined farmhouse. One English purchaser, deciding that the farmer's cowshed spoiled his view, offered to buy it along with the farm. But the farmer wanted more money for the shed than for the farm; the house was his grandparents', falling down and no use to him, he explained, but the cowshed was his livelihood!

Fortified village

Fosdinovo ❻ is the first fortified village you arrive at as you drive towards Aulla on the winding road from Sarzana. Its little piazzas are shaded by huge chestnut trees and the steep twisting streets are dominated by the magnificent castle. It is one of the best preserved castles in the region, despite the fact that it was damaged by Allied fire during World War II. The Germans had a command post there, exploiting its superb strategic position with views from all sides.

It was constructed by the Malaspina family between the 13th and 14th centuries with a complicated network of corridors and loggias. Beautiful frescoed walls and ceilings and furniture have been restored; it is sometimes used for cultural events and is one of the few castles with an interior open to the public on a regular basis.

Aulla ❼ itself is the gateway to the region, where the rivers Magra and Taverone meet, but much of it is war damaged. Of the 10th-century Abbey of San Caprasio only the original apse survives.

Brunella, the *fortezza* of Aulla, broods over the town. It was originally built in the 15th century as a

Map, page 192

BELOW: the fortress at Fosdinovo, one of the region's best preserved castles.

defensive rather than a residential castle with walls 3 metres (10 ft) thick, narrow windows and vaulted ceilings. It was restored earlier this century by Montagu Brown, the British consul in Genoa, and now houses a natural history museum (open Tues–Sun; closed 12–3pm in winter, 12–4pm in summer; entrance fee). It is accessible up a steep driveway off the main Via Nazionale from Aulla, and surrounded by a large park of holm oaks and purple heather.

Fivizzano ❽, a few miles west of Aulla along the 63 road, is a buzzing and attractive market town full of elegant Renaissance palaces and with a distinct air of pride in itself. The young people of Fivizzano are prominent in the movement to revive folk traditions, and they participate in colourful flag-waving performances, dancing and mock duels, and they travel all over Tuscany giving demonstrations.

Nearby is the enchanting castle of **Verrucola**, a completely fortified settlement on the banks of the river which has been superbly restored. Little red-roofed houses and narrow medieval streets cluster around the fortified square keep, with geraniums spilling from window boxes and gardens full of courgettes, beans and tomatoes crammed right down to the river's edge.

The castle is thought to date back as far as the 11th century and is distinguished by its two separate fortified towers, erected when the town was divided between two rulers. The castle and the 15th-century church with its peaceful arched loggia can be visited at some periods of the year.

To the northwest of Fivizzano is **Licciana Nardi** ❾, an 11th-century fortified town. Much of the town wall is still visible with narrow passageways running through immensely thick walls into the village. In the Piazza del Municipio the imposing 16th-century castle dominates the square, and is joined to the grace-

BELOW: springtime wisteria blossom.

ful baroque church by a small bridge spanning the narrow street. There is a small market held once a week in the leafy main square.

Above the nearby Taverone river are the hill villages of **Bastia** and **Cisigliana**, a good base for walking, with high meadows and wonderful views out to sea, perfect for picnics and mushrooming. Bastia has a 15th-century square-bodied fortress, with cylindrical corner turrets, built by the Malaspina and now privately owned.

Along the valley from Licciana is **Crespiano** with a Romanesque church, Santa Maria Assunta di Crespiano, so old that it was restored in 1079.

Walking and riding centre

Comano ⑩ is an important base for walking and riding, and nearby is the Castello of Comano, a ruined malevolent-looking tower surrounded by a tiny farming community, with ducks and chickens wandering the streets, and steep steps up to the tower.

At the end of the valley is **Camporaghena** ⑪, the last outpost before the Apennines, where there is a sad war memorial in the church. When German soldiers came hunting escaped prisoners of war and partisans, the priest rang the church bell as a warning and was summarily shot for his brave deed.

Monti is a tiny village with a particularly charming domesticated castle, complete with geraniums, lace curtains and even a street number on the door. It is well restored with its original gateway, keep and towers and is still apparently used as a summer residence by a surviving member of the Malaspina family. The church of Santa Maria Assunta di Venelia has an apse in *pietra serena* (the local grey "sacred stone") dating from the 12th century.

Pallerone is famous for its crib, which can be seen in the church on request. It is an extraordinary clockwork nativity scene which changes from night to day and has a huge cast of busy clockwork characters, the Holy Family, angels, millers, blacksmiths, and fishermen. It is touching, sentimental and very Italian.

A 16-km (10-mile) drive south of Fivizzano brings you to **Equi Terme,** a popular spa resort smelling strongly of sulphur, with restorative waters that are claimed to have radioactive properties. If you follow the path through the old village tucked into the mountain gorge, you reach a bridge and a waterfall and the high-roofed caves called Buca del Cane, because the remains of paeleolithic men and dogs were found here. Guided tours of the caves are available at certain times.

Close to Aulla is another fine castle, **Podenzana** (closed to the public), a well-proportioned, triangular white building, massively restored in the 18th century after an explosion in the powder room. The castle is at the top of a steep hill and nearby is an excellent local restaurant, Gavarina d'Oro, which specialises in the regional dish of *panigacci*, small chestnut flour pancakes cooked over an open wood fire and served with creamy cheese and home-cured meats.

Quiet villages

Along the main road (SS62) up the Magra valley between Aulla and Pontremoli are many fascinating villages and castles, all within just a few miles. Few of

Map, page 192

TIP

The Lunigiana tourist board catalogue highlights everything from exhibitions and museums to typical food and wine. For a copy or further information, call 0187-830075 Mon and Thur, or fax (24 hours) on 0187-833045.

BELOW: the church of Pieve di Sorano, near Filattiera *(see page 198).*

Map, page 192

A local character in Potremoli.

BELOW: cooling off in the river near Pontremoli.
RIGHT: Bagnone castle.

the small villages have facilities such as shops, restaurants or even bars, so if in need of refreshment try Villafranca or Bagnone.

Villafranca in Lunigiana ⑫ lies in a strategic position near a ford over the River Magra and has some remaining medieval streets. But its 12th-century castle is in ruins, destroyed during World War II, and only parts of the keep and outer walls remain. The church of San Francesco has a terracotta of the School of della Robbia, and there is an interesting Ethnographic Museum in an old water mill near the river, which specialises in exhibits of typical local rural activities such as weaving, crafts and woodwork.

Bagnone ⑬ is a large attractive town of Renaissance palaces, wide streets and cool shady arcades with many little bars and cafés. A honeycomb of houses, arches and passageways leads down to the river bank and tiny gardens. The 15th-century village of Bagnone is clustered on the hillside above, surrounding the cylindrical tower of the Castello and a fine 15th-century campanile. There is an exquisitely carved wooden pulpit in the church of Santi Nicolo da Bagnone.

Symmetrical village

Nearby **Filetto** is a delightful, totally symmetrical, square-walled village with a tower at each corner. Almost every street is linked by covered overhead passages or bridges. Originally a defensive structure, it is now quite cosy, with cats snoozing in corners and village women sitting on the steps sewing and gossiping. Filetto has two piazzas overlooked by palaces.

Malgrate and **Filattiera** ⑭ are also worth a detour and nearby, next to the main highway, is a magnificent Romanesque church, **Pieve di Sorano.** The nave is ruinous and has been turned into a cemetery but in the main apse is a very simple and beautiful little chapel.

Mulazzo ⑮ was headquarters of a branch of the Malaspina family which had territories to the west of the River Magra; their arms are emblazoned over a fine arched doorway which guards the steep steps up to the town. Fragments of the original walls are left and in the upper part of the town the narrow streets widen into charming little squares which are overlooked by elegant loggias and their inhabitants.

The town of **Pontremoli** ⑯ was once divided in two to separate the warring factions of the Guelfs and Ghibellines, and the Castruccio Fortress, built in 1332, similarly divides the town. There are rich medieval town houses and the Church of the Annunziata has a 16th-century octagonal marble temple by Sansovino.

To the north is the **Castello del Piagnaro**, which was part of the original fortifications, and now houses the **Museo Archeologico** (open Tues–Sun; closed 12–2pm in winter, 12–4pm in summer; entrance fee) with its unique collection of *menhirs*, prehistoric and Bronze Age stone monuments. Pontremoli is also famous for its travelling booksellers and awards the Bancarella literary prize each July.

At almost every turn there are more medieval villages, more castles, more breathtaking views. One of the best ways to see this rich and varied region is to take the little train between Aulla and Lucca on its slow journey through the mountains. ❑

LUCCA

Take some mountains and spas, add a few grand villas and beaches, blend in an underrated city full of charm and character – and you begin to paint a picture of Lucca province

Maps:
Area 206
City 204

To the west of Lucca province is "Tuscany by the Sea", a broad strip of land between the sea and the Apennines which contains a rich playground of villas and hotels. To the north is the steeply mountainous Garfagnana region, popular in the past for its variety of spas – a more remedial kind of playground – now more or less forgotten and hardly ever visited by tourists.

The city of **Lucca ❶** (pop. 92,500) has a more realistic outlook on life, with its renowned olive oil industry and increasingly important wine production.

In 1996, the province was hit hard by floods and subsequent landslides. Although many areas were effected to some extent, worst hit were the small villages high up in the hills, where people lost homes, businesses, even families. Scars are still clearly visible around the province today; it is doubtful the damage will ever be fully repaired.

Simpatico city

Driving west along the A11 towards Pisa and the sea, you could be forgiven for thinking that Lucca was one Tuscan city which doesn't merit inspection. Yet to miss Lucca is to miss one of the least appreciated Italian cities, with its wonderful tree-topped walls, its enchanting Gothic and Romanesque churches, but above all the ease with which life is lived. More perhaps than Siena, its ambience is *"simpatico, molto simpatico"*, making it one of the best places to bring a comprehensive tour of Tuscany to an end.

The city **walls** were built at the height of the 16th-century revolution in warfare, when the nature of fighting moved from the offensive to the defensive. The walls of Lucca are the only major city walls in Italy to have survived 19th-century destruction and are an excellent place to conduct *passeggiata* at dusk and to catch sunset behind the Pisan mountains.

For the people of Lucca, the walls represent a fierce fight to preserve their independence. Until the 11th century, Lucca had been the capital of Tuscany. Then for 400 years it defended itself against an ever more belligerent Florence and, even though the Florentines won the title of capital of the region, Lucca never ceded its political and economic autonomy. It managed to remain an independent republic, apart from a brief period of Pisan rule, until the Napoleonic invasion of 1799.

At the other end of the historical scale, Lucca was the most significant Tuscan town in Roman times. The legacy of this history is seen in a plan of the city with its gridiron pattern of streets – so typical of any Roman habitation – and more obviously in the elliptical Piazza Amfiteatro, around which houses were subsequently built. Caesar, Pompey and Crassus, the

Architectural detail on the Duomo of San Martino in Lucca.

TIP

Walking is the only way to explore Lucca, unless you adopt the Luccans' preferred means of transport, the bicycle.

three most influential figures in the last years of the Roman Republic, met here in 56 BC to patch up their differences and to grant Rome a few more years of Republican rule.

The wealth of Lucca, like Florence, was based on banking and, from the late 14th century, its extensive silk industry. As early as the 12th century, bankers were plying the waters of the Mediterranean or travelling north to Bruges, Antwerp and London, buying and then selling silk and woollen cloth. Successful bankers, like the Guinigi family, built substantial city homes. To demonstrate their prosperity some of them erected towers, although only one of these, the **Torre Guinigi** Ⓐ (open daily; entrance fee), remains, distinguished by the oak trees sprouting from the top.

The Guinigi were not the only ones to display their wealth by creating towers. A picture hanging in the Villa Guinigi, also known as the **Museo Nazionale Guinigi** Ⓑ (open Tues–Sun till 2pm; entrance fee), shows that the city was once, like San Gimignano, a forest of towers, and it illustrates just how wealthy late medieval Lucca was. The villa-turned-museum originally lay outside the medieval city walls. Among its treasures, which date mainly from before 1475, is a wonderfully pious *Madonna and Child* in bas-relief. The artist was Matteo Civitalli, a contemporary of Donatello and Lucca's most renowned sculptor.

Walking back into the centre of the town you'll pass the delightful extended **Piazza di San Francesco** Ⓒ with the simple façade of the church at one end and the 17th-century column with the Virgin Mary on top. If the area immediately around the column suggests a picaresque scene from an opera, one's senses are being led in the right direction: Lucca was the birthplace of Giacomo Puccini, who is commemorated with a plaque outside his house in Via di Poggio. Now

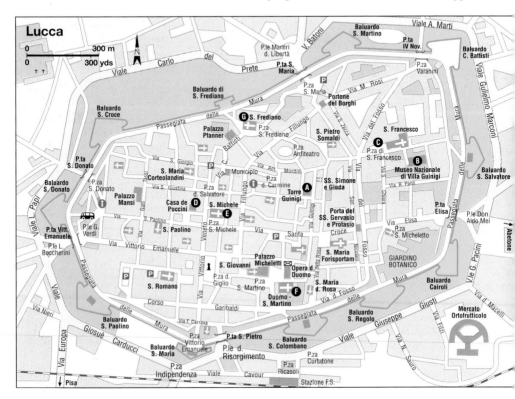

a museum, the **Casa di Puccini** (open Tues–Sun, 10am–1pm; entrance fee) includes exhibits relating to his life and works.

But Lucca's chief attraction is its particularly interesting and beautiful churches. **San Michele** ⓔ, built on the site of the old Roman forum, has one of the most spectacular Pisan Romanesque façades in Italy. The four storeys of intricate arcades rest above some splendid examples of blind-arcading, and the delicate motifs and allegories carved above each arch are especially noteworthy.

The cathedral

The **Duomo of San Martino** ⓕ is also splendid, enhanced by its tower and the particularly attractive piazza – used as a marketplace when the monthly antiques market comes to town – in front of it. The façade was built in the 12th century, and the Gothic interior took 100 years to complete. So Romanesque and Gothic are combined and work surprisingly well together.

The Duomo's main features are a mysterious 13th-century labyrinth, symbolizing life; the *Volto Santo*, a revered 13th-century wooden crucifix believed by some to have been carved by Nicodemus at the time of the Crucifixion; and, in the sacristy, Lucca's masterpiece, the tomb of Ilaria del Carretto by Jacopo della Quercia. To stare at her face is to be transfixed by a sense of quietude and devotion rarely felt with any other sculpture.

The church of **San Frediano** ⓖ is at the north end of the Via Fillungo, a street redolent of the city's medieval past and a popular place for shopping. It is rare to find a mosaic on any church, let alone a Romanesque one, but represented here is the *Annunciation of the Virgin*. Inside, the church is supremely simple, practically austere. There is also an intricate and unusual font.

Map, page 204

According to legend, the artist of the Volto Santo *was helped by angels. The crucifix crossed the Mediterranean miraculously and appeared on the beach in Luni; from there it was taken to Lucca.*

BELOW: Pisan Romanesque façade of San Michele, Lucca.

The original rectangular structure of the Villa Mansi was given its eye-catching portico and double staircase in 1634.

Lucca was a city of organ builders, and there are many examples of fine organ cases – some elaborately decorated – in the churches. Unfortunately, most are in need of costly restoration and there are not many in good working order.

Round the corner is the **Palazzo Pfanner**, which was built in 1667 and is currently being restored (closed to the public indefinitely). With its large 18th-century garden (open daily Easter–October) and its well preserved staircase, it is a perfect contrast to the medieval and religious architecture that so dominates the centre of the city. The critic John Ruskin was so inspired by the architecture of Lucca that he declared that this was where he "literally *began* the study of architecture". He wrote, "Absolutely for the first time I now saw what medieval builders were and what they meant."

Just outside Lucca are even stronger contrasts: the villas **Mansi** (open Tues–Sun; closed 12.30–3pm; entrance fee) and **Torrigiani** (open Wed–Mon; closed 12.30–3pm and Jan–Feb; entrance fee). Mansi, with its statues and busts dotted above windows, in niches, on pediments, looking almost like candles from a distance, is close to fantasy, so ornate is the baroque decoration. Villa Torrigiani is less striking, but has a strong patrician feel. Both villas are set in large open parks.

The Versilia

This coastal region of Italy has always attracted the attention of scholars, poets, writers and artists. It is the area west of Lucca, squeezed between the Apuan Mountains in the east, the sea and the mouth of the Cinquale River in the north, and Lake Massaciuccoli in the south.

The flat, pine-covered landscape has lost a lot of its earlier rustic and remote appeal now that it has been developed and built on so heavily. The sea can be

BELOW: the Villa Torrigiani features beautiful gardens.

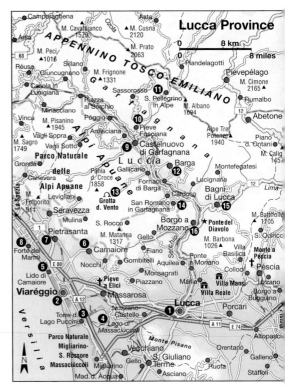

reached only if you pay an entrance fee and want to lie on a sunbed among rows of others, on sand carefully raked and flattened for your added comfort.

Viareggio ❷ is the oldest of the coastal towns in the Versilia. Its origins are Roman and in the Middle Ages it was an important sea landing. In the 19th century it was reputed to build some of the best boats ever launched on the Tyrrhenian Sea, and the boatyards are still very much alive today.

Today Viareggio is best known for its February Carnival. Floats are built to a specified theme and are usually spiced up with political satire and irony. The whole town joins in the football matches, masked balls and fireworks.

To many English visitors, however, Viareggio is best known as the place where, in 1822, the drowned corpse of Percy Bysshe Shelley was washed up after a particularly lethal squall out in the Tyrrhenian Sea. The poet and a friend were on their way from Leghorn (as they called Livorno) to La Spezia.

Viareggio reached its heyday at the turn of the century and there are a number of buildings of this period remaining in the town, such as the **Bagni Margherita** on the seashore, as well as a great many huge *art nouveau* hotels located on the seafront boulevard. During the summer months there is a very lively atmosphere here; not many foreigners tend to visit and the stretch of coastline going towards Forte dei Marmi is well known as the playground for the *Milanesi*.

Puccini's lakeside retreat

Just south of Viareggio, along the Viale dei Tigli, is **Torre del Lago Puccini** ❸. The approach to this lakeside resort passes through one of Viareggio's two pine forests, of which this one, the **Macchia Lucchese**, is the most beautiful.

Maps:
Area 206
City 204

TIP

Those interested in boats would do well to have a wander around the Viareggio dock area of *Dorsena*, which will reveal some enormous luxury floating "gin palaces" in the making.

BELOW: Torre del Lago Puccini.

On **Lake Massaciúccoli**  at Torre del Lago Puccini is Giacomo Puccini's villa, in which were written all his operas except *Turandot*. The area has been rather over-popularised, but when Puccini first came here it was a peaceful backwater where he was able to indulge not only in composing but in his other favourite pastime, which was shooting birds and animals. His villa (open Tues–Sun; closed 1–3pm; entrance fee) displays his musical instruments as well as his guns. Puccini, his wife and his son are all buried in the nearby chapel. Each August, in his memory, Torre del Lago holds a festival of his operas here in a very atmospheric setting – a stage is built onto the lake near his house. The lake, and some of the neighbouring wetlands, form a nature reserve. You can take a pleasant boat trip around the lagoon.

Continuing north from Viareggio, the resorts fall into line in quick succession. **Lido di Camaiore** ❺ is slightly more downmarket than the other places further north but then access to the beach is easier – being virtually free of pay-as-you-enter stretches of sand. From this part of the shore it is easy to reach **Camaiore** ❻ (to the Romans, *Campus Major*), which is about 7 km (4 miles) to the east. The town has an interesting range of architecture, of which the 8th-century **Badia dei Benedettini** with a monumental 14th-century portal and the Romanesque **Collegiata** are the most important.

From Lido di Camaiore the subsequent pockets of watering holes are collectively known as Marina di Pietrasanta. **Pietrasanta** ❼ itself is about 8 km (5 miles) inland from the sea; its name, "Holy Stone", refers to the town's chief product, marble.

Not much happens in Pietrasanta today except for the celebration of the town's main product. It is the Tuscan centre for stone sculptors, who come here

ABOVE: fresco by the 20th-century Colombian artist Botero in Pietra-santa's church of San Martino.
BELOW: beach at Lido di Camaiore.

in droves to work the marble in the privacy of rented studios – private or commercial. A fine white dust covers everything in Pietrasanta, even the wine glasses in the bars of the Piazza Carducci.

Map, page 206

While this town has some of the loveliest monuments in the Versilia, including the 13th-century **Duomo** and the 9th-century **church of SS Giovanni and Felicità**, the **Marina** down below on the shore is bland and unexceptional. The two are joined by a tree-lined avenue which reaches the Marina at Fiumetto. The Marina is really a series of former villages – **Fiumetto**, **Tonfano**, **Montrone** and **le Fucette** – and each offers something different. Fiumetto has a pretty park with an ancient bridge in it, the *Ponte dei Principi*.

Luxurious villas

The gem of the Versilia today is **Forte dei Marmi ❽**, still further to the north. Here the rich old villas of the late 19th century are still occupied as private residences, some *art nouveau*, some ornate and ugly, all forming a suitable backdrop to lives of the utmost luxury. The Agnellis, owners of the Fiat car conglomerate, have houses here. So do holidaying industrialists from Turin and fashion magnates from Milan, and the number of expensive sports cars seen cruising the streets in the early evening is directly proportional to the number of bullet-proof vests required by the drivers and their bodyguards.

Forte dei Marmi grew up around a fort built in 1788 by Leopold I of Tuscany, the remains of which survive in the main square of the town. The shops and cafés around the square somehow still manage to retain something of a small-town atmosphere, even if they do sell some of the most expensive items money can buy.

There are no high-rise buildings, unlike Lido di Camaiore. The highest things

Every year Pietra-santa hosts a large sculpture exhibition in the Consorzio Arigiani, and in the old Istituto d'Arte is a permanent exhibition illustrating the various ways of working marble.

BELOW: the beach at Forte dei Marmi, gem of the Versilia.

TIP

Information on
sporting activities and
guided excursions in
the Garfagnana area
can be obtained from
the Cooperativa
Garfagnana Vacanze
in Castelnuovo di
Garfagnana, tel:
0583-65169.

BELOW: the hills
of Garfagnana,
painted by Adolfo
Tommasi.

are the pine trees in the gardens of the villas, and in the back streets there is still the quiet and solitude that artists, writers, poets and scholars found here in the late 19th century. Patches of beach are freely accessible, while the remainder is made up of smart bathing huts and tropical-style bars with palm-frond roofs, perched on the fine pale grey sand. Here the shore slopes gently into the calm water and bathing is very safe.

In most Italian towns, life is led conspicuously out in the streets – shopping, walking or simply sitting in cafés. At Forte dei Marmi it happens on the beach. Along the sand at the water's edge there is an endless parade of nearly naked bodies strolling languidly in the sun, chatting or simply sporting a fine figure.

Many of the holidaymakers stay in villas over the road from the beach, behind high wooden fences that shield private gardens with swimming pools from prying eyes. These people cross the road in the morning and late in the afternoon simply to stroll; swimming in the sea is out, that's what the private pool is for and at lunchtime the beaches are deserted.

Fortified Garfagnana

The landscape changes dramatically east of Pietrasanta. On the other side of the Alpi Apuane (Apuan Alps) is the **Garfagnana** region, through which runs one major road once very popular with travellers wanting to avoid the risk of catching malaria in the formerly mosquito-infested Versilian lowland by the sea.

The centre of the Garfagnana is the town of **Castelnuovo di Garfagnana** ❾, about 64 km (40 miles) north of Lucca. This fortress town once controlled the route from Genoa to Lucca and Pisa and was under the rule of the Este family of Ferrara until Italian unification. The town also had strategic importance dur-

ing World War II; it suffered badly during this period and a great deal of its town centre was destroyed. However, the Duomo survived and so did the town walls surrounding the church of San Michele, which contains a 14th-century *Madonna* by Giuliano di Simone da Lucca. The **Rocca**, or governor's palace, which dates from the 12th century, is now the town hall.

In the Rocca, in the 16th century, lived Ludovico Ariosto, the epitome of the Renaissance man – successfully combining his talents as a poet with the functions of soldier and statesman. The Este appointed him governor of the district, a post which he evidently hated, and some of the murkier passages in his *Orlando Furioso* may have been influenced by his time at Castelnuovo.

Just north of the town of Castelnuovo, at the foot of the pass which leads up through the rugged heart of the Garfagnana, are the thermal springs of **Pieve Fosciana ⓾**, which produce radioactive water. This is just another variety of the therapeutic springs with which the area is prolifically endowed. The treasures of Fosciana are displayed in the church, including a terracotta *Annunciation* by Luca della Robbia.

Continuing over the pass for about 18 km (11 miles), the first stop is **San Pellegrino in Alpe ⓫**, where there is a **Museo Etnografico** (open Tues–Sun; closed 12–2pm; entrance fee), which highlights elements of peasant life in the Garfagnana. But **Barga ⓬** to the south is by far the most interesting town in the district. The passing of time forgot to take Barga with it and today there is a curious silence in the lanes and alleyways behind its walls.

The Romanesque **Duomo** contains a 13th-century marble pulpit carved by a sculptor from Como called Guido Bigarelli. The pillars supporting the pulpit rest on the backs of lions, while the inlaid decoration and the panels of the pulpit

Map, page 206

BELOW LEFT: ruins of an aqueduct near Barga.
BELOW: Duomo portal, Barga.

Map, page 206

PANE e VINO

itself, on which are scenes from the Scriptures, ensure that this work ranks among Tuscany's finest early Renaissance altars.

However, the real tourist attraction of the area – apart from the July/August opera festival held annually at Barga and the house and tomb of the poet Giovanni Pascoli at Castelvecchio Pascoli – are the subterranean caves at **Grotta del Vento** ⑬ (open daily Apr–Sept for guided tours; entrance fee), near the village of **Fornovolasco**. Nearly three-quarters of a mile (1.2 km) of caverns wend their way through the ground, full of stalactites and stalagmites, every inch of it looking like a stage set from a horror movie.

The cold clammy atmosphere is slightly repugnant, though compelling, and an added theatrical dimension is obtained by the use of coloured lights and echoes. Each visitor must be part of a guided tour because it is fairly easy to lose your way since only a fraction of the caves are illuminated. The terrain is steep and barren and offers the possibility of excellent – but rather dangerous – walks.

San Romano in Garfagnana ⑭ is an interesting town on the way to Bagni di Lucca. It has a large medieval castle and stunning views across the Alta Garfagnana, whose barren beauty is best appreciated with a visit to the nearby **Parco Naturale Demaniale dell'Orecchiella** (open daily Jul–mid-Sept; by appointment Nov–June). This is the preserve of rare flowers, wild boar and deer, and all around are the grandiose peaks of the Apuan Alps.

ABOVE: local staples on offer. **BELOW:** a shady spot for a local youngster.

Byron bathed here

Near this spot, in a valley where the rivers Lima and Serchio meet, is the spa town of **Bagni di Lucca** ⑮. The town has always been known as a source of hot spring water, which contains sulphur and salt. It was very fashionable around the year 1800, when Byron, Shelley and Elizabeth Barrett Browning visited it, but since then it has been quietly forgotten. It has retained, however, an air of quiet respectability and faded elegance and is worth a visit.

In the 19th century the bathhouse was in the Palazzo del Bagno, which is now in a rather neglected state. There are 19 springs in the town as well as two steam vapour grottoes which easily sustain temperatures of up to 47°C (118°F). The open season for the springs lasts from May to September and they are said to be particularly good for anyone suffering from arthritis and rheumatism.

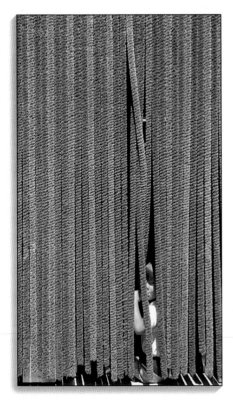

From Bagni di Lucca the road continues along the banks of the River Serchio to **Borgo a Mozzano** ⑯, a hamlet well known for its medieval *Ponte della Maddalena*.

The other name for this hump-backed bridge, which spans the Serchio, is *Ponte del Diavolo* – Devil's Bridge – because the devil is supposed to have built it for the villagers in return for the first soul to cross it on its completion. The crafty villagers cheated the devil by sending over, by night, a pig – with which the devil had to be content.

In reality, this bridge, with arches of five different sizes, was built by Countess Matilda of Tuscany (1046–1115), whose generosity was also responsible for the construction of the Romanesque churches of Diecimo, Pieve di Brancoli and Villa Basilica. ❏

Villas and Gardens

The idea of a country retreat, so popular in Tuscany today, originated with the Romans. The villas were either working farms, which supplied the townhouses with produce, or were planned purely for pleasure. They would be visited for a day's outing and many did not even have bedrooms.

In the 15th century the idea of the country villa was revived by the Medici family, which commissioned magnificent residences and elaborate gardens, modelled on classical ideas. In 1452 Leon Battista Alberti laid down the essential ingredients for a truly well-appointed country retreat: it had to be on a slope, full of light and air, with rooms grouped round an inner hall.

Some are relatively simple structures; others are more extravagant, with whimsical additions, even mock antique ruins and statuary. Often they were copied by visiting Europeans, who applied principles intended for the sunny Mediterranean to more northern climates, with romantic but chilly results.

The Medici villa at Fiesole, which has been described as "the first true Renaissance villa", was designed by the architect Michelozzo for Cosimo the Elder between 1458 and 1461. The design of the hanging gardens, in particular, was very influential and the villa commands a superb view of Florence.

The villa at Poggio a Caiano, near Pistoia, was converted by Giuliano da Sangallo for Lorenzo de'Medici between 1480 and 1485 and it dominates the surrounding countryside. It is characteristically Palladian in style. In the 19th century the gardens were converted according to the fashionable English style, with romantic temples, an aviary, fountains and a mock Gothic ruin.

The 15th-century Villa Gamberaia in Settignano, near Florence, has retained most of its original 18th-century garden and was considered by Harold Acton to be "the most poetic garden in Tuscany".

The area surrounding Lucca is rich in villas: the patrician Villa Torrigiani, the baroque Villa Mansi and the Villa Reale at Marlia are all surrounded by beautiful parks and are open to the public. Marlia was created by the Orsetti family, and it was substantially remodelled by Elisa Bacciocchi, Napoleon's sister. There is a lush park with a lake, which surrounds the formal Italian gardens. Most wonderful of its many fine features is the *teatro di verdura*, an outdoor theatre sculpted from yew, a supreme example of the art of topiary.

Both the house and gardens of the baroque 17th-century Villa Garzoni, near Pescia, can be visited. The gardens are particularly extraordinary: fountains and flower beds are designed in an elaborate formal pattern with parterres and pools, behind which is a complicated series of interconnecting stairs and terraces leading to waterfalls, hidden statues, grottoes and a complicated maze.

Most of these villas are still in appreciative private hands, and often the gardens can be visited even if the house is not open to the public. Wandering through fragrant shrubbery and cool grottoes, past whimsical statuary and fountains can be highly recommended as a delightful diversion on a hot summer's afternoon. ❑

RIGHT: the gardens of Villa Collodi.

PISA

Look beyond the famous leaning tower and you'll discover the numerous other delights this ancient city – and the eponymous province which surrounds it – have to offer

Maps:
Area 222
City 218

The Leaning Tower draws tourists to Pisa like a magnet, many of them pausing to appreciate the religious architecture, others to enjoy the glorious art and history of this Tuscan city. Once a thriving Roman port, Pisa's harbour silted up in the 15th century and it now stands on the Arno river, 10 km (6 miles) from the coast. Great sea battles were fought during the Middle Ages, with the city-state of Pisa becoming first allies then rivals of a number of other states, including Genoa, Lucca, Venice and Florence. At its height, Pisa's power extended to Sardinia, Corsica and the Balearic Islands.

During World War II the city was heavily bombed and has been working ever since to restore its buildings. **Pisa ❶** is halved by the gently curving River Arno, its steep stone banks coloured by floating green algae. Elegant 16th-century *palazzi* along the banks hide the less imposing buildings and general decay in the narrow streets and alleys behind. Two-horse carriages lazily clip-clop along the quiet banks in the middle of the day, when most Pisans are taking their siestas.

The Church of **Santa Maria della Spina ❹** sparkles in the distance. The statues on the sides were carved by followers of Giovanni Pisano, while the central statue of the *Madonna and Child* came from the workshop of Nino Pisano. The chapel once guarded what was believed to be a (*spina*) thorn from the crown of Jesus but that relic, plus the original statues, are now housed in the National Museum.

Crossing the original city bridge, Ponte della Cita-della, the Via Nicola Pisano leads to the **Campo dei Miracoli** (Field of Miracles) **❸**, probably the most perfect assemblage of religious buildings anywhere on earth.

PRECEDING PAGES: the Roman amphitheatre at Volterra. **LEFT:** Leaning Tower of Pisa. **BELOW:** Pisa's Duomo, one of the most important monuments in Italy.

The Leaning Tower

The secret of enjoying Pisa is to see the monuments for the first time from the right place. For the **Campanile** (Leaning Tower) **❻**, the first sight should be through the archway of the Porta Santa Maria, otherwise known as the Porta Nuova. When the sun is shining, the whiteness dazzles; when raining, it glistens.

The best time to visit Italy's most famous landmark is in the early morning, before bus-loads of tourists arrive. The air is fresher then, the heat not too intense, and it provides a magical introduction to the historic buildings.

Visitors come from all over the world to marvel, if only once, at the phenomenon of the 12th-century campanile, or Leaning Tower. In 1989 the tower was closed in response to the increasing tilt. Until one of the Anglo-Italian schemes is successfully implemented, the tower's tempting 294 steps must remain untrod (*see page 220*).

The tower was begun in 1173 by Bonano Pisano,

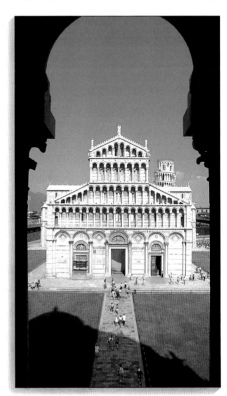

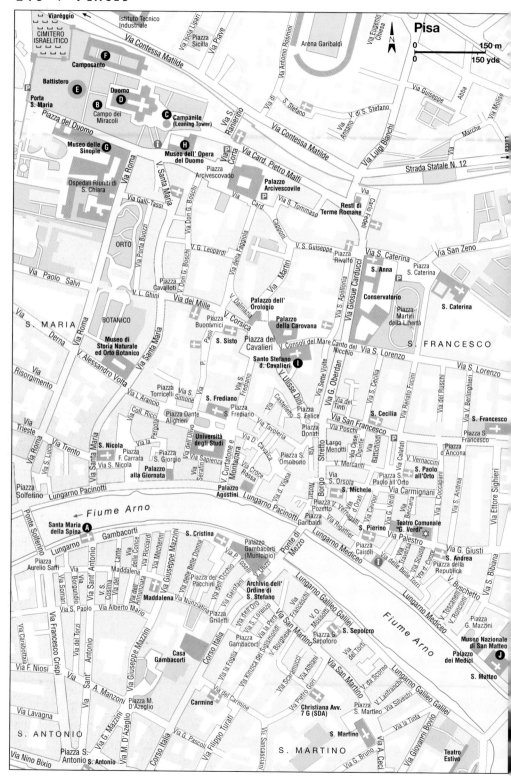

Pisa

the designer of the bronze south transept doors of the Duomo, but almost immediately began to tilt because the alluvial subsoil was unable to take its great weight. When last measured, it was leaning 5.5 metres (18 ft) from vertical.

Map, page 218

The cathedral complex

The **Duomo** ❹, built between 1068 and 1118, is one of the major monuments in Italy. The beautiful white marble façade, the model for the Pisan Romanesque style, is set with mosaics, inlaid marble and glass stones. The tomb of Buscheto, the architect of the building, is on the left of the façade, which was designed by Rainaldo and built in the early 12th century. The central bronze doors, designed by Giovanni da Bologna in 1602, gleam from the caresses of thousands of fingers stroking the figures carved on them.

The main entrance to the Duomo was intended to be through the bronze transept door of the Porta di San Ranieri, near the Campanile. These panels of the life of Christ date from 1180 and show the Greek and Roman influences in the work of Bonano Pisano.

On entering the Duomo the visitor is immediately drawn to the height of the nave, with its ornate golden coffered ceiling, rebuilt after a fire in 1596. At 95 metres (312 ft) long, the nave is supported by 68 Corithinian columns. The interior is impressive, not only for its huge spatial effect but also for the originality of its black and white striped marble walls.

ABOVE: exterior detail of Pisa's Duomo.
BELOW: Kiss of Judas, detail from the Duomo's bronze doors.

The magnificent pulpit, sculpted by Giovanni Pisano between 1302 and 1311, was damaged by fire and removed in 1599, and not reconstructed until 1926. The five detailed reliefs show scenes of the birth of John the Baptist, the life of Christ and the Last Judgement. The six supporting columns are decorated with lifelike statues of biblical figures. The pointed arches draw the eye to a lighted stained-glass window depicting the Virgin Mary.

Across from the Rainaldo façade is the third building of the Duomo complex: the **Baptistry** ❺ or *battistero* (open daily), begun in 1153. It is unfortunate that time and pollution are beginning to take their toll. Statues and busts by Giovanni Pisano, his father, Nicola and Arnolfo di Cambio are being removed from the second tier to the Museo dell'Opera del Duomo while the four massive doors already have wooden replacements.

The spacious interior, with its eight stained glass windows, holds in the centre the 1246 octagonal font of Guido Bigarelli da Como, decorated with squares of ornate black, white and russet oriental design.

The carved **pulpit**, by Giovanni Pisano, has, around the centre column, which is supported by three sculptures, six others – each alternate one resting on a lion's back. The five exquisitely sculptured panels depict scenes of the Nativity, the Message to the Shepherds, the Adoration of the Magi, the Presentation of Jesus in the Temple, the Crucifixion and the Last Judgement.

A visit to the baptistry is not complete without a guide or chorister singing a single note which echoes several times over around the building, lifting even the most atheistic spirit. "Go by night into the Baptistry, having bribed some choirboy to sing for you,

and you shall hear from that marvellous roof a thousand angels singing round the feet of San Raniero," noted the 20th-century English writer Edward Hutton.

The fourth element of the Duomo group is the **Camposanto** , the "sacred field", a cemetery consisting of cloisters surrounding a field of earth taken from the Hill of Calvary by the crusaders. A fire bomb in 1944 destroyed most of its celebrated frescoes. However, the most famous, *The Triumph of Death,* as well as those depicting *Hell* and the *Last Judgement* were saved from the conflagration and are now on display in a room off the north cloister.

Museum collections

The **Museo delle Sinopie** (open daily; till 5.30pm in winter, 8pm in summer; entrance fee) is housed in what was one of the wards of the "New Hospital of Mercy" (Ospedale Nuovo di Misericordia), which was built between 1257 and 1286. *Sinopia* is the name for a preparatory design which was carried out directly on to walls on a special kind of rough plaster, known as *arriccio*.

After preparing the outline of the design, the painter would gradually cover over and paint various parts of it, using a different kind of plaster which was richer in lime (*grassello*) until he had finished the whole work, so the sinopias were destined to disappear for ever.

The fire which followed the bombing of the Camposanto destroyed some of the frescoes and left the others in so precarious a condition that it was necessary to remove them – but that was how the immense sinopias lying beneath the frescoes came to light and were salvaged, and now carefully restored.

Last on the itinerary of the Piazza is the **Museo dell'Opera del Duomo** (open daily; till 5.30pm in winter, 8pm in summer; entrance fee) – the Cathe-

Hanging in the centre of the Duomo on a long corded chain is "Galileo's lamp". The bronze chandelier, with its balancing cherubs (or putti), *supposedly helped Galileo to understand the theories of movement of the pendulum.*

BELOW: inside Pisa's Duomo, one of the first monumental structures of the Middle Ages.

FIGHTING A LOSING BATTLE?

Now leaning by a perilous 5.5 degrees, Pisa's landmark tower is in danger of collapse, shifting with the sun's movements or even reacting to a downpour of rain. Until recently, the tilt was thought to be the result of the way the structure was sinking into the sand and clay foundations. However, the subsidence theory has now been rejected, replaced by the belief that the problem lies in the tower's essential instability, not in the compression of layers of clay.

The breakthrough was the discovery in 1990 that the tower was, in effect, rotating in a vertical plane around the base of the first segment. Since 1992, the tower has been supported by steel bands while the third storey is to be bound by a parachute of horizontal cables. These are only temporary solutions, to be superseded by a plan to arrest the tilt before the millennium. By extracting soil beside the structure, experts hope to right the tower by half a degree, enough to ensure its survival for another millennium while maintaining its lopsided charm.

An ugly chain-link fence has surrounded the tower and the ground immediately around it, making the area look like a messy building site. If the experts are proved right, however, the tower should be open again by the year 2000.

dral Works Museum, housed in the former chapter house. The exhibits are all from monuments in the Duomo square. The main items of the collection can be seen on the ground floor; these are sculptures dating from the 11th, 12th and 13th centuries and are evidence of the artistic currents present in Pisa when, as a republic, it was at the height of its power.

The precious objects in the museum collection – the Duomo treasure and plate – are to be found in Room 9 and in the seminary chapel, together with some very old ecclesiastical garments, heavily embroidered in white, gold, red and black. Here too is Giovanni Pisano's famous *Madonna and Child* in ivory. There is also a fragment of a famous belt that once was the length of the Duomo perimeter, encrusted with enamelled plaques, gemstones and silver crosses.

The archaeological section displays the Etruscan and Roman material looted from the ancient settlements of Pisa and Volterra to decorate the city's new buildings. In Room 1 the 12th-century sculptures taken from the Duomo allow a full appreciation of the artist's work and a clear diagram shows where the fragments originated in the façade. Another unusual art form, in Room 13, is wood marquetry, or intarsias, of which Cristoforo da Lendinara was the greatest master of the 15th-century school of inlaying that was to develop in the Po valley. His two intarsias are one of the favourite themes of the Pisan intarsia workers.

From the Museo dell'Opera del Duomo the Piazza dei Cavalieri is a short walk, but the best viewpoint for this spectacular square is opposite the Palazzo dei Cavalieri at the exit from Via San Frediano. From here the whole of Vasari's glorious 16th-century façade may be appreciated. From six niches above, the Grand Dukes of Tuscany gaze down over the central steps and the fountain topped with Pietro Francavilla's sculpture of Cosimo I.

Map, page 218

ABOVE: statue in the Museo dell'Opera del Duomo.
BELOW: the Ponte di Mezzo, scene of Pisa's annual *Gioco del Ponte*.

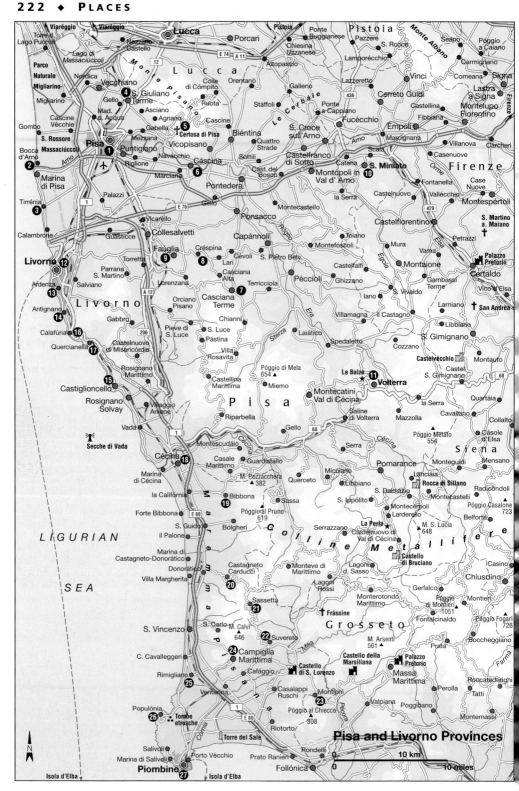

Pisa and Livorno Provinces

LIGURIAN SEA

0   10 km

0   10 miles

N

Vasari (1511–74) designed the tower of the Church of **Santo Stefano dei Cavalieri ❶**, where trophies and spoils of war are displayed. In 1606 Giovanni de' Medici added the marble façade and placed the knights' emblem above the great doorway.

The large, irregular square is sometimes called Piazza dell'Orologio, the name originating from the porcelain clock above the archway, which has cool, stone benches beneath it. In 1284, when the Pisans lost the Battle of Meloria, the Podestà, Count Ugolino, suspected of treachery, was starved to death in the Palace of the Clock.

Maps:
City 218
Area 222

Paintings and pottery

From the Field of Miracles, you can follow the banks of the Arno as far as the Piazza Garibaldi. From here it is a short walk along the river to the **Museo Nazionale di San Matteo ❷** (open daily Tues–Sat; Sun till 2pm; entrance fee). Pisa's National Museum is housed in the converted ex-convent of the Sisters of Saint Matthew, and is renowned for its panel paintings with gold backgrounds – including one of Saint Paul by Masaccio – wooden crucifixes, altar-pieces and medieval Islamic and Pisan pottery.

There is a collection of antique armour used in the *Gioco del Ponte* (a medieval tug-of-war held annually on the last Sunday in June), which comprises breastplates, helmets and other pieces dating from the 15th and 16th centuries. There are also many wooden shields, painted with the colours of the city quarters, which are used in the fight and during the parade.

Another important Pisan festival, held in mid-June every year, is the *Regata di San Ranieri*, where boat races (with competitors in medieval costume) and processions of brilliantly decorated boats are held on the River Arno. The evening before the regatta is the *Luminaria di San Ranieri*, at which tens of thousands of candles and torches are placed on the buildings along the river – a stunning sight when seen after dark.

If you spy some grazing camels on the drive to Marina di Pisa, don't think you've seriously lost your way – they are in fact descendants of a large herd established under Duke Ferdinand II in the mid-17th century.

BELOW: a chat in between lectures near Pisa's university – one of the oldest in Italy.

The pretty road to the coast pauses here and there at railway crossings as it follows the River Arno to the sea. It passes the San Piero a Grado Basilica, where legend has it that St Peter landed when he reached Italy.

At **Bocca d'Arno ❷** the hanging trawlnets from fishing boats and the rods of silent fishermen evoke the atmosphere captured by artists like Nino Costa and Gabriele d'Annunzio.

On both sides of the mouth of the Arno the coastline boasts miles of sandy beaches. Beyond the river mouth is the regional park of San Rossore, with its busy racecourse and enchanting woods. Just in front of the former Royal Estate lies the seaside resort of **Marina di Pisa** with its variety of architectural styles. Concerned newspaper reports of the pollution on this part of the coast are probably true, since industrial waste from the Arno and the sewage of seaside towns fill the Ligurian Sea at this point, but the beaches are kept clean.

Natural barrier

A kilometre or so down the coast at **Tirrenia ❸** is the remaining stretch of Mediterranean pine forest – the one place where no building has been allowed on

The handsome clock tower that looks down over Cascina.

the shore. The evergreen trees act as a natural barrier against the *libeccio*, a strong southwest wind. Thanks to the trees, the wind is reduced to a light, scented breeze of pine and juniper which cools the air on hot, summer days.

As a much larger resort than Marina di Pisa, Tirrenia offers luxury hotels and homely boarding houses. Night clubs, restaurants and sporting facilities for golf, tennis, horse-riding, fishing, windsurfing, sailing and rowing are enjoyed by Tuscans, but few foreigners take holidays along this coast. Each year colourful regattas and boat races are held, and the training centre for the Italian National Olympics is based in Tirrenia.

Midway between Pisa and Lucca, at the foot of the Pisan mountains, is the spa town of **San Giuliano Terme ❹**. The Palazzo Termale (spa building), set in private grounds guarded by high walls, is a national health hospital.

Olives, chestnuts and pines grow in the surrounding fertile countryside and wild horses roam the hills. A number of ruins are dotted among the valleys and at Capoluogo in the Caldaccoli region are eight stone arches remaining from the aqueduct built by Mediceo di Asciano in 1592.

Monastic retreat

Set in lush green countryside, **Certosa di Pisa ❺** (open Tues–Sun; closed pm Sun and public holidays; entrance fee), the Charterhouse of Pisa, was founded in 1366. From the end of that century modifications and additions were continually made to the Carthusian monastery until the final touches were finished in the early 18th century.

BELOW:
a curious onlooker.

The Carthusians were one of the new strict orders who believed that the increasing prosperity of the Cluniac orders was accompanied by a decline in reli-

gious observance. Their architecture reflected this; the monks lived in separate cells within a main enclosure. The centre of monastic life was the Great Cloister, of which the Certosa di Pisa has a particularly fine example.

Work on the frescoes of the church walls began in 1701; Angelo Maria Somazzi from Livorno added fine stucco work, and in 1718 workmen from Carrara carved the marble and renovated the church façade. In 1981 a part of the Charterhouse was allotted to the University of Pisa to house the Museum of Natural and Regional History.

Entering **Cascina** ❻ past fields of sunflowers, grapevines and maize, the roads are lined with plane trees. Cascina is proud of its solid stone walls, dating from 1142, which are depicted in Vasari's energetic painting of the Battle of Cascina, now hanging in the Palazzo Vecchio in Florence.

The town is centred round the production of wooden furniture. At the end of the arcaded main street, Corso Matteotti, there is a large factory with MOSTRA DEL MOBILI displayed in huge letters and containing a permanent furniture exhibition. Yet most of the workshops are tucked away in the pretty side streets, which are usually festooned with seasonal flowers.

Leaving the Mostra and walking up Corso Matteotti, the tiny chapel of **Suore di Carmelitane di Santa Teresa** is on the left. It has beautifully detailed frescoes depicting the creation of the sky and the earth, the expulsion of Abel, the Tower of Babel and St John the Baptist. The nearby Church of the Saints Casciano and Giovanni, *circa* 970, is a graceful building with a simple interior.

Casciana Terme ❼, less than 40 km (25 miles) from Pisa, is surrounded by flourishing vineyards, olive groves and peach orchards. The beautiful hillsides and the mild climate create a relaxing atmosphere for visitors.

Map, page 222

The name of the Carthusian order, which was anglicised as "Charterhouse", was derived from La Grande Chartreuse in Dauphiné.

BELOW: the 18th-century monastery of Certosa di Pisa.

The town exists solely for the spa, which is open from April to November, and the pace of life is leisurely, if somewhat clinical. The thermal waters attract people seeking a break, as well as those "taking the cure".

In 1870 Poggi designed the large spa building, but a bomb destroyed it in World War II, leaving only the façade and the hall intact. In 1968 the building was completely rebuilt around the remains of the original structure.

Gourmets take note: San Miniato is the "truffle capital" of Tuscany, and hosts a truffle and mushroom festival on the third Sunday in October.

The country around Casciana Terme is good for walking, especially in the nearby pine woods of Pineta della Farnia. The village of **Colle Montanino di Ceppato,** which has a 1,000-year-old tower, and **Pariascia,** which has a fortress, are also both within easy reach, and a visit to the **Sanctuary of the Madonnina Dei Monti** might serve to restore the spirit. At **Crespina ❽** and **Fauglia ❾** are several magnificent 19th-century villas, as well as the church of **Chianni** and the nearby **Lari Castle** (open Sun and public holidays 3.30–6.30pm; Mon–Fri by appointment only; tel: 0587 684085), which is heavily adorned with medieval coats of arms and family crests.

A few minutes' drive from Casciana is the co-operative wine cellar *Enoteca di Terricciola,* well-stocked with local wines and those from other parts of Italy. The area around Casciana Terme is known for the production of Chianti Colline Pisane, while the Arno valley from Santa Croce to Cascina and south of San Miniato produces Bianchi San Torpe. The third local wine-producing area is around the town that bears its name – Montescudaio.

Ancient town

In a stillness not usually associated with Italian cities, rests the ancient town of **San Miniato ❿**, whose origins go back to Etruscan and Roman times. It is set on the top of three hills, 192 metres (630 ft) above sea-level, and gazes out upon magnificent views. On one side stretches the large plain of the River Arno with the Apennines towering over the Pisan, Pistoian and Florentine mountains. On the other side, what Carducci described as "the wavy gracefulness of the hills" continues to San Gimignano and Volterra.

The nature and history of the town has always been closely linked to its geographical position, equidistant from the important cities that played a decisive historical role: Pisa, Florence, Lucca, Pistoia, Siena and Volterra.

High on the hillside are the two towers of the **Rocca** (open Tues–Sun; closed 12–3pm; entrance fee), which was rebuilt in the 12th century by Frederick II. Torre di Federico, as it became known, was destroyed in World War II but has been faithfully reconstructed. Dante recounts that it was from this tower that Pietro della Vigna leapt to his death and as punishment was turned into a gnarled and twisted tree.

The oldest tower of the fortress, the Torre di Matilde, was converted into a belltower when the **Duomo** was added, with its Romanesque brick façade and later restructuring. The oldest building in San Miniato is a church built by the Lombards in the 8th century.

The church of **San Francesco** originates from AD 783 but was completely rebuilt in 1276. It is a magnificent example of a Franciscan building. The remains

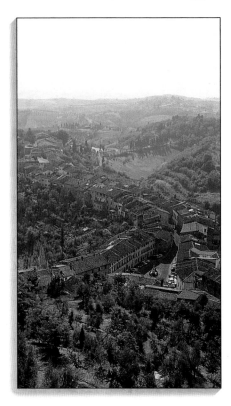

BELOW: there are beautiful views from the hilltop town of San Miniato.

Map, page 222

of a 15th-century fresco depicts Saint Christopher with the Child Jesus. The church, to which a convent was later added was in a state of constant transformation until the 16th century. By using bricks made from local clay, the medieval construction and decorative traditions were maintained.

The **Museo Diocesano d'Arte Sacra** (open winter Sat–Sun; summer Tues–Sun; closed 12–3pm; entrance fee), in the old sacristy of the Duomo, exhibits art and sculpture including works by Lippi, Verrocchio and Tiepolo.

Many local traditions are still maintained. On the feast of St John, when winnowing is over, bonfires of ears of corn and cloves of garlic are lit on all the hills surrounding the town, to keep ill luck away. From the middle of September to the end of Christmas is the season for white truffles (*tuber magnatum pico*). The Association of Trufflers of the San Miniato Hills issue a map showing where to find the aromatic plant, which is dug out of the ground with a type of pole called a *vangheggia*. On four consecutive Sundays in November a huge market and exhibition is mounted to display the catch of the season.

Majestic position

One of the most important towns in Tuscany is **Volterra ⑪**, which has a richly layered history with abundant evidence of its 3,000 years of civilization. It commands a beautiful, windswept and majestic position on a steep ridge 545 metres (1,780 ft) above sea level between the valleys of the Era and Cecina rivers. Walking round the ancient defensive walls is an excellent way to view the town, the Roman remains and the wide sweep of countryside below.

Volterra was the Etruscan city-state of Velathri, one of the confederation of 12 city-states which made up Etruria. It became an important Roman municipality (Volterrae) when Rome annexed Etruria in 351 BC. It followed the new faith of Christianity, and at the fall of the Roman Empire in AD 476 it was already the centre of a vast diocese.

Although predominantly medieval, the town still cherishes abundant evidence of the Etruscan period, including the massive stretches of the city wall. The **Porta all'Arco** (the Arch Gate) is the best preserved Etruscan gateway in Italy, dating from the 4th century BC with sides of huge rectangular stone blocks and three mysterious carved stone heads above the gateway. The Acropolis in the **Enrico Fiumi Archaeological Park** (open daily) on the Plain of Castello shows various periods of human settlements from prehistory to the Middle Ages; also preserved are a large number of hypogea, vases and cinerary urns.

Alabaster excellence

The traditional craftsmanship in alabaster is a legacy from the Etruscans, who made great use of it from the 5th century BC onwards, primarily for their beautifully sculptured urns. Alabaster is one of the most typical products exported from this region, and it is sold at many of the local workshops. Examples of Roman artefacts in the archaeological park include the remains of the **Teatro** in Vallebona, which was started under Augustus but completed during the rule of Tiberius. Recently excavated and partly recon-

San Miniato is full of attractive features like this wall plaque.

BELOW: landscapes are vivid during the sunflower season.

Volterra cathedral's lustrous ceiling.

structed, its features include baths, an enormous rectangular water cistern, a number of sculptures and mosaic flooring.

Evidence of the Middle Ages is demonstrated not only in Volterra's urban structure but in its buildings, the most important of which are in the **Piazza dei Priori**. Here is the tall, 13th-century Palazzo dei Priori, whose façade with its iron flag and torch holders is decorated with coats of arms of the Florentine magistrates; to the right of the square is the Palazzo Pretorio, with its crenellated Torre del Porcellino (Tower of the Little Pig), the name adopted from its decorative bas-reliefs of wild boar.

Family towers

There are other structures of great architectural interest, including the towers of the Buonparenti and Bonaguidi families united by a high arch; the house-towers of Toscano in the small square of the church of San Michele in the Via Guarnacci; the 12th-century **Cattedrale** (open daily; closed 12–2.30pm), which houses works of art from the Middle Ages to the Renaissance; the baptistry, an octagonal building dating from the 13th century, with an elegant marble doorway; and the church of San Francesco and the adjacent chapel of the Croce di Giorno, which was decorated with frescoes by Cenni di Francesco in 1410.

The Renaissance buildings, such as the Palazzo Minucci-Solaini, blend gracefully with the medieval Volterran houses. The conventual complex of San Girolamo has a splendid *Annunciation* by Benvenuto di Giovanni and some della Robbia terracotta statues.

Volterra has three major museums. The **Museo Etrusco Guarnacci** (open Tues–Sun; closed 1–3pm in winter; entrance fee) is one of the most important

BELOW: the simple Romanesque façade of Volterra cathedral.

museums in Italy for its Etruscan exhibits, and is particularly notable for the outstanding collections of alabaster, terracotta and travertine cinerary urns, decorated with many different motifs and sculpted in a great variety of styles.

The Art Gallery and Civic Museum of **Palazzo Minucci-Solaini** (open Tues–Sun; entrance fee) houses valuable paintings of the Sienese and Florentine schools of art. Among the works of Taddeo di Bartolo, Benvenuto di Giovanni and Baldassare Franceschini are such notable works as the *Annunciation* by Luca Signorelli and the *Christ in Glory* by Domenico Ghirlandaio.

The most famous painting in the collection is the *Descent from the Cross* by Rosso Fiorentino (1494–1540), a work of considerable importance and innovation because of the stylisation of the figures and the striking tragedy of the composition. The **Museo d'Arte Sacra** (open daily; closed 1–3pm in summer; open till 1pm in winter; entrance fee) has many ecclesiastical vestments, a collection of gold reliquaries, church bells, illuminated manuscripts and some 13th-century sculptures of the Sienese school of art.

The countryside around Volterra is one of gentle, undulating hills, interrupted in the west by the wild and awe-inspiring spectacle of abrupt crevasses known as the **Balze** (the crags). This is a natural phenomenon created by the continual erosion of layers of sand and clay. Repeated landslides over the centuries finally destroyed the Etruscan and early Christian remains.

Neighbouring **Larderello** is an area at the centre of the borax industry. The landscape is dominated by borax *fumaroles*, machinery which harnesses the volcanic energy of hot springs to generate electricity. It is a curious sight, when approaching Larderello, to see steam escaping from fissures in the ground. The air is heavy with sulphurous fumes for miles around. ❑

Map,
page 222

TIP

The Archeological Park, high on the hilltop site of Volterra's former Etruscan acropolis, is an ideal place for a picnic.

BELOW: the solid defensive city walls of Volterra.

LIVORNO

*The multi-faceted province of Livorno evokes images
of sweet wine, Elba, sandy beaches, Napoleonic myths...
and a few unfortunate industrial ports*

Map,
page 222

W ith barely enough Renaissance art to enliven an overcast beach holiday, **Livorno** should be on the defensive. In fact, the province is as varied as its famed fish soup, *cacciucco*. The fishy ingredients, a little of everything in the right proportions, apply to Livorno's seascapes. Captured in moody canvases by the Tuscan Impressionists, the rocky northern coast is as dramatic as the southern coast is soothing. The mainland stretches from wild, marshy Maremma to the rugged, hilly interior, or the Elban mountains.

Livorno is no architectural desert: a coastline of Pisan watchtowers and Medicean fortresses hides the occasional Roman villa or Etruscan necropolis. Inland, the neglected hilltop villages inspired equally romantic verse from Carducci, Livorno's greatest poet. Livorno is rich in Romanesque and baroque architecture, but the lone sanctuary or homely red-painted farmhouse are truer to the province's individuality.

Livorno City

The city owes its existence to the silting up of Pisa in 1530, and the Livornese joke that, unlike their rivals, the Pisans, they will never be so careless as to let the sea slip away from them. The rivalry between Pisans and the Livornese is legendary and very much alive today. It's even the subject of a monthly satirical magazine, *Il Vernacoliere*. There is also a saying in Livorno: *Meglio un morto in casa che un Pisano all'uscio* – "It is better to have a dead body in your house than a Pisan on the doorstep".

In 1421 the Florentines paid the Genoese 100,000 florins for Livorno, a vast sum for such a malaria-infested and mosquito-ridden village. It was the enlightened Cosimo I who transformed Livorno into the greatest Medicean port in 1575. Cosimo was aided by Buontalenti, whose plan for the "ideal city" envisaged the present star-shaped port with its five bastions.

Grand Duke Ferdinand employed Robert Dudley, the great naval engineer, to build the harbour walls and administer the port. Dudley benefited from Livorno's status as an "open city" with free trade, tax exemption and shelter from persecution.

As late as the 19th century it was an enterprising yet patrician city. Cosmopolitan salons, elegant avenues, Renaissance and baroque villas made it a fashionable port of call for the "Grand Tourists". But after 80 bombing raids in World War II, Livorno resembles a modern necropolis.

Except for the oyster beds laid down by Cosimo, the Medicean port is unchanged. The crumbling red-brick **Fortezza Vecchia** is a patchwork of Livornese history: Antonio da Sangallo's and Buontalenti's mas-

PRECEDING PAGES: ships departing from Livorno. **LEFT:** rocky coast south of Livorno. **BELOW:** a fisherman mending his nets in Livorno's Old Port.

Shoppers stroll along a street in Livorno.

terpiece has Roman remains in its vast Medicean dungeons; 14th-century Pisan walls enclose a small Medicean house and are topped by a Romanesque tower. The **Fortezza Nuova**, built in 1590, completed the Medicis' ambitious fortifications. The murky canals encircling it once led to Pisa. Now restored, the New Fortress hosts conferences, festivals and children's romps through the gardens.

Between the fortresses is **Venezia**, an ill-lit, seedy area not unlike working-class Venice. The canals are lined with 17th-century *palazzi*, crumbling warehouses, fish stands and workshops. The area is not without its charm, however: the *Effetto Venezia* festival is held here in late July/August with performances, concerts and films. Restaurants serve *cacciucco* all day and are open till late.

The area also comes alive in July with the *Carnevale Marinaro*, more of a water pageant than a race. Escorted by swimmers in carnival masks, bedecked boats follow the maze of canals between the two fortresses and sail under the main square, Piazza Repubblica.

Visitors soon realise that the city lives on commerce, not tourism. A baffling one-way street system and gruff hotel and restaurant service reflect the fact that most tourists spend only one night here on their way to the islands, the hills or to Florence. Livorno is often described as a *città particolare*, an unusual city, and it is hard to visualise it as a medieval town or an elegant seaside resort. Unless fascinated by naval engineering and military history, most visitors cannot bridge the gap between Livorno's glorious past and ordinary present.

The rocky west coast

BELOW: ship painting, Livorno.

Most of the city's artistic and literary pretensions lie in **Ardenza** ⓭ and **Antignano** ⓮, now elegant coastal resorts. **Villa Mimbelli** (open Tues–Sun;

entrance fee), based near the naval college, houses a gallery to the "Macchiaioli Movement", the Italian counterpart to Impressionism. While Florence's Pitti Palace has a fuller collection, Lega, Signorini and Fattori are well represented.

This area was home to much of what the Liveronese called "Leghorn's British Factory". In 1819, after the tragic death of their son, Percy and Mary Shelley moved to Villa Valsovana, now a depressing building in the suburbs. The sea views and the dramatic summer storms revived the poet enough to enable him to work on his blank verse drama, *The Cenci* and write his famous *Ode to a Skylark*. Byron, living at Villa Dupouy in Ardenza, was a frequent visitor when not working on *Don Juan*. Ardenza is now a fashionable coastal resort flanked by palms, box hedges and Liberty villas.

From prosperous Antignano, once a mere creek at the foot of the Montenero hills, a road or rickety cable car climbs to the **Sanctuary of Madonna di Montenero** (open daily; closed 12.30–2.30pm), the patron saint of Tuscany. For those who dare look, there are views of Livorno, Elba and even Corsica. Between 1345 and 1774 the original shrine was transformed into a church.

The church is always full of votive offerings from relics to crutches and gold hearts to handwritten promises. Beside the sanctuary is a deep series of watery grottoes. Outside, elixirs are on sale to gullible visitors from beyond the Madonna's parish. Once the ritual stroll and religious observance is over, the locals head for the fish restaurants of **Castiglioncello's** ⓑ with a clear conscience but without elixirs. Dried cod, red mullet and a spicy version of bouillabaisse are best eaten at inland rustic *trattorie*, or cheap dockside bars, not at exorbitant resort restaurants.

Out of season, the high coastal road from Ardenza to Castiglioncello is a

Map, page 222

"The peasants sang as they worked beneath our window during the heat of a very hot summer; and at night the water wheel creaked and the fireflies flashed among the hedges."

– MARY SHELLEY

BELOW: harbour at Castiglioncello.

Visitors will find facilities for a variety of watersports on the beaches along the coast of Livorno province.

BELOW: children enjoy a day on the beach at Marina di Castagneto-Donoratico.

delight, with spectacular views of the wildest coastline in the province. The coast becomes progressively more rugged as Ardenza's hills of neat dwarf oaks give way to rocky creeks cut into deep pine woods.

The road winds past Medici castles, watchtowers and even follies. **Castello del Boccale**, encircled by gulls and rocky paths to the shore, is a Medicean fort converted into a private villa.

At **Calafuria** , an isolated Medicean tower and distorted rock formations provided the Macchiaioli painters with a dramatic setting. But their favourite spot was **Romito**, a Grand Ducal castle later occupied by the French in 1799. It looks like a whimsical folly, a miniature bandstand perched over the sea, but is not open to visitors.

After exposed Romito, the coastline becomes wild and wooded. As **Quercia-nella** comes into view, pine woods run down to the water's edge; small coves, shingle beaches and a narrow harbour struggle for space.

The Lucchese, proud of their flat golden sands, wonder how the Livornese can possibly neglect their own sands below **Cecina** in favour of Castiglioncello's fashionable rocks. However, the people of Livorno seem to place adventure over comfort, just as they prefer a living city to a museum city, modern art to Renaissance art, "vernacular" theatre to classical theatre, the Risorgimento poet Carducci to Florentine Dante. The cunning Livornese also know that there are sandy bays tucked into the rocks.

Cosimo's fort, built on the pine-clad promontory, was designed to keep the pirates at bay, but since the 19th century has drawn all the great Italian Impressionists. In the 1930s, Castiglioncello was popular with film stars.

Rural Maremma

Ignoring Cecina and the vast **California** beach, take the inland road towards Bibbona and the real Maremma beyond. Quiet lanes trace through marshy countryside dotted with red farmhouses and occasional herds of placid white Maremman cattle.

Bibbona is a higgledy-piggledy medieval village traditionally linked to Volterra. One of its simple churches, Santa Maria delle Pietà, has the odd inscription, *Terrible Est Locus Ist* – either written after a touch of Livornese fever or because the church is built on a precarious slope.

Nearby is the **Oasi di Bolgheri**, a nature reserve and bird colony. It is a place apart, neither sea nor land. The "Oasis" is home to moorhens, wild ducks, herons, egrets and migratory birds which might end up as Bolgheri roast duck or thrush *alla Carducci*.

From Bibbona it is a short drive to the tiny chapel of **San Guido** and to medieval **Bolgheri**, the land beloved by Giusè Carducci, one of Italy's finest poets. So potent is his work that Tuscans still tend to see the intensely green valley through Carducci's brooding eyes. The landscape is a shrine to a poet loved as much for his revolutionary fervour and commitment to national unity as for his melancholic verse.

San Guido and Bolgheri are linked by a magnificent avenue of cypresses, almost 5 km (3 miles) long, planted in 1801 by Camillo della Gherardesca. In

Carducci's celebrated poem the tall trees are *quasi in corsa giganti giovinetti*, "galloping young giants" or ranks of upstanding Tuscan soldiers waiting in double file for inspection.

The flatness beyond the trees is broken by low farmhouses, olive trees and the village vineyards. The gateway to the village is the ancient door to the Gherardesca castle. The poet's home was in the village, as was the home of his first love, Maria Banchini. A square called Piazza Bionda Maria recalls his poem, *If Only I'd Married You, Blonde Maria*, a lament which sounds marginally more poetic in Italian.

Lines of Carducci's verse in Bolgheri are as common as Dante inscriptions are in Florence. Busts of Carducci are available at the local shop, sold alongside bottles of Sassicaia, one of Italy's most costly wines, which comes from the Marchesi Incisi estate.

For the resolutely cheerful there is an austere cemetery where the poet's beloved "Nonna Lucia" is buried, "her white solemnity dressed in black" and the only provider of solace in his dismal childhood. For the faint of heart, Bolgheri's excellent wine will dispel Carducci's ghost.

Castagneto Carducci was once a Gherardesca stronghold and a scene of more childhood misery for the young Carducci, but is an attractive hilltop village in its own right. Superficially, little has changed since the Gherardesca lords drained the land, planted the vines and encircled the castle with high stone walls. From its rocky balcony, the town surveys pine forests, plains, golden beaches and two castles. On summer evenings the town is popular with *borghesi* families tempted by the views – and the aromas of sizzling sausages, roast pigeon and hare.

Map, page 222

The neatly parcelled countryside in the Maremma is a result of the 1950 land reforms which were designed to break up the latifundia – *the* latifundia – *the old system of feudal estates. Expropriated land was divided into uneconomical strips, each of which was linked to a cooperative or local farmer.*

BELOW: geraniums in the afternoon sun.

Sassetta ㉑, a bird's nest of a village, was once accessible only to local warriors who thrived on feuds and a diet of game. The area was damned in Dante's *Inferno* as "an impenetrable thicket without paths, leafy patches or apple trees". Since then, Sassetta has sat on its mass of red marble and waited for visitors to penetrate the deep chestnut woods.

Despite the serenity, few have visited its medieval Castello, parish church and alleyways. The locals are no longer ferocious except towards their traditional enemy, Monteverdi Marittima, with whom they share a patron saint, Sant' Andrea, but nothing else. It is a hardy, self-sufficient community with a tradition of weaving, embroidery and pipe making.

An injunction on a Sassetta wall sensibly tells visitors: Lavorate in città, Ristoratevi a Sassetta (*"Work in the city, rest in Sassetta"*).

Thrush hunters.

The *sagra del tordo* is a celebration of the thrush in a place where hunting is both a religious cult and a hobby, carried out in all seasons, legally or otherwise. The last Sunday of October heralds a torchlit procession, a *palio* in costume, and a banquet of roast thrush served with chestnut-flavoured *polenta*. The village displays signs of token tourism: a Zona Climatica board publicises the fresh climate while the summer "information office" is run by eager children.

From Sassetta a winding road through olives, oleanders and woodland leads to **Suvereto** ㉒. The well-preserved villages have much in common, including the same line in advertising. A battered sign encapsulates the region's charm: *La Mattina al Mare, il Pomeriggio ai Monti* ("Mornings at the Sea, Afternoons in the Mountains").

Suvereto was the first "free commune" in Maremma and is proud of its 13th-century Palazzo Comunale with its intact loggia and crenellated tower. The

BELOW: farmhouse in the Maremma.

early Romanesque church of San Giusto combines decorated Byzantine portals with a Pisan façade. Many churches and houses are decorated with the local red, brown or grey variegated marble which has been quarried since medieval times.

Suvereto's urban design, based on rising concentric circles, is simple but effective: each level corresponds to a street, from San Giusto to the towering Rocca above. The steep ascent winds through a rabbit warren of covered passageways. The fortress itself was the scene of a great royal funeral in 1313: Harry VII of Luxembourg died at the Battle of Buonconvento in Siena province but was embalmed here and buried in Pisa.

Map, page 222

The sedate village pours on to the streets for the evening *passeggiata* and, in season, for the *sagra del cinghiale*, a wild boar feast combining food, folklore and spectacle. Early December signals flag-waving displays and crossbow competitions between the rival *rioni* or districts. It all culminates in a feast dedicated to the "King of the woods". The boar is washed down with the Ghimbergo wine which locals claim is "as simple and honest as the people of Suvereto".

This area is **Val di Cornia**, an enchanted region of gently wooded hills, hot springs, lush valleys and old quarries. Orchids and anemones grow on the rocky outcrops while a mix of myrtle, broom and yellow saxifrage cover the slopes.

Up towards **Monte Calvi**, the "Macchiaioli" artists liked to paint the cork trees: the contrast of the fragile leaves and gnarled branches occupied them for days. Wildlife often trotted into the picture, particularly white Maremman oxen and sad-eyed Chianina cows; today it is more likely to be foxes, porcupine and foolish wild boar.

ABOVE: heraldic relic in Campiglia Marittima.
BELOW: Suvereto's Chiesa della Madonna.

At **Montioni** ㉓, a village and spa southeast of Suvereto, Elisa Bacciocchi, Napoleon's sister, used to bathe nude in the hot springs. Pauline, his favourite sister, similarly scandalised the Elban natives.

The ancient baths at **Caldana Terme** are even more impressive than those at Montioni. Both the lake and pool contain ferrous sulphates and natural radioactivity which is apparently "guaranteed to restore youthful vigour in one session".

Campiglia Marittima

In spite of its name, **Campiglia Marittima** ㉔ is a small market and mining town set in the hills. As a "free" commune it was fought over by the Florentines, Pisans and Sienese, all of whom have left heraldic traces on the town walls, four gateways and imposing Rocca. Coats of arms surmount the Gothic arches of Palazzo Pretorio.

The Romanesque church of San Giovanni has an equally turbulent past. When San Fiorenzo's relics were found nearby, Piombino and Campiglia disputed ownership. A test was devised to establish the saint's posthumous sense of home: the relics were put on a cart and the oxen, left to decide where to go, trudged uphill to the saint's present resting place. Naturally the oxen were *Campigliese*.

Campiglia's mineral past is never far from the surface. Apart from viewing the permanent mineral display, visitors can visit a working quarry in **Madonna di Fucinaia** (open Sat, Sun and pub. hols in winter, Tues–Sun in summer, daily during Aug; entrance fee).

The Campigliese boast that their marble contributed to Florence's Duomo is to be taken with a pinch of salt: claiming ownership of national monuments is a common regional habit.

Just outside town is the **Rocca San Silvestro**, the centre of a site quarried since Etruscan times. Recent excavations have revealed traces of copper, lead, silver and tin, and a minerological park is planned to show the historical development of Tuscan mining.

Although mining is an important cultural tradition, food plays a bigger role in the local economy. The simple peasant dishes reflect Campiglia's traditional poverty and dignity. Many dishes – probably the most famous being the *Zuppa Lombarda*, a soup of bread and beans – were imported by the so-called *Lombardi*, seasonal workers from the Emilian or Pistoian hills. These shepherds and woodcutters lived in tenements near the swamps but came inland in the evenings to mix with the locals. In exchange for kindness and dinner, the Lombardi introduced those in the Val di Cornia to chestnut *polenta*, rice soups and *raviolini*.

Local game, sausages and *funghi porcini* were easily incorporated, and Campigliese cuisine has never looked back. The dynamic Suvereto and Campigliese tourist offices will suggest restaurants and *Agriturismo* farm stays where these delights can be sampled.

The Etruscan coast

BELOW: 19th-century village life, by Adolfo Tommasi.

For sightings of flamingoes sheltering under umbrella pines, the **Rimigliano Nature Reserve ㉕** hugs the coast between San Vincenzo and Populonia. If the coast beckons, San Vicenzo's metallic sands and monotonous strip of bungalows can be sacrificed to Populonia's Etruscan city. The Etruscans consider-

ately had themselves buried by a pine-fringed beach, reason enough to visit the only Etruscan city built on the coast.

Behind the sweep of **Baratti Bay** lies **Populonia** ㉖, the last of the 12 Etruscan cities to be founded. The ancient city was divided into two parts: the "acropolis", the religious centre clustered high around the village; and the maritime and industrial centre around the bay. The necropoli cover the slopes between the two centres. When the Maremma revealed its treasures in the 19th century, the contrast between the desolate marshes and the sophisticated tombs stirred locals and scholars alike.

Thanks to its proximity to Elba and to the metal-bearing Campigliese hills, Populonia became a rich industrial city, often called "the ancient Pittsburgh". While Elban iron ore was smelted and then traded within the Etruscan League, minerals from Campiglia were shipped to Corsica, Sardinia and France.

Populonia's secure industrial base meant that, unlike most Etruscan cities, it flourished from the 9th century BC to the Roman age without economic or political upheavals. In the ancient "industrial zone", excavations have uncovered a blast furnace and sophisticated metal-working equipment dating back to the 6th century BC. Foreign slave labour was used to dig water channels, operate the furnace and mint coins. In the 6th century BC Populonia was the first Etruscan city to mint gold, silver and bronze coins, often featuring a lion's head. Sadly, many tombs lie buried or collapsed under the weight of ancient slag heaps. Others have been looted, some recently.

Every few years a new tomb reveals tools, silver coins and bronze jewellery, often designed by resident Greek goldsmiths and gem cutters. Most of the tomb contents are now kept in Florentine museums, but a tiny **Etruscan museum**

Map, page 222

Since Populonia's Etruscan tombs were used continuously, all periods and tomb types are represented: from early oriental "trench" tombs to tiny "niche" tombs. Many of the tombs can actually be entered.

BELOW LEFT: windswept bay of Baratti.
BELOW: Etruscan souvenirs for sale.

(open daily) in Populonia contains some of the sacred objects found in the unlikely named "Tomb of the Harpy".

From Populonia there are smoky views of **Piombino ㉗**, which has been ruled by the Pisans, the noble Appiani family, the ignoble Cesare Borgia and, most effectively, by Elisa Bacciocchi, Princess of Piombino and Lucca and Napoleon's sister. As befits a city which was once the capital of a tiny state, vestiges of old Piombino remain in Piazza Verdi's town walls and in the heavily restored Palazzo Comunale and fortress. Best seen on foot, the city's genteel, dilapidated charm lingers on in quiet squares and Art Deco bars.

The Island of Elba

Known to the Etruscans as *Ilva* ("Iron") and to the Greeks as *Aethalia* ("Soot Island"), **Elba** has exploited its mineral wealth for more than 3,000 years. As the European powers occasionally took an interest in the island's attractive strategic position, waves of Romans, Pisans and Genoese were followed by Spanish, Turkish and French invasions. In 1548 Duke Cosimo I fortified the capital and named it "Cosmopolis" after himself. His great military architect, Giovanni Camerini, designed the star-shaped defensive system and the two defensive forts, Forte della Stella and Forte Falcone.

However, **Portoferraio ❶** is inextricably linked to that other great modern imperialist, Napoleon Bonaparte. He made his official home in two converted windmills above the charming Forte della Stella. Under the terms of the Congress of Vienna in 1814, Elba became a principality of the fallen sovereign.

Napoleon's great empire shrank to his faithful "old guard", pragmatic mother and libertine sister Pauline. Most Elbans were proud to have him

On the eve of his escape from Elba, Napoleon sent for the island governor and reputedly confided, "I am leaving my mother and my sister in your care to show you how much I trust you. I am also placing in your charge this country which means so much to me."

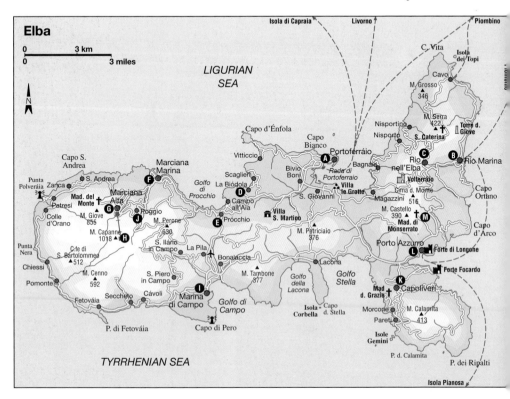

improve the administration, build new roads, develop the mines and expand the island's fleet. The foreign commissioners, however, rightly feared that the "Eagle" might spread its wings: after nine months Napoleon flew, with the connivance of the Elbans. He escaped with no less than 1,000 troops, the Elbans' affection, his sister's diamond necklace and his mother's curt blessing, "Go and fulfil your destiny."

His **Palazzina dei Mulini** (open daily; closed Sun pm, July to mid-Sept open till 11.30pm; closed pub. hols; entrance fee) was lined with silver and books from Fontainebleau and furniture from Elsa's house in Piombino. Most of its charm lies in the period furnishings and Italianate gardens. His country villa, **San Martino** (open daily; closed Sun pm, July to mid-Sept open till 11.30pm; closed pub. hols; entrance fee) was purchased with one of Pauline's handy diamond necklaces. The villa's Classical façade was installed on it in 1851 by the Russian emigré Prince Demidoff. Napoleon's Nile campaigns of 1798–1799 are recalled in the Egyptian-style frescoes in the house, which were painted in 1814. There is a fine garden shaded by evergreen oaks and terraced vineyards.

The 17th-century **Misericordia church** displays one of Napoleon's bronze death-masks and a requiem mass is still said for him on 5 May each year. Napoleon used to say, "When I die, the world will heave a sigh of relief," a sentiment not shared on Elba.

To the east of Portoferraio is Elba's iron heart. Most minerals are concentrated around **Rio Marina** ❸ where open cast mining, polishing and jewellery making still exist. Surrounded by hills rich in ferrous oxide, the whole port has a pinkish hue, including the 16th-century tower of San Rocco.

More than 700 exhibits are on display in the **Museo Mineralogica** (open

Maps:
Area 222
Elba 242

The emblem of Elba's most famous resident, Napoleon, seen at San Martino villa.

BELOW: harbour of Portoferraio.

BELOW: taking
a break at Rio
Marina.

mid-Mar–mid-Oct; closed 12–3pm and Sun pm; entrance fee), and visitors can
buy jewellery made from local semi-precious stones in several shops.

Inland, **Rio nell'Elba** is a strange, rather wild village perched on a couple
of ledges among desolate mountain slopes. Seemingly untouched by tourism, its
misfortunes can perhaps be traced to its destruction by Barbarossa's pirates and
abduction into slavery of the entire population.

Many of the rocky beaches are mineralogical treasure hunts. A line of parked
cars signals hazardous tracks down steep cliffs to the sea. From Rio to Cavo in
the northeast, the road cuts through woods and moorland. Paths trail through
gorse, heather and the wild flowers of the maquis.

The spectacular drive westward from Portoferraio to Marciana Marina passes
a number of popular beaches, including Le Ghiaie, noted for its multicoloured
pebbles, and **La Biodola** , considered the chicest beach on Elba and containing deckchairs filled with rich bronzed Florentines in Valentino swimwear.

At La Biodola and **Procchio** , a more egalitarian paradise, the rocky ocean
bottom means clear, sediment free water. Between Procchio and Marciana
Marina is "La Paolina", a rock named after Napoleon's sister, whose passion for
nude sunbathing still scandalises the natives today.

Marciana Marina has evolved smoothly from fishing village to elegant
resort. Set amidst magnolias, palms and oleanders at the end of a long valley, the
resort narrowly avoids picture-postcard beauty. The thin, pastel-coloured houses
in the old quarter are reminiscent of those on the Ligurian coast. On 12 August
the port explodes in a firework display to honour Santa Chiara, the patron saint.

Marciana Alta , perched above, is the island's best preserved medieval
town. Chestnut woods frame the red-tiled rooftops, narrow alleys and crumbling

Pisan fortress. The local "Antiquarium" displays Etruscan sacred objects as well as Roman oil lamps and ivory statues found in shipwrecks.

From Marciana, a cable car lurches over crags and chasms to the summit of **Monte Capanne** . Even in high summer this wooded mountain area is quiet and breezy. Hot springs and old hermit caves often come in sociable pairs. Depending on the season, patches of orchids, snapdragons and helianthemums are as common as the cedars and chestnuts. Even the coastal vegetation is more exotic than in the east; eucalyptus and magnolia rather than vines or rough maquis.

Map, page 242

Medieval villages

From Marciana to **Marina di Campo** in the south, the high road winds past the neglected village of **Poggio** to **Monte Perone** nature reserve, vineyards and the plains behind Marina. With its expanse of golden sands, Marina is a loud, rather tacky resort near the airport.

However, two dusty medieval villages nestle in the hills behind. Fortified by the Pisans in the 12th century, **San Ilario** and **San Piero in Campo** conceal Romanesque churches and hermitages. A tangy *panzanella* or crisp *crostone* blows the cobwebs away.

Capoliveri is a traditional inland village with a Roman and Medieval past as dramatic as its location high on the southern promontory. Carved into the iron mountain of **Monte Calamita**, Capoliveri is also an old mining village. The black, iron-bearing lodestone still plays havoc with the compasses of passing ships, but is ideal for the production of sweet red Aleatico, said to be the favourite wine of Napoleon Bonaparte.

Often independent, Capoliveri was the only village to reject Napoleon in

BELOW: heading up to the heights of Monte Capanne in the cable car.

RICH IN MINERALS

The island of Elba, up to the late 19th century, was known as a "mineralogical paradise", and today it is still a prime site for minerals including hematite, pyrite and tourmaline. Many of the minerals found here are ferrous, including black lodestone, yellow pyrites and blackish-red ilvaites. Semi-precious stones are also worked, including green quartz, black onyx and pink or pale green beryl. The proper mineral name for most gem tourmalines, in fact, is "Elbaite", named after the island where it was found long ago.

Scientifically, Elbaite is classified as "lithium tourmaline" to differentiate it from tourmalines of different compositions. Large crystals of gem tourmaline occur in a great range of colours, but the type found on Elba is of the pink-green variety, one of the most desirable colours. Rio Marina, on the eastern shore of the island, is where almost all mining activity occurs in Elba today, and the Museo Mineralogica there not only exhibits many area finds but also explains the geology of the island.

There is also a large Elban collection of minerals – well over 6,000 items – in the Natural History Museum of Florence, and the Smithsonian Institution in the United States also features Elban tourmalines in their Gem and Mineral Collection, part of the National Museum of Natural History.

Map, page 242

1814. The story is that only the intercession of a local beauty saved the village. It soon became part of Napoleon's hunting estate and is still noted for its dishes of woodcock, pheasant and hare.

The hills are covered with heath, fern and juniper; the scent of thyme and rosemary are never far away. Roads from the hills to the sea often turn into cart tracks but are worth pursuing unless specifically marked *strada privata*; this is often the only access to the loveliest beaches. **Innamorata** is a sandy inlet linked to the romance between a nymph and a fisherman. Believing her lover drowned in a shipwreck, the nymph drowned herself; he survived and asked the gods to turn him into a seagull so he could seek her out.

From the village there are views of **Pianosa**, **Montecristo**, **Gorgona** and **Capraia** islands. Inaccessible Pianosa and Gorgona are prisons, now filled with Mafiosi caught after the 1991–94 crime blitz. Montecristo is a nature reserve; Capraia is a miniature Elba without its history or architecture.

Capoliveri also surveys fashionable **Porto Azzurro ❶**, the main town on the east coast of Elba and once part of the Spanish protectorate. The vast Forte Longone, constructed in 1603 as a Spanish naval base, is now a top security prison. Visitors can purchase crafts from the prison shop, the scene of a mass break-out in 1987. Forte Focardo, its sister fortress across the bay, has uninviting ramparts running down a sheer cliff.

ABOVE: Elban wines.
BELOW: swimming off Porto Azurro.
RIGHT: the coves along Elba's coast can be stunning.

By day, Porto Azzurro has a rather uninspiring seafront. In the evening, however, it is a favoured place for a leisurely promenade (the famous *passeggiata*), designer shopping and people-watching. It is also a top place for sampling some of the local seafood specialities: such as a *cacciucco* (soup) of octopus, scorpion, dogfish and prawns; *riso nero* or "black rice" (risotto made with the dark ink of cuttlefish or squid), perhaps followed by *schiaccia briaca* ("drunken cake"), made with hazelnuts and Aleatico wine.

Distinctive wines

There is also dry Elba Bianco, sweet Moscato, a heady white, or Elba Rosso, similar to Chianti. The distinct flavour is due to the iron, phosphorous, arsenic and natural radioactivity in the fertile soil. After enough Elban wine, one's impressions of Porto Azzurro are of harbour lights, cheerful bustle and gently bobbing boats.

Behind Porto Azzurro is the most mystical spot on the island, the remote sanctuary of **Madonna di Monserrato ⓜ** (open daily; mid-July–mid-Sept). It was built in the Toledan style by a Spanish governor, Ponce de Léon, in 1606. A steep, rocky track leads high up the mountain to the tiny red-domed church precariously balanced among the crags. Despite mountain goats cavorting on impossible ledges, the place has great solemnity and few visitors.

The Spanish façade and belltower find echoes in the Black Madonna inside, which is a copy of an early Spanish painting. Every September, an Elban pilgrimage celebrates the *Festa della Madonna* with a walk past ravines and isolated grottoes to the church. At the foot of the hills is a rustic restaurant with service as leisurely as an Elban Sunday. ❑

GROSSETO

The largest and perhaps least known of Tuscany's provinces, Grosseto has some of the most beautiful stretches of coast and wilderness areas in the entire region

Map, page 252

Grosseto's remarkable landscape is wonderfully varied, ranging from the flat plains around Grosseto, now drained, to the thickly wooded peak of Monte Amiata, capped with snow throughout the winter months, to the smooth hills bordering the province of nearby Siena.

The coastline has an unrivalled mix of Mediterranean flora and fauna; three areas (Monti dell' Uccellina, Monte Argentario and Monte Amiata) have been converted into nature parks.

The region is dominated by the marshy plain of the **Maremma**, "the swamp by the sea". Until quite recently travel books tended to warn visitors away from the area, but the marshes have now been successfully reclaimed and it has become a popular tourist spot, especially for nature lovers. (*See also "Wild Tuscany", page 85.*)

Etruscan influence

Evidence of Roman and Etruscan settlements in the area is considerable. One of the most important Etruscan cities, Vetulonia, is close to Grosseto, as are the once-prosperous settlements of Cosa and Roselle.

By medieval times the coastal plain had become quite unsafe and unhealthy, partly due to the plundering of Saracens from the sea, partly because of the malarial swamps. In the early 14th century the whole area fell under the power of Siena. Towards the end of the 16th century, Grosseto became part of the Grand Duchy of Tuscany, until the formation of Italy in 1860.

The capital of the province, **Grosseto ❶**, was built as a fortified citadel only around AD 950, when the Saracens looted the former capital, Roselle, less than 12 kms (8 miles) away. The city has expanded beyond its walls only in the last part of this century. Mainly because of its unhealthy climate, Grosseto – now primarily an administrative centre – was for a long time no more than a military citadel, and was never as big as Massa Marittima or Pitigliano.

The old town of Grosseto is quite small, contained within an ancient six-sided citadel created by the Aldobrandeschi family in the 11th century, and surrounded by brick walls added by the Medici in the 15th century.

There is a 14th-century **Duomo** on the main square, at the end of the traditional *corso*, where all the best shops and a café are to be found.

The Duomo, dedicated to San Lorenzo, was built towards the end of the 13th century on a church constructed about 100 years earlier. It is a mixture of Romanesque and Gothic styles, with a rose window and three magnificent doors with Romanesque arches in

PRECEDING PAGES: sunflowers in the Maremma.
LEFT: a hunters' picnic.
BELOW: Grosseto gargoyle.

the main façade. There is an adjoining 15th-century campanile and a museum displaying a *Madonna dell' Uccellino* of the Lorenzetti School, and a *Madonna delle Ciliege*, which is considered a Sassetta masterpiece.

Next to the Duomo in the Palazzo del Licio is the **Museo Archeologico** (call 0564-455132 for opening hours), one of the richest museums in the area; it has a fine collection of pre-Etruscan, Etruscan and Roman artifacts.

The museum is also the place to pick up maps of the key archaeological sites where the finds were made: Roselle (12 km/8 miles northeast of the city), Vetulonia, Talamone, Pitigliano and Saturnia to the south.

Tuscany's most important excavated archaeological site is at **Bagno Roselle ②** (open daily; entrance fee), with a nearly intact circuit of Romano-Etruscan walls, a Roman forum, paved streets, basilicas, villas and baths. **Vetulonia ③**, originally the Etruscan city of Vatluna, has remains of Roman houses and a Mithraeum. The museum is closed for restoration, but you can visit the archaeological park (open daily Apr–Sept; Tues and Thur from Oct–Mar; entrance fee).

The coast

Grosseto is in the middle of a flat plain formed by the Ombrone river and is about 17 km (10 miles) from the sea. Many Grossetans have a second home along the nearby coast, either in congested **Marina di Grosseto ④** or in the more snobbish and quieter **Principina a Mare ⑤** hidden in a beautiful pine forest.

Some prefer the old fishing village of **Castiglione della Pescaia ⑥**, where they can keep a sailing boat, ideally located at the foot of the mountains north of Grosseto. The harbour, crowded with fishermen's and tourists' boats, is believed to be the Etruscan *Hasta*, or *Portus Traianus* in Roman times. Overlooking the port is the Rocca Aragonese, with its walls and towers dating back to the 14th century.

Slightly north of the same promontory lies exclusive **Punta Ala ⑦**, a semi-private resort with good hotels, golf clubs, horse-riding and polo facilities. A little further along the coast, before Follonica, is a lovely quiet bay, **Cala Violino**, so-called because of its squeaky musical sand.

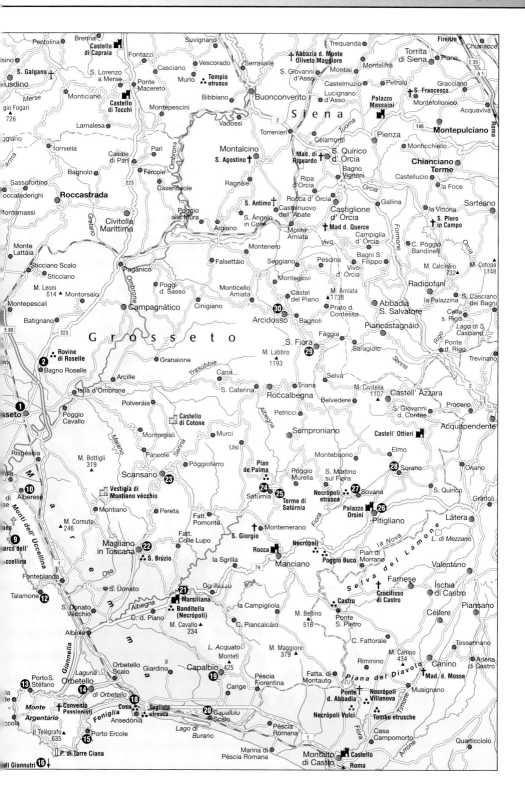

A flag-waving lamb is the symbol of Massa Marittima's "new town" or Città Nuova, *which dates from the 13th and 14th centuries. The "old town", or* Città Vecchia, *dates from the 11th to 13th centuries.*

BELOW: walls of Massa Marittima.

Massa Marittima ❽ is about 24 km (15 miles) inland, despite its maritime name. It is one of the most astounding Tuscan cities, perched on top of a high hill on the edge of the Colline Metallifere, or "ore-bearing mountains", which divide the province of Grosseto from Siena. It was the most important town in the Maremma until the 17th century when the land silted up, and was originally called Massa; but the name of Massa Maremma or Massa Marittima has been introduced to distinguish it from Massa in Massa-Carrara province.

Massa Marittima was built around the 10th century, after the decline of ancient Populonia (*see page 241*), which was too exposed to plundering from the sea. It was known for its copper and silver mines even in Etruscan times, and the rich variety of metals available was a major factor in the economic development of the city. The affluence of medieval Massa Marittima is apparent in its rigorous town planning, and in the concentration of public buildings (*palazzi*) around the Duomo. In the main square – the spectacular **Piazza Garibaldi**, one of the finest squares in Tuscany – are Palazzo Vescovile (seat of the bishop), Palazzo Pretorio (seat of the governor, now also an interesting museum), Palazzo del Comune (town hall), Zecca Cittadina (the mint), Fonte Pubblica (public fountain) and Palazzo dell' Abbondanza (the public granary).

The **Duomo** is an example of Pisan Romanesque architecture with marvellous reliefs of *Madonna delle Grazie*, ascribed to Duccio Di Buoninsegna (1316) and the *Arca di San Cerbone* (St Cerbone's ark), a masterpiece of the Sienese school of sculpture, dating back to 1324. There is a 4th-century sarcophagus in the Duomo and St Cerbone (who died in AD 380) is buried in the crypt.

A memorable experience – and a lot easier to see than Siena's *Palio* – is the traditional *Balestro del Girfalco*, every last Sunday in May and every second

Sunday in August. Here the three *terzieri* of Massa (old city, new city and the outer *Borgo*) struggle for victory in a shooting contest using mechanical falcons with ancient crossbows.

The nearby **Colline Metallifere** are rich in metal ores, and were the focus of the Industrial Revolution in the area, but by the end of the 19th century mining and related industries were already in decline, and now these mountains are a remote and lonely region. The ancient mines and factories now in ruins present a surreal picture, hidden away in thick forests littered with heaps of coloured metals. If you are interested, in Massa Marittima there is a **mining museum** (open Tues–Sun in summer; closed 11am–3pm; open by appointment in winter; tel: 0566-902289; entrance fee), located in the Palazzetto delle Armi. It is also possible to organise a visit to a real mine very near the city.

The South

Beyond the river Ombrone, the **Parco dell'Uccellina** ❾, also known as the **Parco Naturale della Maremma**, covers about 20 km (12 miles) of the coastal mountains and the marshland around the mouth of the river Ombrone. The park is entered at **Alberese** ❿, **Marina di Alberese** ⓫ or **Talamone** ⓬, a walled coastal resort. Its most noticeable peculiarity is the tradition of *butteri* – the only Italian cowboys. They actually won a challenge with Buffalo Bill at the end of the last century; to commemorate the event, an annual rodeo is held in August, which brings American cowboys to Alberese, a small village in the heart of the wild coastal prairie.

Other local festivals include the *Torneo del Buttero*, in Alberese, the *Sagra del Cinghiale* (boar fair) in Montepescali, the *Sagra del Gnocco* (gnocchi fair, a culi-

Map, page 252

A malaria outbreak in the 1500s caused Massa Marittima to go into decline, and the mines there weren't reopened until the 19th century after the swamps were drained. The result is that the town still looks very much as it did in the Middle Ages.

BELOW: the Duomo of Massa Marittima.

*Distinctive cork tree
on the promontory of
Monte Argentario.*

nary speciality) and a summer opera festival in Batignano, the *Sagra della Gastronomia* (gastronomic fair) in Manciano and the *Sagra della Trippa* (tripe fair) in Montemerano.

Activities within the nature park include canoeing along the Ombrone river, sailing along the coast, trekking or riding across the mountains, and visiting the noble ruins of San Rabano and the many towers on top of the mountains overlooking the sea, each with its story of marauding pirates and hidden treasures, going back to the times of the Saracens and Spanish galleons.

The beaches within Monti dell'Uccellina are among the most beautiful and unspoilt in Tuscany. To preserve this wilderness, the number of visitors are limited during the summer, and cars cannot reach the beaches. Transport from Alberese is arranged on buses.

South of Monti dell'Uccellina is **Monte Argentario**. This promontory was once an island. The name of Argentario comes from *argentarius* (money-lender), since it was owned by Roman money-lenders in the 4th century. The island became attached to the mainland by two long sandbanks, containing a lagoon. The main city of the area, Orbetello, is sited on a peninsula which projects into the lagoon from the mainland.

From 1556 until 1815, Monte Argentario was politically detached from the Grand Duchy of Tuscany, existing as a separate state, under Spanish rule. It encompassed the whole promontory and the existing ports of Orbetello, Porto Santo Stefano, Porto Ercole, Talamone and Porto Azzurro, on the island of Elba, and many Spanish fortifications still remain here.

This complex landscape is a beautiful region for walking, with a wide variety of flora and fauna, and you can see magnificent sunsets and views as far as

BELOW: a solitary spot in the Maremma.

Corsica from the peak of Argentario. Although the area was badly damaged by fire in mid-1996, the vegetation has now grown back and there seems to have been no permanent damage.

Among the fortunate inhabitants of these hills are the *Passionisti* monks. In keeping with the monastic traditions of central Italy, the monks reserve some cells for pious guests, and the traveller may leave with a precious memento: *Amaro dei frati dell'Argentario*, a special liqueur produced by the monks.

Map, page 252

Rocky coast

The coastline is rocky and precipitous with breathtaking descents to the sea beneath. The most easily accessible beach is the 7-km (5-mile) **Feniglia**, but it is also very popular and therefore is often crowded. (It was also where the riotous genius Caravaggio died on his way back to Rome in 1610.) The sandbank backing the Feniglia forms another lovely and accessible beach, the **Giannella**. There are many other hidden coves and beaches, but a boat is needed to reach them; it is an ideal location for scuba diving and underwater photography.

Porto Santo Stefano ⓭ is now the most important harbour in the area, and little fishing boats nestle against huge yachts in the crowded harbour. Although scarred by World War II bombing, it is still a picturesque town with many boutiques, bars and excellent *gelaterie*.

Orbetello ⓮, the state capital, stretches along a very narrow peninsula, surrounded by Spanish walls built over the previous Etruscan fortifications. The city still has a maritime atmosphere, in spite of being now almost 5 km (3 miles) from the sea. The individuality of Orbetello is reflected in its cuisine, with a mixture of three traditions: seafood, freshwater fish from the lagoon, such as the

TIP

To escape the crowds on the Feniglia beach, just walk a bit further along its extensive sands: the crowds are lazy and tend to keep close to the nearest bars.

BELOW: beach at Porto San Stefano.

exquisite *anguilla fumata* (smoked eel), and game such as wild boar from the hillside and surrounding marshes.

Island excursions

On the southern side of Monte Argentario, **Porto Ercole** ⓯ (smaller, prettier and more elegant than Santo Stefano) has a 16th-century Spanish fortress on the hill overlooking the harbour.

The woodland around the town of Capalbio is managed as a game reserve. A game festival is held here in September each year.

Santo Stefano has ferry connections with two interesting islands, Giannutri and Giglio. On **Giannutri** ⓰, a tiny, virtually uninhabited island 22km (14 miles) away, one can imagine pirates finding refuge long ago. On the island are the ruins of a Roman villa which belonged to the Domizii Enobarbi family during the 1st century. The villa has columns, mosaics, baths and a private pier.

Giglio ⓱, half an hour's sail off the coast, is the second largest in Tuscany after Elba and has an impenetrable coastline with only one easy port, Giglio Porto. Among the vineyards producing grapes for the very strong, distinctive local wine, *Ansonaco*, Giglio Castello dominates the landscape. It is a fortified settlement, with arches and dark passages, and stairs carved from the rock.

Giglio has a number of sandy beaches and is covered in typical Mediterranean vegetation: aromatic herbs and plants, and orange and lemon groves. It is ideal for all water sports, but because of this and because it is close to Rome it is very popular and is better visited out of season.

Giannutri and Giglio are just two islands in the "Archipelago Toscano", which also includes Elba, Capraia and the inaccessible islands of Pianosa, Gorgona (where there are prisons) and Montecristo (a highly protected wildlife sanctuary). The entire archipelago has been declared a nature reserve, covering certain parts

BELOW:
fishing boats at Porto Ercole.

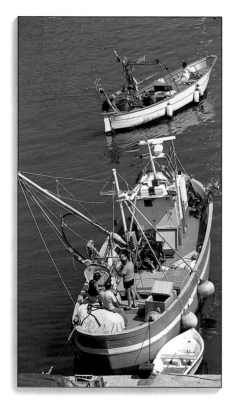

of the islands themselves and the surrounding water – a move that, while obviously done to protect the environment, has created much controversy amongst both those involved with the tourist industry and local fishermen, whose rights have been restricted. Although swimming has not been affected, there are some areas where boats are not allowed to drop anchor.

Returning to the coast, there are the important Roman remains of **Cosa** ⓲, built on top of what was originally an Etruscan settlement. The city has been excavated and the site contains a main street, a forum, a walled acropolis and capitolium from which there are magnificent views out to sea; the site is somewhat overgrown and has a melancholy air.

Below the promontory is the silted-up Roman port and the **Tagliata Etrusca**, the Etruscan Cut – which is in fact Roman, built as a canal to drain Lake Burano.

Inland from Monte Argentario is **Capalbio** ⓳, one of the first towns on the hills bordering Latium (the region in which Rome is situated). It is the heart of the Maremma and famous for its brigands. One notorious *bandito*, Domenico Tiburzi, a local Robin Hood, was executed in 1896. There was disagreement over whether he could be buried in consecrated land and eventually a typical Italian compromise was reached: he was buried at the edge of the cemetery with his head in sacred ground, the rest of his body outside.

Capalbio is much appreciated by Roman intelligentsia, who have bought up every corner of the village as a fashionable summer refuge from the capital. It is also famous for its food, and several excellent restaurants specialise in local dishes of wild boar and other game. Nearby is the magical **Giardino dei Tarocchi**/Pescia Fiorentina, or Tarot Garden, (open daily; mid-May–Oct), created by French sculptor Niki de Saint Phalle and inspired by the symbolism of the tarot. Open in summer, this park displays fantastic, brightly coloured figures covered in mirror and mosaic, glinting in the sun.

Capalbio Scalo ❷⓪ is a few hundred metres from Lake Burano, where there is a lake and small nature park, a favourite stopping place for thousands of birds migrating from the former Yugoslavia to North Africa. Bird-watching (seagulls, coots, pheasants and blackbirds, among others) is the main attraction for visitors, but the flora is also quite varied.

Fortified towns

Across the densely wooded hills north of Capalbio is the flat plain of the River Albegna, now completely drained, which leads to the castle of **Marsiliana** ❷❶, once an Etruscan town and now the only property left to the Corsini family, who originally owned the entire area. Most of these swamps were expropriated by the state, drained and then distributed to small landowners.

Not far from the coast, **Magliano in Toscana** ❷❷ still has intact city walls, built in the 15th century. Both civil and religious architecture show a strong Romanesque influence, with Gothic and Renaissance additions. A perfect example of the blend of styles is San Giovanni Battista, a Romanesque church, with Gothic side windows and a Renaissance façade.

A few miles inland, **Scansano** ❷❸, now a quiet town with a separate fortified

Map, page 252

BELOW:
one of the famous
butteri (cowboys)
of the region.

section (*oppido*) on top of a modest hill, used to be the summer capital of the province, when all administrative powers were moved from malarial Grosseto during the hot season.

Travelling eastwards across hills and moors inhabited by *butteri* (cowboys) and their cattle, you arrive at **Saturnia ㉔**, about 32 km (20 miles) from the coast. Saturnia is a quiet little town, drowsy under the immense weight of its past. It was the Etruscan Aurinia, and then came under Roman control in 280 BC.

The atmosphere here is so attractive that a number of northern Italians have settled in the area and run speciality shops in the village, which is centred around a large oak-ringed piazza. Saturnia and surrounding villages have some notable *trattorie*.

Through the old Porta Romana, half hidden by vegetation, you can walk about 3 km (2 miles) down the hill along a Roman road to **Terme di Saturnia ㉕**, a modern spa, where you can experience the healing waters coming from the earth beneath the distant Monte Amiata. You can swim in the thermal pools or in the hot waterfall at Cascate del Gorello, on the Montemerano road.

This southern part of Tuscany is in the process of gentrification and many Romans and foreigners living in Rome buy property here. One reason why the area is so attractive is that for centuries it has been neglected by the main traffic routes, one on the coast along the Roman Via Aurelia, and one inland along Roman Via Cassia, both going north from Rome. The old Via Clodia, between the coast and Via Cassia, almost disappeared, cutting out important Saturnia and other towns like Sovana, Sorano and Pitigliano – all of which are well worth including on a holiday itinerary.

The most important town in the area is **Pitigliano ㉖**, which in the mid-18th

BELOW: Pitigliano, with its distinctive caves cut out of the cliff.

century was one of the main cities in southern Tuscany. After a drive along a particularly tortuous road, Pitigliano rises up before you, a spectacular sight. It has the distinct shape of a crib, built on a hill of volcanic tufa with wine and olive oil cellars carved out of caves in the hillside.

The town is centred around a magnificent fortified palazzo, built by the Orsini in the 16th century. **Palazzo Orsini** is a separate citadel, linked to the town by a vast, arched aqueduct and close to the new **Etruscan museum** (open Thur–Tues; entrance fee).

Pitigliano used to be called "little Jerusalem" because it was a refuge for Jews fleeing from religious persecution in the Papal states. Even today the Jewish section of the city – 60 narrow streets crossing two main ones – is still quite distinct. Tiny streets and winding alleys intersect and the backs of the houses form a sheer drop to the valley below. It is one of the few places in Catholic Italy where you can find kosher wine or turkey "ham" (*billo*), another Jewish speciality. *Bianco di Pitigliano* from the tufa wine cellars is also well-known.

Sovana ㉗, a few miles away, is a tiny village rich in history. There is an important Etruscan necropolis as well as Roman ruins hidden in the surrounding woods, but a local guide is recommended to show you the way around.

No visit to this area would be complete without a walk in the old streets of **Sorano** ㉘, which is also built on a tufa outcrop. Unfortunately some of the buildings have begun to collapse into the steep valleys around the city, but the great majority of Sorano can be seen without danger.

Visible from every corner of the province on a clear day, particularly in a snowy winter, is **Monte Amiata**, the highest peak in Tuscany south of Florence. It is a dormant volcano, with hot geysers on its slopes and underground waters that supply the spa at Saturnia. Monte Amiata is a paradise for mountain trekkers, and a refreshing escape during the hot summer months.

The area's third main town, **Santa Fiora** ㉙, is particularly delightful, and has fine works of art in the 12th-century Santa Fiora and Santa Lucilla churches, including ceramics by Andrea and Luca della Robbia.

Arcidosso ㉚ was the birthplace of a man called David Lazzaretti, "The Prophet of the Amiata". In the 19th century Lazzaretti created a revolutionary social and religious movement with its headquarters on **Monte Labro**, a lonely peak which forms part of a nature reserve where deer, chamois and wolves roam, and protected trees and wildflowers grow. The best time is autumn, when the crowds have left and the wild mushrooms appear.

Local dishes

Maremmana cuisine is not particularly sophisticated but it is unique. Local dishes include *prosciutto di cinghiale*, boar ham; *acquacotta*, a celery and tomato soup, served on top of a slice of stale bread scented with garlic and garnished with a poached egg; *scottiglia*, a mixture of various meats, such as boar and deer, cooked with olives; *pecorino* cheeses, Monte Amiata chestnuts, *anice* biscuits and *ricotta* cheese. Good local wines include *Morellino di Scansano*, *Bianco di Pitigliano*, and *Ansonaco di Argentario*. ❑

Map, page 252

TIP

Pitigliano's unique skyline can be seen to its best advantage from the church of Madonna della Grazie.

BELOW: skiing on Monte Amiata.

SIENA

The well-known tall towers of Siena and San Gimignano and the vineyards of Chianti aside, this is a province that glories in its hidden villages, separate identity and artistic treasures

Maps:
Area 272
City 266

From its striped marble cathedral to its tunnelled alleys, brilliant Campo and black-and-white city emblem, **Siena ❶** is a *chiaroscuro* city. In its surging towers it is truly Gothic. Where Florence is boldly horizontal, Siena is soaringly vertical; where Florence has large squares and masculine statues, Siena has hidden gardens and romantic wells. Florentine art is perspective and innovation while Sienese art is sensitivity and conservatism. Siena is often considered the feminine foil to Florentine masculinity.

Approached by night, Siena's towers resemble "firebrands that are the last to die in the ashes of the night". Federigo Tozzi, the most Sienese of authors, also praised the city's radiant femininity. Even by day, the glow of rose-coloured brick warms the narrow passageways and arches. The motto of the Shell Contrada – "It's the red of the coral that burns in my heart" – could refer to the Campo, the centre of Sienese life.

For such a feminine city, Siena has a decidedly warlike reputation nourished by sieges, city-state rivalry and *Palio* battles. The average Sienese is no ethereal Botticelli nymph but dark, stocky and swarthy. Only in Sienese painting is pale theatricality the norm.

In keeping with Sienese mystique, the city's origins are shrouded in myths of wolves and martyred saints. According to legend, the city was founded by Senius, son of Remus; hence the she-wolf symbols in the city. Saint Ansano brought Christianity to Roman Siena and, although he was promptly tossed into a vat of hot tar and beheaded, he has left a legacy of mysticism traced through Saints Catherine and Bernardino to the present-day cult of the Madonna. The power of the church came to a dramatic end when the populace rose against the Ecclesiastical Council and established an independent republic in 1147. The 12th century was marked by emerging rivalry in which the Florentine Guelfs usually triumphed over the Sienese Ghibellines.

PRECEDING PAGES: *contrada* procession in the Piazza del Campo, Siena, by Vincenzo Rustici. **LEFT:** *Palio* banners in the Piazza. **BELOW:** Romulus and Remus.

Cultural superiors

In 1260 the battle of Montaperti routed the Florentines and won the Sienese 10 years of cultural supremacy which saw the foundation of the university and the charitable "fraternities". The Council of the Twenty-Four – a form of power-sharing between nobles and the working class – was followed by the Council of the Nine, an oligarchy of merchants which ruled until 1335.

Although modern historians judge the "Nine" self-seeking and profligate, under their rule the finest works of art were either commissioned or completed, including the famous Campo, the Palazzo Pubblico and Duccio's *Maestà*.

Three companies of women fought alongside men in the Siege of Siena of 1554, causing Charles V's general to exclaim "I would rather have defeated Rome with Sienese women than with Roman soldiers."

The ancient republic survived until 1529 when the reconciliation between the pope and the emperor ended the Guelf-Ghibelline feud. The occupying Spanish demolished the city towers, symbols of freedom and fratricide, and used the masonry to build the present fortress. The final blow to the republic was the long Siege of Siena by Emperor Charles V and Cosimo I in 1554.

After the Sienese defeat, the government-in-exile survived in Montalcino until 1559, but the city of Siena became absorbed into the Tuscan dukedom. As an untrusted member of the Tuscan empire, impoverished Siena turned in on itself until the 20th century.

War survivors

Soon afterwards, the city, unlike the countryside, challenged fascist appointees. In July 1944 American and French troops surrounded Siena and forced the city to surrender. General Monsambert instructed troops not to "let any shells fall on Siena, otherwise you'll be shot". The State Archives in Palazzo Piccolomini

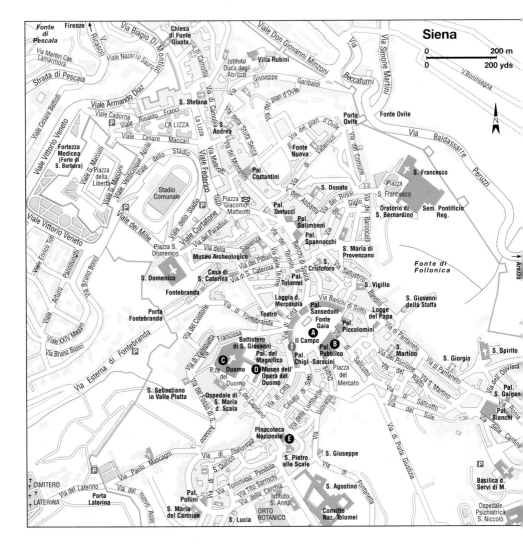

(open Mon–Sat till 1pm), provide a pictorial history of Siena through illuminated manuscripts and paintings. An inscription on the city gates reads, "Siena opens her heart to you wider than this door." But such openness is illusory: Siena offers hospitality but not intimacy. Its cultural aloofness owes much to the *contrade*, the 17 city wards representing self-sustaining cities within the Sienese empire.

Immune to influence and praise, the city takes care of its own from birth to death. The Sienese prefer to work for paternalistic local employers such as *Monte dei Paschi*, founded in 1472 and known as "the oldest bank in the world" and "the city father".

Change is anathema to the city: traditional landowning, financial speculation, trade and tourism are more appealing than new technology or industry. Siena has made a virtue of conservatism; stringent medieval building regulations protect the fabric of the city; tourism is decidedly low-key; old family firms such as *Nannini*'s cake shop do a roaring trade with locals (and also produced Gianna Nannini, Italy's best-known female singer). It is a city with the psychology of a village and the grandeur of a nation.

All roads lead to **Il Campo** Ⓐ, Siena's shell-like piazza. It is at its most theatrical in the late afternoon, after a day spent in the shadows of the city walls and inner courtyards. After so much dark, the huge pool of light draws even the most modest visitor to blunder on to centre stage.

ABOVE: Siena has all sorts of quirky details worth looking out for.
BELOW: interior of Siena's Duomo.

The Palazzo Pubblico

One's eyes adjust to the red-brick piazza, a fountain depicting the Sienese she-wolf and to the **Palazzo Pubblico** Ⓑ, the dignified Town Hall surmounted by the slender Torre del Mangia (open daily from 10am; entrance fee). The Town Hall, built in 1310, is a Gothic masterpiece of rose-coloured brick and silver-grey travertine. Each ogival arch is crowned by the *balzana*, Siena's black-and-white emblem representing the mystery and purity of the Madonna's life. The distinctive tower is named after the first bellringer, Mangiaguadagni – the "spendthrift" – and is flanked by a chapel constructed as a thanksgiving after the plague.

Inside the Palazzo Pubblico is the **Museo Civico** (open daily; closed at 1.30pm in winter; closed pub. hols; entrance fee), where Simone Martini, Duccio's successor, had to create his masterpiece twice since he painted it on a wall backing on to a damp salt warehouse. His *Maestà*, a poetic evocation of the Madonna on a filigree throne, has a rich tapestry-like quality, not unlike the French arras, *The Lady and the Unicorn*. The muted blues, reds and ivory add a gauzy softness. Martini echoes Giotto's conception of perspective yet clothes his Madonna in diaphanous robes, concealing her spirituality in dazzling decoration.

Opposite is Martini's famous *Guidoriccio*, the haughty diamond-spangled *condottiero* reproduced on calendars and *panforte* boxes. But despite Sienese denials, this famous Trecento work is probably a Quattrocento painting concealing Martini's original. Since the Sienese Republic feared a military takeover in 1318, it would have been odd to commission a portrait of a captain for the Town Hall.

Map, page 266

In the next room is a genuine civic masterpiece, Ambrogio Lorenzetti's *Effects of Good and Bad Government*, painted in 1338 as an idealised tribute to the Council of the Nine. The narrative realism and vivid facial expressions give the allegory emotional resonance. A wise old man symbolises the Common Good while a patchwork of neat fields, tame boar and busy hoers suggests order and prosperity. Bad Government is a desolate place, razed to the ground by a diabolical tyrant, the Sienese she-wolf at his feet.

From above, the fishbone design of the Campo forms nine different shades of pink, recalling the Noveschi or "Nine". Below, the Sienese awaited news of Montaperti, the Spanish siege, and the German deportation of local Jews. In 1980 Pope John Paul II preached on the same spot where Saint Bernardino denounced witchcraft, superstition and the power of the Sienese Republic. Church and state are well matched here: the Mangia Tower and the Duomo belltower confront each other from the same height.

The **Duomo** is in Castelvecchio, the oldest part of the city. It is Siena's most controversial monument, either a symphony in black and white marble or a tasteless iced cake. It began in 1220 as a round-arched Romanesque church but soon acquired a Gothic façade festooned with pinnacles. Bands of black, white and green marble were inlaid with pink stone and topped by Giovanni Pisano's naturalistic statues.

The interior is creativity run riot – Oriental abstraction, Byzantine formality, Gothic flight and Romanesque austerity. A giddy *chiaroscuro* effect is created by the black-and-white walls reaching up to the starry blue vaults.

The **floor** is even more inspiring: major Sienese craftsmen worked on the marble *pavimentazione* between 1372 and 1562. Although the oldest are mar-

Ruskin dismissed Siena's cathedral as "over-striped, over-crocketed, over-gabled, a piece of costly confectionery and faithless vanity." Wagner, the composer, was more attuned to its operatic intensity and was apparently driven to tears by the building's alien, restless beauty.

BELOW: Siena's distinctive – and also controversial – Duomo.

ble engravings, the finest are Matteo di Giovanni's pensive Sibyls and marble mosaics by Beccafumi. In order to preserve the floors, many of the most interesting scenes are covered by hardboard for most of the year.

Map, page 266

Subtle dazzler

Nicola Pisano's octagonal marble pulpit is a Gothic masterpiece: built in 1226, it is a dramatic and fluid progression from his solemn **pulpit** in Pisa Cathedral. Within the Duomo is the frescoed **Libreria Piccolomini** (open daily; closed 1–2.30pm in winter; entrance fee), the most ornate Renaissance room in Tuscany. Sienese consider the dazzling interior subtle and refined.

The present Duomo would have been the transept of the new one, a scheme devised in the Golden Age and abandoned after the 1348 plague. Beside the Baptistry of San Giovanni, the skeletal remains of the **Duomo Nuovo** are home to the **Museo dell'Opera del Duomo** (open daily; closes at 1.30pm in winter; entrance fee) and Pisano's original statues for the façade. In a dramatically lit room above is Duccio's *Maestà* , which was escorted from the artist's workshop to the Duomo in a torchlit procession; the largest known medieval panel painting graced the High Altar until 1506. Duccio chose Madonna blue for the Virgin's cloak to match the blue stained glass windows in the Duomo.

The largest panel depicts the Madonna enthroned among saints and angels, and, since the separation of the painting, faces scenes from the Passion. Although Byzantine Gothic in style, the *Maestà* is suffused with melancholy charm. The delicate gold and red colouring is matched by Duccio's grace of line which influenced Sienese painting for the next two centuries.

The Sienese believe that Giotto copied Duccio but sacrificed beauty to naturalism. The small panels around the walls do, however, reveal some of Giotto's truthfulness and sense of perspective. The modest status of the Trecento painter was that of a master craftsman whose only reward was the devotion of the populace. As Siena's best-loved work, the *Maestà* achieves just that for its creator.

Opposite the Duomo on the piazza is the **Ospedale Santa Maria della Scala** (open daily; closed some pub. hols; entrance fee). This former pilgrims' hospital, believed to have been founded in the 9th century and, in its day, one of the most important hospitals in the world, has recently been transformed into a museum, and there are plans to turn it into an arts centre and exhibition space with restoration facilities. Used as a practising hospital until quite recently, frescoes by Domenico di Bartolo adorn the main ward. The city's **Museo Archeologico** (open daily am; closed 2nd and 4th Sun of the month; entrance fee), with its significant collection of Etruscan and Roman remains, has been rehoused here, and other rooms host temporary exhibitions.

The **Pinacoteca Nazionale** 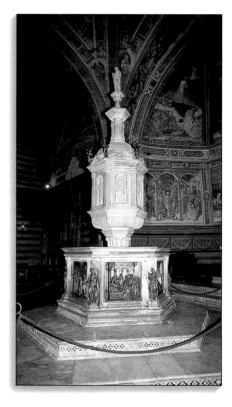 (open daily; Sun and Mon till 1pm and 1.30pm respectively; entrance fee) contains the finest collection of Sienese "Primitives" in the suitably Gothic Palazzo Buonsignori. The early rooms are full of Madonnas, apple-cheeked, pale, remote or warmly human. The beautiful repetition of Siena's favourite theme focuses attention on the style

TIP

Take advantage of Siena's "multi-entrance" ticket, the *Biglietto di Ingresso Cumulativo*, which allows entry to a number of museums over three days.

BELOW: the Early Renaissance font in the Baptistry of San Giovanni in the Duomo.

and vivid colouring. Matteo di Giovanni's stylised Madonnas shift to Lorenzetti's affectionate *Annunciation* and to Ugolino di Neri's radiant *Madonna*. Neroccio di Bartolomeo's *Madonna* is as truthful as a Masaccio.

As a variant, the grisly deaths of obscure saints compete with a huge medieval crucifix with a naturalistic spurt of blood. The famous landscapes and surreal Persian city attributed to Lorenzetti were probably painted by Sassetta a century later. But his *Madonna dei Carmelitani* is a sweeping cavalcade of Sienese life, as is the entire gallery.

Slightly outside the historic centre of the city, on Vicolo del Tiratoio, is the **Casa di Santa Caterina** (Costa di Sant' Antonio; open daily; closed 12.30–3.30pm), the home of Catherine Benincase (1347–80), proclaimed Italy's Patron Saint in 1939. All the places she visited, from the day of her birth, have been consecrated. The house, garden and her father's dye-works now form the "Sanctuary of St Catherine".

Also of interest, particularly to wine connoisseurs, is the **Fortezza Medicea**, off the Viale Maccari. The 16th-century red-brick fortress now houses an open-air theatre, provides glorious views of the countryside and contains the *Enoteca Italica* (open Tues–Sat 12pm–1am and Mon 12–8pm). The latter, a permanent exhibition of Italian wines and a wine shop, offers visitors the chance to sample and buy from a wide range of Tuscan wines and have any questions answered about the wine-making process.

Contrade passions

The Sienese claim that Siena is three cities: "illustrious", "homely" and "dream-like". Illustrious Siena is public knowledge but homely Siena belongs to the *con-*

ABOVE: detail from the city's dignified Palazzo Pubblico.
BELOW: Siena's unmistakable Campo.

trade churches, fountains and tabernacles. Fontebranda, Saint Catherine's fountain, is the oldest and most impressive of the city's enclosed fountains.

Despite its public grandeur, much of Siena is resolutely working-class. All over the city, the importance of the various *contrade* is evident. Little marble or ceramic plaques set into the wall in the various districts testify to which *contrada* you are in (dolphin, caterpillar, giraffe, goose and so on). Little hidden fountains have also been built for each *contrada*.

Contrade passions outweigh individual loyalty. The sense of rivalry between the factions during the *Palio* (*see page 294*) is intensified, and the various districts of the city can be awash with tears of joy or despair depending on the result of the race.

In Brucco *contrada* pockets of narrow housing, friendly shops and dignified poverty are disguised by old-world charm and wishful thinking. The tiny tabernacles reflect spontaneous affection for the Madonna. Sodoma's *Madonna del Corvo* marks the spot where a crow dropped dead with the plague, thus infecting the entire city.

Dreamlike Siena embraces the cult of the Madonna and the mystique of the *Palio*. It can be sensed in the box-like *contrade* churches and in Saint Catherine's sanctuary rather than in the grander churches of San Francesco and San Domenico. The Duomo and the Campo are broad enough to accommodate all the Sienas.

But the Sienese are not borne down by the weight of the past. Siena is a sensuous city. On a drowsy summer's afternoon near the Campo, the flapping pigeons perch on a rushing fountain; the air smells of roasted chestnuts; a child eats a piece of sweet, spicy *panforte* and the Chigi choir can be heard practising. Siena is Italy's last surviving city-state – provincial and universal, a fitting capital.

Map, page 266

TIP

With one week's notice, you can visit any of the *contrada* (district) museums that celebrate the *Palio* and the ancient city traditions. Tel: 0577-42209.

BELOW: a more unsual view of Siena.

Beautiful towers

Becoming one of the most visited towns in Siena in recent years, the romantic but often packed town of **San Gimignano** ❷ presents an unforgettable Tuscan scene. The approach to the many-towered hilltop town 40 km (25 miles) northwest of Siena, west of sprawling Poggibonsi, is memorable as the famous San Gimignano towers come into view behind olives, cypresses and vines.

The 12th- and 13th-century towers were designed as keeps by the *magnati*, or nobles, during the Guelf-Ghibelline feuds. The original conflict between the Ghibelline Salvucci family and the Guelf Ardinghelli family degenerated into more localised disputes between rival factions. As height meant prestige, power and status, towers were as big as the nobles' egos. Only 13 of the original 76 *belli torri* are left standing today.

Earthy pleasures

The local 14th-century poet Folgore, who wrote during a period of relative wealth, described the city's earthy pleasures, including "silk sheets, sugared nuts, sweets and sparkling wine".

The arrival of the Black Death in 1348, however, put an end to silk sheets in San Gimignano until the 20th century. The diminished population fell under Florentine control and this important city became an economic backwater, bypassed by the Renaissance. While more civilised cities were exchanging towers for *palazzi*, San Gimignano destroyed nothing and built nothing. The city's misfortune has made it the best preserved medieval city in Tuscany.

The Romanesque **Collegiata** does not have the status of a cathedral because there is no longer a bishop. Inside, Benozzo Gozzoli's fresco of a plump St Sebastian in agony is worth seeing. The radiant aisles are dedicated to two cycles of Biblical frescoes painted concurrently by two 15th-century artists.

Bartolo di Fredi's Old Testament frescoes along the church's north aisle are vivid, intimate and full of careless violence. *The Parting of the Red Sea* is

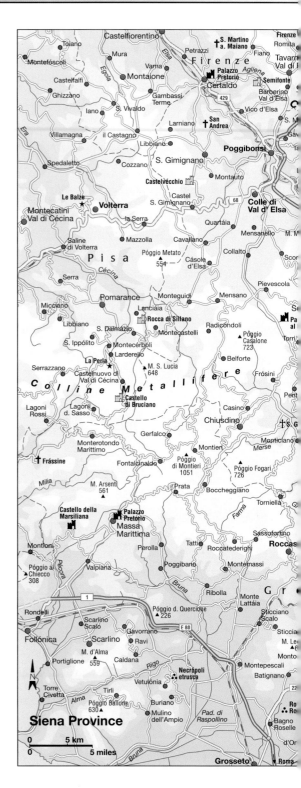

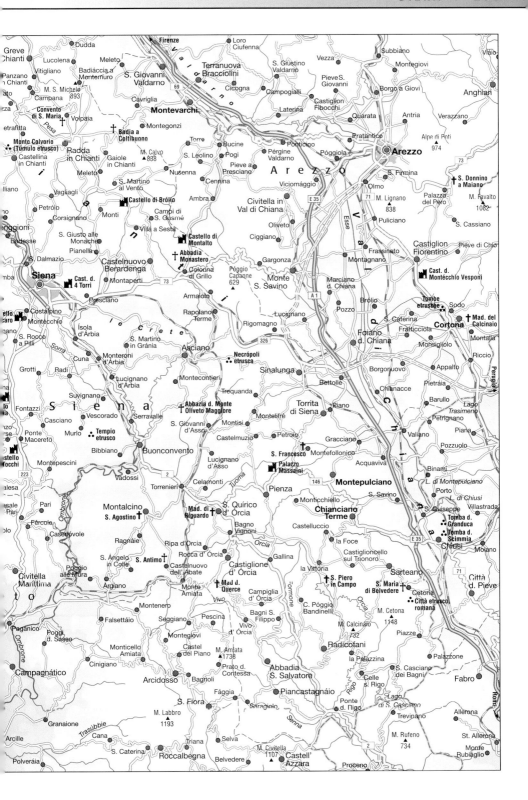

Look out for some of San Gimignano's edible specialities, on offer in local shops.

an animated jumble of flying and floating bodies, like a happy Hieronymus Bosch. There is a childlike but lively narrative in all the frescoes. For people raised on too many words and too little religion, it is fun trying to work out the significance of the Biblical stories through a pictorial narrative.

The variety of Biblical animals is astonishing: expressive camels, dogs and sheep often have more emotional resonance than the human subjects. As in Siena Cathedral there is a ceiling of faded stars to complete the magic. This was perhaps Barna di Siena's last view as he fell off his scaffolding and died.

In **Santa Fina's Chapel** off the south aisle, Ghirlandaio's frescoes of the local saint are rather too flowery. Legend has it that when she died in March 1253, violets sprang up on her coffin and on the towers.

Next to the Collegiata is the combined **Museo d'Arte Sacra e Museo Etrusco** (open daily; Mar–Oct; closed 1–2.30pm; closed Mon Nov–Feb; entrance fee), containing sacred vestments and other religious fragments from the 13th and 14th centuries, as well as a small collection of local Etruscan treasures.

Also in the **Piazza del Duomo** is the crenellated Palazzo del Popolo, housing the **Museo Civico** (open daily; Mar–Oct; closed 1–2.30pm and Mon in winter; entrance fee; tel: 0577-940340) with its countless Sienese "masters" and "schools of". On the second floor, the Camera del Podestà contains domestic and profane scenes by Filippuccio. Amongst the gentle erotica is a picture of a semi-nude couple wearing wooden nightcaps and similar expressions. The nearby **Piazza della Cisterna** is a lovely triangular square with a 13th-century well and medieval *palazzi*.

The final visit should be a short walk along the city walls to the 14th-century fortress. This semi-derelict **Rocca** has views over tiered gardens and olive groves winding down to the "Vernaccia" vineyards. As you leave, do not be surprised by the smell of sulphur – it is only Monte Amiata doing her stuff again.

Sleeping countryside

The **Chianti** is a spiritual rather than a geographical location. Its shifting borders reflect the fluctuations in Florentine and Sienese power but its soul remains where it has always been: on Florentine soil. The Sienese countryside is a bit wilder, the valleys deeper and the hills higher, but it is essentially sleepy, overly civilised Florentine Chianti.

Unlike the southern part of the province, the Chianti is not an area for artistic or architectural set-pieces. Instead, it is a place whose turbulent history has shaped a scene of utter tranquillity, a harmony of tame hills and gentle people.

In a place where nothing is essential viewing, everywhere is a glorious detour. **Castellina in Chianti** ❸ is conveniently sited on the Chiantigiana, the winding route linking Florence and Siena. Castellina surveys symmetrical vineyards and wooded groves, a landscape dotted with low stone houses and Renaissance villas.

New wine estates have been built from the remains of medieval castles. Villas have lazily domesticated the original castle or tower, but names like "La Rocca" or "La Torre" reveal the original function.

Map, page 272

Castellina's name also reveals its medieval function as a Florentine outpost. In the late 13th century it was the first site of the Chianti League, a group of three Florentine feudal castles, each responsible for a third of the territory. The castle is now a fortified town hall hiding a small Etruscan museum and a warren of atmospheric back streets with half-glimpsed views of the Chianti hills.

The other attraction is the *Enoteca Vini Gallo Nero* (Via della Rocca 13), the wine-tasting centre which gives advice on wine tours and *vendita diretta*, direct sales. (*See also "The Chianti Wine Trail", page 174.*)

Radda in Chianti ❹ retains its medieval street plan and imposing town hall. As in Castellina, the spontaneous rural architecture is more rewarding. Classical Medici villas with 16th-century windows and wells compete with romantic villas, constructed magpie fashion from castles or Etruscan ruins. One 17th-century masterpiece is Villa Vistarenni, a white beacon of sophistication unimaginable in the countryside south of Siena.

The elegant loggias, the openness of the architecture, symbolise the increasing safety of the countryside and its proximity to urban Florence. In the tranquil Chianti, the country is richer and more civilised than the town. The reverse is true of the urban-inspired communes south of Siena.

Outside Radda is **Volpaia ❺**, the most picturesque village in the Chianti. A tortuous road climbs to the medieval village with its towers, ruined castle and Brunelleschi-style church. If Chianti villages and towns have little sense of identity and few artistic treasures today, it is because they came into being with fully-fledged Florentine and Sienese identities, while military outposts like Radda had no time to develop artistically. Only the Chianti abbeys, endowed separately, had the independence to shape their own culture.

The Consorzio dello Gallo Nero was founded in the Fattoria Vignale just outside Radda in Chianti in 1924, and since that time the black cockerel has been the symbol of the Chianti League, which has been headquartered in Radda since 1415.

BELOW: San Gimignano looks impressive from whichever direction you approach.

TIP

Two very good
products to invest in at
the Castello di Brolio
are the *Galestro* white
wine, or the *Riserva
del Barone*, a noble
red wine which needs
at least five years to
mature.

BELOW: the red
earth of the Sienese
landscape.

Between Radda and Gaiole is the aptly-named **Badia a Coltibuono** ❻ (open
May–Oct; closed am, Sun and pub. hols; closed Aug), Abbey of the Good Har-
vest, set among pines, oaks, chestnuts and vines. Since the Dissolution of the
Monasteries in 1810, this medieval abbey has belonged to one family.

Although the lovely 15th-century cloisters, chapel and frescoed ceilings are
only visible to guests enrolled on a Tuscan cooking course, the 12th-century
walls and belltower are harmonious enough. Below the abbey are cellars filled
with Chianti Classico, the abbey's traditional living.

No less famous is the aromatic chestnut blossom honey or the *vergine* olive
oil. Much of the produce can be bought on the premises or savoured in the excellent abbey restaurant.

Gaiole in Chianti ❼, the baby baron of the Chianti League, is a newer river-
side development in a wooded valley. It is a popular *villeggiatura*, a summer
escape for hot Florentines in search of family-run hotels, home cooking and
the familiar *gallo nero* (black cock) wine symbol.

History lies in wait at Meleto and Vertine, unusual castles, and Barbischio, a
medieval village, is a short walk away. Tempting footpaths marked *Sentieri del
Chianti* lead all the way to Siena. With vineyards rising up gentle slopes, tranquil Gaiole and sleepy Greve are traditional Chianti.

The countryside from Gaiole south to Siena and east to Arezzo is higher,
wilder and wetter. The wooded peaks of the Chianti Sienese are vibrantly green
and fresh with scents of thyme, rosemary and pine kernels. Deep chestnut woods
provide ideal cover for wild boar, recently reintroduced.

Of the many Florentine castles in the woods, **Castello di Brolio** ❽ (open
daily for guided tours; entrance fee) is the most impressive – not least because

of its views over the original Chianti vineyards stretching as far as Siena and Monte Amiata. On the medieval chessboard, every Florentine castle faced its Sienese shadow. If the surviving castles are Florentine, it is because Siena lost the match and all its pieces. While Sienese Cereto and Cettamura are small heaps, Florentine Brolio and Meleto are resplendent.

As a Florentine outpost, Castello di Brolio's past spans Guelf-Ghibelline conflicts, sacking by the Sienese in 1529 and German occupation and Allied bombing during World War II. The medieval walls are the castle's most striking feature, along with the 14th-century chapel set in lush grounds. Brolio has long been controlled by the Ricasoli, Chianti landowners since the eighth century. Baron Bettino Ricasoli, Italian Premier in 1861, founded the modern Chianti wine industry, a business continued by the present family. The common saying, "When Brolio stirs, Siena shakes", still holds true today – not least in the wine trade.

The Chianti is a place for pottering and chance encounters, one of which is tiny **Campi di San Gusmé ⓦ**, just south of Brolio. A short climb leads to a small tower, Romanesque church and views of tumbledown castles, villas and vineyards. The tower was designed to be higher than the tallest cypresses encircling it, but, not surprisingly, the trees grew and the tower did not.

A Renaissance dolls' house

In contrast to the Chianti, towns south of Siena were never dependent on powerful Sienese and Florentine masters for their identity. The southern towns developed independently around local noblemen or industries and expressed their differences artistically. Shifting allegiances and even political domination

Map, page 272

BELOW LEFT: rape field in full bloom.
BELOW: old gateway in Pienza, a hilltop Renaissance jewel.

Amore *has no age limitations.*

BELOW: Pienza's Piazza Pio II, over-looked by the Duomo and Palazzo Piccolomini.

did not mean an acceptance of new, extraneous values but only an entrenchment in local culture and traditions.

Pienza is an exquisite Renaissance dolls' house. Although created by a humanist Pope, Pius II, Pienza is almost too perfect to be human and too precious to be spiritual. Every fountain, piazza and painting is harmonious. Model citizens walk through streets as romantic as their names: Via dell' Amore, Via del Bacio, Via della Fortuna – streets of "love", "kisses" and "fortune".

Pienza's origins date back to 1458. When E.S. Piccolomini was elected Pope, he could not resist playing God in his home village, Corsignano. He chose the noted Florentine architect, Bernardo Rossellino, to ennoble the hamlet in accordance with humanist principles. When the first masterpiece in modern town planning emerged late and over budget, the Pope reduced his fraudulent architect to tears with his words, "You did well, Bernardo, in lying to us about the expense involved in the work… Your deceit has built these glorious structures; which are praised by all except the few consumed with envy."

Bernardo Rossellino was rewarded with a scarlet robe, 100 ducats and some new commissions. The decision to build a cathedral enabled the Pope to rechristen Corsignano the village as Pienza the city – named, modestly, after himself. The result is what locals call a *città d'autore*, a city inspired by one vision. After Pienza, other cities in Tuscany or elsewhere are liable to look cluttered and confused.

Symmetrical centre

Much of the symmetry lies in the cathedral square, **Piazza Pio II**, and the slightly listing Duomo adds to the charm. Despite a Renaissance façade, the

interior is late Gothic and decorated with mystical paintings from the Sienese school. In one central alcove is a chilling *Assumption* by Vecchietta in which Saint Agatha holds a cup containing her breasts, torn off by the executioner.

The Duomo's façade, the gracious arches, the well and the Palazzo Piccolomini, the Pope's home, are just as Pius left them when he set off to fight the crusades and never returned. On summer nights, impromptu concerts are often held in the ill-lit square: the tilted church, the ghostly musicians and the solidity of Pius's presence can have an unnerving effect.

Palazzo Piccolomini (open Tues–Sun; closed 12.30–3pm; guided tours only; entrance fee; tel: 0578-748503), now a museum, is lined with grand and homely treasures, including a library and arms collection.

Still, an image of domestic clutter prevails. In the Pope's bedroom, the intriguing book-holder, as cumbersome as a church lectern, is proof that the Pope did not read in bed. The library opens onto a tranquil loggia with Etruscan urns, hanging gardens and a panorama across the Orcia valley to Monte Amiata.

If overwhelmed by beauty or hunger, one can retreat to the restaurants behind the main square. Pienza is famous for its homemade cheeses, especially *pecorino* and *ricotta*. "Lucrezia Borgia" biscuits provide an antidote to a surfeit of piety.

Just outside Pienza is the **Pieve di Corsignano**, a simple but coherent Romanesque church where Pope Pius II was baptised. You can ask for the key at the Pienza tourist office.

Cinquecento pearls

The winding road from Pienza up to **Montepulciano** ⓫ – visible for miles around, with houses cluttering the sides of the hump of a hill on which it is

"In our change-loving Italy, where no ancient dynasty exists, a servant can become king."

– POPE PIUS II

BELOW: Church of San Biagio, Montepulciano.

built – is lined with *vendita diretta* signs, offering *pecorino* and wine. If Pienza belongs to Rossellino, Montepulciano is Antonio da Sangallo's masterpiece.

Traffic is now banned from inside the city walls but just outside and below the walls, at the end of a long line of cypresses, lies **San Biagio**, the Renaissance building most at ease with its setting. The isolation focuses attention on the honey-coloured *travertine*, the Greek Cross design, the dome and the purity of the line. Sangallo's design skills rival Bramante's, not just in the church, the elegant well, the porticoed Canon's House, but elsewhere in the city. The airy interior has a deeply classical feel, more akin to the Roman Pantheon than to a small Tuscan church.

From San Biagio there is a short walk to **Santa Maria delle Grazie**, a 16th-century church whose Renaissance organ is still played at concerts. After Pienza, Montepulciano's asymmetrical design and spontaneous development give it the architectural tension that the earlier city lacks.

Pienza's reverence of Pope Pius is surpassed by Montepulciano's devotion to Poliziano. The renowned scholar, poet and resident tutor to Lorenzo de' Medici's children was named after the Latin term for the town. The tradition of scholarship is upheld in the city's annual Renaissance Convention. Likewise, early morning buses are filled with 2,000 young Poliziano coming to receive a "humanistic education".

As a humanist, Poliziano was "bent on doing over the whole house of Italian civilisation from top to bottom". But Mary McCarthy's view of him as a querulous interior designer does not reflect Poliziano's deep love of the Montepulciano countryside. The spring landscape inspired Botticelli's painting *Primavera* and Poliziano's *Stanzas*.

BELOW: the Palazzo del Comune in Montepulciano.

Fatal ecstasy

Poliziano's claims that maidens would be "safe in the shady arbours among so many young men" were probably correct. Poliziano himself is rumoured to have died in ecstasy while playing a love song on the lute to a "beardless youth".

Map, page 272

Poliziano's house is just off the main square, **Piazza Grande**, the highest part of town and the highest spot culturally. In August, the square becomes a stage for concerts and traditional Bruscello plays, originally performed by peasants on the threshing floor.

On the last Sunday in August the route is filled with sturdy *Poliziani* pushing heavy barrels uphill. The barrel race, *Bravio delle Botti*, started out as a Sienese *Palio*, but after numerous accidents the horse race was transformed into a pageant and an equally violent barrel race.

Florentine design has shaped the grand façades on Piazza Grande, but earlier Sienese Gothic touches are present in the interiors, double arches and doorways. Both styles reflect the city's buffeting between the two city-states and the eventual supremacy of Florence. The **Palazzo Comunale** (town hall) has a Florentine Michelozzo façade adorning Sienese turrets. The tower (open Mon–Sat till 1.30pm), modelled on that of Florence's Palazzo Vecchio, surveys the whole province: from Monte Amiata to Siena and even Lake Trasimeno. Once in the Palazzo, do not be deterred by the presence of a police station and the absence of a custodian: the view is legally yours in the morning.

ABOVE: ancient *cisterna* in Montepulciano. **BELOW:** the 16th-century Palazzo Tarugi, overlooking Piazza Grande.

Contessa's secret

Sangallo's **Palazzo Contucci**, on the other side of the square, is a secret. Ring the concealed bell and an elderly housekeeper or the Contessa herself will point

to palatial 18th-century ceilings before alluding to the real treasure here: the vast Contucci cellars below.

In the Cantina, Adamo, the wine master, will be delighted to expand on the entire noble history of the Contucci family and on his essential role on the Vino Nobile Wine Tasting Committee. Vino Nobile, a smooth red wine with a hint of violets, was "ennobled" in 1549 when Pope Paul III's sommelier proclaimed it "a most perfect wine, a wine for lords". In Montepulciano today, naive or noble-looking purchasers are often recommended the 1887 vintage. Vino Nobile is excellent with two local peasant dishes: *bruschetta*, a toasted garlic bread drenched in olive oil, or *panzanella*, a bread salad with herbs.

The Renaissance **Palazzo Bucelli**, closed to visitors, is a reminder of the city's Etruscan origins, dating back to Lars Porsenna, the mythical king of the Etruscans. The Palazzo, decorated with a mosaic of Etruscan urns and pots, is a sign of what civilised Tuscans call "urban decoration" and unenlightened foreigners call theft. The Poliziani are not alone in rifling tombs for useful garden furniture.

You can easily drive or even walk from Montepulciano to **Montefollonico ⓬**, a medieval village with one of the best restaurants in Italy, La Chiusa. Montefollonico is just one of Siena's hidden villages which, a world apart from the much vaunted and much visited "Cinquecento Pearls", are scattered among the rolling landscape of Siena province, each with a separate identity and artistic treasures espied almost incidentally over the brow of a hill.

Near Montepulciano a circular itinerary unites tiny villages once ruled by the Cacciaconti barons. Otherwise, the only link is that each tiny village considers itself civilised and the others feudal.

BELOW: slopes of carefully tended vineyards.

Petroio ⑬, set on a rocky, wooded promontory, is a grand fortified village on an old pilgrim route. In recent years it has been undergoing a revival thanks to its terracotta – examples of which adorn the city walls, Palazzo Pretorio and the medieval towers. Look out for the Canon's House, which contains a remarkable *Madonna and Child* by Taddio di Bartolo.

Map, page 272

Near the village is the intact **Abbadia a Sicille**, built by the Knights Templar as a refuge for knights on the way to the Holy Land. The adjoining Romanesque church is decorated with two Maltese crosses, but an Olivetan coat of arms marks the abolition of the Templars.

The high road to **Castelmuzio** ⑭ is dotted with *Divieto di Caccia* warnings to Sienese businessmen out to hunt boar at weekends. Quite seriously, it is advisable to wear bright clothes for walking across country in the hunting season.

Castelmuzio, set among farmland and woods, is a medieval village wrapped up in itself, its museum of Sacred Art and its direct line to San Bernardo. Narrow shops in winding streets sell honey, salami and cheese made by an ageing population of church-goers.

Once a Cacciaconti fortress, aristocratic **Montisi** ⑮ commands a view over two valleys. Montisi is a feudal and feuding village, sure of its superiority over "*primitivo*" San Giovanni d'Asso in the valley. Dwellers in the Castello, or "high town", have survived many attempts to tame them over the years and also withstood German bombing raids in World War II.

Although the "low town" has a few young families and newer attitudes, the "high town" is a relic of medieval Italy. While some peasants still sell eggs individually, the distinguished *Colonnello* sells the noble local wine, Vino Rosso dei Cacciaconti, through his housekeeper.

BELOW: an expert tests one of the many fine wines produced in the Chianti Classico region.

The village offers intriguing alleys, views, restaurants and two tiny Romanesque churches, one decorated with a Scuola di Duccio crucifix. A few apparently stark, uninviting farmhouses conceal wonderful frescoes and the occasional private chapel.

One can return to Montepulciano via **Sinalunga** ⑯, a schizophrenic Tuscan town with a hideous "low town" but a pleasant "old town". The town's original name, Asinalunga, echoes its shape, "the long donkey". But in the lively market, pigs, not donkeys, are in evidence: the entire population can be seen devouring *porchetta*, the local speciality of roast pig flavoured with rosemary.

The mysterious craters

Siena province's strangest area lies to the west of these villages. From Buonconvento to Rapolano Terme is a primeval landscape. Appropriately called **Crete**, this area is a moonscape of interlocking pale clay hummocks and treeless gullies. In winter it is cold, bleak and even more crater-like. Locals speak of these infertile furrows as *maligne crete*, in the same vein as the American "Badlands". Sienese city dwellers love this barren landscape and are successfully discouraging local farmers from accepting European Union funds to flatten the land and grow wheat.

There is an extraordinary range of ill-concealed wildlife in the area: by day, wild deer roam by the

Ombrone river; by night, porcupines and foxes are about in the woods. If intrepid walkers venture out in the late autumn evening they may meet a strange character with a couple of dogs, a torch and a harness. He is a truffle hunter, sniffing out truffles in the dampest ditches.

More legal are the Sardinian peasants selling cheese. Unlike many Tuscans, Sardinians are prepared to live in remote, infertile places. Sadly, the local population associate the "Sardi" with only three things: *pecorino*, horseriding and kidnapping.

Tobias Smollett, the "choleric philistine", hated Buonconvento. But then his horses had just run off, he was hungry, and he knew nothing of truffles.

Buonconvento ⑰, situated on a plain in the heart of the Crete, is a place for hunting and eating. It is also a quiet historical town, known for its *muraria*, the imposing red 14th-century walls and grand wooden gates. In 1366 Siena rebuilt the walls because, as a Sienese outpost, Buonconvento had been devastated. Today the town is essentially a place for a leisurely introduction to truffles or game; or for a summer picnic in the peaceful gardens beside the town walls.

In between Buonconvento and **Monte Oliveto Maggiore** ⑱, the rugged landscape is dotted with striking hill-top farmhouses. It is an empty road along which pheasants suddenly appear. Called the Accona Desert in medieval times, it retains its spiritual remoteness.

Hermits' order

After so much pale, undulating land, the red abbey of Monte Oliveto (open daily; closed 12–3.15pm) is glimpsed through a wood of pines, oaks and olive trees. If the land appears to fall away from the abbey, it is not far from the truth: land erosion and frequent landslides provide a natural defence to the abbey's mystical centre.

BELOW: the abbey of Monte Oliveto Maggiore.

In 1313 Tolomei, a wealthy Sienese, abandoned the law for a life of prayer in the wilderness, taking with him two fellow hermits. After a vision of white-robed monks, Tolomei established an Olivetan Order under Benedictine rule. The monks followed Saint Benedict's precept that "a real monk is one who lives by his own labour". Fortunately, a meagre diet, fervent prayer and lack of conversation stimulated the monks to artistic endeavour in the form of wood carving, sculpture and manuscript design. As a noted artistic centre, the abbey invited Luca Signorelli and Il Sodoma to decorate the Renaissance style cloisters with scenes from St Benedict's life.

The moated gateway, adorned with della Robbia terracottas, leads through cypresses and meaningful "*Silenzio!*" signs to the monks' domain. To see the wonderful if over-restored frescoes is more difficult than it looks, but once inside the main cloister, or Chiostro Grande, St Benedict's life unfolds in surprisingly profane ways. Of the two contemporaries, Signorelli had the more spiritual approach. But his loveliest work is a domestic scene portraying two monks being served by girls at an inn. St Benedict guessed that the monks had broken the monastic rule by eating outside the monastery. The fresco's expressive grace lies in the monks' absorption and in the sculptural sensuousness of one woman's neck. In 1497, after only nine frescoes were completed, Luca Signorelli left the rest for Il Sodoma to execute. The Olivetan monks' interfering ways were no match for the freedom, novelty and financial rewards dangled by Orvieto Cathedral.

Vasari adored Signorelli's spirituality as much as he loathed Il Sodoma's exuberance, hedonistic lifestyle and "licentious" fondness for "boys and beardless youths" which earned him his nickname in the first place. Il Sodoma's confident homosexuality helped him to flout the conventions of religious art.

One fresco originally depicted naked courtesans out to seduce the monks but the livid Abbot insisted on Sodoma "dressing" the courtesans. In his self-portrait, Sodoma has an actor's sense of his audience, a complicity shared by the pets at his feet.

Sodoma's love of what Vasari called his Noah's Ark of "badgers, squirrels, apes, dwarf asses and Elba ponies" is often present, but his landscapes only come to life with the temptations of the flesh. His gaze rarely focuses on the main subject but is deflected by the turn of an attractive leg, a mischievous smile, a perky badger or a soldier's buttocks. Needless to say, the inhibited monks preferred Signorelli's work to that of the man they labelled "*Il Mataccio*", imbecile or madman.

The excitement of Sodoma aside, Monte Oliveto is a spiritual retreat. The austere refectory, the library cluttered with ancient manuscripts and books, the exquisite marquetry work of the choir stalls are as peaceful as the hidden walks deep into the woods. A restaurant and former monastic cells are also available for overnight visitors.

The watery valley

The **Val d'Orcia** is a poor but beautiful rural area bordering southern Crete. The villages have suffered from

Map, page 272

TIP

Female visitors to the abbey of Monte Oliveto need to be aware that even bare wrists need to be covered by one of the monks' stock of headscarves.

BELOW: the 14th-century heavy timber gates at Buonconvento.

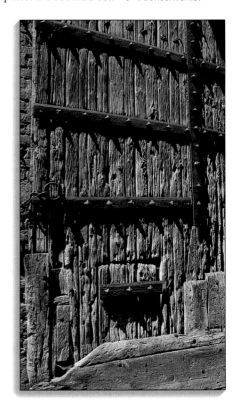

the desertion of the countryside in the 1950s and 1960s. The abandoned farmhouses used to be green oases near the barren Crete. Since the peasants had to be self-sufficient under the *mezzadria* system, every patch of land was cultivated, from the rosemary and camomile by the house to the enclosed orchard.

Conservationists practise *Agriturismo* and developers plan leisure centres. As local politician Fabio Pellegrini said: "Beware of linking the beauty of the countryside with the living conditions of the peasants – such a harmony has never existed."

An artistic celebration of local habits.

San Quirico d'Orcia ⑲ is a dignified valley town still waiting for its heyday. It survived an attack by Cesare Borgia's troops in 1502 and a World War II bombardment of its formal Collegiata and city walls. The Romanesque **Collegiata**, made from sandstone and local travertine, has three remarkable portals. The finest is the south portal, which is exquisitely decorated with lions and caryatids by the Giovanni Pisano school. Inside, a Sano di Pietro triptych incorporates the town's red-and-gold coat of arms.

From San Quirico d'Orcia, an exciting rough walk leads to three medieval fortresses – Ripa d'Orcia, Rocca d'Orcia and Castiglione d'Orcia. After the turning to the shabby medieval town of Bagno Vignoni, **Ripa d'Orcia** ⑳, an enchanted castle set among cypress groves, comes into view. Although goats and pheasants are the commonplace fauna here, the locals nevertheless make claims that wolves roam the area. After failing to see a wolf, the intrepid traveller clambers on to **Rocca d'Orcia** ㉑, a fortified village once owned by the warring Salimbeni clan.

BELOW:
fortified village of
Rocca d'Orcia.

The energetic can press on to **Castiglione d'Orcia** for more of the same. Wonderful views and exhaustion can be assumed. On a winter visit in 1332,

Saint Catherine of Siena felt God had abandoned her to the howling winds; a sensation still true today.

Just beyond San Quirico is **Bagno Vignoni** ㉒, a tiny but energetic spa station. In the middle of a severe medieval piazza, bubbling warm water gushes into an enclosed stone pool. The hot springs were used by Romans and became public baths in medieval times. Saint Catherine perhaps bathed here on her day off between miracles or saving the Papacy.

The new baths in Hotel Posta Marcucci are open at night on summer weekends. From the pool, all senses are fulfilled at once: the imposing Rocca d'Orcia looms above; outside the pool of light, the sound of sheep and crickets reverberates; the softness of the hot chalky water dissolves tiredness; and the smell of sulphur evaporates into the night air. The locals add the bizarre touch: while formation swimmers "dance" in time to Big Band music, spectators stare upwards for shooting stars, a feature on dark nights in mid-August. After a swim, a short *passeggiata* around the old baths shows the well-restored square at its most romantic.

The Etruscan towns

Although set among attractive low hills, **Chiusi** ㉓ comes across as a rather unprepossessing town, devoid of Renaissance charm. The "low town" is a commercial centre and the shabby "high town" is endearing but overwhelmed by its glorious Etruscan past.

Then, as now, the **Chiusini** were farmers, merchants and craftsmen, a spirit which predominates over artistry. Yet with a little Etruscan knowledge and much curiosity, the town is as fascinating as any in Tuscany. It boasts a complete

Map, page 272

The arthritic Lorenzo de' Medici and Saint Catherine of Siena, who suffered from a form of tuberculosis, both bathed in the medicinal waters of Bagno Vignoni in the hope of relieving their ailments.

BELOW:
the hot springs of Bagno Vignoni.

underground city; an unrivalled collection of female cinerary urns; and the only tomb paintings in their original setting in Tuscany.

As one of the greatest city-states in the Etruscan League, Chiusi, or "Kamars", controlled the area from Lago di Trasimeno to Monte Amiata. After reaching its zenith as a trading centre in the 7th century BC, Etruscan Kamars became submerged by Roman Clusium and then by medieval Chiusi.

The old city survives on three levels of civilisation: the Etruscan necropolis beneath the city hills; the Roman street grid system below the cathedral; and the medieval city above. If the locals seem unimpressed by modern Chiusi, it is simply because they remember that their king, Lars Porsenna, conquered Rome in 508 BC. The city's decline was hastened by its proximity to malaria-ridden marshes. Drainage works started by Cosimo de' Medici and continued today have created a healthier commercial climate within the grand Etruscan walls.

The National Etruscan Museum

The **National Etruscan Museum** (open daily till 2pm, Sun till 1pm; also open pm during the summer; entrance fee; tel: 0578-20177) is a wonderfully confusing experience, concealing one of the finest collections of its kind in Italy. Still, the collection as it stands attests to the vitality of Kamars and shows a distinctly female bias in the outstanding female canopic jars, cinerary urns and rounded *cippi* tombstones. The containers have Egyptian-style lids resembling human or animal heads. The Etruscans borrowed freely from the Greeks and Egyptians; the imitation Greek vases are less rational but more vigorous than the originals.

A speciality of Chiusi is *bucchero*, glossy black earthenware, often in the form of vases with figures in relief. This pottery has a sophisticated metallic fin-

BELOW: Chiusi's cathedral, built from Etruscan and Roman fragments.

ish which cannot be reproduced by modern craftsmen. Although much of the domestic pottery has a naturalness verging on the commonplace, the sarcophagi, the cinerary urns and the crouching sphinx reveal an underlying obsession with death and the appeasement of shadowy spirits.

In the Chiusi **Duomo**, three civilisations are visible at once: the "barbaric" Romanesque cathedral is built from Etruscan and Roman fragments; and the antique cistern beneath the belltower is from the 1st century BC. After fanciful speculation on the Etruscan galleries running beneath the town, a visit to the tombs can be arranged with the museum curator. Before this, look out for signs of "urban decoration": genuine Etruscan urns and sculptures in local gardens. The Etruscan physiognomy can also be spotted in the ironic smile or oblique glance of the bartender.

The tombs contain sarcophagi, cinerary urns and, in the case of the Monkey Tomb, rare wall paintings depicting athletic games and domestic scenes. Outside the town, ignore the two unremarkable towers, Beccati Questo and Beccati Quello, translated in Chiusi's tourist brochures as the "Get an Eyeful of This One" and "Get an Eyeful of That One" towers. Get a mouthful of the local fish instead.

After underground Chiusi, **Chianciano Terme** ❷ is a breath of fresh air. It has the healthiest and wealthiest climate in Tuscany: hills, spas, pine forests, and more doctors and fur coats per square metre than elsewhere in Italy. "Chianciano for a Healthy Liver," the signs into town invite, exhort or cajole. The "high" spa town is where Italians have flocked since Roman times to enjoy the unique powers of *Acqua Santa*: as one of the world's top spas, Chianciano is a seriously rich town.

Map, page 272

ABOVE AND BELOW: Chiusi's glorious Etruscan past is featured in its National Etruscan Museum.

TIP

The parish Church of St Peter in Radicofani houses several works of art, including Francesco di Valdambrino's wooden statue, *Madonna del Castello*, as well as two paintings by Andrea della Robbia in each side-altar. Other works of art are in the nearby Church of Agata.

This southern part of Siena province is positively bursting with Etruscan remains, and digging produces a continual flow of exciting finds. In Chianciano, well-marked walks lead to several recently discovered tombs and temples, and a new, excellent **Etruscan museum** (open Tues–Sun in Apr–Oct; Sat and Sun in winter, weekdays by appointment; tel: 0578-31384; entrance fee) contains many important and impressive finds, including an intact monumental tomb of a princess lined with bronze and adorned with various gold and bronze artifacts. The large museum also features the remains from a spa complex dating from the 1st century BC, which was discovered in Chianciano.

Near the town are some of the loveliest walks and drives in Tuscany. Many walks start from **La Foce**, a 15th-century farmhouse which overlooks the fertile Val di Chiana and the desolate craters of the Val d'Orcia. The superb gardens here (open Wed 3–7pm; entrance fee) were designed by the famous landscape gardener Cecil Pinsent. There are views across an Etruscan site to Monte Amiata and Monte Cetona. Its excellent strategic position meant that its owners, the Anglo-Italian Origos, used it as the partisans' refuge during World War II. Ongoing excavations on the property have uncovered some 200 – largely unviolated – Etruscan tombs.

From there, a rough track leads to Petraporciana, the partisans' hidden headquarters and to a primeval forest. This *faggeta* is full of giant oaks, cyclamens, wild orchids or snowdrops: a perfect short spring or autumn walk.

Beside La Foce is **Castelluccio**, a castle – and summer concert venue – which commands the best-loved view in the province: a sinuous line of cypresses plotting an Etruscan route across the craters. When Britain's Prince Charles stayed at Villa La Foce, proud locals were not surprised to see him painting this view.

A short walk leads to Pocce Lattaie and prehistoric caves with dripping stalagtites shaped like teats or nipples. These pagan caves were used in fertility rites and propitiatory offerings made to the gods. To tread where no prince has ever trod, be prepared to hire a guide (and a torch) from Chianciano.

Routes up to Monte Amiata

From Chianciano, an idyllic rural drive leads through Castelluccio to Sarteano and Cetona, two small medieval and Etruscan towns. These views of desolate *crete*, fortified farmhouses and hazy Monte Amiata are captured by Paolo Busato in his celebrated photographs. It is worth sacrificing a hired car to the dirt roads, but the nervous can take the more direct route to Sarteano.

Castiglioncello sul Trionoro ㉕ is a tiny village with a *castello* and a church containing a Trecento Madonna. The village is set amid vast expanses of abandoned countryside in which Etruscan remains are uncovered by chance every few years.

Spilling over its double ring of city walls, **Sarteano** ㉖ is a popular thermal centre which has retained its traditional identity. The town offers Etruscan remains, a grandiose 13th-century Rocca and crumbling Renaissance *palazzi* built into the city walls. An interesting **Etruscan museum** (open Tues–Sun; times vary; tel: 0578-269261 for information) has recently

BELOW: horsey detail at La Foce.

opened up in the town – but, contrary to rumours, the tomb of the Etruscan king, Porsenna, has never been discovered. In August each year, Sarteano holds a famous *Giostra* or tournament.

Map, page 272

Cetona ㉗ clings on to a richly wooded hill and, with the lowest incomes in the province, is struggling to survive. The grand 18th-century houses on the plains are a relic of past prosperity. The town's star attractions are a medieval fortress and a villa owned by the fashion designer Valentino.

Although Cetona is noted for its textiles and copies of Etruscan vases, it now relies on *Agriturismo* to keep its population from leaving. A short stay in a local farm with mountain walks and *bruschetti* drenched in olive oil is recommended.

The varied approaches to Monte Amiata, southern Tuscany's highest peak, are at least as good as what awaits you on arrival. The fast Pienza to Abbadia San Salvatore route allows for a detour to Siena's loveliest thermal baths, **Bagni San Filippo** ㉘. A turning to the right shortly before Abbadia leads to a cluster of houses and orchards and the sulphurous smell indicates the thermal centre.

The winding walk down to the pool passes a pediluvium before reaching a magnificent rocky waterfall and a modern pool. Mud and massage treatments are available for those not already coated in chalky white masks. Although Italians are quite happy swimming in hot baths in the height of summer, visitors tend to collapse with exhaustion after two lengths.

The historic streets of Montalcino.

The alternative route via Sarteano and **Radicofani** ㉙ was the one taken by both Dickens and Montaigne to a location second only to Volterra for natural drama. While the mountain villages have sports and leisure industries to thank for their revival, the villages on the edge of Amiata seem to be in permanent limbo, trapped rather than enhanced by a medieval identity – and, in Radicofani's case, a medieval economy.

BELOW: the neo-classical cathedral in Montalcino.

Sea of stones

Dickens found Radicofani "as barren, as stony, and as wild as Cornwall, in England". Perched on a craggy basalt rock 766 metres (2,513 ft) above sea level, it is the only place in Italy to possess a triple Medicean wall. The town overlooks *Il Mare di Sassi*, the "sea of stones" suitable only for very hardy sheep.

Radicofani is linked to the exploits of Ghino di Tacco, the "gentle outlaw" immortalised by Dante and Boccaccio. Exiled Ghino controlled the town from Radicofani Castle, built by Hadrian IV, the only English Pope. A fierce basalt sculpture of Ghino stands in this forbidding town of low stone houses with external stairways, blind alleys and severe façades. Although an 18th-century earthquake destroyed much of the town, enough atmosphere remains.

The drive from Radicofani to **Abbadia San Salvatore** ㉚ is via Le Conie, a tortuous road known as "Amiata's sentry". For those not interested in skiing, mountain walks and disused mercury mines, Abbadia is best known for its much overrated **Abbazia** and its medieval "high town".

The Romanesque San Salvatore is all that remains of a once magnificent abbey. Unfortunately it has been heavily restored, once in 16th-century baroque and again in 1925. A 12th-century crucifix and the crypt

with 36 columns remain relatively unspoilt. Geometric symbols, grapes, palm leaves, animals, and gordian knots decorate the pillars.

From Abbadia, a winding road with sharp bends and sheer drops leads to the summit of **Monte Amiata**, 1,738 metres (5,700 ft) high. The wooded area around the extinct volcano has attractive walks and, since hunting is banned, there is plenty of opportunity for animal spotting. The Fosso della Cocca, a leafy tunnel, is the best place for unusual wildlife and vegetation.

Although **Castel del Piano** ③, in neighbouring Grosseto province and set among pine forests and wild raspberries, is the oldest settlement in the area, **Piancastagnaio** is a better base. Perched among chestnut groves, the town offers a newly restored Rocca, Franciscan monastery and odd villages.

Pope Pius II, on a visit to Amiata from Pienza in 1462, wrote: "The soft spring waters run through mountain spots more beautiful than nymphs or fauns could have found." Given the sulphurous odour, the nymphs must have had colds at the time.

Quintessential Sienese

In both temperament and identity, **Montalcino** ㉜ is certainly the most Sienese town in the province. In essence, its history is a microcosm of all Sienese history. From a distance Montalcino even looks like a Sienese Trecento painting: the landscape could be a background to a saint's life; in the foreground would be the fortress and scenes of rejoicing and celebration after an historic victory.

Montalcino has been known as "the last rock of Communal freedom" since its time as the Sienese capital in exile between 1555 and 1559. After the fall of Siena, exiles gathered around Piero Strozzi and the Sienese flag. As a reward,

BELOW:
Romanesque abbey
of Sant'Antimo.

Montalcinesi standard bearers have the place of honour in the procession preceding the *Palio* in Siena.

The magnificent 14th-century **Rocca** (open Tues–Sunday; closed 1–2pm) is the key to Montalcino's pride. The approach is through olive groves and the slopes famous for Brunello wine. But the asymmetrical fortress, astride a spur of land, dominates the landscape. From its gardens there is a sense of boundless space and absolute freedom.

In winter, the wind howls over the massive walls and drives visitors to a different type of fortification in the *Enoteca* bar inside. This "National Wine Library" naturally serves Brunello, the first wine in Italy to be given the DOCG *Denominazione* for excellence.

The fortress still contains the tattered flag of the old Sienese Republic. Depicting the Virgin and Child, it represents the Republic's struggle for liberty. Visiting Sienese have been known to weep on seeing the *stendardo*.

Visiting Montalcino is not a trip, it is a pilgrimage. Oddly enough, Montalcino's history has come full circle: after countless changes to its boundaries, it is now in possession of exactly the same land as in medieval times. Its liberal and left-wing traditions have also survived: in the 1920s the town had a proud anti-fascist record and held out against the Germans until 1945.

Architecturally, Montalcino offers a neo-classical cathedral, a Gothic loggia, a Romanesque church and a myriad of intriguing alleys. The Duccio and della Robbia schools are well-served by the Civic and Sacred Museums. Sano di Pietro's *Madonna dell' Umiltà* is particularly moving. Most significant is the Palazzo Comunale, a mass of *Fiorentinità* finished off by a Sienese tower to prove that the Sienese always surpass the Florentines. In spring, the area is very green, but yellow rape seed, poppies, sunflowers and grapes soon retaliate. Before leaving, try *pici*, home-made spaghetti, and sweet *sospiri* ("sighs") in a *fin de siècle* bar.

Other attractions

Nearby is **Sant'Antimo** ㉝, the remains of a Romanesque abbey founded by Charlemagne. If the church is closed, try the sacristan in **Castelnuovo dell'Abate** ㉞, the village up the hill. Designed in the French and Lombard style, the abbey is built from local travertine, which resembles alabaster or onyx.

But what sets Sant'Antimo apart is the interior. It has a translucent quality and, as the light changes, turns luminously golden, white and brown. Its setting, amidst cypresses in a peaceful valley, inspired Charles Tomlinson to write of the wind in the cypresses as "a continual breathing, an underwater floating of foliage" chasing its shadowy reflection against the stone tower.

Not far away, **Sant'Angelo in Colle** ㉟, a fortified hilltop village, once cast a dramatic shadow over Grosseto and other enemies. Until 1265 it was a Sienese outpost, but the tower is all that remains. Today it is a quiet medieval village with time and consideration for peaceful visitors.

Modern Siena province ends just there. As a frontier castle, Sant'Angelo looked down onto the plain which falls into Grosseto. After Siena province, Grosseto can look deceptively flat. ❏

Map, page 272

TIP

A good souvenir of Montalcino – apart from a bottle of Brunello – are the local green-and-white ceramic products, which can be bought in the village as well as in the Rocca.

BELOW: interior of the abbey of Sant'Antimo.

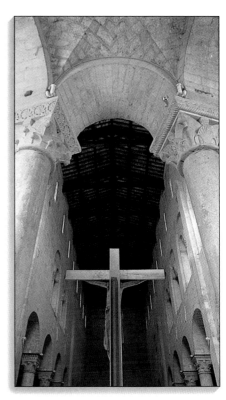

THE PASSION OF SIENA'S PALIO

In little more than a minute, the Campo is filled with unbearable happiness and irrational despair as centuries-old loyalties are put to the test

It is strange how a race that lasts just 90 seconds can require 12 months' planning, a lifetime's patience and the involvement of an entire city. But Siena's famous *Palio* does just that, as it has done since the 13th century, when an August *Palio* made its debut. At that time, the contest took the form of a bareback race the length of the city. The bareback race run around the Siena's main square, the Piazza del Campo, was introduced in the 17th century. Today the *Palio* is held twice a year, in early July and mid-August.

The *Palio*, which has been run in times of war, famine and plague, stops for nothing. In the 1300s, criminals were released from jail to celebrate the festival. When the fascists were gaining ground in 1919, Siena postponed council elections until after the *Palio*. In 1943, British soldiers in a Tunisian prisoner-of-war camp feared a riot when they banned Sienese prisoners from staging a *Palio*; Sienese fervour eventually triumphed.

IMPORTANT PREPARATIONS

Although, as the Sienese say, "*Il Palio corre tutto l'anno*" ("The *Palio* runs all year"), the final preparations boil down to three days, during which there is the drawing by lots of the horse for each competing ward (*contrada*), the choice of the jockeys (who often hail from the Maremma) and then the six trial races – the last of which is held on the morning of the *Palio* itself and is called the *provaccia*, or "terrible trial". On the eve of the race, a tense "propitiatory" dinner is held in each *contrada*. Although many do pack into the Campo for the actual race, other citizens cannot bear to watch it and instead cluster around the TV set in the *contrada* square or go to church to pray.

▷ **FLAG-WAVING FEATS**
A highlight of the *Palio* pageantry is the spectacular display of the flag-wavers, famous throughout Italy for their elaborate manoeuvres of twirling and hurling the huge standards dozens of feet in the air.

△ **CONTRADE ON PARADE**
Siena's 17 existing *contrade* are all represented in the *Palio*'s colourful *Corteo Storico* or Historical Parade. Those taking part don costumes symbolic of their particular *contrada*.

◁ **MEDIEVAL FINERY**
The words "*C'è terra in piazza*" ("There's earth in the Campo") are the signal to remove the colourful costumes from Siena's museums to feature in the great Historical Parade.

△ **BLESSINGS BESTOWED**
On the day of the *Palio*, the horses are taken to each *contrada* church for a blessing. The priest holds the horse's head and commands it, "*Vai e torni vincitore!*" ("Go and return victorious!").

THE POWER OF THE *CONTRADE*

In Siena the *contrada* rules: ask a Sienese where he is from and he will say, "*Ma sono della Lupa*" ("But I'm from the Wolf Contrada"). The first loyalty is to the city in the head, not to the city on the map.

Ten out of Siena's 17 *contrade* take part in each *Palio*: the seven who did not run in the previous race and three selected by lot. Each *contrada* appoints a captain and two lieutenants to run the campaign. In the *Palio*, the illegal becomes legal: bribery, kidnapping, plots and the doping of horses is common.

Each of the *contrade* in the city has its own standard, many of which are displayed around the city during the *Palio* and play an important role in the ceremonial aspect of the event.

Flags, or standards, are a central theme of the *Palio* event. In fact, the "*palio*" itself – the trophy of victory for which everyone is striving – is a standard: a silk flag emblazoned with the image of the Madonna and the coats-of-arms of the city, ironically referred to by the Sienese as the *cencio*, or rag. The *contrada* which wins the event retains possession of the *palio* standard until the next race.

▷ ANYTHING GOES
The ruthless race lurches round the Campo three times. If a riderless horse wins, the animal is almost deified, is given the place of honour in the victory banquet and has its hooves painted gold.

◁ HISTORICAL PAGEANTRY
The Historical Parade, which is staged in the run-up to the main race, retraces Siena's centuries of struggle against Florence, from the glorious victory against its rival in 1260 to the ghastly defeat in 1560.

AREZZO

Known for its gold, art and antiques, Arezzo city is one of the wealthiest in Tuscany, and the province is equally well-off in terms of prosperous farms and medieval villages

Maps:
Area 302
City 300

The landscape of the province of Arezzo is rugged with steep valleys that form a kind of backwoods, hiding its towns and villages from public view. The north is a remote area of chestnut woods, vineyards and monasteries; to the south are the prosperous farms of the Val di Chiana.

Arezzo ❶, the Roman Arretium, was originally an Etruscan city but in 294 BC it became a military rest station on the Via Cassia between Rome and Florence. The principal Roman site is the **amphitheatre** ❹ (open daily), off the Via Margaritone, built in the 1st century BC. Now turned into a park, the huge site was much plundered to build the city walls and churches.

Although the view of the town from the south is quite unremarkable, from the north and the west Arezzo looks the classic hill town, surrounded by a high wall and crowned by the **Duomo** ❸.

The Duomo's construction, mainly from the late 13th to the early 16th centuries, has been described as one of the most perfect expressions of Gothic architecture in Italy. The Gothic façade, however, is fake and dates from 1914.

Internally there are clustered columns, pointed arches and beautiful 16th-century stained glass windows by Guillaume de Marcillat, a French artist who made Arezzo his home. Other great works here are the 14th-century cenotaph of Guido Tarlati, which flanks the St Mary Magdalene fresco by Piero della Francesca. The **Museo del Duomo** ❸ (open Thur–Sat 10am–noon; other days by appointment; tel: 0575-23991; entrance fee), behind the cathedral, contains medieval crucifixes and Vasari frescoes.

PRECEDING PAGES:
view from Cortona.
LEFT: Via del Pileati
in Arezzo.
BELOW: the perfect
place to pose:
Arezzo's Piazza
Grande.

Antiques fair

On the first Sunday of every month Arezzo holds an antiques fair which is one of the largest and oldest in Italy. Stalls run around the base of the Duomo, down the cobbled main street in the old quarter, the **Corso Italia** ❿, and into the Piazza Grande.

Don't miss a visit to the **church of San Francesco** ❸ (open daily; closed 12–1.30pm) in Piazza San Francesco, where you can see Piero della Francesca's powerful and haunting fresco cycle *The Legend of the True Cross*. This is the greatest work in Arezzo, painted between 1452–66 and restored for the 500th anniversary of the artist's death in 1992. The powerful and haunting series of painting includes a 15th-century representation of Arezzo.

The **Museo Archeologico** ❺ (open Mon–Sat till 2pm; entrance fee) features some of the best examples anywhere of the red-glazed Coralline ware for which Arezzo has long been famous.

The **Museo Statale d'Arte Medioevale e Moderna** ❸ (open daily; entrance fee), housed in the 15th-

An example of the kind of pottery for which Arezzo's archaeological museum is renowned.

BELOW: façade detail of Arezzo's Santa Maria della Pieve church.

century Palazzo Bruni, has a varied collection that includes an excellent display of majolica pottery, frescoes, paintings and examples of the long-popular Arezzo goldsmiths' work.

In fact, the town itself still has a large number of jewellers, though not as many as there are antique shops and furniture restorers. Both are to be found in the vicinity of the **Piazza Grande** ⓗ behind the church of **Santa Maria della Pieve** ⓘ, a great Romanesque church with a Pisan-Lucchese façade.

On one side of the essentially medieval piazza is Vasari's **Palazzo delle Logge** which, when it was built in 1573, changed the entire appearance of the medieval square. The piazza is also the scene of the colourful *Giostra del Saracino*, or Joust of the Saracen, on the first Sunday in September (*see page 124*).

Some great intellectuals lived in Arezzo – Maecenas, the rich friend and patron of Virgil and Horace; Petrarch; Guido d'Arezzo, the inventor of musical notation; and Giorgio Vasari, the 16th-century documenter of Italian painters' lives. A reconstruction of Petrarch's house can be visited, as can Vasari's house (open daily; Sun till 12.30pm).

As Arezzo can be seen in one day and the hotels are not of a very high standard, a good plan is to commute from Monte San Savino or from Cortona.

A dream town

The Upper Tiber Valley is tightly enclosed at its northern end by Alpe di Catenaia and the Alpe della Luna. According to tradition, **Sansepolcro** ❷ was built in the foothills of these Apennine peaks, near the Tiber, on the whim of two 10th-century pilgrims, Arcano and Giles, who had been inspired in a dream. Having just arrived back from Palestine with relics of the Holy Sepulchre, they built a

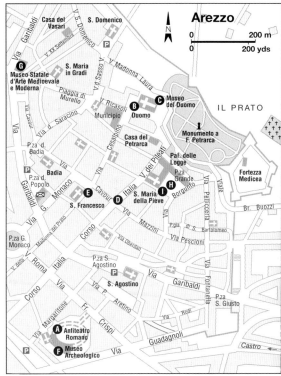

chapel on the site of the present Duomo and dedicated it to the Holy Sepulchre; the Borgo of Sansepolcro is the progeny of this.

Sansepolcro is famous for two things. It was the birthplace of Piero della Francesca, one of the greatest painters of the 15th century, and it is the source of much of Italy's pasta. Buitoni factories on the outskirts produce miles of spaghetti and macaroni, carrying the name of Sansepolcro all over the world.

The old town huddled behind crumbling ramparts is an important artistic centre. The narrow quiet streets are linked by four ancient gates, the best preserved of which is the Porta Fiorentina. At the town centre, at the junction of Piazza Torre di Berta and the Via Matteotti, is the **Duomo**. Dedicated to St John the Evangelist, it began life in the 11th century as a monastic abbey.

Rich interior

A wide range of excellent artworks cover the walls of the interior including a tabernacle by the della Robbia School. Perugino's *Ascension of Jesus* is also here. The Torre di Berta itself was a 12th-century tower, built at the most ancient point of the city. This was blown up by the retreating Germans in 1944.

Luckily this ruthless vandalism failed to destroy the other important buildings in this part of the town: the 16th-century Palazzo delle Laudi (the town hall) and the Palazzo Gherardi, begun in 1300, both in the Via Matteotti; and the Palazzo Pretorio opposite the Piazza Garibaldi.

The survival of Piero della Francesca's greatest work, the *Resurrection*, was under threat from destruction by the Allies during World War II as they bombarded Sansepolcro, believing that the Germans were still occupying the town. Today this intense, brooding fresco, which was saved by citizens placing sand-

Maps:
Area 302
City 300

The most important of Sansepolcro's four ancient gates used to be the Bastione del Nord, designed in the 15th century by Buontalenti.

BELOW: antiques market in Piazza Grande, Arezzo.

bags against it, is in the **Museo Civico** (open daily; closed 1–2.30pm; entrance fee) in Via degli Aggiunti. It stands opposite della Francesca's polyptych of the *Madonna della Misericordia*, another of this artist's most important works. In the *Resurrection* Christ and the soldiers are as rough and as rustic as della Francesca's Madonna del Parto in the **Museo Madonna del Parto** (open Tues–Sun; closed 1–2pm; entrance fee) in **Monterchi ❸**, which lies a few miles south of Sansepolcro.

The Madonna, heavily pregnant, and obviously aching after nearly nine months of carrying a child, has unbuttoned the front of her dress, while above two angels hold up the entrance to the tent in which she stands.

Birthplace of Michelangelo

Northwest of Sansepolcro, on a steep slope above the Tiber, is the hamlet of **Caprese ❹**, birthplace of Michelangelo. Protected by an almost complete set of walls, this clutter of rustic buildings – which includes the Buonarroti house,

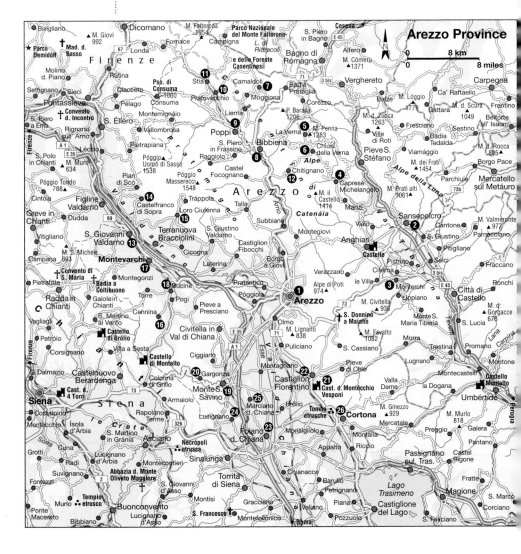

the old town hall where Michelangelo's father was the Florentine governor, and the tiny chapel in which Michelangelo was baptised – are interesting more for their connections than for their contents.

Map, page 302

At its remoter edges this region cannot be greatly different from how it was on the day that St Francis took to a lonely, desolate crag crowned with beeches on the wooded slopes of **Monte Penna** at **La Verna ❺**, using a niche between two huge boulders as a hermitage. The mountain was given to the Franciscan order as a free gift by a local devotee, Count Orlando da Chiusi di Casentino, who had been inspired by one of St Francis's sermons. On this spot in 1224 St Francis is supposed to have received the stigmata while he was praying. Today a Franciscan sanctuary still occupies the rock and an air of solitude remains. Assembled around a tiny piazza is a collection of monastic buildings, including one large church containing yet more fine terracotta sculptures by the gifted della Robbia family.

The journey to La Verna today from the town of **Chiusi della Verna ❻** down below is as much of a pilgrimage as it was in the Middle Ages. A crazy twisting road drives higher up through the birch and fir forest, providing a cool retreat from the summer heat.

Caprese's town hall contains full-size reproductions of Michelangelo's works and an assortment of memorabilia. Outside in the garden is a sculpture park of very questionable tributes to the master from other, more recent artists.

Intimations of mortality

The Casentino is the uppermost stretch of the Arno Valley. It is shut in by high mountains and so most access routes are tiny winding roads which have to be traversed in second gear and extremely slowly.

Sixteen kilometres (10 miles) northeast of La Verna, high in the mountains of the Casentino, is another more ancient monastery called **Camaldoli ❼** (open

BELOW: Caprese, birthplace of Michelangelo.

daily). It was founded in 1012 by San Romualdo (St Rumbold), a former member of the Benedictine order, as a reaction to what he felt was the lax and luxurious life led by most Benedictines in their monasteries. The monastery has a pharmacy in which very little has altered since the Middle Ages. An alligator hangs from the rafters and rows of dusty pots, pestles and mortars nestle up to an upright coffin with a glass lid in which is a skeleton.

Etched into the glass lid of the coffin displayed at the Camaldoli monastery is the inscription: "In this glass you see yourself, foolish mortal. Any other glass is not telling the truth."

Another 300 metres (1,000 ft) up the mountain above the monastery is the **Eremo di Camaldoli** (open daily), a hermitage consisting of nothing more than a small baroque church and eight cells, each surrounded by a high wall and a tiny garden. Here the hermits are still obeying the rules their founder laid down for them in the Dark Ages. One or two of them have been incarcerated in solitude for up to 15 years.

Bibbiena

A brief sojourn in the loneliness of Camaldoli would easily be balanced by a visit to noisy **Bibbiena ❽**, a typical Tuscan hill town, and one of the more important centres in the area which, unlike most other hill towns these days, is still prey to insane traffic jams.

In the church of Santa Maria del Sasso are two richly decorated panels by Giovanni della Robbia, and in the church of Santa Ipolito and San Donato there is a triptych by Bicci di Lorenzo. Nearby is the rustic Palazzo Dovizi, home of Cardinal Dovizi who, as Cardinal Bibbiena, became the secretary of Pope Leo X.

BELOW:
"Still Life 1".

Today Bibbiena is best known for its own particular brand of salami and a lively variety of shops and bars. From the main piazza there are distant views to Camaldoli and to Poppi, the latter the gateway to an interesting district of castles and fortified towns, all of which retain traces of the barbarous quality of life led by the inhabitants of this part of Tuscany in the late Middle Ages.

The region was continually fought over by the Guelf Florentines and the Ghibelline Aretines, and a decisive battle in 1289 which firmly established the dominance of the former over the latter is marked by a column on a site called Campaldino, just between Castel San Niccolò and Poppi.

Poppi ❾ glowers over the surrounding countryside from its hilltop perch. At its highest point is the particularly brutal-looking, and now decaying, Palazzo Pretorio, formerly a castle of the Counts Guidi.

The streets of the town are lined with arcades joined by steep steps and decorated with finely carved capitals and cut stone seats. The silence of Poppi today is a reminder of the fact that young people are constantly being drawn to the bright lights of the cities. At Poppi only old men sit about in the cafés and there is none of the ebullience and noise of Bibbiena and Arezzo.

Off in the distance, on a hill above the village of **Pratovecchio ❿** is the 11th-century **Castello di Romena** (open mid-May–mid-Oct, Sun and pub. hols; closed 12–3pm), once again a former possession of the Guidi family to whom most of the Casentino belonged. The Guidi sheltered Dante here after his expulsion from Florence at the beginning of the 14th century. Of the 14 towers that Dante would have seen at the castle, only three now remain. **Pieve di Romena**, a stone's throw from the castle and standing on a lonely slope below the castle, is one of the most important Romanesque churches in Tuscany.

Beneath its apse, excavations have revealed the remains of an Etruscan building as well as two earlier churches. Finely executed Romanesque capitals on the top of the gigantic granite columns of the nave make references to the four evangelists and to St Peter. Most notable of all is the present apse of this building, which dates from 1152. The key to the church is kept by the farmer's wife, who lives in the house directly over the road.

At **Stia ⓫** is the **Castello di Porciano** (open by appointment only; tel: 0575-58633), which looks down over the valley to the Castello di Romena and further on to Poppi, also in the possession of the Guidi. Whereas these monuments are all easily accessible, the fortified remains at Castel Castagnaia, with the nearby ruined Roman temple, both to the west of Stia, are harder to reach. The road peters out and a walk through rough, stony countryside is necessary in order to get to them.

Another of the Guidi castles was in the tiny village of Montemignaio. Today only a few remains of this building exist, but in the village church is Ghirlandaio's *Virgin and Child with the Four Church Elders*.

South of Bibbiena is yet another important castle at Focognano on the south-western slope of the Pratomagno. One of the few castles in the region to have been restored is at **Chitignano ⓬**, just a few miles to the east of Focognano. The medieval remains were rebuilt in the 18th century. There are other ruined castles at Talla and Subbiano – at the latter Castelnuovo has a 15th-century tower which overlooks the main road and is of particular interest.

Map, page 302

An alluring stack of local cheeses.

BELOW: "Still Life 2".

Warlike bishops

The Valdarno region was the other much fought-over battle ground of the Ghibellines and the Guelfs in the Middle Ages. At the close of the 13th century pressure was exerted on the Florentines by the warlike Aretine bishops who controlled powerful and well-fortified castles in the Arno valley, such as at Cennina. In an effort to resist them, the Florentines built three fortresses, which were really fortified towns, at San Giovanni Valdarno, Terranuovo and Castelfranco di Sopra.

San Giovanni Valdarno ⓭ was fortified as a bulwark against the Aretines. Today it is a lively industrial centre with a prominent display of architectural and artistic wealth. The central piazza was designed by Arnolfo di Cambio; the church of Santa Maria della Grazia here contains Masaccio's *Virgin and Child with the Four Saints*.

Arnolfo was also responsible for the Palazzo Comunale in the middle of the piazza, and facing Santa Maria della Grazia. Just outside the town is the Renaissance monastery of Montecarlo, in which is preserved the *Annunciation* by Fra Angelico.

Castelfranco di Sopra ⓮, in contrast to San Giovanni Valdarno, still retains its military character; the fortified Porta Fiorentina is as forbidding as it ever was, but these days the only thing the walls protect is an antique atmosphere. Most of the 14th-century streets and buildings have survived.

Castiglion Fibocchi defended the ancient road from the Valdarno to the Casentino, and all that remains from this period is a tower and some castellated walls. The medieval nucleus spawned a village, little altered, and the fine Renaissance residences here are as varied as those of Castelfranco di Sopra.

BELOW: a farm worker's house.

VAL DI CHIANA AND ITS CATTLE

The Val di Chiana is the most extensive of all the valleys in the Apennine range. The entire valley between the towns of Monte San Savino and Cortona was once covered in water. It was drained by the Etruscans – and, some say, Cosimo I – and all that remains is Lake Trasimeno, just across the Tuscan border in Umbria.

By the late Middle Ages the whole area had become a swamp, and for refuge from malaria, as well as from marauding, hostile armies, the people took to the hills, barricading themselves behind high defensive walls on precipitous outcrops of rock. Val di Chiana today is known first and foremost as an area of rich farmland, and most towns within it have become prosperous through agriculture. The farmland is mainly used to rear one of Italy's two prized breeds of cattle for meat – Chianina, which is native to Tuscany. (The other is Razza Piemontese from Piedmont.)

The Chianina grows quickly to a large size, so that it is butchered when the steer is a grown calf. The meat is firm and tasty, with a distinctive flavour. To any beef-loving Italian, *bistecca alla Fiorentina* – a huge, tender Val di Chiana T-bone steak, grilled over an open fire seasoned with nothing more than crushed peppercorns, salt, and a hint of garlic and olive oil, served very rare – is the *ultimate* steak.

Etruscan heritage

Under scrutiny, the Valdarno reveals an even more ancient heritage than the comparatively recent warring of the Middle Ages. The villages of **Loro Ciuf-fenna** ⓯ and **Cennina** ⓰ bear names derived from Etruscan dialect. A more medieval rusticity is evident in their village alleyways and ruined castle fortifications. The far-distant past feels closest early in the morning when the mist covers the floor of the valley, looking like water from the height of the surrounding hills.

In prehistoric times the Arno basin was a lake, and farmers today frequently dig up fossil remains and bones of animals which have long been extinct. At **Montevarchi** ⓱, south of San Giovanni Valdarno, is the important **Accademia Valdarnese** (open Tues–Sun; closed 12–4pm and Sun pm; entrance fee), a museum of prehistory which houses an impressive collection of fossilised remains from the Pliocene period, discovered in this stretch of the Arno valley. Apart from the museum and the church, there is not much to detain the traveller here, though at tiny **Galatrona** in the hills to the south of the town, above **Bucine** ⓲, is a beautiful hexagonal font in the parish church. It is covered with reliefs of the life of St John the Baptist.

Pristine medieval town

Monte San Savino ⓳, on the edge of the Val di Chiana, has been a citadel since Etruscan times, although the fortifications that survive date actually from the Middle Ages. In 1325 the inhabitants were unable to fend off a ruthless Aretine mob who razed the town to the ground for displaying Guelf tendencies. It was subsequently rebuilt and not much happened there until its formerly

Map, page 302

Montevarchi contains a bizarre relic: a phial of the milk of the Virgin, which is kept on the altar of the Madonna del Latte.

BELOW: Monte san Savino.

strong Jewish community was wiped out – many of them burnt at the stake – for resisting the French army in 1799.

Progress has hardly touched Monte San Savino; it retains medieval and Renaissance houses, of which the **Palazzo Comunale**, with a façade by Antonio da Sangallo the Elder and a fine museum, is the most important. It was originally built as the Palazzo di Monte for Cardinal Antonio di Monte in 1515.

The other important edifices in the town are the **Loggia del Mercato** by Sansovino and the churches of Santa Chiara and Sant' Agostino. The wild hills of the country to the northwest of the town shelter a feudal retreat, the **Castello di Gargonza ⑳** on the west slope of Monte Palazzuolo.

Dante is known to have been at the Castello di Gargonza in 1304 when it was used as a gathering point for Ghibellines from Arezzo and Florence.

This 13th-century castle, in fact a *borgo* or walled village, dominates the Chiana valley and is the centre of a vast wooded estate producing oil and wine. For nearly 400 years from 1385 a varied history shunted this castle about from one ownership to another.

Still privately owned, the walled precinct contains a number of small cell-like peasant houses which have been well-restored as a hotel complex and notable restaurant run by the Guicciardini family. Tiny stone streets, a chapel dedicated to the saints Tiburzio and Susanna, a massive baronial tower, attractive gardens and a magnificent view down to the Chiana, all make Gargonza a very pleasant retreat.

English mercenary

BELOW: Cortona's Basilica of Santa Margherita (*see page 310*) contains the body of the mystic Santa Margherita.

Another castle, originally a *borgo* as well, and at one time not unlike Gargonza in character, is the **Castello di Montecchio Vesponi ㉑**, which crowns a peak above the main road from Castiglion Fiorentino to Cortona, just south of Arezzo.

The owners of this gargantuan, castellated building – which is seriously dilapidated in parts – won an award for the restoration of its 8th-century tower.

This castle was once the property of the English *condottiero* Sir John Hawkwood, who had been hired by Florence to capture Arezzo in 1384. Montecchio was his reward. Nowadays it is only occasionally open to the public, but you can always drive up to the walls and walk around the outside.

Map, page 302

From here you can see in the distance **Castiglion Fiorentino 22** with its medieval girdle of walls dominated by the Cassero fortress. In this village there is an unusually high number of churches, of which no less than five are worth a visit. The most important are **Pieve San Giuliana**, which contains Signorelli's *Deposition of Christ*, and **San Francesco**, which is part Romanesque and part Gothic, with a 17th-century cloister attached to one side.

Just outside the village is a fine octagonal church called Santa Maria della Consolazione. The Palazzo Comunale within the walls contains works which have been taken from all the surrounding churches – paintings, sculpture and goldsmiths work – an unbelievable quantity of treasures for such a small place.

Southeast Arezzo

The southeastern part of the province of Arezzo contains three other interesting little towns: Foiano della Chiana, and Lucignano Marciano della Chiana.

Foiana 23 clings to the side of the hill and from afar it is a very picturesque little place. Much of it is 15th and 16th century, though traces of medieval defences can be seen around the edge of the town. The etymology of the town's name reveals a Roman origin, and just over 3 km (2 miles) to the northeast of the centre are the remains of what is believed to have been a Roman bathhouse, at Cisternella.

South of Monte San Savino, **Lucignano 24** was originally an Etruscan stronghold, though today its overriding characteristic is a very peculiar medieval town plan which arranged the streets concentrically around a castle that was rebuilt in the 15th century.

With only a few exceptions the town's buildings, predominantly 13th- to 18th-century, are perfectly preserved, as is its Gothic church of San Francesco. In the 14th-century **Palazzo Comunale** (open Tues–Sun; closed 12.30–3pm; entrance fee) are frescoes from the Sienese and Aretine schools as well as some examples of finely worked gold ornaments for which the province of Arezzo has long been famous.

Marciano 25, a tiny village of great character, was also fortified in the Middle Ages and most of these fortifications still survive unchanged. Much of the castle remains and so do the walls and a gateway with a clock tower built into it. Three km (2 miles) to the southeast is the octagonal chapel of San Vittorio, designed by Vasari in 1572 to mark the spot where the Florentines defeated the Sienese in 1554.

The most important town in the province of Arezzo is **Cortona 26**. It sits at a height of 650 metres (2,130 ft) above the Val di Chiana, perched on a ridge on the side of Monte Sant'Egidio. Cortona is really a massive fortress, which is accessible only via a dizzy road of hairpin bends and loops.

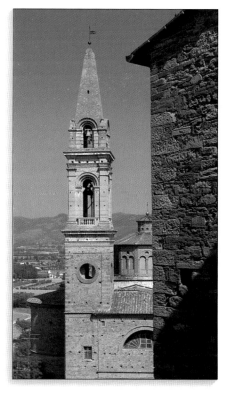

BELOW: Castiglion Fiorentino.

Map, page 302

ABOVE: Cortona bell-tower.
RIGHT: Tuscan villa.
BELOW: long, late afternoon shadows along a tree-lined Tuscan road.

The town is so high that it is perceptibly cooler here than in the plain below. Although the town is characteristically medieval, it was at one time a fortress belonging to the Umbrian tribe, predating even the Etruscans, whose considerable relics are scattered around the Porta Colonia at the end of Via Dardano.

The Romans colonised it, the Aretines sacked it in 1258 and in 1409 it was sold to the Florentines, which linked it from then onwards to the fortunes of the Grand Duchy of Tuscany.

The road from the plain to the city winds up through terraced olive groves scattered about with villas and farms surrounded by ilexes and cypresses, monasteries and churches. The first church on the way is the domed **Santa Maria della Grazia**, on the slopes beneath the town.

Beyond it is the **Porta Sant' Agostino** from which Via Guelfa leads to the Piazza Repubblica at the heart of the town. Here the 13th-century Palazzo Comunale adjoins the Palazzo Pretorio, a 13th-century mansion rebuilt in the 17th century, facing the **Piazza Signorelli**, on which is the rewarding **Museo dell'Accademia Etrusca** (open Tues–Sun; closed 1–4pm; entrance fee), containing a number of major Etruscan artifacts and medieval paintings.

But it is the **Museo Diocesano** (open Tues–Sun; closed 1–3pm; entrance fee) in the Piazza Duomo that houses the greatest masterpieces – Fra Angelico's *Annunciation*, a Duccio *Madonna*, a Lorenzetti *Crucifix* and Luca Signorelli's *Deposition.*

Signorelli was born in Cortona, and the **Chiesa di San Niccolò** in a tiny courtyard below the Medici fortress appropriately houses his standard of *The Deposition.* The **Church of San Francesco** contains the body of St Francis of Assisi's follower and disciple, Brother Elia Coppi of Cortona who, after the death of St Francis, was responsible for sweeping away the ideal of poverty, and bringing the Franciscan Order into line with the materialistic world.

Pilgrimages

The **Basilica of Santa Margherita**, which towers over Cortona from above, contains the near perfectly preserved body of the mystic Santa Margherita, who died in 1297. She was eventually received into the Third Order of St Francis. The local citizens still make pilgrimages up the winding stone-flagged streets of the town to her tomb to pray during hard times.

Cortona's narrow streets turn into steep flights of shallow steps down which it is easy, although not desirable, to drive a small car. The overhanging houses of the Via del Gesù are quaint, even rustic, while scattered around are a number of especially fine medieval palaces: the 18th-century **Palazzo Ferreti** in the Via Nazionale, and Brunelleschi's **Palazzo Lovari** and **Palazzo Mancini** in the Via Guelfa.

In some ways, the province of Arezzo neatly epitomises the region of Tuscany itself: full of contrasts – hills and valleys; traditional and modern ways of life; quiet, peaceful villages and bustling, noisy cities. Like all of Tuscany, it too has its artistic and architectural treasures and a proud populace to look after them for generations of Tuscans – and appreciative visitors – to come. ❏

INSIGHT GUIDES

Travel Tips

Simply travelling safely

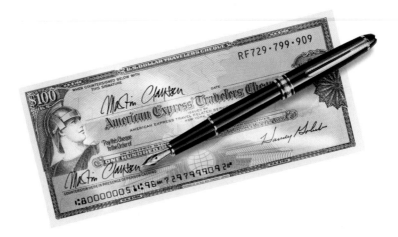

American Express Travellers Cheques

- are recognised as one of the safest and most convenient ways to protect your money when travelling abroad

- are more widely accepted than any other travellers cheque brand

- are available in eleven currencies

- are supported by a 24 hour worldwide refund service and

- a 24 hour Express Helpline service provides assistance and information when travelling abroad

- are accepted in millions of shops, hotels and restaurants throughout the world

Travellers Cheques

CONTENTS

Getting Acquainted

The Place

Situation Approximately 43°N, 11°E, on the same latitude as Boston, Massachusetts, and Vladivostok, Russia.

Population The population of Tuscany is approximately 3.5 million, out of a total population of 58 million in Italy. None of the cities is populous: 450,000 live in Florence, 176,000 in Livorno.

Area Tuscany (Toscana) roughly covers the area of northwestern Italy known as Etruria in ancient times, lying between the Apennine mountains and the Ligurian and Tyrrhenian seas. Much of its 22,992 sq. km (8,876 sq. miles) is mountainous, drained by the Arno and the Ombrone rivers. The Arno, the principal river, flows through the region's capital, Florence, located 80 km (50 miles) from the sea. Livorno is the main port. Tuscany also includes several islands, the largest of which is Elba (868 sq. km/225 sq. miles).

Religion The state religion is Roman Catholicism, and even the smallest village has its own church. Other denominations also hold services.

Language Italian.

Time Zone Central European Time (GMT plus 1 hour).

Currency Lira.

Weights & Measures Metric.

Electricity 220 volts. You will need an adaptor to operate British three-pin appliances and a transformer to use 100–120 volt appliances.

International Dialling Code 00 39.

Climate

The Tuscan climate is pleasantly mild in the spring and autumn, cool and wet in the winter, and very hot near the sea and on low-lying land in the summer, with a pleasant warmth in the hills. There is very little wind except for on the Tyrrhenian coastline around Marina di Pisa and Tirrenia, but surprise storms can be very heavy at any time of the year, and flooding in a number of places has caused severe damage in the past. The rainfall in Tuscany is generally higher than in most other parts of Italy. The temperature is slightly lower than in other areas, making it more agreeable in summer though somewhat colder in winter.

The weather in Florence can be extreme. The city is built in a bowl, surrounded by hills, with the Arno cutting through it, and this accounts for the high degree of humidity that is often a feature of mid-summer. The worst of the humidity is likely to occur between mid-July and mid-August with temperatures climbing well into the 90s Fahrenheit (30s Celsius). Dampness is a characteristic of winter weather, and it can get very cold.

Government

Italy is a republic headed by a president who holds office for seven years. There are two houses of Parliament, the Chamber of Deputies, and the Senate. Power is distributed among 20 regions of which Tuscany is one. Tuscany itself is divided into 10 provinces: Florence, Pistoia, Prato, Lucca, Massa-Carrara, Pisa, Livorno, Grosseto, Siena and Arezzo. The regional capital is Florence.

The Economy

The landscape of Tuscany is widely considered to be gently agricultural, but there are also rugged mountains in the north which encompass the marble quarries of the Apuan Alps, the valleys of the Garfagnana and the ski resorts of the Apennines. To the south are the flat alluvial plains of Grosseto as well as metal mining and power stations. Agriculture, however, remains the mainstay of the economy with the region's wine and olive oil world-famous. Tourism also plays a vital part in the local economy as visitors flock to an unrivalled centre of art and architecture.

Culture & Customs

Italy is the world's fifth economic power on the basis of purchasing power but a report on social trends notes that, since Italy became prosperous, manners and morals have been changing for the worse. Still, Tuscans are generally friendly and will appreciate efforts to speak the language. An attempt to rush or pressure them, however, will be regarded as the

Public Holidays

- **1 January** – *Capodanno* (New Year's Day)
- 6 January – *La Befana* (Epiphany).
- **Easter** – *Pasqua*.
- **Easter Monday** – *Pasquetta*.
- **25 April** – *Anniversario della Liberazione* (Liberation Day).
- **1 May** – *Festa del Lavoro* (Labour Day).
- **24 June** – *San Giovanni* (St John the Baptist) – in Florence only.
- **15 August** – *Ferragosto* (Assumption of the Blessed Virgin Mary).
- **1 November** – *Ognissanti* (All Saints' Day).
- **8 December** – *Immacolata Concezione* (Immaculate Conception).
- **25 December** – *Natale* (Christmas Day).
- **26 December** – *Santo Stefano* (Boxing Day).

height of bad taste, and whatever you want will take longer. Almost everything is done on the basis of personal favours or contacts so any personal recommendations you can muster will always come in useful.

Business Hours

Shops in the main cities open Monday–Friday 8.30am–1pm and 3.30–7.30pm. Some open on Saturday, but all are closed on Sunday. Some shops in coastal resorts and tourist centres now stay open all day in summer and have limited Saturday and Sunday opening. Food shops are closed on Wednesday afternoons in winter and Saturday afternoons in summer. Clothes shops are closed on Monday mornings.

On Italian national holidays, all shops, offices and schools are closed. Some cities celebrate their own saint's day, but shops and offices usually stay open.

Planning the Trip

Visas & Passports

Subjects from European Union countries require either a passport or a Visitor's Identification Card to enter Italy. A visa is not required.

Holders of passports from most other countries do not require visas for stays of less than three months, except for nationals of Eastern European countries, who need to obtain visas from the Italian Embassy in their own country.

Police Registration

A person may stay in Italy for three months as a tourist, but police registration is required within three days of entering Italy. If staying at a hotel, the management will attend to the formality. Although this regulation seems to be rarely observed, it is advisable that you carry a set of passport photos in case you need them for registration.

You are legally obliged to carry a form of identification (passport, driving licence, etc.) with you at all times. This rule is often flouted but bear in mind that it would be unwise to call the police or attempt to report a problem (e.g. theft) unless you are carrying appropriate identification.

Customs Regulations

Examination of luggage, passports, currency and hand baggage takes place on both entering and leaving Italy at

Animal Quarantine

Two certificates have to be produced for dogs and cats accompanying travellers: **(1)** a bilingual (English/Italian) Certificate of Health from a Veterinary Inspector of the Ministry of Agriculture, Fisheries and Food stating that the animal is free of any clinical signs of disease, and, **(2)** a certificate to show the animal had been vaccinated against rabies not less than 20 days, and not more than 11 months, prior to the date of issue of the health certificate.

airports, ports and frontiers. Formalities are also carried on trains. Registered luggage may be sent to towns with Customs Offices: examination takes place at the destination.

The following may be imported duty-free for personal use: clothing, books, camping equipment, fishing tackle, two cameras with 10 rolls of film each or 24 plates, one cine-camera with 10 rolls of film (film is expensive in Italy), one canoe or similar boat less than 5.5 metres in length, and sports equipment (skis, rackets, etc.). One portable typewriter, one record-player with a reasonable number of records, one pram, one musical instrument, one tape recorder with a portable radio and portable television set (subject to a licence fee to be paid at the Customs), and personal jewellery (it is advisable to have jewels listed and kept with the passport to avoid problems on exit).

Items other than those listed above can be imported duty-free on condition that the owner can prove that they are essential for his/her profession or trade (medical equipment, art material, samples, etc.). All items listed must be for personal use only and must neither be sold or traded.

Professional photographers must carry an ATA Carnet (issued in the UK through the London Chamber of Commerce, 33 Queen Street, London EC4R 1BX, tel: 0171-248 4444) for temporary importation of equipment.

Health

With form E111 from the Department of Health (available from main UK post offices), UK visitors are entitled to reciprocal medical treatment in Italy. There are similar arrangements for citizens of other European Union countries. As few Italians have faith in their own state health service, it may be advisable to take out insurance for private treatment in case of accident.

Holiday insurance policies and private patients schemes give full cover during your stay abroad and are recommended for non-EU visitors.

In high summer, the weather can be very hot; sunscreen, shady hats and mosquito repellent are recommended.

See *Medical Services* for emergency telephone and contact numbers.

Money Matters

The monetary unit is the Italian *lira* (plural *lire*), abbreviated to Lit. (or L.). Notes are issued for 1,000, 2,000, 5,000, 10,000, 50,000, 100,000 and 500,000 lire. Coins are in denominations of 50, 100, 200, 500 and 1,000 lire; 5, 10 and 20 lire coins, as well as *gettoni* – telephone tokens – are now obsolete.

Foreign currency up to the value of 1 million lire may be taken out of the country. To export more than this amount, a declaration form V2 must be obtained from the Customs police when entering Italy, stating the quantity of foreign currency brought in.

Traveller's Cheques

The use of dollar or sterling traveller's cheques is advised and all major companies' cheques are accepted, including Eurocheques, a popular option. Traveller's cheques are gradually being replaced by credit cards. Both can be used to obtain cash in any commercial bank and in exchange for goods and services in shops and hotels.

Credit Cards

Most credit cards, including Visa, American Express and Mastercard are accepted in hotels, restaurants and shops, for air and train tickets and for cash in any bank. The American Express office in Florence is at Via Dante Alighieri 22r, tel: 055-50981.

Exchange Rates

Exchange rates are displayed outside banks and exchange offices. They are also printed in daily newspapers. It is customary to get more lire for other currencies in the summer months, but the rate fluctuates according to world markets. There is one rate to buy lire and one to sell. £1 is very roughly equivalent to about L.2,900; $1 is approximately equivalent to about L.1,750.

Banks

Working hours are 8.30am–1.30pm and at varied times between 2.30–4.30pm. Banks are closed Saturday and Sunday. The following are the main branches in Tuscany's major cities.

Florence
Banca Commerciale Italiana, Via Tornabuoni 16.
Banca d'America e d'Italia, Via Strozzi 16.
Banca d'Italia, Via dell'Oriuolo 37/39.
Credito Italiano, Via Vecchietti 11.

Cassa di Risparmio, Via Bufalini 6.

Siena
Banca Nazionale dell'Agricoltura, Via Banchi di Sopra 56–58.
Banca Nazionale del Lavoro, Via Vittorio Veneto 43.
Banca di Roma, Via Banchi di Sotto.
Cassa di Risparmio di Firenze, Piazza Tolomei.

Exchange Offices

Exchange offices are allowed to change only from foreign currency into Italian lire. These are some main outlets.

Florence
Change Underground, Piazza Stazione 14, Int. 37 (under the station).
Frama, Via Calzaiuoli 79r. Charges a hefty commission.
Post Office, Via Pellicceria 3 (1st floor). Open 8.15am–1.30pm Monday–Friday, 8.15am–12.30pm Saturday.

Siena
Viaggi Seti (Piazza del Campo 56) – changes notes and traveller's cheques.
Coop "Siena Hotels Promotion" (Piazza San Domenico) – changes notes, traveller's cheques and Eurocheques.
Biglietteria Stazione Ferroviaria (railway station ticket office, Piazza Rosselli) – open daily 7am–8.30pm, including holidays. Changes notes and traveller's cheques.

What To Bring

Towns like Florence, Lucca and Siena are sophisticated, so take something smart for shopping or dining out, although jackets and ties are rarely required for men. It can rain unexpectedly wherever you are, so a raincoat is an essential piece of clothing; it should be large enough to cover anything worn, and light enough to be folded and carried.

Planespotting

Get a passport ✈ get some cheap tickets ✈ get a plane ✈ get some sun ✈ get a tan
get some friends ✈ get another plane ✈ get some laughs ✈ get some great photos
get another plane ✈ get some memories ✈ get some weird clothes ✈ get to the clubs
get another plane ✈ get some more sun ✈ get some strange food ✈ get another plane
get some adventure ✈ get some thrills ✈ get to the sea ✈ get another plane
get to the cities ✈ get to the action ✈ get away ✈ get Young Europe Special ✈ get a life!

Young Europe Special –

 tickets are sold in packages of four to ten.

See Europe from only £49 for the first flight coupon! This price *includes* UK airport departure tax but not any other security charges/airport taxes applicable to your selected European destinations.

Get a free info pack by:

Filling in the coupon below and sending it to us FREEPOST.

Calling us on 0800 214 493.

Finding us on the Internet at:

http://www.lufthansa.co.uk

What are *YOU* doing this year?

⊘ **Lufthansa**   **BM British Midland**   **SAS**

YES is available to UK and Ireland residents aged 12-26 or full-time students under 31 and can be booked via your local USIT, Campus Travel or STA Travel office.

Insight Guides portray destinations in depth, providing the complete picture and the top photography

Insight Pocket Guides focus on the best choices for places to see and things to do and include large fold-out maps

Insight Compact Guides' portability makes them the perfect books to carry with you for on-the-spot reference

Three types of guide for all types of travel

INSIGHT GUIDES Different people need different kinds of information. Some want *background information* to help them prepare for the trip. Others seek *personal recommendations* from someone who knows the destination well. And others look for *compactly presented data* for on-the-spot reference. With three carefully designed series, Insight Guides offer readers the perfect choice. Insight Guides will turn your visit into an experience.

The world's largest collection of visual travel guides

Decent dress is required when visiting religious buildings: men and women are expected to have their arms covered, and shorts are frowned upon. Women often carry a headscarf as a simple head covering. Sun hats are also recommended as protection.

Shoes need to be sturdy but comfortable and suitable for walking – especially on cobbled streets and for climbing steps.

Binoculars are a good idea for nature studies and viewing architectural details.

Maps
Touring Club Italiano does a good fold-out map of the Tuscany region showing major and minor roads. The Siena and Florence tourist offices supply reasonable city maps.

Getting There

By Air
Tuscany is fairly well off for airports. Apart from the airport at Pisa, a short train journey from Florence, there is also the international airport of Peretola (also known as Amerigo Vespucci), which serves Florence. Flights to Peretola tend to be more expensive than flights to Pisa. Pisa handles a number of charter companies, in addition to scheduled flights (e.g. Alitalia, Air France and British Airways), while Peretola serves mainly business travellers.

Alitalia (AZ), British Airways (BA) and Ryan Air operate competitively priced flights between the UK and Pisa. In addition, a number of charter companies, notably Italy Sky Shuttle, run keenly priced flights to Pisa. Flights to Bologna and Rome are also worth considering (and are cheaper). These are reasonable options if your destination is on a direct train route from Rome/Bologna. Meridiana fly to Florence from London Gatwick and Barcelona. Sabena links Brussels and Florence Peretola.

Airlines

For further information about flights to Italy, telephone the following:
Italy's Sky Shuttle (London office), tel: 0181-748 1333/4999; fax 0181-748 6381.
Alitalia (Florence office), tel: 055-27888. (Pisa office), tel: 050-501570.
For information and bookings while in Italy, call toll free: 1478-65643.

Air France operates flights between Florence and Paris.

North America: As yet, there are no direct flights between North America and Tuscany, but, via London, Brussels or Amsterdam, you can get to Florence from almost anywhere now. TWA and Air Canada are among the North American carriers who operate flights to Milan and Rome. The excellent airport train linking Fiumicino Airport (Rome) with Rome railway station (Termini) and good train connections northwards to Florence mean that this is a perfectly acceptable option for visitors from the US.

Fares available on scheduled services are:
Normal fares: the most expensive but with no restrictions.
Eurobudget: return reservations may be left open.
Apex Fares: return only. Reservations are made and tickets are issued at the same time. The stay in Italy must include a Saturday night.
Superpex: the least expensive; return only. Reservations must be made at least 14 days prior to departure and tickets are issued at the same time. The stay in Italy must include at least one Saturday night. From North America, the restrictions include a minimum of one week's, and a maximum of 90 days', stay.

British Airways (Pisa office), tel: 050-501838. Alternatively, within Italy call toll free: 1478-812266.
Ryan Air, tel: 0541-569569 (within the UK).
TWA (Florence office), tel: 055-2396856.
Airport information, Florence Peretola (Amerigo Vespucci airport), tel: 055-373498.
Pisa (Galileo Galilei airport), tel: 050-500707.

By Rail
Tickets: Tickets for Italian trains are issued in the UK by Italian State Railways, CIT, Marco Polo House, 3–5 Lansdowne Road, Croydon, Surrey, tel: 0181-686 0677/5533. In the US, contact CIT, 666 Fifth Avenue, New York, NY 10103, tel: 800-223 0230. In Canada, contact CIT, 1450 City Counsellors, Suite 750, Montreal, Quebec H3A 2E6, tel: (514) 845 9101. These organisations will provide details of rail travel, including the availability of special tickets restricted to foreigners who purchase the ticket in their home country.

In addition to first and second class, there are some useful special tickets, including the **Inter Rail Ticket** (*Tessera Inter Rail*) for people under 26. It allows them unlimited travel for one month in 22 countries of Europe, with a reduction of 50 percent in Italy and 30 percent in the UK.

See the *Domestic Travel* (*By Rail*) section for more information on conditions and rail services.

By Road
Channel Crossing by Car: To cross the Channel to Italy, the most convenient and direct car ferries are from Dover to Calais, and Folkestone to Calais or Boulogne; you can also sail to Ostend from Dover. Other useful ferries include Newhaven–Dieppe

and Portsmouth–Le Havre or Caen. Poole–Cherbourg is another alternative. The Channel Tunnel transports cars on the Le Shuttle train service between Folkestone and Calais.

The AA or RAC will give up-to-date advice on Channel crossings, with or without a car.

By Coach

European Coach Service: Given the cheapness of charter flights to Tuscany, this is a less used option. A regular coach service is operated by National Express for a European journey from London (Victoria Coach Station, Buckingham Palace Road) via Dover – Paris – Mont Blanc – Aosta – Turin – Genoa – Milan – Bologna – Florence (Via Santa Caterina da Siena) to Rome. Details of bookings can be obtained from National Express, Victoria Coach Station, London, SW1, tel: 0990-808080.

Package Holidays

The Italian State Tourist Office, 1 Princes Street, London W1R 8AY, tel: 0171-408 1254, can supply free maps and brochures on a wide range of holidays and activities, and produces a useful booklet, *La Mia Italia*, with practical information on unusual travel itineraries.

Italiatour is Alitalia's package tour operator, offering holidays based on scheduled Alitalia flights from Heathrow to six Italian airports, including Pisa. For brochures and further information, write to 205 Holland Park Avenue, London W11 4XV, tel: 0171-605 7500. **Citalia** also offers holidays covering the whole of Italy, tel: 0181-686 0677. Package deals, especially weekend breaks, are reasonable.

Magic of Italy, 227 Shepherd's Bush Road, London W6 7AS, tel: 0181-748 7575, is an established company which runs good-quality package tours (with a great degree of independence).

Specialist Holidays

Language Courses

There are numerous language schools, mostly in Florence and Siena. The reputable ones are run by Siena and Florence universities or are organised by long-established centres, such as the British Institute. These are some worth trying:

Centro di Cultura per Stranieri dell'Università di Firenze, Via Vittorio Emanuele II 64, 50134 Florence, tel: 055-472139.
Koinè, Via Pandolfini 27, Florence, tel: 055-213881.
Leonardo da Vinci, Via Brunelleschi 4, Florence, tel: 055-294420.
Machiavelli, Piazza Santo Spirito 4, Firenze, tel: 055-2396966

As the "purest Italian language" is spoken in Siena, the **Italian Language and Culture School for Foreigners** (*Università per Stranieri*), Piazzetta Grassi 2, Siena 53100, tel: 0577-49260, runs courses for foreigners and Italians who are permanent residents abroad. It is a recognised Institute of Higher Education for Language and Culture, awarding a diploma to successful students. Also in Siena is the **Centro Internazionale Dante Alighieri**, La Lizza 10, 53100 Siena, tel: 0577-46421.

Art Tours

Prospect Art Tours, 454–458 Chiswick High Road, London W4 5TT, tel: 0181-995 2151, is a specialised upmarket company which runs sophisticated art tours to Tuscany.

Art Courses

At the **Università Internazionale dell'Arte**, Villa Il Ventaglio, Via delle Forbici 24/26, 50133 Florence, tel: 055-570216, various art appreciation courses are held, which include specialisation in museum collections, conservation and restoration, design and graphic design.

Istituto d'Arte di Firenze, Via dell'Alloro 14r, tel: 055-283142, offers courses in drawing, design, photography, painting, watercolours, sculpture, restoration, ceramics and jewellery-making.
British Institute, Piazza Strozzi 2, tel: 055-284031, conducts art and language courses. This is the centre with the best reputation for such courses in Florence. It also has an excellent English and Italian library at Palazzo Lanfredini, Lungarno Guicciardini 9, tel: 055-284032, to which one can have temporary membership (one section was donated in 1994 by the late Harold Acton).
Istituto per l'Arte e Restauro, Palazzo Spinelli, Borgo Santa Croce 10, tel: 055-246001. This art restoration school has a reputation for being the best in Italy and offers restoration courses in Italian.

Fashion Institutes

Centro Moda, Via Faenza 109, tel: 055-219331/2/3.
Polimoda, Via Pisana 71, tel: 055-717173.

Music

The **Accademia Musicale Chigiana** (Chigiana Academy of Music), Via di Città 89, 53100 Siena, tel: 0577-46152, provides proficiency courses (based on the classical repertoire) in July and August for young performers.

A theoretical and practical course on jazz music is held annually at the **Seminari Nazionali Senesi**, Via Vallerozzi 77, 53100 Siena, tel: 0577-47552. This training centre is one of the best-known for jazz in Europe.

Ceramic Workshops

In Sorano, an ancient medieval village in the Maremma, pottery courses of one or two weeks' duration are held between June and September and during the Easter and Christmas holidays. Various techniques, including majolica firing, bucchero firing (ancient Etruscan technique), reduction and wood firing are taught. Full information from: **Studio Pandora**, Andrea Sola, Via della Fortezza 13, 58010 Sorano (GR), tel: 041-5205116.

Cookery Courses

Scuola di Arte Culinaria "Cordon Bleu", Via di Mezzo 55r (near the Cathedral), Florence, tel: 055-2345468. Also contact Badia a Coltibuono, tel: 0577-749424. Italian cookery classes, noon–3pm for three consecutive days, are given by an Italian cook with an interpreter. Lessons can be held in both English and German on request. For further information contact the Italian Institute in London, tel: 0171-235 1461.

Green Tourism

Tuscany is a perfect destination for holidays involving hiking, cycling or some other outdoor activity. See the *Wild Tuscany* essay on pages 85–9 and the *Outdoor Activities* in the Travel tips section starting on page 350 for more information on the best areas and other details.

In recent years, a number of specialist tour operators have started offering cycling and hiking tours of Tuscany. Some include a house party element, attempting to combine people of similar backgrounds and tastes. Others mix the outdoor side with more leisurely pursuits, such as painting, cookery or history of art courses (suitable for those with less energetic partners!). The tours range greatly in terms of accommodation (from classic villas to simple farms). Nonetheless, the quality (and price) is usually well above that offered by a two-star hotel.

These holidays tend to be all-inclusive, except for optional excursions. Some packages involve staying in different accommodation along the route; in this case, the company generally transports your luggage for you from hotel to hotel.

A fairly expensive but highly recommended UK company which arranges walks and other outdoor tours in Tuscany is **The Alternative Travel Group Limited**, 69–71 Banbury Road, Oxford OX2 6PE, tel: 01865-315678; fax: 01865-315697. Its walking holidays are designed for anyone – not just serious walkers – and all transport and hotel accommodation is arranged.

You should also contact such companies as **Cycling for Softies** and **Explore**. For a full list of reputable companies specialising in adventure, nature, walking and cycling tours, contact your national ENIT (Italian Tourist Board) office. The Italian Alpine Club (CAI), the principal walking organisation in Italy, is also worth contacting *(see listing on page 350)*.

Useful Addresses

(see listing on page 350)

UNITED KINGDOM

Accademia Italiana: 24 Rutland Gate, London SW7 1BB, tel: 0171-225 3474. Italian art exhibitions, events, bookshop and restaurant.
Italian Embassy: 14 Three Kings Yard, London W1Y 2EH, tel: 0171-312 2200. General enquiries, Commercial Office and residence.
Italian Consulate: 38 Eaton Place, London SWIX 8AN, tel: 0171-235 9371.
Italian Institute: 39 Belgrave Square, London SWIX 8NT, tel: 0171-235 1461. Advice on culture, events, language and art courses in London and Italy.
Italian Trade Centre (ICE): 37 Sackville Street, London W1X 2DQ, tel: 0171-734 2412.

Italian Chamber of Commerce: Rooms 418–427 Walmar House, 296 Regent Street, London W1R 5HS. Tel: 0171-637 3153.
Italian State Railways (CIT): Marco Polo House, 3–5 Lansdowne Road, Croydon, Surrey, Tel: 0181-686 0677.
Italian State Tourist Office (ENIT): 1 Princes Street, London W1R 8AY. Tel: 0171-408 1254.
Alitalia (Italian Airlines): 27 Piccadilly, London W1, tel: 0181-745 8200; Heathrow Airport, Tel: 0181-745 8400: arrivals. Tel: 01426-914139, departures information.
Italian Sky Shuttle (flights): 227 Shepherd's Bush Road, London W6 7AS. Tel: 0181-748 1333.

NORTH AMERICA

Italian State Tourist Office: Store 56, Plaza 3, Place Ville Marie, Montreal, Quebec, Canada. Tel: (514) 866-7667.
Italian State Tourist Office: 630 Fifth Avenue, Suite 1565, New York, NY 10111. Tel: (212) 245-4822.
Italian State Tourist Office: 360 Post Street, Suite 801, San Francisco, California, CA 94108. Tel: (415) 392-6206.
Italian State Tourist Office: 500 N. Michigan Avenue, Chicago, Illinois, IL 60611. Tel: (312) 644-0990.

Practical Tips

Media

Italy Each large Italian town has its own newspaper. *La Stampa*, *Il Corriere della Sera*, and *La Repubblica* also have a national following. *La Nazione* is the paper favoured by most Tuscans for regional matters.

Television is deregulated in Italy. In addition to the state network, RAI (which offers three channels), there are about 1,000 channels of which the main ones are Canale 5, Rete 4, Italia 1, Telemontecarlo and Video Music. There are about 500 radio stations, including many regional ones.

There are several useful publications for visitors to Tuscany:
● *Events*, a monthly listings magazine in English and Italian.
● *Firenze Spettacolo*, a monthly listings magazine in Italian (with some listings also in English), focusing on nightlife, clubs, bars and the live arts in Florence.
● *Toscana Qui*, a serious but informative magazine (published every two months in Italian), covering such topical issues as restoration work, the arts scene and Tuscan environmental issues.
● *Firenze ieri, oggi, domani*, a monthly magazine in Italian for cultural/topical issues.

Postal Services

Main post offices in major towns are open all day, otherwise the hours are 8am–1.30pm (12.30pm Saturday). Stamps are sold at post offices and tobacconist's shops (*tabacchi*). There are post-boxes in most main streets, at post offices and at railway stations.

CAI post is a service for sending important documents worldwide in 24/48 hours. This service is only available at major post offices. In Florence these are at Via Pellicceria 3 (main post office) and Via Alamanni 20r (by the station).

Poste Restante

Correspondence addressed c/o Post Office with FERMO POSTA added to the name of the locality will be held for collection. Letters are held at the local Central Post Office and will be handed over from the Fermo Posta counter on proof of identification – usually a passport – and a fee.

Telecommunications

Italy has plenty of public telephones and almost every bar has a public phone, but not all can be used for long-distance calls. The phone kiosks at railway stations take coins and cards. The minimum amount of money needed for a call is L.200.

Telephone cards (*schede*) can be purchased from a machine or at PTP (*Posto Telefonico Pubblico*) offices. They are available for the sums of L.5,000, L.10,000 and L.15,000 and are increasingly taking over from other methods of payment for public telephone calls. Indeed, many telephone boxes now take only cards, so you would be wise to always carry one with you. Telephone cards can be bought from *tabacchi* or newspaper kiosks.

In bars and telephone centres at bus and railway stations, payment is often by *scatti* (units) – you talk first and pay later.

There is direct dialling to most countries in the world from Italy. To call the UK, dial 00 44 then the area code number, dropping the initial zero.

To make calls within Italy, first use the three- or four-number city codes (including the initial zero), even if you are calling locally. When calling Italy from outside the country, you should retain the initial zero of the local city code – a new rule introduced in the summer of 1998.

Directories are easy to understand and give comprehensive information. Alternatively, from a private telephone, you can dial 12 for Information.

Telegrams, Telexes and Faxes
Most large hotels offer all three services. Telegrams and telexes may be sent from any TELECOM office, post office or railway station. Only main offices and stations have fax facilities.

INTALCABLE provides international telegram services. Both internal and overseas telegrams may be dictated over the phone.

Photocopying machines can be found at main rail stations in cities like Florence and Pisa.

Tourist Offices

General tourist information is available at the Azienda di Promozione Turistica (APT), the main tourist office in each provincial capital. In addition, there is a tourist office (*Ufficio di Turismo*) in most towns. In small places, the *Comune* holds tourist information and some commercial banks and travel agencies publish tourist guides. The Touring Club Italiano (TCI), with offices in almost every town, provides free information about the area.

Arezzo Province
Arezzo: Piazza della Repubblica 28, 52100, tel: 0575-377678.
Cortona: Via Nazionale 70, tel: 0575-630352.
Florence Province
Florence: Via Cavour 1r, 50129, tel: 055-290832; & Borgo Santa Croce 29r, tel: 055-2340444.
Fiesole: Piazza Mino 36, 50014, tel: 055-598720.

Grosseto Province

Grosseto: Via Monterosa 206, 58100, tel: 0564-454510.

Livorno Province

Livorno: Piazza Cavour 6, 57100, tel: 0586-898111. There is also the Harbour Information Office, Porto di Livorno, tel: 0586-895320, open 15 June–15 September.

Elba: Calata Mazzini 26, 67037 Portoferraio, tel: 0565-914671.

Lucca Province

Lucca: Vecchia Porta San Donato, Piazzale Verdi, 55100, tel: 0583-419689.

Bagni di Lucca: Via Umberto 1, tel: 0583-87946.

Versilia: Viale Carducci 10, 55049 Viareggio, tel: 0584-869015.

Massa-Carrara Province

Marina di Massa: Lungomare Vespucci 23, 54037, tel: 0585-240046.

Carrara: Piazza 2 Giugno 14, 54033, tel: 0585-70894.

Marina di Carrara: Piazza G. Marconi 6/b, 54036, tel: 0585-632218.

Pisa Province

Pisa: Piazza della Stazione, tel: 050-42291.

Volterra: Piazza dei Priori, tel: 0588-86150.

Pistoia Province

Pistoia: Piazza Duomo 1, 51100, tel: 0573-21622.

San Marcello Pistoiese: Via Marconi 28, 50128 tel: 0573-630145.

Prato Province

Prato: Via Cairoli 48, 50047, tel: 0574-24112.

Siena Province

Siena: Piazza del Campo 56, 53100, tel: 0577-280551; fax: 0577-270676.

Women Travellers

The difficulties encountered by women travelling in Italy are sometimes overstated. However, women do, especially if they are young and blonde, often have to put up with much male attention. Ignoring whistles and questions is the best way to get rid of unwanted attention. The less you look like a tourist, the fewer problems you are likely to have.

Embassies

Australia: Via Alessandria 215, Rome.
Tel: 06-852721.

Germany: Borgo SS Apostoli 22, Florence.
Tel: 055-294722.

Netherlands: Via Cavour 81, Florence.
Tel: 055-475249.

UK: Palazzo Castelbarco, Lungarno Corsini 2, Florence.
Tel: 055-284133; fax: 055-219112.

US: Lungarno Amerigo Vespucci 38, Florence.
Tel: 055-2398276.

Doing Business

Business transactions are unfortunately long-winded and bureaucratic. The *Comune* (City Council) normally monitors anything requiring legislation; most paperwork is processed by a lawyer and is issued in triplicate, complete with official stamps (everything must be authorised). Note: Most public sector offices are open only in the mornings. To conduct any sort of business, make the first approach in writing a long time ahead. If possible, acquire credentials and contacts who can act as referees (the so-called *raccommandata* is all-powerful).

Be prepared to wait in endless queues, sign several documents and receipts, and lose much time. Even sending a parcel or withdrawing cash on a credit card is a lengthy process. Use a "hole-in-the-wall" instead (which you may find out of order).

In business transactions, be prepared for unorthodox methods of negotiation or settlement: payment may be required in goods or in foreign currency. If you can get someone else to take on the transaction for you, do so, it is worth every extra lira!

Business travellers should also try to buy a copy of *Italy* (Cassell Business Companions), which is an invaluable guide to the language and business of operating in Italy.

Travellers With Disabilities

Despite difficult cobbled streets and poor wheelchair access to many tourist attractions and hotels, many people with disabilities visit Florence and Tuscany every year.

However, unaccompanied visitors will usually experience some difficulty, so it is best to travel with a companion.

Conditions and disability awareness are improving slowly in Tuscany (as well as in Italy in general), although the situation is certainly not ideal, and access is not always easy. More museums now have lifts, ramps and adapted toilets, newer trains are accessible (although wheelchair users may need help when boarding), and recent laws require restaurants, bars and hotels to provide the relevant facilities. These laws, however, do not always cover access to those facilities. This sometimes results in the absurdity of a new wheelchair accessible room being located on the fourth or fifth floor of a hotel with a lift that is too narrow to admit a wheelchair.

For drivers with disabilities, there are plenty of reserved parking places in towns, and these are free.

In the United Kingdom, you can obtain further information from RADAR, 25 Mortimer Street, London W1M 8AB, tel: 0171-250 3222. In the United States, contact SATH, 347 5th Avenue, Suite 610, NY 10016, tel: (212) 447-7284.

Tipping

Below are some general guide-lines for tipping in Italy:

• L.100 for coffee or other drinks at an ordinary bar, L.500 for drinking at a table, and L.1,000 for consuming at a hotel bar.

• L.1,000 each for cloakroom attendants and ushers in a cinema or theatre .

• In hotels, tip doormen about L.500 for ordering you a taxi, chamber staff L.3,000–4,000 per week and the concierge L.1,000 or more, according to the help given and length of stay; other staff who carry luggage, provide room ser-vice, help with parking or clean-ing your car and so on. should get at least L.2,000.

• Hairdressers should receive L.3,000–5,000 depend-ing on the cutting, styling or treatment given.

• add about 10 percent to a taxi fare.

• In restaurants, the service charge of normally 15–20 per-cent is added automatically to the bill. (You may wish to note that according to Italian law, you should keep the bill with you until you are at least 100 metres (300 ft) from the restaurant.

Weights & Measures

The metric system is used for weights and measures.

To convert:	Multiply by:
Centimetres to inches	0.4
Metres to feet	3.3
Metres to yards	1.1
Kilometres to miles	0.6
Gallons to litres	4.5
Kilograms to pounds	2.2

• Italians refer to 100 grams as *un etto;* 200 grams are therefore *due etti.*

• Liquid measurements are in litres. One litre is 1.75 imper-ial pints.

• Temperatures are given in Celsius (Centigrade).

An extra tip is not necessary, although it is customary in city establishments to round up the amount on the bill, perhaps giving about five percent to the waiter or waitress (who will not necessarily benefit from the automatic service charge.

Medical Services

Chemist's Shops: The staff in chemist's shops (*farmacie*) are usually very knowledgeable about common illnesses and sell far more medicines without prescrip-tion than their colleagues in other Western countries (even so, most drugs still require a prescription).

Every *farmacia* has a list of the local pharmacies which are open at night and on Sundays. Chemist's shops which are open 24 hours (*farmacie aperte 24 ore su 24*) in Florence are:

Farmacia Comunale 13, in Florence station, tel: 055-289435/216761.

Farmacia Molteni, Via Calza-iuoli 7r, Florence, tel: 055-289490/215472.

Farmacia all'Insegna del Moro, Piazza San Giovanni 20r, tel: 055-211343.

In addition, you can call 182 to find out which chemists are on the night rota.

First Aid Service (*Pronto Soccorso*) with a doctor is found at airports, railway stations and in all hospitals.You can also try the following addresses in the main cities:

Emergency Numbers

Fire Brigade: 115.
Medical Aid/Ambulance: 118.
Police Immediate Action: 112.
General Emergency Fire, Police or Ambulance (replies are in foreigh languages in the main cities): 113.
Automobile Club d'Italia (ACI)
• 24-hour car breakdown: 116.
• 24-hour information line in English: 06-4477.

USEFUL FLORENCE CONTACTS
Heart Emergency Mobile Coronary Unit: 055-214444.
Night-time and Holiday Ambulances (*Misericordia*) Piazza Duomo 2: 055-212222.

Tourist Medical Service 24-hour home visits, with English-or French-speaking doctors: Via Lorenzo Il Magnifico 59, tel 055-475411.
Lost Property: 055-3283942.
Automobile Club d'Italia (ACI): 055-24861.
Towing Away if your car is towed away, call 055-308249.
Police Headquarters the place to visit in the event of thefts, lost passports, etc.: Via Zara 2, tel: 055-49771.
Radio Soccorso Misericordia, Piazza Duomo 20, Florence, tel: 055–212222, or dial 118 in an emergency.

Associazione Volontari Ospedalieri, Florence, tel: 055-2344567. This group of volun-teers will translate (free) for foreign patients.

USEFUL SIENA CONTACTS
Siena Hospital Nuovo Policlinico di Siena, Località le Scotte, Viale Bracci, tel: 0577-586111.
Pronto Soccorso (Misericor-dia), Via del Porrione 49, Siena, tel: 0577-280028, or dial 118 in an emergency.
Lost Property Via Casato di Sotto 23, tel: 0577-292426.

When you're

bitten by the travel bug,

make sure you're protected.

Check into a British Airways Travel Clinic.

British Airways Travel Clinics provide travellers with:
- A complete vaccination service and essential travel health-care items
- Up-dated travel health information and advice

Call **01276 685040** for details of your nearest Travel Clinic.

BRITISH AIRWAYS
TRAVEL CLINICS

*plus another
190 titles covering
almost every corner
of the world...*

The world's largest collection of visual travel guides

INSIGHT GUIDES You notice the photography first – stunning pictures which don't just illustrate the text but communicate directly life as it is lived by locals. But then you discover that the text is a joy to read, illuminating a destination's history and culture as well as evaluating places and activities. Next you find that Insight Guides are highly practical, with specially drawn maps and a carefully structured listings section. How's that for versatility?

Insight Guides turn a visit into an experience

Security & Crime

Petty crime is a recognised problem in Italy, particularly the snatching of handbags and jewellery in the street. Always carry valuables securely either in a money belt or handbag which can be worn strapped across the body. One popular scam is for bags to be snatched by thieves driving past on a moped or motorbike.

Cars are also vulnerable, so avoid leaving personal belongings in view and always lock the doors and boot. Car radios are a common target, so take your radio with you if you have one of the detatchable types; most Italians do – you often see local people going for their evening stroll with a radio tucked under their arm.

Make sure you report any thefts to the police, since you will need evidence of the crime to claim insurance.

Website Information

General Information:
http://www.enit.it
Museums:
http://www.enit.it/musei
Hotels:
hhtp://dbase.ipzs.it/enit/albergi/homealberghi.htm
Travel Agencies:
http://risc.ipzs.it/agtu
Events:
http://www.enit.it/avvenimenti
Virtual Magazine (Italy Tourism on line):
http://www.enit.it/rivista

Getting Around

On Arrival

Pisa Airport The international airport, Galileo Gallilei (tel: 050-500707) in Pisa has its own railway station. Trains take five minutes into Pisa Centrale and one hour for the 80 km (50 miles) to Florence. Bus No. 5 also links the airport with Pisa Centrale rail station. Car hire is available from the airport, and so are taxis. A new toll-free *superstrada* links Pisa airport with Florence.

Peretola (Amerigo Vespucci) International Airport (see *Getting There*) is situated in the northwestern suburb of Florence (tel: 055-373498) and is connected by bus to the SITA bus company depot not far from Santa Maria Novella rail station; the journey time is about 15 minutes.

By Air

ATI is the internal airline and offers routes between 26 Italian cities. If you make an outward journey on a Saturday and return on the following Sunday, there is a discount of some sort (the actual figure varies) on all Alitalia and ATI domestic services.

Infants under two years, accompanied by an adult, get a 90 percent discount on a full fare; children over two and under 12 receive 33 percent discount; and 12–21-year-olds enjoy a 10 percent discount on Apex fares.

By Rail

The state-subsidised railway network is a relatively cheap (although prices have increased substantially recently) and convenient form of transport for travelling between major cities in Tuscany. The principal Rome–Milan line is convenient for Bologna, Florence and Arezzo, while the Rome–Genoa line serves Pisa, Livorno and Grosseto. The Florence–Siena route is much faster by coach than by train.

Note that Pisa and Florence both have several train stations: **Pisa Centrale** station serves Pisa city while **Pisa Aeroporto** serves the airport. In Florence, **Santa Maria Novella** is the main station for the city, although the second station, **Rifredi**, is served by several *Eurostar* trains.

Categories of Trains

Eurostar: these swish, high-speed trains have replaced the *Pendolinos*. There are first- and second-class carriages, both with heavy supplements on top of the ordinary rail fare. It is obligatory to reserve a seat.
Eurocity: these trains link major Italian cities with other European cities – in Germany and Switzerland, for instance. A supplement is payable. A buffet car and refreshment trolleys are usually available.
Intercity: this fast service links major Italian cities. A supplement is payable and reservations are required. Buffet car.
Interregionali: these interregional trains link cities within different regions (e.g. Tuscany and Umbria) and stop reasonably frequently. Some have refreshment trolleys.
Regionali: these regional trains link towns within the same region (e.g. Tuscany) and stop at every station.

Tickets

Booking: Reservations are mandatory for superior trains (Eurostar, Eurocity and Intercity services) and tickets should be purchased in advance. Other tickets with compulsory supplements should be purchased at least three hours in advance. You now have to stamp (*convalidare*) your rail ticket before beginning the journey at one of the small machines at the head of the platforms. Failure to do so may result in a fine. If you board a train without a ticket, one can be bought from a conductor, with a penalty payment of 20 percent. You can also pay the conductor directly if you wish to upgrade to first class or a *couchette* (should there be places available).

Expect long queues for tickets at major stations, but, for a small fee, tickets can also be purchased from many travel agents. There are now automatic ticket machines at major stations, although they are often out of order. Payment can be made by cash or credit cards.

Wagons Lits/Carrozze Letto (sleeping cars) are found on long-distance trains within Italy, as well as on trains to countries like Austria, France, Germany, Spain and Switzerland. Reservations are essential.

There are a wide variety of train tickets and special offers available:

Chilometrico: this is the best-value of the long-standing Italian ticket deals, providing a discount of over 15 percent. Valid for two months, the ticket can be used by up to five people at the same time and allows 3,000 km (1,864 miles) of travel, spread over a maximum of 20 journeys. A first-class ticket costs L.338,000, while a second-class costs L.206,000.

Group fares: groups of between 6 and 24 people can benefit from a 20 percent discount. The group leader's ticket is free.

Youth fares: students between 12 and 26 can buy a yearly "green card" (*Carta Verde*) for L.40,000. This season ticket entitles them to a 20 percent discount.

Children's fares: children under four travel free; children aged between 4–12 are eligible for a 50 percent discount on all trains but must pay the full price of the supplement for Intercity and Eurocity trains.

Pensioners' fares: the over-60s can buy a *Carta d'Argento* for L.40,000. Valid for a year, this "silver card" entitles them to a 20 percent discount on all train tickets.

Booklets of tickets (*Carta Prima*): eight tickets valid for a two-month period for use by two people can be purchased. There are two types: one for journeys for up to 350 km (218 miles), and the other for longer journeys, with savings of up to 50 percent.

Train Information

For train information anywhere in Italy, tel: 478-88088 (daily 7am–9pm).

Railway Stations

The main railway stations are open 24 hours a day and are integrated with road and sea transport. They provide numerous services, including telecommunications, left luggage, food and drink, tourist information and porters (average charge L.3,000 per case; luggage trolleys are hard to find). Most large stations have *alberghi diurni* (day hotels) that provide restrooms, dressing rooms, baths, showers and hairdressers for the convenience of travellers.

Florence: The train information office at Santa Maria Novella station is at the end of tracks 9 and 10. The train reservation office and money exchange office are inside the main station hall. Both open daily from 7am–9pm. The left luggage counter is usually very busy. Each piece of luggage is left at your own risk, and badly packed or awkwardly shaped packages are likely to be damaged by the unco-operative staff (L.10,000 per day per bag).

There is an Air Terminal at Santa Maria Novella (near platform 5), where you can check in for Pisa airport (tel: 055-216073).

Siena: The railway station is the centre for most communications. There is an information office, telex, left luggage (and bicycles), photocopier and restaurant. Immediately outside the station is a bus ticket office and a tourist office. However, Siena's station is outside the town centre. More useful, and with faster services and a greater range of local destinations, is the coach service, with coaches leaving from Piazza San Domenico to Florence and various other Tuscan towns.

By Coach

Coaches are very comfortable and often quicker, though usually more expensive, than trains. Numerous sightseeing tours are offered in all the main cities, with morning tours usually running 9am–noon and afternoon tours 2.30–6.30pm. Details are available locally.

Addresses of bus/coach companies are:

ACIT, Piazza Sant'Antonio, Pisa, tel: 050-501038. (For travel in Pisa Province.)

LAZZI, Piazza Adua, Florence, tel: 055-351061, (for travel in Tuscany), and at Piazza V Emanuele II, Pisa, tel: 050-46288.

SITA, Via S. Caterina da Siena 15, Florence, tel: 055-483651 (for travel in Tuscany and other parts of Italy).

Water Transport

Sea transport from Italian ports has decreased in recent years, but occasionally passenger liners dock at Livorno and it is still a busy commercial port.

Yachts and small cruisers moor at Marina di Pisa, a few miles from Pisa.

Two car-ferry services operate regularly to the Island of Elba: **Narvarma**, Viale Elba 4, Portoferraio, tel: 0586-914133. **Toremar**, Via Calafati 6, Livorno, tel: 0586-22772.

Together they offer up to 20 services a day in high season (less other times) in each direction. The first departure in the morning from Piombino is 6.15am and the last back from Portoferraio is 6.50pm. Fares range from L.15,000–44,000.

In the summer, additional services run from Livorno and there are hydrofoil services from Piombino (Piombino–Cavo, 20 minutes; Piombino–Portoferraio, 40 minutes).

City Transport

Buses

Buses within each province are cheap and plentiful. Tickets can normally be purchased at designated offices, tobacconist shops, bars and newspaper stands. A set amount, varying between L.1,000–2,000, is payable for one journey, each province setting its own fare level. Tickets are purchased in booklets or singly, and have to be clipped by a machine on the bus at the start of a journey. Failure to do so risks a fine of 50 times the price of the ticket, payable either on the spot or within a month.

In **Florence**, a range of tickets is available from the ATAF office by Santa Maria Novella station): 60-minute ticket (L.1,500); multiple ticket (four singles – L.5,800); 3-hour ticket (L.2,500) and 24-hour ticket (L.6,000).

Rather confusingly for English-speakers, **Siena's** city/regional bus service is called TRA-IN.

All the times of buses within **Pisa** province are clearly displayed on a board in the APT office in the city's Piazza Garibaldi. Just outside Pisa Centrale Station, on the left, is a ticket window where bus tickets are sold.

All provincial bus services are routed past the railway station in every town.

Taxis

Taxis are plentiful in all towns and tourist resorts. They wait in special taxi-ranks at railway stations and main parts of the city but can always be called by telephone. If you call a taxi by phone, the cost of the journey begins then. (In Florence, tel: 4390 or 4798 for Radio Taxi.) Meters display the fares. The fixed starting charge varies (L.4,000–5,000).

There are extra charges for night service, Sunday and public holidays, luggage and journeys outside the town area.

In Florence, there are taxi ranks in Via Pellicceria, Piazza di San Marco and Piazza Santa Trinità.

Cycling

Bicycles can be hired in the main cities and cost around L.20,000 per day. You may be asked to leave an identity card or passport. Choose one with good brakes and a stand. Mopeds cost around L.50,000 per day.

Below is a list of possible outlets for bike hire:

Florence: Florence by Bike, Via della Scala 12/r, tel: 055-264035. Or Motorent (also mopeds), Via San Zanobi 9/r, tel: 055-490113.

Siena: Perozzi, Via del Romitorio 5 (near the Lizza park), tel: 0577-223157.

Lucca: Barbetti, Via Antieatro 23, tel: 0583-954444; Noleggio Biciclette, Piazzale Verdi.

Driving

Italy holds one of the worst records in Europe for road accidents. Drivers in the north tend to drive very fast, regardless of the number of cars on the road or the conditions. The high level of traffic in city centres means many areas, particularly round historic sights, are closed to most vehicles.

Since cities like Florence, Montepulciano and Pistoia have introduced partial or complete city-centre driving bans (at least for non-residents), it makes sense to leave the car in the car parks on the edge of the historic centre.

State highways in Tuscany include the No. 1 "Aurelia", which runs north–south, to the west of Pisa. There are also national motorways (*autostrade*): the A11, the "Firenze-mare", and the A12, the "Sestri Levante-Livorno". Both of these are toll roads. The two *superstrade* (Florence–Siena and the new Florence–Pisa–Livorno) are toll-free.

CAR HIRE

You can rent cars from major rental companies (Hertz, Avis, Europcar, etc.) in most cities and resorts, with different rates and conditions. The smaller local firms offer cheaper rates but cars can only be booked on the spot. Generally, booking from the UK, perhaps as part of a fly-drive package, is much cheaper than hiring on arrival. Even with four or five people sharing, hiring a car can be a fairly expensive exercise.

Rates generally allow unlimited mileage and include breakdown service. Basic insurance is included but additional cover is available at fixed rates.

Most firms require a deposit equal to the estimated cost of the hire. They often take and hold a credit card payment, which serves as the charge on return of the car.

Cars may be hired from the following outlets and also at Pisa and Florence airports, as well as at the railway station at Florence. In Florence, most of the car hire companies have offices on or near Borgo Ognissanti.

Florence
Avis, Borgo Ognissanti 128r, tel: 055-2398826.
Eurodollar, Via il Prato 80r, tel: 055-2382482. There is also a branch at Florence Airport, tel: 055-309790.
Maggiore, Via Maso Finiguerra 31r, tel: 055-294578. Also at Florence Airport, tel: 055-311256.
Hertz, Via Maso Finiguerra 33r, tel: 055-282260.

Siena
Hertz, c/o Albergo Lea, Viale XXIV Maggio, tel: 0577-45085.
Avis, Via Simone Martini 36, tel: 0577-270305.

LICENCES AND INSURANCE
Licences: Drivers must have a driving licence issued by a nation with a reciprocal agreement with Italy. The pink EU licence does not officially need an Italian translation. All other licences do need a translation, obtainable (free) from motoring organisations and Italian tourist offices.
Insurance: you are strongly

advised to obtain a Green Card (international motor insurance certificate) from your own insurance company at least 10 days before travelling. For minimum cover, they may be bought at ferry terminals in Britain and at the Customs Office at any border. Also seek out breakdown insurance, which offers some compensation for the hire of replacement vehicles and transport home if your car breaks down.

RULES OF THE ROAD
The Italian highway code is aligned to the Geneva Convention and Italy uses international road signs. Some rules come as no surprise – e.g. traffic travels on the right-hand side of the road and the wearing of seatbelts is compulsory – but there are a few local differences:

Road signs: ALT is a stop line painted on the road for road junctions; STOP is for a pedestrian crossing.

Side mirrors: these are compulsory on the left-hand side of the car, for both right–and–left-hand drive vehicles. Drivers may be required to have one fitted.

Precedence: at crossroads, motorists must give precedence to vehicles on their right, except on recently built roundabouts, when those already on the roundabout have priority.

Trams and trains always take

precedence from left to right.

If a motorist approaching a crossroads finds a precedence sign (a triangle with the point downwards) or a Stop sign, he/she must give precedence to all vehicles coming from both the right and left.

Parking: Outside cities and towns, parking on the right-hand side of the road is allowed, except on motorways, at crossroads, on curves and near hilly ground not having full visibility.

In Florence, there is free parking outside the city with shuttle services into the centre. Parking meters are considered unsightly, but there are a few and they are on the increase. Illegally parked vehicles will be towed away, and you will have to pay a fine.

RUSH HOURS
The busiest time in the cities is 8am–1pm, when most business is done. There is a lull in the afternoon until 3pm and traffic is heavy again 4–8pm.

On country roads and motorways, heavy traffic builds up leading into the cities in the mornings and out again in the evenings around 7pm. In the summer, roads leading to the coast on Saturday mornings are especially busy, and, on late Sunday afternoons, enormous queues can form on routes into the cities, with people returning from a day or weekend away.

Italian Automobile Club (ACI)

The Italian Automobile Club, or ACI, is the equivalent of the RAC or AA in the UK. Iti will rescue any foreign drivers who break down in Tuscany for a reasonable charge.

The ACI's head office is at Via Marsala, 8, 00185 Roma, tel: 06-4477 (24-hour information line in English). Its addresses in Tuscany, where drivers may obtain useful maps and road information, are:

Arezzo: Viale L. Signorelli 24a. Tel: 0575-303601; fax: 0575-303620.
Florence: Viale Amendola, 36. Tel: 055-24861; fax: 055-2343257.
Grosseto: Via Mazzini, 105. Tel: 0564-415777; fax: 0564-415449.
Livorno: Via G. Verdi, 32. Tel: 0586-898775; fax: 0586-898387.
Lucca: Via Catalani, 59, Tel: 0583-582626;

fax: 0583-418058.
Massa-Carrara: Via Aurelia Ovest 193.
Tel: 0585-830515; fax: 0585-831944.
Pisa: Via Cisanello 168.
Tel: 050-950111; fax: 050-950399.
Pistoia: Via Racciardetto, 2. Tel: 0573-975786; fax: 0573-34377.
Siena: Viale Vittorio Veneto, 47. Tel: 0577-49001; fax: 0577-49003.

Driving Speeds

The following speed limits apply to cars in Italy:
• **Urban areas**: 50kmph/30mph
• **Roads outside urban areas**: 90kmph/55mph
• **Dual carriageways outside urban areas**: 110kmph/70mph
• **Motorways (*autostrade*)**: 130kmph/80mph (110kmph/70mph for vehicles of less than 1100cc.)

In addition, each province declares local speed limits: in most, these are lower at weekends and in summer.

MOTORWAY TOLLS

Tharges for driving on motorways in Italy can be considerable. A ticket is taken from a machine on entering and payment is made at the end or at intermediate stages. An attendant takes the toll and gives change. To save time, be prepared with handfuls of coins and L.1,000/2,000 notes. Within Tuscany, there is a charge on the A11 from Florence to Pisa of L.6,500 for cars; from Florence to Lucca, L.5,500.

Access signs to the motorways, unlike those of other European countries, are in green, not blue.

For more information on tolls, charges and routes, as well as traffic, contact Centro Servizi Firenze-Ovest, tel: 055-420 0444; fax: 055-420 3234.

BREAKDOWNS AND ACCIDENTS

Tn case of a breakdown on an Italian road, dial 116 at the nearest telephone box. Tell the operator where you are, the registration number and the type of car and the nearest Automobile Club d'Italia (ACI) office will be informed for immediate assistance. They are usually very efficient.

On motorways, telephones are 2 km (1 mile) apart, with special buttons to call for the police and medical assistance. Both have to be contacted if an accident involves an injury.

Warning signs: if your car breaks down, or if you stop or block the road for any reason, you must try to move your vehicle right off the road. If this is impossible, you are required to warn other vehicles by placing a red triangular danger sign at least 50 metres (150 ft) behind the vehicle. All vehicles must carry these signs, which can be obtained on hire from all ACI offices at the border by paying a deposit of L.5,000.

PETROL STATIONS

Tn Florence, petrol stations and garages which open at night include:
AGIP, Via Antonio del Pollaiuolo. Self-service.
Tamoil, Via Senese. Self-service.
Texaco, Viale Guidoni. Self-service.

At self-service petrol stations you will need L.10,000 and L.50,000 notes.

Where to Stay

Choosing a Hotel

The quality and range of accommodation in Tuscany is extremely varied, with a choice between a city *palazzo*, grand country villa, or historic family-run hotel. Alternatively, visitors can choose to stay in a rented apartment or villa, sample an increasingly popular farm-stay holiday (*agriturismo*) or even, in the most popular cities, a private home stay. (This is not known as bed and breakfast since breakfast is not usually provided.)

The region has a reasonable range of accommodation but hotel rooms generally need to be booked well in advance in Florence and Siena. During local summer festivals, particularly the Sienese *Palio* and Arezzo *Giostra*, rooms are scarce. Attractive accommodation in the centre of Volterra and San Gimignano is popular, so early booking is advisable.

There is a huge variation in what you get for your money from place to place. A moderately priced hotel in Florence may be an adequate 3-star *pensione*, whereas the same money could buy you a luxury 4-star room in a grand country house off the tourist track.

In towns, "high season" does not necessarily include July and August. In Florence, for instance, many of the more expensive hotels cut their prices during these months. Furthermore, remember it can sometimes pay to bargain.

Many hotels with restaurants insist on a half- or full-board arrangement, especially in the high season. This ploy is particularly prevalent on the islands (e.g. Elba), in seaside resorts (e.g. Forte dei Marmi), in spa resorts (e.g. Montecatini Terme and Chianciano Terme), and where accommodation is in short supply.

Hotel Listing

The following list of recommended hotels is arranged in alphabetical order by town or city. In the case of Florence, where so many hotels are available, the listing is subdivided into price categories. Other cities' hotels have price indicators at the end of their descriptions. These refer to the cost of a standard double room for one night during high season, usually including breakfast, and the ranges are as follows:

$ = below L.175,000
$$ = L.175,000–300,000
$$$ = L.300,000–450.000
$$$$ = over L.450,000

For villa and apartment rental, rural accommodation, farm stays, budget accommodation and rooms in private homes, see the specific categories that follow the general hotel listings.

Abetone
Boscolungo
Via Brennero 224.
Tel: 0573-60582
Pensione with swimming pool. Open 20 June–15 September; minimum stay: one week. $
Regina
Via Uccelliero 9.
Tel: 0573-60007.
Pleasant 19th-century villa within an attractive setting: a 3-star hotel. $

Arezzo
Continentale
Piazza G. Monaco 7.
Tel: 0575-20251
Fax: 0575-350485
A centrally located 3-star hotel,

decorated in a modern, elegant style. $
Hotel Europa
Via Spinello 43.
Tel: 0575-357701
Fax: 0575-357703
Conveniently near railway station.L.150 and L.15
Val di Colle
Località Bagnoro.
Tel: 0575-365167
A meticulously restored 14th-century house, 4 km (2.5 miles) from the centre. Antique furniture rubs shoulders with modern art. Eight beautiful bedrooms. $$

Artimino
Paggeria Medicea
Viale Papa Giovanni XXIII 3.
Tel: 055-8718081
Fax: 055-8718080
Grand hotel in the former stables of a restored Medici villa, nestling between olive groves and vineyards near Carmignano, just west of Florence. Hunting and fishing on site. Very good restaurant. $$$

Bagno Vignoni
Hotel Posta Marcucci
Tel: 0577-887112
Fax: 0577-887119
Hotel noted for its spa facilities, close to the famous medieval pool. Fine views of the ancient fortress from the water. $$

Candeli
Villa La Massa
Via La Massa 24.
Tel: 055-6510101
Fax: 055-6510109
Seven km (4 miles) north of Florence, this cluster of beautifully converted 17th-century villas radiates elegance. Riverside restaurant; swimming and tennis. $$$$

Cascina
Hotel Villa Guelfi
Via Tosco Romagnola 941, Località Santa Anna Cascina.
Tel: 050-775182
Fax: 050-760888
Villa built in typical Pisan 19th-century style. $

Castagneto Carducci
La Torre
Tel: 0565-775268
Cheap, country hotel with a separate restaurant offering wild boar dishes. $

Castellina In Chianti
Belvedere di San Leonino
Località San Leonino.
Tel: 0577-740887
Fax: 0577-740924
Imposing 15th-century country house surrounded by olive trees and vineyards. Pool. $
Collelungo
Tel: 0577-740489
Lovingly restored stone farmhouse divided into comfortable apartments for two–four people. Barbecue and pool. Minimum stay: three nights. $$
Le Piazze
Località Le Piazze.
Tel: 0577-743190
Fax: 0577-743191
Converted 17th-century farmhouse with terraces and gardens. Rustic furnishings; luxurious bathrooms. Meals on request. $$
Salivolpi
Via Fiorentina 89.
Tel: 0577-740484
Fax: 0577-740998
Well-restored farmhouse with an appealing garden and uncontrived rustic decor – original beams, whitewashed walls, terracotta tiles and decorative ironwork. $
Tenuta di Ricavo
Località Ricavo.
Tel: 0577-740221
Fax: 0577-741014
Open March–October: a highly rated hotel occupying a series of rustic houses in a medieval hamlet, 5 km (3 miles) from Castellina. Pool; good quality restaurant. $$
Villa Casalecchi
Località Casalecchi.
Tel: 0577-740240
Fax: 0577-741111
Open March–October. 3-star hotel, set in a 19th-century villa, surrounded by oak trees. Pool, tennis courts, restaurant. $$

Certaldo Alto
Osteria del Vicario
Via Rivellino 3.
Tel/fax: 055-668228
Well-known restaurant with five simple rooms in a pretty hilltop town. The food is creative. $

Chianciano Terme
Hotel Michelangelo
Via delle Piane.
Tel: 0578-64004
Fax: 0578-60480
Modern 4-star hotel in a fine setting, with large grounds, a pool, sauna, tennis courts and good restaurants, including a rooftop restaurant in summer. Popular with Italians. Open April–mid-October. $$

Chiusi
Centrale Hotel
Tel: 0578-20118/222043
Renovated hotel convenient for the railway station (direct trains to Florence). $$

Colle di Val d'Elsa
Villa Belvedere
Località Belvedere.
Tel: 0577-920966
Fax: 0557-924128
A delightful 18th-century villa surrounded by a large park. Excellent restaurant. $$

Cortona
Il Falconiere
Località San Martino.
Tel: 0575-612679
Fax: 0575-612927
Luxurious country retreat set in gardens and olive groves. The first-class restaurant is set in the old lemonary. $$$
San Michele
Via Guelfa 15.
Tel: 0575-604348
Fax: 0575-630147
Centrally situated, comfortable hotel housed in an impressively restored Renaissance palace. High quality furnishings. $$

Elba
Le Acacie
Località Maregno, Capoliveri.
Tel: 0565-966111

Hotel Prices

The price categories refer to the cost of a double room during high season, usually including breakfast.

$ = below L.175,000
$$ = L.175,000–300,000
$$$ = L.300,000–450.000
$$$$ = over L.450,000

Fax: 0565-967062
Three-star, Mediterranean-style hotel set in an attractive part of the island. $$
Capo Sud
Lacona.
Tel: 0565-964021
Fax: 0565-964263
Cluster of little villas, quite remotely set behind a private beach. Restaurant, bar, pool. $$
Costa dei Gabbiani
Capoliveri.
Tel: 0565-935122
Fax: 0565-925333
Resort complex bordering a protected coastline and occupying a vast estate. Guests can stay in villas, apartments or rooms. Swimming, horse-riding, golf and archery are on offer. Open all year. $$
Dei Coralli
Via degli Etruschi, Marina di Campo.
Tel: 0565-976336
Fax: 0565-977748
Three-star hotel 100 metres (300 ft) from the beach in one of the most popular resorts on the island. $
Fabbricia
Località Magazzini, Portoferraio.
Tel: 0565-933181
Fax: 0565-933185
Four-star hotel situated 9 km (5.5 miles) from Portoferraio. Modern but decorated in island style, and set in an ancient olive grove. Adjacent beach. $$
La Hermitage
Biodola.
Tel: 0565-969911
Fax: 0565-969984
Bungalows in pinewoods by a beach. Lively. $$

Fiesole
Pensione Bencistà
Via Benedetto da Maiano 4.
Tel/fax: 055-59163
Sprawling but delightful 14th-century villa with a homely atmosphere, decorated with antiques and rustic furnishings. Reliable restaurant; half-board is compulsory. Flower-bedecked terrace with panoramic views over Florence. $$
Villa Fiesole
Via Fra Giovanni Angelico 35.
Tel: 055-597252
Fax: 055-599133
Comfortable but chic hotel near Villa San Michele (see below), and much cheaper. Full wheel-chair access. $$$
Villa San Michele
Via Doccia 4.
Tel: 055-59451
Fax: 055-598734
One of the finest hotels in Tuscany. Supposedly designed by Michelangelo, this ex-monastery enjoys harmonious lines and heavenly views, particularly from the *loggia* (and restaurant). Spacious grounds; pool; piano bar. The plush suites have jacuzzis. $$$$

Florence

Deluxe ($$$$)
Astoria
Via del Giglio 9.
Tel: 055-2398095
Fax: 055-214632
Completely refurbished hotel near the station. The grand dimensions and elaborate decor are popular with up-market tour groups.
Excelsior
Piazza Ognissanti 3.
Tel: 055-264201
Fax: 055-210278
The grandest hotel in Florence – a lavishly furnished 19th-century building on the banks of the Arno. Celebrities and business executives often stay here. You can look forward to sumptuous bedrooms, many with grand marble bathrooms, and there is a panoramic rooftop restaurant.

Hotels in Florence

Hotel beds in the centre of Florence are usually scarce so try to book ahead. Failing that, rooms can be booked at the information office in Santa Maria Novella train station. The ITA office (Informazioni Turistiche Alberghi) is situated in the main concourse and is open 9am–9pm (slightly reduced hours in winter).

The cheapest hotels tend to be situated around Santa Maria Novella and the station areas, which is not particularly salubrious at night. Only in Florence can dingy hotels still get away with being situated on the top floor of a lift-free *palazzo* and closing the doors to guests at midnight.

However, at the other end of the scale, the city has some of the loveliest hotels in Tuscany, with frescoed interiors or sweeping views over the city. In the upper price bracket, the essential decision is between staying in an historic centrally located *palazzo* in the city or a beautifully appointed villa in the hills.

If the letter "r" appears after numbers, it refers to *rosso* (red) and denotes a business address. Confusingly, Florentine addresses operate a dual numbering system, with "red" numbers usually denoting businesses and blue or black numbers usually denoting residential addresses.

Florence Hotels contd
Grand Hotel
Piazza Ognissanti 1.
Tel: 055-288781
Fax: 055-217400
Smaller than its sister hotel (the Excelsior, across the square) but almost as grand. Queen Victoria and other foreign royalty stayed here in the 19th century. Refurbished several years ago.
Grand Hotel Villa Cora
Viale Machiavelli 18.
Tel: 055-2298451
Fax: 055-229086
Quiet, elegant hotel in a huge park on a hill above Florence. Free limo service; pool.
Helvetia & Bristol
Via dei Pescioni 2.
Tel: 055-287814
Fax: 055-288353
Possibly the best of the luxury small hotels in the city, with many illustrious names numbered amongst its guests. Supremely comfortable rooms and suites; excellent restaurant. Delightful winter garden.
Hotel Regency
Piazza Massimo d'Azeglio 3.
Tel: 055-245247
Fax: 055-2342938
Five-star luxury in a small hotel

situated in a quiet, leafy square, a short walk from the sights. Cool, shady garden. Good restaurant.
J&J
Via di Mezzo 20.
Tel: 055-240951
Fax: 055-240282
The setting of this small hotel – in a modest street near Santa Croce – belies the luxury within. All 19 rooms and suites are highly individual, romantic and chic. Lovely old cloister for summer breakfasts.
Montebello Splendid
Via Montebello 60.
Tel: 055-2398051
Fax: 055-211867
Comfortable and sober hotel with an attractive garden, in the 18th-century residential area west of the Ponte Vecchio.
Torre di Bellosguardo
Via Roti Michelozzi 2.
Tel: 055-2298145
Fax: 055-229008
Bellosguardo ("beautiful view"), the hill on which this Renaissance villa was built, is only 15 minutes' walk up from Porta Romana, but a world away. Superb gardens; pool; frescoed reception rooms.

Villa Medici
Via Il Prato 42.
Tel: 055-2381331
Fax: 055-2381336
Convenient hotel near the train station with a pool, gardens and large airy bedrooms.

EXPENSIVE ($$$)
Hermitage
Vicolo Marzio 1, Piazza del Pesce.
Tel: 055-287216
Fax: 055-212208
A delightful hotel, recently expanded, behind the Ponte Vecchio. Personal attention from staff. Lovely roof garden views over the city.
Hotel Baglioni
Piazza Unità 6.
Tel: 055-23580
Fax: 055-2358895
Classic hotel retaining its air of discreet elegance while providing extremely comfortable rooms. Very popular with the business community.
Kraft
Via Solferino 2.
Tel: 055-284273
Fax: 055-2398267
Ideally placed for music lovers, a stone's throw from the opera house, and performers often stay here. It has the only rooftop pool in the city.
Loggiato dei Serviti
Piazza della SS Annunziata 3.
Tel: 055-289592
Fax: 055-289595
Atmospheric hotel facing the Innocenti hospital across a traffic-free piazza. Sangallo's 16th-century palazzo houses 29 rooms and suites, all different and tastefully furnished. One of the city's best-loved and most refined hotels. No garden.
Monna Lisa
Borgo Pinti 27.
Tel: 055-2479751
Fax: 055-2479755
This Renaissance *palazzo*, furnished with antiques, drawings and sculpture, is a particular favourite with visitors. There is a delightful garden and private parking.

Plaza Hotel Lucchesi
Lungarno della Zecca Vecchia 38.
Tel: 055-264141
Comfortable and very efficiently run hotel overlooking the Arno.
Villa Belvedere
Via Benedetto Castelli 3.
Tel: 055-222501
Fax: 055-223163
Exceptionally friendly and modern hotel; south of the city. Sunny rooms, a pretty garden and lovely views across Florence. Pool and tennis court.

Hotel Prices

The price categories refer to the cost of a double room during high season, usually including breakfast.

$ = below L.175,000
$$ = L.175,000–300,000
$$$ = L.300,000–450.000
$$$$ = over L.450,000

MODERATE ($$)

Annalena
Via Romana 34.
Tel: 055-222402
Fax: 055-222403
A discreet *pensione* in a 15th-century *palazzo*, situated opposite the rear entrance to the Boboli Gardens. Some rooms have balconies looking onto the horticultural centre.
Aprile
Via della Scala 6.
Tel: 055-216237
Fax: 055-280947
Much more appealing than most hotels near the station, this is an ex-Medici palace complete with frescoes, a pleasant breakfast room and garden. Rooms range from simple to reasonably grand.
Beacci-Tornabuoni
Via de' Tornabuoni 3.
Tel: 055-212645
Fax: 055-283594
Deluxe guest house, comfortable and very welcoming, although some rooms are on the small side. Flower-filled rooftop terrace for breakfast

and drinks. Half-board terms compulsory. Particularly popular with Americans.
Botticelli
Via Taddea 8.
Tel: 055-290905
Fax: 055-294322
New hotel close to the central market. It is both comfortable and appealing, with all the mod cons you could want but also well-preserved 16th-century features, including frescoes.
Classic
Viale Machiavelli 25.
Tel: 055-229351
Fax: 055-229353
Elegant, pinkwashed villa with lovely rooms, a conservatory and pretty gardens, situated just above the Porta Romana. Excellent value.
Mario's
Via Faenza 89.
Tel: 055-216801
Fax: 055-212039
One of the most attractive of the many *pensioni* in Via Faenza, behind the central market. Decorated in rustic Tuscan style, with comfortable bedrooms (quieter at the rear). Friendly.
Morandi alla Crocetta
Via Laura 50.
Tel: 055-2344747
Fax: 055-2480954
Tiny *pensione* tucked away in a backstreet near the university, housed in a former convent. Antiques, parquet flooring and colourful rugs; ten bedrooms, two with private terraces. Book well in advance.
Palazzo Benci
Via Faenza 6r.
Tel: 055-213848
Fax: 055-288308
Patrician *palazzo*, traditionally the seat of the Benci family, recently restored but retaining original features. Tiny garden.
Porta Faenza
Via Faenza 77.
Tel: 055-214287
Comfortable, family-run hotel with all modern conveniences, situated near the central market. Private garage (rare in this part of town).

Silla
Via de'Renai 5.
Tel: 055-2342888
Fax: 055-2341437
An elegant arched courtyard leads to this first-floor hotel in a quiet, relatively leafy area south of and overlooking the Arno.
Splendor
Via San Gallo 30.
Tel: 055-483427
Fax: 055-461276
Attractive little neo-classical *palazzo* near Piazza San Marco, with sumptuous public rooms. Simpler bedrooms, most with private baths; lovely breakfast room leading onto a terrace.
Torre Guelfa
Borgo SS Apostoli 8.
Tel: 055-2396338
Fax: 055-2398577
Quite elegant, recently refurbished hotel with a grand "salon", pastel-shaded bedrooms, a sunny breakfast room and the tallest privately owned tower in the city.
Villa Azalee
Viale Fratelli Rosselli 44.
Tel: 055-214242
Fax: 055-268264
Pleasant, 19th-century villa near the station, with the feel of a private house, set in a garden full of azaleas and camelias. Private garage; bicycles for hire.

INEXPENSIVE ($)

Alessandra
Borgo SS Apostoli 17.
Tel: 055-283438
Fax: 055-210619
An old-fashioned, simple *pensione* conveniently near the Ponte Vecchio. Many of the 25 spacious rooms have antiques.
Casci
Via Cavour 13.
Tel: 055-211686
Fax: 055-239 6461
Frescoed *quattrocento palazzo*, family-run and enjoying a welcoming atmosphere. Five minutes' walk north of the Duomo.
Fiorino
Via Osteria del Guanto 6.
Tel/fax: 055-210579
Basic and unpretentious.

Florence Hotels contd

Firenze
Piazza Donati 4.
Tel: 055-214203
Fax: 055-212370
Refurbished *pensione* with modern, if unexciting, rooms, all with baths and TV. Just off the central Via del Corso. Low prices for the position and facilities.

Giada
Canto de'Nelli 2.
Tel: 055-215317
Friendly *pensione* near San Lorenzo market. Some rooms overlook the Medici Chapels.

Liana
Via Alfieri 18.
Tel: 055-245303
Fax: 055-2344596
Simple hotel some way north of centre in the former British Embassy. Quiet, pleasant, but slightly faded. Rooms vary from the simple to the more elegant. Fresh flowers and private car park.

Pensione Bretagna
Lungarno Corsini 6.
Tel: 055-263618
Suitably, this is a favourite with British business travellers.

Pensione Sorelle Bandini
Piazza Santo Spirito 9.
Tel: 055-215308
Fax: 055-282761
Extremely popular *pensione*, despite its rather shabby appearance and (some) uncomfortable beds. It overlooks a lively piazza. Ask for the room with direct access.

Residence Johanna
Via Bonifacio Lupi 14.
Tel: 055-481896
Fax: 055-482721
Excellent value residence (even though there are few mod cons and breakfasts are do-it-yourself) in an unmarked apartment building in a quiet street near Piazza Libertà.

Residence Johanna Cinque Giornate
Via delle Cinque Giornate 12.
Tel: 055-473377
Run along the same lines as its sister hotel (above), but with slightly higher prices to reflect the extras: a garden, free private parking, bathrooms in every room and a TV/sitting room.

Gaiole In Chianti

Castello di Spaltenna
Tel: 0577-749483
Fax: 0577-749269
Formidable fortified monastery, now a luxurious hotel with an excellent restaurant. Supremely comfortable, individualistic rooms. $$$

Hotel Prices

The price categories refer to the cost of a double room during high season, usually including breakfast.

$ = below L.175,000
$$ = L.175,000–300,000
$$$ = L.300,000–450.000
$$$$ = over L.450,000

Galluzzo

La Fattoressa
Via Volterrana 58.
Tel/fax: 055-2048418
Old farmhouse and outbuildings converted into simple but comfortable accommodation. Very conveniently situated for the *autostrada*. $

Relais Certosa
Via Colle Romole 2.
Tel: 055-204 7171
Fax: 055-268575
Former hunting lodge (once attached to the Carthusian monastery) near Florence, now a welcoming residence, with spacious grounds and tennis courts. $$$

Gargonza

Castello di Gargonza
Monte San Savino.
Tel: 0575-847021
Fax: 0575-847054
Attractive fortified village – with a frescoed chapel and castle walls – near Arezzo, converted into a hotel with separate apartments. 13th-century buildings overlook the Valdichiana. Restaurant speciality is game. $$

Giglio

Pardini's Hermitage
Giglio Porto.
Tel: 0564-809034
Fax: 0564-809177
Pleasant island retreat, accessible by boat from Giglio Porto. Offers a relaxed atmosphere, friendly welcome and good facilities. There is direct access to rocky shore swimming. Half-board only is available. $$

Greve In Chianti

Villa San Giovese
Piazza Bucciarelli 5, Panzano.
Tel: 055-852461
Fax: 055-852463
Well-restored villa in the Florentine Chianti, offering additional rooms in a converted traditional farmhouse. Noted restaurant and wines. Closed Jan–Feb. $$

Livorno

Palazzo
Viale Italia 195.
Tel: 0586-805371
Fax: 0586-803206
Restored 19th-century hotel with spacious bedrooms and public rooms. $$$

Lucca

Diana
Via del Molinetto 11.
Tel: 0583-492202
Centrally located hotel off Piazza San Martino: a pleasant budget option. $

Hotel Cinzia
Via della Dogana 9.
Tel: 0583-491323
A clean and peaceful hotel in a central position, even cheaper than the one above. $

Hotel Celide
Via Giusti 27.
Tel: 0583-954106
Good, modern hotel outside the city walls. $$

La Luna
Via Fillungo, angolo Corte Compagni 12.
Tel: 0583-493634
Fax: 0583-490021
A family-run hotel in the historic centre. $$

Piccolo Hotel Puccini
Via di Poggio 9.
Tel: 0583-55421
Fax: 0583-53487
A small hotel just around the corner from Puccini's birthplace and crammed with mementos of the maestro. Offers excellent value and exceptionally helpful staff. $
Stipino
Via Romana 95.
Tel: 0583-495077
Fax: 0583-490309
Simply decorated, 2-star hotel graced with a personal touch. $
Universo
Piazza del Giglio 1.
Tel/fax: 0583-493678
Large Victorian hotel where Ruskin always stayed. $$$
Villa La Principessa Elisa
Via Nuova per Pisa, Massa Pisana.
Tel: 0583-379737
Fax: 0583- 379019
Gracious villa near Lucca with bright blue and white paintwork, now a luxury hotel. Precious antiques and expensive fabrics abound. Restaurant in a 19th-century conservatory. Pool. $$$–$$$$
Villa Rinascimento
Località Santa Maria del Giudice.
Tel: 0583-378392
Fax: 0583-370238
Rustic villa with a lovely garden and pool, on a hillside 9 km (5 miles) west of Lucca. $

Luigiana
Del Pino
Bastia di Licciana Nardi.
Tel: 0187-475041
A quiet, comfortable modern *pensione* in a mountain village, surrounded by pine trees. Full board available. $
Il Giardinetto
Via Roma 151, Fivizzano.
Tel: 0585-92060
Rather eccentric hotel, full of character and characters (including some permanent residents). Old-fashioned Tuscan food. $

The Maremma
Hotel Agnelli
S Quirico di Sorano.
Tel: 0564-619015
Hotel and pizzeria near Vitozza, 5 km (3 miles) from Sorano. $
Albergo Ristorante Scilla
Via del Duomo 5, Sovana.
Tel: 0564-616531
Central restaurant/hotel. $
Albergo Ristorante Taverna Etrusca
Piazza del Pretorio, Sovana.
Tel: 0564-616183
Excellent small restaurant with rooms. $
Villa Aquaviva
Località Aquaviva, Montemerano.
Tel/fax: 0564-602890
Family-run guest house near Saturnia, with a lovely garden and comfortable rooms. $

Marina di Carrara
Hotel Mediterraneo
Via Genova 24.
Tel: 0585-635222/54036
Large, modern hotel one block from the waterfront. Being situated near the marble port, it can be rather noisy at times. $$$

Marina di Pisa
Albergo Manzi
Lungomare 25.
Tel: 050-36593
Reasonable hotel right on the seafront. $
Pensione Milena
Via Padre Agostino 14.
Tel: 050-36863
Full board and a minimum of one week's stay are required. $$

Massa Marittima
Duca del Mare
Piazza Dante Alighieri 1/2.
Tel: 0566-902284
Simple accommodation. Half-board is obligatory in August. $

Massa Pisana
Villa La Principessa
Via Nuova per Pisa 1616.
Tel: 0583-370037
Fax: 0583-379019
Exclusive mansion open April–October. Old-fashioned elegance; modern comforts. $$$

Molino del Piano
Hotel il Trebbiolo
Via del Trebbiolo 8.
Tel: 055-8300098
Fax: 055-8300583
Delightful 3-star hotel 14 km (9 miles) from Florence: an ochre-coloured villa amidst olive groves and vines. Relaxed atmosphere; good cuisine. $$

Monsummano Terme
Grotta Giusti
Via Grotta Giusti 171.
Tel: 0572-51165
Fax: 0572-51269
Handsome villa in parkland with its own thermal spring. Pool and spa facilities. Open 1 March–30 November. $$$
La Speranza
Via Grotta Giusti 62.
Tel: 0572-51313
Pensione with a private, well-maintained garden. $
Mugello
Villa Campestri, Via di Campestri 19/22, Vicchio.
Tel: 055-8490107
Fax: 055-8490108
Square villa immersed in greenery, with a marvellous view of the Apennines. Pool; restaurant; horse riding; walking. $$

Montecatini Terme
Florio
Via Montebello 41.
Tel: 0572-78632
Hotel with its own garden. $
Grand Hotel Plaza e Locanda Maggiore
Piazza del Popolo 7.
Tel: 0572 75831
Four-star hotel with a wide range of facilities including a pool. $$
Torreta
Viale Bustichini 63.
Tel: 0572-70305
A decent hotel with a swimming pool. $$

Monteriggioni
Monteriggioni
Via 1 Maggio 4.
Tel: 0577-305009
Fax: 0577-305011
A couple of village houses have been converted into a pleasant

and comfortable hotel with a garden and pool, in a pretty walled town 10 km (6 miles) north of Siena. $$

Panzano in Chianti
Villa Le Barone
Via San Leolino 19.
Tel: 055-852621
Fax: 055-852277
Aristocratic villa filled with family antiques, with the feel of a private house. Pool; tennis court; good restaurant. Half-board rates. $$$

Pescai
Azienda Marzalla
Via Collecchio 1.
Tel: 0572-490751
Fax: 0572-478332
Unpretentious, family-run *agriturismo* outlet in the hills. Pool; pleasant *trattoria* nearby.

Pisa
Ariston
Via Maffi 42.
Tel: 050-561834
Fax: 050-561891
Restrained, yet welcoming, 3-star hotel facing the Leaning Tower. $
Bologna
Via Mazzini 57.
Tel: 050-502120
Fax: 050-43070
Established, well-furnished 2-star hotel. Car park. $
California Park Hotel
Madonna dell'Acqua.
Tel: 050-890726
Fax: 050-890727
Rooms are in the numerous small villas scattered throughout the grounds. Swimming pool. Located 3 km/1.5 miles outside Pisa. $$

Pisa Hotels

Pisa has a number of good hotels in the inexpensive category but a shortage of exceptional moderate hotels and a total lack of truly luxurious accommodation.

Jolly Hotel Cavalieri
Piazza della Stazione 2.
Tel: 050-43290
Fax: 050-502242
One of the Jolly 4-star chain, opposite the station. $$$
D'Azeglio
Piazza V Emanuele 18b.
Tel: 050-500310
Four-star hotel. $$
Grand Hotel Duomo
Via Santa Maria 94.
Tel: 050-561894
Fax: 050-560418
Comfortable hotel with a business-type atmosphere. Restaurant; private garage. $$$
Hotel Giardino
Via C. Cammeo.
Tel: 050-562101
Tucked behind the corner bar and self-service restaurant at the Porta Nuova. English- and French-speaking. $
La Pace
Galleria B di Viale Gramsci 4.
Tel: 050-29351/502266
Very clean hotel. $$
Pisa Hotel
Via Manzoni 22.
Tel: 050-44551
Hotel offering good service and comfort. $
Royal Victoria
Lungarno Pacinotti 12.
Tel: 050-940111
Fax: 050-940180
The most characterful hotel in the city, opened in 1842 and host to Dickens and other Grand Tourists. Old-fashioned atmosphere. Rooms overlooking the Arno are in great demand. Private garage. $$
Terminus e Plaza
Via Colombo 45.
Tel/fax: 050-500303
Three-star hotel convenient for the train station. $
Touring
Via Puccini 24.
Tel: 050-46374
Fax: 050-502148
Well-run hotel with a classic feel. $$
Villa Kinzica
Piazza Arcivescovado 2.
Tel: 050-560419
Fax: 050-551204

Hotel Prices

The price categories refer to the cost of a double room during high season, usually including breakfast.

$ = below L.175,000
$$ = L.175,000–300,000
$$$ = L.300,000–450.000
$$$$ = over L.450,000

Remarkably positioned hotel, right under the Leaning Tower, but some rooms need attention. Own restaurant/pizzeria. $$

Pistoia
Il Convento
Via San Quirico 33.
Tel: 0573-452651
Fax: 0573-453578
Tranquil and comfortable hotel, once a Franciscan monastery. Features include a lovely garden, swimming pool, restaurant and even a chapel. Five km (3 miles) from town. $$
Hotel Patria
Via Crispi 8.
Tel: 0573-25187
Charming small hotel in the city's historic centre. Parking permits available. $
Leon Bianco
Via Panciatichi 2.
Tel/fax: 0573-26675
Set in the historic centre, this quiet, renovated hotel is a sensible choice. $$
Villa Vannini
Villa di Pitecchio.
Tel: 0573-42031
Fax: 0573-26331
Delightful villa in the woods, some 6 km (4 miles) north of Pistoia, with the atmosphere of a private house. Elegant and comfortable bedrooms; fine food; wonderful walks in the nearby forest. Good value. $$

Porto Ercole
Don Pedro
Via Panoramica 7.
Tel/fax: 0564-033914
Three-star family-run hotel with fine views. Open April–October. Guests must take full-board. $$

Hotel Il Pellicano
Località Cala dei Santi.
Tel: 0564-833801
Fax: 0564-833418
Chic hotel enjoying a superb, isolated clifftop position. Bedrooms are housed in various buildings; terraces lead down to the private beach. Weekly barbecues in summer. $$$–$$$$

Prato
Villa Rucellai
Via di Canneto 16.
Tel: 0574-460392
Mellow, medieval villa, now an informal but elegant place to stay. Family house atmosphere. $$

Radda in Chianti
Relais Fattoria Vignale
Via Pianigiani 15.
Tel: 0577-738300
Fax: 0577-738592
Old, stone farmhouse with discreetly elegant decor; relaxed and comfortable. Excellent wine produced on site; restaurant; pool. $$

Regello
Villa Rigacci
Vaggio 76.
Tel: 055-8656718
Fax: 055-8656537
Country house hotel in a pleasant setting, handy for the Rome–Florence motorway. Sophisticated Mediterranean food; pool. $$$

Rigoli
Villa Corliano
Via Statale 50, San Giuliano Terme.
Tel: 050-818193
Fax: 050-818341
Faded villa of grand dimensions, halfway between Pisa and Lucca. Informal, with plenty of atmosphere. Restaurant attached. $

San Gimignano
L'Antico Pozzo
Via San Matteo 87.
Tel: 0577-942014
Fax: 0577-942117
Old town house, carefully

restored and simply but tastefully furnished. $$
La Cisterna
Piazza della Cisterna 24.
Tel: 0577-940328
Fax: 0577-942080
Trecento palazzo in the heart of the *centro storico*. Atmospheric, fine restaurant; Tuscan cuisine. One of the most popular hotels in the town. $$
Hotel Pescille
Località Pescille.
Tel/fax: 0577-940186
Converted manor house three km (2 miles) southwest of San Gimignano. Pool; tennis. $$
Le Renaie
Località Pancole.
Tel: 0577-955044
Fax: 0577-955126
Modern farmhouse in a peaceful setting 5 km (3 miles) from San Gimignano. Rustic decor. Pool; restaurant; tennis nearby. $
Villa San Paolo
Strada per Certaldo.
Tel: 0577-955100
Fax: 0577-955113
Nineteenth-century hillside villa, 5 km (3 miles) from San Gimignano, with attractive rooms and terraced grounds. Closed January–February. $$$

San Quirco d'Orcia
Castello di Ripa d'Orcia
Località Castiglione d'Orcia.
Tel: 0577-897376
Fax: 0577-898038
Medieval village, dominated by a tower, where some houses have been converted into hotel rooms and apartments. *Trattoria* with panoramic terrace views. $$

Sesto Fiorentino
Villa Villoresi
Via Campi 2, Colonnata di Sesto Fiorentino.
Tel: 055-443692
Fax: 055-442063
Gracious villa, a world away from the ugly Florence industrial suburb of Sesto which surrounds it. Complete with chandeliers and frescoes, plus the longest loggia in Tuscany. Restaurant and pool. $$$

Except for in July and August (during the *Palio* festivities), it is usually much easier to find accommodation in Siena than in Florence, but note that several of Siena's most luxurious hotels lie outside the city walls. To see the whole range of accommodation on offer in Siena and Siena Province, ask for the latest edition of *Hotel, Campeggi, Ostelli, Agriturismo*, a booklet available free from Siena tourist offices.

Siena
Albergo Centrale
Via Calzoleria 24.
Tel: 0577-280379
Clean and spacious. $
Albergo Chiusarelli
Via Curtatone 15.
Tel: 0577-280562
Fax: 0577-271177
Slightly decaying, genteel villa in a garden with a car park. Near the bus station. $$
Albergo Tre Donzelle
Via delle Donzelle 5.
Tel: 0577-280358
Good value and position. $
Antica Torre
Via Fieravecchia 7.
Tel/fax: 0577-222255
A tiny, atmospheric hotel – essentially a conversion of a 17th-century tower. Early booking is advised. $
Duomo
Via Stalloreggi 38.
Tel: 0577-289088
Fax: 0577-43043
Situated right in the heart of the historic centre, close to Siena's magnificent cathedral, this 18th-century *palazzo* has a cloistered, intimate atmosphere. $$
Certosa di Maggiano
Via Certosa 82.
Tel: 0577-288180
Fax: 0577-288189
A 14th-century former Carthusian monastery – the oldest in Tuscany – id now a 5-star hotel adorned with antiques. Has a

Siena Hotels **contd**

prestigious restaurant. Original features, lovingly restored, include the chapel, cloisters and antiquarian library. $$$$

Garden
Via Custoza 2.
Tel: 0577-47056
Fax: 0577-46050
Sixteenth-century patrician villa, now a 3-star hotel with a formal, Italian garden and a pool. Four-star rooms available in a dependence. $$–$$$

Palazzo Ravizza
Pian dei Mantellini 34.
Tel: 0577-280462
Recently refurbished town house with lovely gardens and a good restaurant. Well-chosen antiques and pretty fabrics in the bedrooms. Welcoming public rooms. $$

Park Hotel
Via Marciano 16.
Tel: 0577-44803
Fax: 0577-49020
Splendid 16th-century Tuscan villa with an exclusive, 5-star atmosphere and a famous restaurant, L'Olivo. $$$

Piccolo Hotel Etruria
Via delle Donzelle 3.
Tel: 0577-288088
Fax: 0577-288461
Friendly hotel with new, simple but clean rooms divided between two town houses. $

Santa Caterina
Via Enea Silvio Piccolomini 7.
Tel: 0577-221105
Fax: 0577-271087
Friendly hotel set in a garden just outside the city walls, near Porta Romana. Roadside rooms can be noisy. $$

Villa Scacciapensieri
Via di Scacciapensieri 10.
Tel: 0577-41441
Fax: 0577-270854
A supremely elegant villa hotel in lovely grounds 3 km (1.5 miles) north of the city. Has a sophisticated interior, bedrooms with rural views, and a panoramic city view from the restaurant terrace. $$$

Sinalunga
Locanda dell'Amorosa
Tel: 0577-679497
Fax: 0577-678216
Renaissance village, complete with chapel, converted into a first-class hotel. Romantic setting; superb restaurant in adapted stables. $$$

Hotel Prices

The price categories refer to the cost of a double room during high season, usually including breakfast.

$ = below L.175,000
$$ = L.175,000–300,000
$$$ = L.300,000–450.000
$$$$ = over L.450,000

Sovicille
Borgo Pretale
Località Pretale.
Tel: 0577-345401
Fax: 0577-345625
Renovated fortified village divided into myriad apartments and topped by a massive medieval tower, situated in woods southwest of Siena. Facilities are good but prices are high. $$$

Tirrenia
Atlantico Continental Hotel
Viale Belvedere.
Tel: 050-37031
Four-star luxury-class hotel with pool, private beach and tennis court. $$$

Bristol
Via delle Felci 38.
Tel: 050-37161.
Three-star, unpretentious and comfortable hotel. $$

Gran Hotel Golf
Via dell'Edera.
Tel: 050-37545
Four-star hotel with its own golf course. $$

Trespiano
Villa Le Rondini
Via Bolognese Vecchia 224.
Tel: 055-400081
Fax: 055-268212

Secluded villa notable for its wonderful setting, overlooking the Arno Valley 4 km (2.5 miles) from Florence. There are lovely views over the city from the swimming pool, set in an olive grove. Restaurant. Bus link to the city. $$

Viareggio
Plaza
Piazza d'Azeglio 1.
Tel: 0584-44449
Newly refurbished hotel, one of the most luxurious in this seaside resort. $$$

Volterra
Etruria
Via Matteotti 32.
Tel/fax: 0588-87377
An ancient building incorporating Etruscan elements. A family atmosphere adds to the hotel's charm. $

Nazionale
Via dei Marchesi 11.
Tel: 0588-86284
Fax: 0588-84097
Ancient *palazzo*, a hotel since 1860: a charming blend of old and modern. $

San Lino
Via San Lino 26.
Tel: 0588-85250
Fax: 0588-80620
Monastic building whose original austerity has been softened by a successful conversion into a 4-star hotel. $$

Villa Nencini
Borgo Santo Stefano 55.
Tel: 0588-86386
Fax: 0588-86686
Pleasant stone villa just outside the town, with a garden and pool. $$

Villa Rioddi
Località Rioddi.
Tel: 0588-88053
Fax: 0588-88074
Accommodation in this 15th-century villa includes four apartments. Simple furnishings; pleasant garden and swimming pool. $

Camping

There are a number of well-run campsites in Tuscany. A list of sites with a location map, **Carta d'Italia Parchi di Campeggio**, can be obtained free of charge by writing to: Centro Internazionale Prenotazioni, Federcampeggio, Casella Postale 23, 50041 Calenzano (Firenze). Most seaside resorts in Tuscany have campsites of various levels where you can often hire tents or caravans. Contact the local tourist office for information. Below are details of some campsites in the main centres.

Florence
For more information on all sites in Florence, write to Federazione Italiana del Campeggio, Casella Postale 649, 50100 Florence.
Camping Italiani e Stranieri
Viale Michelangelo 80.
Tel: 055-6811977
Open Apr–Oct, crowded in high season. No. 13 bus from station. Good facilities; 500 tents.
Camping Panoramico
Via Peramonda, Fiesole.
Tel: 050-599069
Terraced site overlooking Florence. Open all year.
Camping Villa Camerata
Viale Righi 2/4.
Tel: 055-610300
Open Apr–Oct. No. 17B bus from station.

Pisa
Campeggio Torre Pendente
Viale delle Cascine 86.
Tel: 050-560665
Open mid-Mar–Sept. No. 5 bus from the station.
Camping Internazionale
Via Litorenea, Marina di Pisa.
Tel: 050-36553
Facilities include a private beach, bar and pizzeria.

Siena
Campeggio "Siena Colleverde"
Strada di Scacciapensieri 47.
Tel: 0577-280044.
Open end Mar–end Oct. Two km (1 mile) from the city; no. 8 bus.

There are also companies which organise campsite holidays in Tuscany In the UK, these include the following:
Eurocamp, 28 Princess Street, Knutsford, Cheshire WA16 6BU, tel: 01565-626262.
Keycamp, 92–96 Lind Road, Sutton, Surrey SM1 4PL, tel: 0181-395 4000.

Caravan and Camper Hire: in Tuscany, this is available from **Caravanmec**, Via Cupola 281, Peretola, Florence, tel: 055-315101, although there are other companies too.

Private Home Stays

This is a fairly new development in Tuscany but is a good way of experiencing closer contact with the locals while paying modest prices. In Florence and Siena, where the system is reasonably sophisticated, the private homes are carefully graded from simple to luxurious, with prices varying accordingly.

In Florence, contact AGAP (Associazione Gestori Alloggi Privati) at Via de' Neri 9, 50122 Florence, tel: 055-284100. In Siena, request the *Affitta-camere* (private lodgings) booklet of addresses from the tourist office (APT, Via di Città 43, Siena, tel: 0577-280551). The list includes private accommodation in the whole of Siena Province, including San Gimignano, Montalcino and the Sienese Chianti.

Farm Stays

Farm stays (*agriturismo*) are an excellent way of experiencing the wonderful Tuscan countryside while staying on a farm or a wine estate. Standards vary from simple, rustic accommodation at low prices to relatively luxurious surroundings, complete with private wings and swimming pool. It is best to insist on a description or a photo of the farm since many

may be modern and fail to match up with the visitor's romantic image of Tuscany. Some farms, however, are genuine 16th-century wine and oil estates. There is usually the chance to buy local produce on site and meals are sometimes provided. You need to check the accommodation on offer carefully since this may range from the provision of a few rooms to a vast number of separate self-contained apartments. For obvious reasons, you will normally need a car to make the most of a farm stay.

One of the best (illustrated) guides to farm stays is *Vacanza e Natura, La Guida di Terranostra*, covering the whole of Italy and revised annually. If you speak basic Italian, it is worth obtaining, thanks to its comprehensive use of pictorial symbols to explain the farms.

Reservations: to book a Terranostra farm in Tuscany, telephone your selection from the above book or call 055-280539. The national Terra-nostra organisation in Rome can also supply details of properties in Tuscany: Terranostra, Via XXIV Maggio 43, Rome, tel: 06-4682370/4682420. Most local tourist offices also provide lists of local *Agriturismo* possibilities but pin them down as to the precise nature of the accommodation (location, size, age and atmosphere of the estate).

The regional *Agriturismo* booking centre is Agriturist Ufficio Regionale, Piazza di San Firenze 3, 50122 Florence, tel: 055-287838. In Siena, the booking centre is Agriturist Provinciale, Via della Sapienza 39, tel: 0577-47669. The Italian head office is Agriturist, Corso Vittorio Emanuele 101, Rome, tel: 06-6852342.

Rural Stays

These overlap with farm stays but can include country houses or even entire restored medieval villages (such as Sovicille, near Siena). In general, there is a working farm attached to the accommodation or at least the opportunity to sample or buy wine, oil and local products grown on the estate. As with farm stays, accommodation can be in simple rooms or self-contained apartments. The owners often use the profits from letting to reinvest in the restoration of the family estate or village. With rural stays, the emphasis is on country living in traditional buildings rather than in luxurious villa accommodation.

Some typical rural stays are listed in *Vacanza e Natura, La Guida di Terranostra* (see Farm Stays), while others can be booked through local tourist offices. Many of the owners may speak basic English, French or German, but at least a smattering of Italian is appreciated. Always request detailed descriptions and directions.

The following are typical examples of rural stays:

La Ripolina, Località Pieve di Piana, 53022 Buonconvento, Siena Province. Contact Laura Cresti, tel: 0577-282280; fax: 0577-282954. (Correspondence address: c/o Cresti, Via del Vecchietta 156, 53100 Siena). Most of the holiday apartments are in converted farmhouses; one is actually in a fortified abbey with its 10th-century wall. Farm produce available.

Green Farm, Località Albavola, Madonna dell'Acqua, Via Vecchia Pietrasantina 11, 56017 San Giuliano Terme, Pisa Province, tel: 050-890671/055-280539. This traditional rural estate near the Pisan coast offers Tuscan dishes, farm produce, horse-riding and nature rambles.

San Savino, Val di Chio, Località Santa Lucia 89/a, 52043 Castiglion Fiorentino, Arezzo Province. Contact Maria Assunta Casagni, tel: 0575-651000/055-280539. This 11th-century monastery over-

looks a lake, olive groves and woods and offers several apartments (plus pool and stables).

Castles & Monasteries

Accommodation is available in a variety of castles, palaces and monasteries. Standards will vary from very simple (and cheap) to luxurious. A list of places can be obtained from the ENIT (Italian State Tourist Offices abroad) or enquire at the local tourist office.

Villa & Apartment Rentals

Particularly recommended for the Lunigiana region of northern Tuscany is "Hello Italy", a small company with a good selection of villas and houses of various sizes. The owners live locally and provide a summer "club house" for visitors, as well as very detailed information about the region. (They can also help with property hunting in the area.)

Italy office: Via del Borgo, Tavernelle 54010, tel: 0187-425114.
UK office: East Horsley, Surrey, tel: 01483-285002.

Prices vary enormously, depending on the season and the luxuriousness of the accommodation. In general, prices range from a simple four-person villa in the low season for about L.800,000 to a magnificent secluded villa for about L.4,000,000 in the high season.

The following agencies deal with rentals:

American Agency
Via Porta Rossa 33r, 50129 Florence.
Tel: 055-495070.

The Best in Italy
Via Ugo Foscolo 72, 50124 Florence.
Tel: 055-223064.
Fax: 055-2298912.
A luxurious lettings agency run by Conte Girolama Brandolini d'Adda and his wife, Contessa

Simonetta, offering villas or *palazzi* with pools, stables and other such luxuries.
Solemar
Via Cavour 80, 50129 Florence. Tel: 055-239361.
Casa Club
Via dei Termini 83, 53100 Siena. Tel: 0577-44041.

Youth Hostels

A list of Youth Hostels is available from ENIT (Italian National Tourist Offices) and places can be booked through them or through local Tuscan tourist offices. Alternatively, contact the Associazione Italiana Alberghi per la Gioventù, Via Cavour 44, 00184 Rome, tel: 06-4871152.

The main city youth hostels in Tuscany are:

Florence
Archi Rossi, Via Faenza 94r, tel: 055-290804.
Europa Villa Camerata, Viale Augusto Righi 2–4, 50137 Florence, tel: 055-601451;
Santa Monaca Hostel, Via Santa Monaca 6, tel: 050-296704/268338.

Siena
Ostello della Gioventù "Guido Riccio", Via Fiorentina 17, Località Stellino, tel: 0577-52212. It is appealing but lies 2 km (1 mile) outside the city: catch bus no. 10 or no. 15 from Piazza Matteotti and ask to be let off at Lo Stellino.

Pisa
Centro Turistico Madonna dell'Acqua, Via Pietrasanta 15, Pisa, tel: 050-890622. It is a few km out of town, so take bus no. 3 from the station.

Lucca
Ostello "Il Sercio", Via del Brennero 673, Salicchi, tel: 0583-341811. It is 2 km (1.5 miles) north of Lucca, accessible on bus no. 6.

Where to Eat

Eating Out

Eating patterns in Italy are changing. Many fewer Italians partake of a full lunch on a daily basis, partly due to increased health awareness, partly due to restricted lunch hours. There are now plenty of alternatives to a full restaurant meal where locals will eat. A *tavola calda* is a self-service restaurant with hot and cold dishes at resonable prices – try to avoid those in the most touristy areas. Tuscan towns and cities also usually have a fair share of "*Vinaio*" bars. These are old-fashioned wine bars where all sorts of snacks (or more substantial dishes) are available. These often have a more genuine atmosphere than the *tavola calda*s. Many bars also serve a limited selection of salads, pastas and meat dishes at lunchtime, designed to satisfy office workers who are limited for time.

Sales Tax

Sales tax, known in Italy as IVA, will be included in your restaurant bill. *Pane e coperto*, which includes bread, etc. will also normally be included as a small extra charge.

Restaurant Listing

The following listing of recommended restaurants includes an indication of the prices you may expect to pay per head for a three-course meal including house wine. These, of course, are only guidelines and the bill can vary considerably depending on your choice of food and wine.

$ = below L.40,000
$$ = L.40,000–65,000
$$$ = L.65,000–85,000
$$$$ = over L.85,000

For the more expensive restaurants you are advised to book in advance, especially during the summer months.

Abetone
La Capannina
Via Brennero 520.
Tel: 0573-60562
Friendly restaurant affording spectacular Apennine views and serving fresh local dishes. $$

Arezzo
Antica Osteria L'Agania
Via Mazzini 10.
Tel: 0575-25381
Family-run *trattoria* serving good, homely Tuscan fare. Closed Monday. $
Buca di San Francesco
Piazza San Francesco 1.
Tel: 0575-23271
Fax: 0575-360588
A famous cellar restaurant adjoining San Francesco church, with *Trecento* frescoes and a Roman-Etruscan pavement below. The lovely, medieval atmosphere is matched by straightforward, rustic, tasty cuisine. Closed Monday evening and Tuesday. $$
Il Cantuccio
Via Madonna del Prato 76.
Tel: 0575-26830
Vaulted basement restaurant run by the Volpi family who produce their own wine and olive oil. Try the *bistecca*, perhaps with deep-fried porcini mushrooms. Closed Wednesday. $$

La Capannaccia
Località Campriano.
Tel: 0575-361759
Farmhouse immersed in trees and vines, with a big open fire on which tasty meats are grilled. Simple, rustic food and local wine. Closed Sunday evening and Monday. $
Il Torrino
Strada dei Due Mari 1.
Tel: 0575-360264
Eight km along the San Sepolchro road: a restaurant with a wonderful view and good food. Truffles in season. Closed Monday. $$

Artimino
Biagio Pignatta
Paggeria Medicea, Viale Papa Giovanni XXIII.
Tel: 055-8718086
Part of a four-star hotel which occupies the former stables of a Medici villa. Dishes with historical origins a speciality. $$$
Da Delfina
Via della Chiesa 1.
Tel: 055-8718074
Seasonal ingredients of high quality are served in this elegant setting, overlooking the Medici villa. Tuscan food, often with a twist. Closed Sunday evening and Monday. $$$

Carrara
Locanda Apuana
Via Comunale 1, Colonnata.
Tel: 0585-768003
The famous *lardo di Colonnata* (lard flavoured with rosemary, salt and pepper) is made opposite this *locanda* and will appear on the table if you order *antipasto*. The other house specialities are also often worth considering. Closed Tuesday and sometimes in winter. $
Soldaini
Via Mazzini 11.
Tel: 0585-71459
Simple yet elegant cuisine. Closed Monday. $$
Il Trillo
Via Vecchia Bergola 3, Località Castegnetola.
Tel: 0585-46755

Carrara Restaurants contd

A restaurant in the hills above industrial Massa, 7 km (4 miles) south of Carrara, Il Trillo is set in a lemon grove with sea views. The food is traditional and plentiful. Try the mixed *antipasto*. $

Certaldo Alto
Osteria del Vicario
Via Rivellino 3.
Tel: 0571-668228
Pleasantly set in Romanesque cloisters, this restaurant serves inventive variations on both Tuscan and international dishes. Closed Wednesday. $$.

Cetona
Frateria di Padre Egidio
Convento di San Francesco.
Tel: 0578-238015
Franciscan monastery dating from 1212, now an unusual setting for a top class hotel and restaurant. The set menu (nine courses) changes daily and is very original. Exceptional wine list. Worth the considerable expense. Closed Tuesday. $$$$

Cerbaia
La Tenda Rossa
Piazza del Monumento.
Tel: 055-826132
One of the best restaurants in the Florence area, serving elegant and creative food. Excellent wine list. Worth the trek for a special treat. Closed Thursday lunch, Wednesday and August. $$$$

Florence
VERY EXPENSIVE ($$$$)
Alle Murate
Via Ghibellina 52r.
Tel: 055-240618
Cosy restaurant, fashionable with young Florentines. Creative Tuscan and international dishes; elegant but relaxed atmosphere. Serves fine wines. Closed Monday and August.

Enoteca Pinchiorri
Via Ghibellina 87.
Tel: 055-242777
Reservations are essential at "Italy's finest restaurant", as is elegant dress. Enoteca Pinchiorri occupies a 15th-century palace with fine courtyard for *al fresco* meals. You can expect excellent *nouvelle cuisine* and remarkably rare wines. Closed Monday and Wednesday lunch, Sunday and August.

Relais Le Jardin, Hotel Regency
Piazza Massimo d'Azeglio 3.
Tel: 055-245247
Top-notch food in exclusive hotel restaurant, overlooking a garden. Elegant dress required. Closed Sunday.

Tuscan Specialities

Some of the dishes to expect on a Tuscan menu are:

HORS D'OEUVRES (ANTIPASTI)
Bruschetta (also known as *fettunta*): a slice of Tuscan bread rubbed with garlic and served with lashings of local olive oil drizzled over the top. It is also served with a topping of tomato or white beans.
Crostini: rounds of toasted bread; the traditional Tuscan topping is a rough paté of chicken livers cooked with anchovies and capers.

FIRST COURSES (PRIMI)
Ribollita: a hearty, dense soup of white beans and vegetables thickened with bread.
Pappa al pomodoro: another bread-based "soup", this time flavoured with tomatoes, garlic and basil. Both the above come with thick, pungent olive oil dripped over the top.
Pasta e fagioli: a thick soup of pureéd white beans flavoured with garlic and rosemary in which pasta is cooked.

Panzanella: a summer salad of bread, tomatoes, cucumber, red onions and basil. Dressed with olive oil and a little vinegar, this is a surprisingly refreshing alternative to pasta.
Pappardelle alla lepre: thick, egg pasta strips with hare sauce.

MAIN COURSES (SECONDI)
Bistecca alla fiorentina: the most famous of all Tuscan meat dishes. Often vast (you can order one by the number of people that are going to eat it), this T-bone steak is ideally grilled over an open wood fire, sprinkled with freshly ground black pepper.
Tagliata: a tender piece of steak, char-grilled, sliced and often topped with rocket (*rucola*) leaves.
Trippa alla fiorentina: tripe stewed with tomatoes and garlic.
Lampredotto: intestines usually eaten from a stall in a roll with *salsa verde*.
Cacciucco alla livornese: a rich, spicy fish stew which is served on toasted bread.

Tortino di Carciofia: a thick omelette with artichokes.
Baccalà alla livornese: salt cod cooked in a garlicky tomato sauce.
Cinghiale in umido: a rich wild boar stew; a dish traditionally from the Maremma.
Salsicce e fagioli: baked beans and sausages (really!), but the beans are slow cooked with tomato and garlic, and the sausages are thick and spicy. The two are combined in a hearty stew.
Fagioli all'uccelletto: white haricot beans stewed in tomato and flavoured with sage and garlic.

DESSERTS (DOLCI)
Schiacciata alla fiorentina: a simple sponge cake traditionally eaten around carnival time.
Panforte di Siena: a chewy confection made of honey, candied fruits, almonds and cloves, nowadays sold all over the world.
Castagnaccio: a chestnut cake with pine nuts and sultanas.
Ricciarelli: a very delicate biscuit of honey and almonds from Siena.

Sabatini
Via de' Panzani 9a.
Tel: 055-282802/211559
Fax: 055-210293
This highly traditional restaurant was once the star Florentine haunt and, although it has been overtaken by more fashionable or imaginative restaurants, it remains a sophisticated choice for classic Tuscan cuisine and sober international dishes. Closed Monday.

EXPENSIVE ($$$)
Caffè Concerto
Lungarno Colombo 7.
Tel: 055-677377
Very pleasantly set restaurant on the north bank of the Arno, some way from the centre, with a wood panelled interior. Imaginative, but not overly so, food. Closed Sunday and mid-August.

Cibreo
Via de' Macci 118r.
Tel: 055-2341100
Justly famed, elegant but relaxed restaurant, one of the most popular in the city. Pure Tuscan cuisine, with a creative twist. No pasta, but a selection of superb soups and other *primi*. Closed Sunday and Monday.

Garga
Via del Moro 50–52.
Tel: 055-2398898
This cosy, cramped *trattoria* is run by an Italian-Canadian couple. Against a background of frescoed walls and cut flowers, the trendy or bohemian clientele enjoy *bistecca alla fiorentina*, fish dishes and other varied fare.

Da Stefano
Via Senese 271, Galluzzo.
Tel: 055-2049105
Seafood restaurant in the unremarkable suburb of Galluzzo (towards Siena), serving the freshest fish. Only open for dinner; closed Sunday and August.

Taverna del Bronzino
Via delle Ruote 25/27r.
Tel: 055-495220
Classically comfortable restaurant in a quiet sidestreet, some

way from the centre. Elegantly served traditional food. Try the black *tortellini*, flavoured with truffle. Closed Sunday and August.

Restaurant Prices

The price categories refer to the cost per head for a three-course meal including house wine.

$ = below L.40,000
$$ = L.40,000–65,000
$$$ = L.65,000–85,000
$$$$ = over L.85,000

MODERATE ($$)
Alla Vecchia Bettola
Viale Ariosto 32–34/r.
Tel: 055-224158
South of the river, away from the centre: the marble-topped tables and wooden benches are popular with Florentines filling up on good, rustic food. Closed Sunday.

Angiolino
Via Santo Spirito 36r.
Tel: 055-2398976
Bustling restaurant serving generous helpings of Florentine food. Closed Sunday evening and Monday.

Baldovino
Via S. Giuseppe 22/r.
Tel: 055-241773
Located just off Piazza Santa Croce, at Baldovino you can eat anything from a salad to a full meal, without sacrificing quality. Refreshingly modern decor, young Scottish owner. Closed Sunday.

Bibe
Via delle Bagnese 1/r.
Tel: 055-2049085
You need transport for the short journey to this above average rustic *trattoria* which has a delightful garden for *al fresco* meals. Magnificent puddings. Closed Thursday lunch and Wednesday.

Buca Mario
Piazza Ottaviani 16r.
Tel: 055-214179

Cellar restaurant with good home-made pasta and grilled meats. Very popular with tourists. Closed Wednesday, Thursday lunch, and three weeks in July.

Cantinetta Antinori
Piazza Antinori 3.
Tel: 055-292234
Restaurant in a 15th-century *palazzo*, serving typical Tuscan snacks and meals with wines from the well-known Antinori estates. A good place for a light lunch at the bar or a fuller meal in the elegant dining room. Closed weekends.

Coco Lezzone
Via del Parioncino 26r.
Tel: 055-287178
Traditional food of the highest quality. Ingredients are always very fresh and the menu changes somewhat with the seasons. Closed Sunday and Tuesday evening.

Dulcamara
Via Dante Castiglione 2, Località Cercina.
Tel: 055-4255021
Restaurant set in a shady garden, with an enclosed verandah for cooler evenings. Good, imaginative food in a truly relaxed atmosphere. Vegetarian options. Open for dinner only, except on Sunday; closed Monday, except in August.

Latini
Via dei Palchetti 6r.
Tel: 055-210916
You can't book for this popular, noisy *trattoria* and there is often a long queue. Communal tables; enjoyable atmosphere. Not a good choice for vegetarians: huge plates of meat are specialities. Closed Monday and August.

Mamma Gina
Borgo San Jacopo 37r.
Tel: 055-2396009
Set in a Renaissance *palazzo*, this *trattoria* produces hearty Tuscan dishes. Closed Sunday.

Osteria Caffè Italiano
Via Isole delle Stinche 11/13r.
Tel: 055-289368
One of the new "in" places,

Florence restaurants contd

under the same directorship as Alle Murate (above). Short menu but high standards. Open 10am "till late". Closed Monday.

Osteria dei Cento Poveri
Via Palazzuolo 31r.
Tel: 055-218846
Don't be put off by the number of tourists in this rustically cosy *osteria*: the food, a mixture of Tuscan and Pugliese, is excellent. Open kitchen Closed Wednesday lunch and Tuesday.

Pane e Vino
Via San Niccolò 70r.
Tel: 055-2476956
Pleasant, informal restaurant with an interesting menu (including a daily "*Menu Degustazione*" with six courses) and excellent wines. Open till midnight (rare in Florence). Closed Sunday.

INEXPENSIVE ($)

All'Antico Ristoro di Cambi
Via S. Onofrio 1r.
Tel: 055-217134
Busy, rustic *trattoria* serving genuine Florentine food, popular with local intellectuals. Terrace in summer. Closed Sunday, and a week in mid-August.

Le Belle Donne
Via delle Belle Donne 16/r.
Tel: 055-2382609
Tiny hole-in-the-wall restaurant with a marvellous counter display of fresh fruit and vegetables. Always crowded. The menu is written on a board and features Florentine standards with some variations. Closed Saturday and Sunday.

Borgo Antico
Piazza Santa Spirito 6r.
Tel: 055-210437
Trendy hang-out for young Florentines. Good pizzas and pasta, but also full meals. Loud music inside, but a lovely terrace on the piazza for summer dining.

Cantinetta da Verrazzano
Via de' Tavolini 18-20.
Tel: 055-268590
Pleasant, wood-panelled coffee house and wine bar in the cen-

Restaurant Prices

The price categories refer to the cost per head for a three-course meal including house wine.

$ = below L.40,000
$$ = L.40,000–65,000
$$$ = L.65,000–85,000
$$$$ = over L.85,000

tre of town. Delicious sandwiches and snacks; wines from the Verrazzano estate. Closed Sunday.

La Casalinga
Via del Michelozzo 9r.
Tel: 055-218624
One of the best value eateries in town. Plentiful helpings of home cooking attract locals as well as visitors. Family-run. Closed Sunday.

Da Burde
Via Pistoiese 6/r.
Tel: 055-317206
Authentic Tuscan *trattoria* someway along the old Pistoia road, with home-made soups, pastas and puddings. Closed evenings and Sunday.

Da Nerbone
Mercato Centrale di San Lorenzo.
Tel: 055-219949
Authentic market eatery as old as the market itself. The clientele includes the local stallholders. Dishes like tripe and *lampredotto*, as well as usual *trattoria* fare. There are a few tables. Closed evenings and Sunday.

Da Ruggero
Via Senese 89r.
Tel: 055-220542
Comfortingly small, old-fashioned *trattoria* on the old Siena road. Traditional food and decor. Booking essential. Closed Tuesday and Wednesday.

Da Sergio
Piazza San Lorenzo 8r.
Tel: 055-281941
Big, airy *trattoria*, hidden behind a row of stalls. A haunt of market workers and discerning

tourists. Short, simple, seasonal menu; fish is featured Tuesday–Thursday. No desserts served. Open for lunch only; closed Sunday.

Enoteca de' Giraldi
Via de' Giraldi 4/r.
Tel: 055-216518
A pleasant wine bar in a high-ceilinged, former stable building, which once formed part of the Palazzo Borghese. There is an interesting selection of Tuscan wines. Handy for the Bargello.

Gaugin
Via degli Alfani 24r.
Tel: 055-2340616
Creative vegetarian food with several Middle Eastern dishes on the menu, in a pleasant and relaxed setting.

Le Mossacce
Via del Proconsolo 55r.
Tel: 055-294361
Trattoria between the Cathedral and the Bargello, serving pasta dishes and basic Tuscan fare. Popular lunchtimes with office workers. Closed Saturday and Sunday.

Il Pizzaiuolo
Via dei Macci 113/r.
Tel: 055-241171
The name means "pizza maker" and the varied pizzas are wonderful, but there's plenty more besides. Try the *antipasto della casa*. Popular; booking recommended. Closed Tuesday and August.

Ruth's
Via Farini 2a.
Tel: 055-2480888
Pleasant and airy restaurant serving vegetarian food. Closed Friday pm and Saturday lunch.

Santa Lucia
Via Ponte alla Mosse 102r.
Tel: 055-353255
Authentically Neapolitan, no-frills *trattoria*, serving the best pizzas in town. Good seafood, too. Booking essential.

Tarocchi
Via dei Renai 14r.
Tel: 055-234 3912
Pizzeria with lively, friendly atmosphere . Closed Monday.

Coffee and Ice Cream in Florence

Ice Cream Parlours
No visit to Florence would be complete without tasting an ice cream made on the premises. Choose ice cream parlours (*gelateria*) with a *Produzione Propria* (home-made) sign or credentials. A selection of good *gelaterie* are:

Bar Ricchi, Piazza Santo Spirito.
Festival del Gelato, Via del Corso 75r.
Perché No, Via Tavolini 194, near the Cathedral.
Vivoli, Via Isola delle Stinche 7.

Closed Sunday afternoon and Monday. Recently enlarged. No seats but a lot of atmosphere.

Popular cafés include:
Caffè Italiano, Via della Condotta 56/r. Central for drinks and light lunches. The pleasant upstairs room has seating.
Giacosa, Via de' Tornabuoni 83. Upmarket café where the young affluent eat home-made pastries with the best cappuccino in Florence. Closed Monday.
Gilli, Piazza della Repubblica 36–39/r. Lavishly decorated

café at which to sit and watch the world go by. Expensive.
Giubbe Rosse, Piazza della Repubblica. Once favoured by writers and poets, and still popular with a more mixed crowd. Has an open-air café and a dining room serving snacks or full meals.
Hemingway, Piazza Piattellina 9/r. Pleasant, airy bar situated in the Oltrarno (over the river). Open 4pm–late.
Rivoire, Piazza della Signoria 5. Views of the Palazzo Vecchio and a lovely marble interior but prices are high. Closed Monday.

Trattoria Cibreo
Piazza Ghiberti 35.
Tel: 055-2341100
Annexe of the restaurant of the same name (*see Expensive, above*), but with meals at half the price. Few frills, but the food is basically the same as in the main restaurant. No bookings. Closed Sunday and Monday.
Trattoria Da Za-Za
Piazza del Mercato Centrale 26r.
Tel: 055-215411
Good, earthy food and delicious home-made puddings. The riotous atmosphere is enjoyed by both locals and tourists. Closed Sunday.
Trattoria del Carmine
Piazza del Carmine 18/r.
Tel: 055-218601
Small, traditional *trattoria* in the Oltrarno. Part of the long menu changes seasonally; all tastes catered for. Good Tuscan soups; huge portions of home-made lasagne. Closed Sunday.

Gaiole In Chianti
Badia a Coltibuono
Tel: 0577-749424
Fax: 0577-749235
Set on a glorious rural wine estate 5 km (3 miles) from Gaiole, complete with 11th-century abbey. Specialities include home-made pasta with wild duck sauce and *antipasto della*

Badia. Wine and oil from the estate is for sale. Popular with tourists on the Chianti trail. Closed Monday, and January and February. $$
Il Carlino d'Oro
Località San Regolo.
Tel: 0577-747136
Family-run *trattoria*, far removed from the tourists that swarm around this part of the Chianti. Try the deep-fried chicken and rabbit. Open for lunch only (except in August); closed Monday. $
Castello di Spaltenna
Tel: 0577-749483
Fax: 0577-749269
Magnificent restaurant in a hotel converted from a fortified monastery. Dishes use fresh local ingredients and food is cooked in a wood-burning stove. Closed Monday. $$$$

Grosseto
Il Canto del Gallo
Via Mazzini 29.
Tel: 0564-414589
Tiny *trattoria* in the old town walls. Interesting cooking with, unusually, vegetables featuring strongly. Closed Sunday. $$
Da Remo
Rispescia Stazione 5/7, Rispescia.
Tel: 0564-405015
Unassuming bar/*trattoria* on the

edge of a small village, 10 km (6 miles) south of Grosseto. Super fresh fish. Try the generous mixed antipasti. Closed Wednesday. $$

Livorno
Enoteca DOC
Via Goldoni 42.
Tel: 0586-887583
Good, central place for wine, snacks and light meals, fish or otherwise. Open for lunch only; closed Monday. $
Gennarino
Via Santa Fortunata 11.
Tel: 0586-888093
Classic fish restaurant serving local specialities such as *triglia* (red mullet) *alla livornese* (with garlic and mushrooms). Closed Wednesday, and February. $$

Lucca
Antico Caffè della Mura
Piazzale V. Emanuele.
Tel: 0583-47962
Elegant garden restaurant and caffè on the city walls. Napery is crisp and white; glasses gleam. Extensive menu, with specialities like rabbit in mint sauce. Closed Tuesday. $$$
Buatino
Via del Borgo Giannotti 508.
Tel: 0583-343207
Trattoria just outside the city walls, offering excellent value,

Lucca Restaurants contd

largely traditional meals. Tasty roast pork. Background jazz. Prices are even lower lunchtime. Closed Sunday. $
La Buca di Sant'Antonio
Via della Cervia 1.
Tel: 0583-55881
Very famous restaurant serving Lucchese and Garfagnana classic dishes (try the *fettuccine* with pigeon sauce), as well as dishes with a more modern slant. Closed Sunday evening and Monday. $$
Giglio
Piazza del Giglio 2.
Tel: 0583-494058
Fax: 0583-55881
With the reputation for being Lucca's best seafood restaurant, this charming spot spills out on to the piazza. Comfortable interior with a fine traditional fireplace, which is obviously best appreciated in winter. Closed Tuesday evening, Wednesday and February. $$
La Mora
Località Ponte a Moriano.
Tel: 0583-406402
The 15-minute drive north of Lucca (on the Barga road) is worth the effort for the superb food. Seasonal local ingredients are inventively prepared and beautifully presented. $$$
Gli Orti di Via Elisa
Via Elisa 17.
Tel: 0583-491241
Good choice for a quick lunch: a busy *trattoria* with a wide choice of pasta and pizzas, plus a self-service salad bar. $
Solferino
San Macario in Piano.
Tel: 0583-59118
Some 6 km (4 miles) from Lucca, this is rated among the best restaurants in rural Tuscany. There are two sections: one serves more sophisticated dishes; the other is an *osteria* with cheaper, simpler fare and local wine. Closed Thursday lunch, Wednesday and two weeks in August. $$/$$$

Marina di Pisa
Da Gino
Via Curzolari 2.
Tel: 050-35408
Excellent fish restaurant near the sea. Closed Monday evening and Tuesday. $$$

Montecatini Terme
Enoteca Da Giovanni
Via Garibaldi 25.
Tel: 0572-71695
Not surprisingly, the wine list of the Enoteca is extensive, but the food merits a visit in itself. Plenty of choice of meat and fish. The annexe, known as the Cucina da Giovanni, serves more traditional Tuscan fare and is cheaper. Closed Monday. $$$
Locanda Narciso
Via Marruota 79.
Tel: 0572-72765
Trattoria offering some variation on the Tuscan theme. Game and truffles feature in the autumn. Closed Thursday. $$

Montemerano
Da Caiano
Via Canonica 3.
Tel: 0564-602817
Pretty restaurant in Grosseto province, one of the best in Tuscany. Exquisite and creative food, specialising in wild mushrooms and truffles; complementary wine list. $$$$

Montepulciano
La Grotta
Località San Biagio.
Tel: 0578-757607
Once the home of architect Sangallo, and right next to his stunningly positioned church of San Biagio. Rustic Tuscan dishes, with French influence from the owner. Closed Wednesday. $$$

Monteriggioni
Il Pozzo
Piazza Roma 2.
Tel: 0577-304127
Famous restaurant full of foreigners in summer, but deservedly popular, in a gem of a little walled town. Dishes from

Tuscany and further afield. Closed Sunday evening and Monday. $$$

Pescia
Cecco
Via Forti 96.
Tel: 0572-477955
Mushrooms, asparagus and truffles feature here, and the fish is also good. Closed Monday. $$
Monte a Pescia
Località Monte a Pescia.
Tel: 0572-478887
Trattoria specialising in meats grilled over an open fire. Lovely terrace overlooking olive trees and hills. Closed Wednesday. $

Pisa
Al Ristoro dei Vecchi Macelli,
Via Volturno 49.
Tel: 050-20424
Famous restaurant with a cosy ambience. Try the *Menu di Primi*, which involves a succession of pasta dishes. Closed Sunday lunch and Wednesday. $$$
L'Artilafo
Via Volturno 38.
Tel: 050-27010
Pleasant restaurant serving creative variations on a Tuscan theme. Open only for dinner; closed Wednesday. $$
La Mescita
Via Cavalca 2.
Tel: 050-544294
There's a new, less traditional look for this wine bar/*trattoria*, situated near the market. Good wines; cheese and cold meats snacks; small selection of regularly changing hot dishes. Closed Monday. $
Osteria dei Cavalieri
Via San Frediano 16.
Tel: 050-580858
Modern restaurant near Piazza dei Cavalieri, serving fish and meat dishes. A simpler menu is offered at lunchtimes. Closed Saturday lunch, Sunday and August. $$
Pergoletta
Via delle Belle Torri 36.
Tel: 050-542458
Set in a fortified tower-house,

this is a welcoming restaurant with a garden. Most typical are the grills and soups. Closed Monday. $
Sergio
Lungarno Pacinotti 1.
Tel: 050-580580
Elaborate food in a famous restaurant. Closed Sunday, January and the last two weeks in July. $$$
Trattoria Asmara
Via Cammeo 27.
Tel: 050-552711
The French proprietor has made this into a bistro, with pretty pink tablecloths, superb food and walls covered in paintings by artists who make it their regular haunt. Situated at the Porta Nuova. Closed Friday. $
Trattoria Kostas
Via del Borghetto 39.
Tel: 050-571467
Restaurant serving (but not exclusively) several Greek specialities. Try the *ravioli* stuffed with Savoy cabbage in a cheesy sauce. Closed Monday and August. $$

Pistoia
Il Castagno di Pier Angelo
Via Castagno, Località Pitecchio.
Tel: 0573-42214
Delightfully set in the hills, 20 km (12 miles) north of Pistoia: a friendly restaurant highly recommended for its basically Tuscan food. The dishes are seasonal and change frequently. $$
Il Ritrovo di Iccio
Via dei Fabbri 5/7.
Tel: 0573-366935
Friendly restaurant in the historic centre, featuring piano music and Tuscan cooking, plus Roman dishes like *gran faro* (wheat broth). $$
La Limonaia
Via di Gello 9a.
Tel: 0573-400453
Old lemonary transformed into an appealing, rustic *trattoria* a little way from the centre of town. Unusual herbs and flavourings pep up the Tuscan food. Closed Monday evening and Tuesday. $

Porto Ercole
Bacco in Toscana
Via San Paolo delle Croce 6.
Tel: 0564-833078
Good selection of seafood in a trendy port. The mixed *antipasti* and the lobster are both recommended. Only open for dinner; closed Monday–Wednesday in winter. $$$

Restaurant Prices

The price categories refer to the cost per head for a three-course meal including house wine.

$ = below L.40,000
$$ = L.40,000–65,000
$$$ = L.65,000–85,000
$$$$ = over L.85,000

Porto Santo Stefano
Dal Greco
Via del Molo 1/2.
Tel: 0564-814885
Intimate fish restaurant with a few tables on the quayside (book these). Generous and interesting *antipasti*. $$$

Prato
Osvaldo Baroncelli
Via Fra Bartolomeo 13.
Tel: 0574-23810
Fine, well-established restaurant which mixes traditional and innovative choices. Fine wine list. Closed Sunday. $$$

Radda In Chianti
Al Chiasso dei Portici
Chiasso dei Portici 1.
Tel: 0577-738774
Traditional *trattoria* beneath the town walls. Short menu of rustic dishes. Closed Tuesday. $
Vignale
Fattoria Vignale, Via XX Settembre 23.
Tel: 0577-738094
Fax: 0577-738730
Restaurant housed in a converted farm-building used for olive-pressing, serving refined Tuscan cuisine, with imaginative versions of regional dishes.

However, prices are high and tourists abound. Closed Thursday and November–March. $$$

San Gimignano
Dorandò
Vicolo dell'Oro 2.
Tel: 0577-941862
Stylish, friendly restaurant specialising in recipes with ancient origins. Notes on the Etruscan or Renaissance recipes are provided. Closed Monday $$$
Osteria delle Catene
Via Mainardi 18.
Tel: 0577-941966
Another of the new wave of *trattorie* where traditional and contemporary ideas successfully co-exist. Try the local white Vernaccia wine. Closed Wednesday and January. $$

San Vincenzo
Gambero Rosso
Piazza della Vittoria.
Tel: 0565-701021
Elegant restaurant overlooking the sea; one of Tuscany's best. Fish features prominently. The wine list is around 100 pages long. Worth saving up for. $$$$

Siena
Al Marsili
Via del Castoro 3.
Tel: 0577-47154
Fax: 0577-47338
Elegant restaurant in an ancient building with the wine cellars cut deep into the limestone. Sophisticated cuisine, including *gnocchi* in duck sauce. Closed Monday. $$
Castelvecchio
Via Castelvecchio 65.
Tel: 0577-49586
Restaurant converted from ancient stables in the oldest part of the city. Contemporary dishes with traditional flavours. Interesting wine list. Closed on Tuesday. $$
Certosa di Maggiano
Via Certosa 82.
Tel: 0577-288189
This converted Carthusian monastery serves gourmet food in a magical setting: a cloistered

Siena Restaurants **contd**

courtyard overlooking Siena.
$$$$
Da Guido
Vicolo del Pettinaio.
Tel: 0577-28042
Fax: 0577-271370
Veritable Sienese institution, set
in medieval premises and long
popular with visiting VIPs. Tradi-
tional Sienese cuisine. Closed
Wednesday and January. $$–$$$
Il Ghibellino
Via dei Pellegrini 26.
Tel: 0577-288079
Pleasantly rustic *trattoria* near
the Piazza del Campo, with a
seasonal menu of traditional
dishes. Closed Monday. $$
La Torre
Via Salicotto 7–9.
Tel: 0577-287545
Family-run restaurant and popu-
lar young haunt below the Torre
del Mangia. Closed Tuesday and
part of August. $
Osteria Il Carroccio
Via Casato di Sotto 32.
Tel: 0577-41165
Well-run, tiny, quaint and highly
typical *trattoria* serving simple
local dishes. Closed Wednesday
and February. $
Osteria Le Chiacchera
Costa di S. Antonio 4.
Tel: 0577-280631
Small, rustic *osteria* offering
Sienese fare (try the thick *pici*),
on a steep street leading down
to Santa Caterina. Closed Tues-
day. $
Osteria Le Logge
Via del Porrione 33.
Tel: 0577-48013
Restaurant set in a 19th-century
grocer's shop, with an authentic
dark wood and marble interior.
On the menu are duck and fen-
nel, chicken and lemon and
such exotic dishes as stuffed
guinea fowl (*faraona*). The
house olive oil and wines are
produced by the owners. Closed
Sunday. $$
Papei
Piazza del Mercato 6.
Tel: 0577-280894
Ideal place for sampling genuine

Tuscan Wines

The *Denominazione di Origine
Controllata* (DOC) *e Garantita*
(DOCG) is a system of controlling Italian wine by EU rules
similar to the French *Appella-
tion Contrôlée*, but it does not
always guarantee top quality.
Chianti, the best-known wine in
Italy, and Brunello di Montal-

Sienese home cooking in generous helpings. There's a variety
of grilled meats, too. Closed
Monday. $$
Tullio ai Tre Cristi
Vicolo di Provenzano 1–7.
Tel: 0577-280608
Restaurant where frescoed
walls add to the atmosphere.
Closed Monday and January. $

Sinalunga
Locanda dell'Amorosa
Tel: 0577-679497
Fax: 0577-678216
Superb restaurant romantically
set in the stables of a medieval
estate. The food is a mix of trad-
itional and new, with a good
choice. There is no better place
to eat a *bistecca chianina*
(farmed locally). Closed Tuesday
lunch. $$$

Tirrenia
Dante e Ivana
Viale del Tirreno 207c.
Tel/fax: 050-32549
Pleasant fish restaurant with an
open kitchen and a tank from
which to choose the ingredients
of your meal. Closed Sunday. $$$

Viareggio
L'Oca Bianca
Via Coppino 409.
Tel: 0584-388477
Possibly Viareggio's finest
restaurant, with a creative and
original seafood menu. Exquisite
service; exceptional wine list.
Near the port. Closed Wednes-
day lunch and Tuesday. $$$
Il Porto
Via Coppino 319.
Tel: 0584-383878

cino and Nobile di Montepulciano, all from Tuscany, have
been awarded the status of
DOCG. Other DOC and Vino di
Tavola wines that are often of
excellent quality are Vernaccia,
Aleatico, Bianco Pisano San
Torpè and the red and white
wines from Montescudaio.

Cheaper than many of the good
fish restaurants in town and
famous for its visually spectacu-
lar steamed crustaceans. $$
Romano
Via Mazzini 122.
Tel: 0584-31382
Elegant and formal, yet welcom-
ing, restaurant with a pleasant
garden. Excellent seafood –
some of the best in Tuscany –
creatively put together. Reserva-
tions required. Closed Monday
and January. $$$
Trattoria La Darsena
Via Vigilio 154/156.
Tel: 0584-392785
Modest *trattoria* hidden away in
the backstreets among the boatyards, serving the freshest
seafood at remarkably low
prices (particularly lunchtime
when boatyard workers are in).
The antipasti is almost a meal
in itself. Closed Monday evening
and Sunday. $–$$

Volterra
Badò
Borgo San Lazzaro 9.
Tel: 0588-86477
Simple, family-run *trattoria* spe-
cialising in game. Try the wild
boar stew, or the mushrooms.
Open for lunch only; closed
Wednesday. $
Il Sacco Fiorentino
Piazza XX Settembre 18.
Tel: 0588-88537
Pleasant and welcoming eatery
in two parts: one side is a *trat-
toria* serving interesting Tuscan
fare; the other is a wine bar with
a shorter, cheaper, more trad-
itional menu and snacks. Closed
Wednesday. $–$$

Culture

Archaeological Sites

There are various places of archaeological interest in Tuscany. These include **Etruscan** (8th–2nd century BC) sites at Volterra, Fiesole, Arezzo, Chiusi, Vetulonia and on the island of Elba. There is an archaeological museum in Florence and other museums in Volterra, Chiusi, Cortona, Asciano, Grosseto and Massa Marittima.

Notable **Roman** (8th century BC–5th century AD) remains can be seen at Fiesole, Cosa, Roselle, Volterra and Arezzo.

Art and Architecture

Architecture
Tuscany is a veritable treasure trove of architectural history (see the feature on *pages 111–16*).
• Churches and civil buildings from the **Romanesque** period can be found at Pisa, Florence, Lucca, Siena, Pistoia and Arezzo.
• The most important **Gothic** buildings are in Florence, Siena, Pisa, Pistoia and Arezzo.
• Tuscany also abounds in religious and secular **Renaissance** buildings, Florence being the most important centre.

Art
Renaissance art is of course what Tuscany is most famous for. The most outstanding Renaissance collections are in Florence, in the **Uffizi Gallery**, the **Pitti Palace Gallery** and the **San Marco Museum**.

Works of art from the late Renaissance and Mannerist periods, the baroque, the neo-classical and romantic, and also the 20th century are exhibited at most art galleries and museums in main cities.

Sightseeing

Details of important museums and art galleries, together with opening hours and entrance fees, are included in the *Places* section of this book.

Special tickets: Be sure to take advantage of the "multi-entrance" tickets promoted by local tourist authorities: one example is Siena's "*Biglietto di Ingresso Cumulativo*" allowing you entry to a number of museums over a three-day period.

Florence also offers a ticket for its six communal museums, valid for six months (see below).

Florence
A free monthly publication, *Florence Today*, is published in Italian and English and lists current exhibitions. It also has informative articles about museums and places of interest.

The Friends of Florentine Museums Association (Via degli Alfani 39) has 12,000 members. They arrange museum visits 9–11pm in the summer, with orchestral recitals, to allow Florentine workers to visit museums during the tourist season, and for tourists to get a further insight into Florentine culture. In response to popular demand, the authorities have extended the opening hours of museums in summer. Many have special evening opening times. Contact the Florence tourist office for details.

Entry prices for museums and galleries range from L.3,000–12,000, with the Uffizi the most expensive. State museums (such as the Uffizi) are closed on Monday while most other museums close on Tuesday or Wednesday. Get the *Biglietto Cumulativo*, a ticket which allows you to see all *Musei Comunali* (the city council-run museums) on one ticket.

Also, every year, Florence offers a free museum week (*La Settimana di Beni Culturali*), when all the state museums are open free of charge. Look out for this in December or April.

Pisa
The main sites may be easily visited on foot or by local bus but taking a horse and carriage is a pleasant introduction to the city. Prices are negotiable, but generally start around L.30,000 for a half-hour ride along the Arno, to the Piazza Cavalieri and the Piazza del Duomo. A recommended time is about 2pm, when the streets are quiet and the tourist crowds are having their midday meal. Buy a joint ticket to see all the sights on the Campo dei Miracoli.

Siena
The tourist office can provide a list of authorised guides. Opening hours and entrance fees may vary. With one week's notice, you can visit any of the *Contrada* (district) museums that celebrate the *Palio* and the ancient city traditions, tel: 0577-42209.

War Cemeteries

Tuscany has seen its share of war during the 20th century, and there are several cemeteries where the war dead are buried.

There is an **American War Cemetery**, near Falciani (about 8 km/5 miles south of Florence, towards Siena), tel: 055-2020020. It is open daily till 5pm and later during the summer. The **British Commonwealth War Cemetery** is on road No. 67 near Girone, 7 km (4 miles) east of Florence, towards Arezzo, and is open 9am–5pm (9am–1pm on Sundays). The **German War Cemetery** is near Traversa, just beyond the Futa pass, and is open 8.30am–noon and 2–7pm.

Music, Ballet & Opera

To keep up-to-date with events, buy *Firenze Spettacolo*, the monthly listings magazine. (Although it is in Italian, the listings themselves are quite straightforward.) Alternatively, obtain *Events*, another popular listings magazine and check the entertainment pages of *La Nazione*, the regional newspaper. If you read Italian well, then get *Toscana Qui*, and *Firenze ieri, oggi, domani*.

Florence
The *Maggio Musicale* music festival, held from mid-May to the end of June, is a big event with top names in concert, ballet and opera performing in various venues throughout the city. Tickets are available from the Teatro Comunale, Corso Italia 16, tel: 055-211158, and this is where most of the events are staged, although concerts, formal and informal, are held throughout the summer in cloisters, piazzas or in the Boboli Gardens.

The opera season opens at the end of September or beginning of October. During the *Estate Fiesolana* – Fiesole's summer festival – concerts, opera, ballet and theatre are held in the town's Roman amphitheatre. Classical concerts are also held in many of the city churches.

The principal venue for quality chamber music concerts in Florence is the **Teatro della Pergola**, Via della Pergola (tel: 055-2479651), which is a superb example of a 17th-century theatre (inaugurated in 1656). These concerts are generally held at weekends, and are well publicised.

The **Fiesole Music School** in San Domenico also holds a concert series (tel: 055-599725 for information), and the Orchestra Regionale Toscana's lively concert series runs December–May. They also perform regularly in

other Tuscan provinces (tel: 055-242767 for details).

Florence's **Teatro Verdi**, Via Verdi (tel: 055-212320) is the venue for a wider range of entertainment, from light opera and ballet to jazz and rock concerts.

To find out what rock, jazz and Latin American music is on offer, check in the latest issue of *Firenze Spettacolo* listings magazine.

Pisa
In May and June, concerts are held at various annual festivals and fairs, especially during the *Gioco del Ponte* on the last Sunday in June.

Siena
The **Accademia Musicale Chigiana** (Chigiana Academy of Music), Via di Città 89, 53100 Siena (tel: 0577-46152) provides proficiency courses in July and August for young performers, both Italian and foreign.

Public performances of rare, unpublished and new music are held in August each year during the Sienese Music Week. They include opera, symphonic concerts and chamber orchestras.

A theoretical and practical course in jazz music is held annually at the Seminari Nazionali Senesi, Via Vallerozzi 77, 53100 Siena, tel: 0577-47552. This training centre is among the best-known for jazz music in Europe.

Theatre

To find out what plays are on, buy *La Repubblica* newspaper on Tuesday. The main theatres are the **Teatro della Pergola**, Via della Pergola 18, tel: 055-247-9651 and **Teatro Niccolini**, Via Ricasoli, tel: 055-213282. Most productions are in Italian.

The **Teatro Metastasio** in Prato is one of the best places in Tuscany to see prose, tel: 0574-608501. There are also numerous smaller companies performing regularly in Florence.

Look out for the listings in *Firenze Spettacolo*.

A useful ticket agency is Box Office, Via Faenza 139r, Florence, tel: 055-210804. It is best to go in person to buy tickets for all events from opera to rock music.

Cinema

The cinema is well attended by Italians. There are numerous foreign films, sometimes in English or other foreign languages with Italian subtitles.

In summer, open-air cinemas are set up in country towns and in quiet city squares, such as the one in Lucca.

The main English-language cinema in Florence is the **Astro**, Piazza Simone, near Santa Croce, which shows films every night except Monday. Astro films are not always the latest. There are two cinemas that show foreign films in their original versions: the **Goldini Original Sound**, Via dei Serragli (tel: 055-222473) on Wednesdays, and the **Odeon**, Piazza Strozzi (tel: 055-214068) on Mondays.

Diary of Events

AREZZO
First weekend of every month: Antique fair in the square.
Sunday in mid-June: *Giostra del Saracino* – Saracen's Joust. Mounted knights representing the four districts of the city attack a wooden effigy of a Turk. Procession beforehand.

CORTONA
July/August: Cortona Summer Festival with a full artistic programme.
15 August: *Sagra della Bistecca* – Feast of the Beefsteak.
September (first half of the month): antiques exhibition.

FLORENCE
Easter Day: *Scoppio del Carro*, the Explosion of the "Carriage" (actually fireworks on a float) and the emergence of a dove. Colourful musical processions.
Ascension Day: *Festa del Grillo*, Festival of the Crickets in the Cascine park. Sale of crickets and sweets.
End of April: Flower Show, Parterre, near Piazza Libertà – a riot of colour.
May and June: *Maggio Musicale Fiorentino* – performances of opera, ballet and concerts to a high standard, much patronised by the Florentines themselves.
24 June: *San Giovanni* – Florence's patron saint's day, with a holiday in the city and an evening firework display near Piazzale Michelangelo. *Calcio in costume* (*Calcio Fiorentino*) – football in medieval costume in Piazza Santa Croce. Three other matches are also played in June/July.
7 September: night festival of the *Rificolona* (lanterns) – procession of carts, lanterns and singers.

LIVORNO
Late July/August: *Effetto Venezia* – lively 10-day festival in the city's Venetian quarter. The little canals provide a suggestive setting for shows, street theatre, music and food. The local fish stew (*cacciucco*) is sold from stalls.

LUCCA
September: *Luminaria di Santa Croce* – a religious procession.

LUCIGNANO
Last two Sundays in May: *Maggiolata Lucignanese* – festival that includes a procession of carts decorated with allegorical scenes in flowers.

MASSA MARITTIMA
Sunday following May 20 and the **second Sunday in August**: *Balestro del Girifalco* – a-crossbow competition involving a mechanical falcon.

MONTICCHIELLO
Last 15 days of July: *Il Teatro Povero* – "The Poor Theatre" presents a drama written and acted by everyone about the local history and culture of the farmer.

PIENZA
August/September: "Meeting with a Master of Art" in the council chamber of the Town Hall. Many famous artists have displayed their work here.
First Sunday of September: *Fiera del Cacio* – a fair devoted to sheepmilk cheese – for which Pienza is renowned.

PISA
May and **June**: concerts at various annual festivals and fairs, especially during the *Gioco del Ponte* on the last Sunday of June.
16–17 June: *Luminaria di San Ranieri* – thousands of candles are displayed on buildings along the Arno creating a spectacle after dark. Boat race in the evening of the second day.

PISTOIA
25 July: *Giostra dell'Orso* – Joust of the Bear in Piazza del Duomo. A mock battle takes place between a wooden bear and 12 knights in costume.

SIENA
28–30 April: Feast of St Catherine.
July 2 and **16 August**: *Palio* – traditional horse race. For tickets and hotel bookings, write to the tourist office six months in advance. Visits may be made to the museums of the 17 *contrade* (districts) of Siena by giving at least one week's notice (list of museums from the tourist office).
Mid July–August: *Incontri in Terra di Siena* – chamber music festival featuring concerts of international quality, held in stunning settings south of Siena such as Castelluccio, Pienza, Montepulciano and Sinalunga.
August: Sienese Music Week – public performances of opera, symphonic concerts and chamber music.

TORRE DEL LAGO
July and August: Puccini Opera Festival, near the composer's villa on Lake Massaciuccoli.

VIAREGGIO
February: *Carnevale* – one of the best carnivals in Italy.

VOLTERRA
First Sunday in September: *Torneo di Tiro con la Balestra* – crossbow tournament in Piazza dei Priori.
End of September: *Fiera Regionale degli Uccelli* – regional bird fair.

Nightlife

Italians enjoy playing and listening to music: violin players stroll round restaurants, and small bands often play at gatherings in preference to taped music. Summer discos are set up in resorts, and dancing usually takes place outside a restaurant or bar. All the cities have a wide variety of music and entertainment on offer, but nightclubs open or close down with some regularity, so you should ask around for recommendations.

To keep up with the ever-changing Tuscan scene, buy *Firenze Spettacolo*, the listings magazine, or the Tuesday edition of *La Repubblica*.

Bars and Live Music

The following places are all in Florence. Note that most places are closed on Monday.

Be Bop, Via dei Servi 76c. Cocktail bar with live music: country, blues and jazz. Entrance free.

Caffè, Piazza Pitti 9, tel: 051-296241. Chic and refined: a cosy spot to chat to friends, during the day or evening.

Caffèdeco, Piazza della Libertà 45. This stylish, Art Deco style, this stylish bar is popular with jazz-lovers.

Caffè Donatello, Piazza Donatello. Opens at 7pm for cocktails, drinks and dinner; from 10pm live music, poetry, cabaret and rock 'n' roll.

Caffè Voltaire, Via della Scala 9r (near Santa Maria Novella). Florentine "open space", offering live entertainment from blues to poetry, salsa to samba.

Chiodo Fisso Club, Via Dante Alighieri 16r, tel: 055-238 1290.

Well-established club, with live music every night.

Dolce Vita, Piazza del Carmine. Fashionable bar in the bohemian Oltrarno quarter.

Hemingway, Piazza Piattellina 9r, tel: 055-284781. Beautifully decorated café where you can snack, drink or sample the superb chocolates. Comfy chairs and books to browse through.

The Jazz Café, Via Nuova dei Caccini 3, tel: 055-2479700. Relaxed basement bar with live music on Fridays and Saturdays.

Meccanò Meccanò, Piazzale delle Cascine, tel: 055-331371. Huge late-night spot with a piano bar, disco and restaurant. Themed music.

The Roof Terrace, Hotel Kraft, Via Solferino 2. Pleasant, even romantic, spot with a wonderful view over the city.

Tabasco (Gay), Piazza Santa Cecilia 3, tel: 055-213000. Men only; this was the first gay bar in Italy. Discos.

Nightclubs

FLORENCE

Central Park, Parco delle Cascine. Possibly the trendiest disco in Florence.

Jackie O', Via dell'Erta Canina 24b, tel: 055-2342442. For thirtysomethings.

Maracana, Via Faenza 4. A lively Latino club playing mostly salsa and samba. Closed Monday.

Space Electronic, Via Palazzuolo 37, tel: 055-293082. Lasers and videos are the hallmarks; this is the usual hangout of foreign teenagers and would-be Latin lovers.

Villa Kasar, Lungarno Colombo, tel: 051-676912. Popular with celebrities. You are advised to check the nature of the night's entertainment before turning up. Closed Monday.

SIENA

Jet Set, Via Pantaneto 13, tel: 0577-288378.

Club Enoteca, Fortezza Medicea, tel: 0577-288497.

Outdoor Activities

Sources of Information

For information about Green Tourism and outdoor activities, first contact nearest office of ENIT, the national Italian tourist.

For trekking or cycling routes (with map and suggested hostels and mountain refuges), request the *Turismo Natura Toscana* booklet (available in various languages) from Regione Toscana, Via di Novoli 26, 50127 Firenze, tel: 055-4383822; fax: 055-4383064. (It also includes suggestions for other activities, from horse-riding to climbing and caving.)

In English, the most comprehensive guide to green tourism is *Wild Italy* (by Tim Jepson, Sheldrake Press, 1994). Recommended local guides (in various languages) are: *Italia a Cavallo* (*Italy on Horseback*) published by Edizioni Demomedia and available from bookstores (or tel: 055-282162; fax: 055-289063; or call 167-467692, a toll-free number from within Italy). The same publishers also produce *Toscana Verde* (*Green Tuscany*), *The Chianti* and *Il Mangia Firenze* (*Eating in Florence Province*).

Hiking

Hiking (usually called 'trekking' in Italian) is an increasingly popular activity in Tuscany. Serious hikers can follow the Italian Alpine Club (CAI) paths, which criss cross the region. The Tuscan branch of CAI is in Prato, tel: 0574-24760; fax: 0574-27028, or you can contact the local tourist office for information.

Two long-distance paths, **Apuane Trekking** (a four-day trek) and the **Grande Escursione Apenninica** (GEA, taking 25 days end to end), have well-marked trails and can be joined at various points. If following a long-distance mountain trail, always make sure that your destinations or local contacts are informed of your expected arrival times.

Shorter waymarked trails (such as those in the Maremma or the Chianti regions) tend to be less well indicated, so take good local maps (such as those produced by CAI). This is worth doing since many Italian paths can be misleading.

All walkers should bear in mind that there is no public right of way across private property. Although individual landowners can be lenient, it is worth checking routes with CAI, a tourist office or reputable guides. Be particularly vigilant during the hunting season, particularly on Sundays. As Tim Jepson says in *Wild Italy*, "the thunder of guns on a Sunday morning remains a fact of rural Italian life".

Each local tourist office produces information on farm stays and public transport (variable in quality and reliability). Depending on the region, there are also opportunities for such activities as cycling, horse-riding, mountaineering, caving and watersports.

If travelling without a car, then some forward planning is required – particularly given the tedium, patchiness and general unreliability of public transport in Tuscany. City to city transport is generally fine (often quicker by bus than train) but rural transport is deeply deficient: either of the "two buses a day" variety or simply non-existent.

AREAS TO EXPLORE

The following are guidelines to some of the more accessible areas of natural beauty.

Abetone and the Tuscan Emilian border

Abetone makes a good base for green tourism in any season, and for exploring this forested mountain region, sometimes known as the Alto Appennino. The town has a profusion of traditional or modern Swiss chalet-style hotels.

The picturesque medieval centres of Fiumalbo and Cutigliano make good alternative bases but possess fewer facilities and lack Abetone's more dramatic alpine views.

Transport: by public transport, it is usually easier and quicker to reach Abetone by bus from Modena (in Emilia-Romagna) than by other routes.

Apuan Alps (Alpi Apuane)

Maps and information on mountain refuges are available from Massa, Carrara and most coastal tourist offices. Numerous day hikes are available through the Alps, with typical starting points being the villages of Stazzema and Levigliano on the western flanks of the mountains. Almost as appealing is a car journey along the winding mountain roads towards the interior.

Lunigiana and Garfagnana

Serious hikers should request the Trekking in Lunigiana map, with long-distance trails beginning in Aulla, Fosdinovo, Frignoli and Sassalbo.

To appreciate the rural atmosphere, avoid staying in such fashionable coastal resorts as Forte dei Marmi. Instead, choose the Garfagnana hinterland, where Castelnuovo di Garfagnana is picturesque and Barga, the main town, makes a pleasant base. Both are convenient for Parco dell'Orecchiella, the national park, 15 km (9 miles) north of Castelnuovo di Garfagnana. San Pellegrino in Alpe, 16 km (9.5 miles) northeast of Castelnuovo, is appealing in summer and winter.

Transport: Coastal transport is good, with transport into the Garfagnana hinterland less so. However, for those who wish to explore Garfagnana and Lunigiana by train or bicycle, a small branch line connects Lucca with Aulla and allows bicycles to be transported on the train.

The Maremma

If you are keen on comfort and a chic coastal atmosphere, you should stay in hotels in Santo Stefano, Talamone or Orbetello. Otherwise, opt for a ranch or farm near the park itself (*see Where to Stay*).

Transport: By public transport, visitors should go to Orbetello (by bus or train) or to Monte Argentario (by bus from Grosseto). To visit the nature reserve is trickier: by train to Alberese station (only a couple of trains a day, from Grosseto), then a taxi.

The Mugello

Request the *Green Heart of Tuscany* booklet from Promo-Mugello, Centro Commerciale Mugello, Piazza Martin Luther King 5, Borgo San Lorenzo, Florence Province 50032, tel: 055-8458742; fax: 055-8495772. Alternatively, in Italy you can call this toll-free number: 167-405891.

Avoid staying in Borgo San Lorenzo, the main town, which is not particularly attractive, or in the semi-industrialised valleys, which do not feel remotely rural. Instead, choose the countryside or such villages as Vicchio. The result is access to a landscape in many ways lovelier than the over-rated Chianti. Transport: For those who wish to explore the Mugello by train or bicycle, the Faenza–Florence train service stops at stations along the Apennine ridge (Vicchio, Marradi, Ronta), ideal places to begin trekking.

Green Sites

These include nature reserves, caves, botanical gardens and museums of rural life. The classification of Italian conservation areas is chaotic and confusing. In theory, the Arcipelago Toscano (Tuscan Archipelago, including Elb and the other islands) is a National Park but in reality much remains unprotected. Illegal hunting continues in the larger parks. The best-run sanctuaries tend to be the smallest, often those administered by the Worldwide Fund for Nature (WWF) or by LIPU, the Italian bird protection society (for which there is a great need).

Abetone

On the Tuscan-Emilian border Abetone is the main ski and summer resort in the northern Apennines (*see page 354*). It is also the centre for information on GEA long-distance trails and shorter botanical rambles. There is a small but appealing botanical garden too. For details, contact the Abetone tourist office.

The Apuan Alps and Lunigiana

The **Frignoli Botanical Gardens** near Sassalbo (tel: 0585-949688) boast an arboretum and display the full range of plants grown in the Apuan Alps. In **Aulla**, in Lunigiana, there is an interesting natural history museum and ecological centre set in historic Brunella castle (tel: 0187-400252), as well as neighbouring botanical gardens. From Aulla, visitors can organise tours of glacial moraines, karst gorges and caves.

Garfagnana

Here, **Parco dell'Orecchiella**, 15 km (9 miles) north of Castelnuovo di Garfagnana, is the chief regional park in the Lucca stretch of the Apennines. The main entry point is Corfino. There are also **botanical gardens** nearby, at Villa Collemansina,

Pania di Corfino (tel: 0584-62994). The local visitors' centre includes a civilised mountain refuge and suggested nature trails (Bosi Picchiotti Ilda, tel: 0583-619010). For general information, you should contact the Comunità Montana Garfagnana (tel: 0583-65169) or the tourist office in Barga, the region's main town.

The **Orrido dei Bottri reserve** is a narrow gorge with sheer cliff faces that can be crossed by serious hikers.

Livorno Province

In Livorno, the **Oasi di Bolgheri** is certainly the best bird and wildlife sanctuary, a mixture of scrub, lakes and marshy grasslands. This WWF reserve is home to native and migratory birds, including the lapwing, osprey, reed-warbler, grey herons, black-winged stilts and the rare lesser-spotted eagle. It is also a haven for small mammals, including the wild boar. The reserve lies 10 km (6 miles) south of Cecina and is reached by train to Bolgheri. Contact Marina di Cecina or Livorno provincial tourist offices for details.

Lucca Province

Bottaccio wood, outside Castelvecchio di Compito, is a marshland nature reserve good for birds and best visited in spring (tel: 0583-955834).

The Maremma

In the Maremma region, the **Parco Naturale della Maremma,** or Parco dell'Uccellina, (tel: 0564-407098), is closed to traffic. Entry points are Marina di Alberese (the coast) or Alberese (the landward side, with the park ticket office and small museum). The Marina entrance gives access to the park via the excellent beach. The Alberese entrance provides access to the park on foot or by means of the park shuttle bus. In addition to short trails, there

are longer trails of 5 or 4 km (3 or 2.5 miles), lasting about three hours). The waymarked paths are not wholly reliable. It is advisable to bring drinking water and a picnic. In Alberese, canoes can be hired to explore the irrigation canals, and horse-riding is also available. Like Siena and the Chianti, this is a place for gentle rambles, particularly on horseback.

In the Maremma, **Lago di Burano** (tel: 0564-898829), further south, offers one of the best bird-watching opportunities in Tuscany. This is the southern-most of two lagoons (enclosing wildlife reserves) beside the peninsula of Monte Argentario. This WWF lagoon is home to falcons, cormorants, the black-winged stilt, purple and grey herons, with peregrines, ospreys and marsh harriers using the lagoons as feeding grounds. Visits are usually possible on Thursday and Sunday, 1 August–31 May. (By road, the reserve is 0.5 km from the Capalbio Scalo exit on the SS1; by rail, travel to the small Capalbio station). For details of opening times, contact the Maremma national park (as above) or Grosseto provincial tourist office.

The Mugello

In the Mugello, the hamlet of Grezzano has **Casa d'Erci**, which is a farmhouse converted into a museum of rural life and peasant culture, including early looms and a charcoal-burner's hut. Check current opening times on 055-8458742; or in Italy, on 167-405891 (toll-free).

Pisa Province

Here, the lakeside habitat at **Lago di Massaciuccoli** is home for migratory and wintering wildfowl as well as native species, including flamingoes, geese, ducks, cranes and terns. The region's lone surviving lagoon has suffered from intensive shooting but survives nonetheless. For details of opening times and organised tours, contact Pisa provincial tourist office.

Horse-riding

There are over 40 centres belonging to the National Association of Equestrian Tourism (ANTE) where it is possible to spend your holiday on horseback. For further information, write to: ANTE, Largo Messico 13, Rome, or to the Federazione Italiana Sport Equestri, Viale Tiziano 70, Rome, tel: 06-3233826.

Here are some suggestions for riding near Tuscany's main cities:

Maneggio Marinella, Via di Macia 21, Calenzano, Florence, tel: 055-8878066.

Club Ippico Fattria di Maiano, Via Cave di Maiano, Fiesole, tel: 055-599539.

La Certosa, Via Roma, Calci, near Pisa, tel: 050-938447.

Club Ippico Senese, Località Pian del Lago, Siena, tel: 0577-318677.

For horse-riding centres in other parts of Tuscany, contact the **Centro Ippico Toscano**, tel: 055-315621.

Hunting & Shooting

Shooting birds and animals is not everyone's cup of tea, but it is a popular sport in Italy. Nevertheless, the activity is not encouraged by the tourist boards, and there are strict rules on the importation and use of firearms.

Information may be obtained from the **Federazione Italiana Caccia**, Viale Tiziano 70, Rome, tel: 06-394871.

The Maremma and the Volterra are areas for wild boar hunting and there are several reserves for shooting pheasant.

For target shooting, try **Tiro a Segno Nazionale**, Strada di Peragna, Torre Fiorentina, tel: 0577-52417.

Spas

Tuscany has a large number of spas, catering for different ailments.

Most spas charge a daily entrance fee of around L.30,000. Extra treatments such as mudbaths cost about L.30,000 each per session. The cost of a complete cure depends on the number of treatments involved and obviously the standard of accommodation. At Montecatini Terme, for example, accommodation ranges from simple pensions to 5-star hotels.

You can see a doctor before taking a cure and some treatments such as the mudbath should only be undertaken with medical advice.

The major spas include Bagni di Lucca, Casciana Terme, Bagno Vignoni, Chianciano Terme, Monsummano Terme, Montecatini Terme, San Carlo Terme, Terme di Saturnia and Petriolo.

Sport

Taking Part

It is possible to play any popular sport either at private clubs or at municipal centres run by the National Olympic Committee (CONI). There are tennis courts at most resorts, and swimming, scuba diving, windsurfing and boating on the coast. In villages, bowls (*boccie*) and cards are popular; gambling, often for high stakes, is widespread, though illegal, except in approved casinos and betting shops.

Fishing

Sport fishing can be practised both from the shore and from a boat. In some ports, a special permit is required from the Harbourmaster's Office.

Only those over 16 are allowed to use underwater guns and such equipment. When submerged, an underwater fisherman is required to indicate the fact with a float bearing a red flag with a yellow diagonal stripe, and must operate within a radius of 50 metres (164 ft) of the support barge or the float bearing the flag.

Fishing is prohibited within 500 metres (1,640 ft) of a beach used by bathers and within 50 metres (164 ft) of fishing installations and ships at anchor.

Freshwater fishing in rivers and lakes for trout, grayling, char, chub, carp, tench, pike, perch, roach, etc. is generally satisfactory. Foreigners need a temporary membership of FIPS (Federazione Italiana della

Pesca Sportiva) and a government licence issued by the Provincial Administration. A licence for rod-fishing, with or without a reel, costs about £1.50 and is valid for one year. Every provincial town has an office to give advice and notice of restrictions on fishing times and places.

Golf

There are better things to do in Tuscany than play golf, but there are some decent courses. The best of these include the following:

Florence
Golf Club Ugolino, 50015 Grassina, tel: 055-230 1096. Eighteen holes on a course set in an olive grove.
Golf Club Montelupo, tel: 0571-541004, 25 km (16 miles) west of Florence. Nine holes on the banks of the River Arno. Closed Tuesday.

Tirrenia
Cosmopolitan Golf and Country Club, tel: 050-33085. Nine-hole course.
Punta Ala:
Tel: 0564-922121. Eighteen-hole course.

Tennis

Tennis is a popular sport in Italy. If you wish to play a game, try these clubs:
Circolo Carraia, Via Monti alle Croci, Florence, tel: 055-2346353.
Zodiac, Via Grandi 2, Tavernuzze (near Florence), tel: 055-2022850.
Circolo Tennis Siena, Località Vico Alto, Siena, tel: 0577-333464.

Skiing

Tuscany has a major ski resort at Abetone in the Apennines, north of Pistoia. The skiing area extends over four valleys and 30 km (19 miles) of trails. Tourist information on ski passes, pistes, etc. may be obtained from Azienda Autonoma Soggiorno e Turismo, Abetone, tel: 0573-60231.

Watersports

At all Tuscan sea resorts, it is possible to water-ski and row with hired boats. Yacht chartering facilities are also available in the resorts of Marina di Pisa and Tirrenia.

Warning: sharks have occasionally been sighted off the Tuscan coast and a diver has been killed by one that measured 6 metres (20 ft) long ... so beware! Ask local life-guards if you are concerned.

Skindiving

This is a very popular activity in Tuscany, the best areas being around the Argentario on the southern coast, and the islands Giglio, Giannutri, Elba and Capraia. Recent legislation has restricted diving activities in certain areas, but it can, nonetheless, be a rewarding experience. There is red coral, a huge variety of Mediterranean underwater flora and even a couple of wrecks off Giannutri.

Many of the seaside ports in the area have diving clubs which take boats out regularly, especially at weekends. Ask about these in the local tourist offices, or try the diving centres listed here:
Elba Diving Centre, Marciana Marina, tel: 0565-904256.
Giglio Diving Club, Giglio Porto, tel: 0564-804064.

Swimming Pools

Most luxury hotels have swimming pools and there are public pools in most towns. If you wish to use a particular hotel pool but are not a guest, it is worth calling to ask if you can use it; sometimes you will have to pay a small fee for the privilege.

The following swimming pools are in Florence:
Piscina Costoli, Viale Paoli, Campo di Marte, tel: 050-669744. This is in the north of the city.
Piscina Comunale Bellariva, Lungarno Colombo 6, tel: 050-677521. Open-air during the summer.
Piscina Le Pavoniere, Viale degli Olmi, tel: 050-367506. Set in the Cascine park, this is one of the most appealing pools. Only open in summer.

Siena has its own **Piscina Comunale**, Piazza G. Amendola, tel: 0577-47496.

Spectator Sports

The main spectator sports in Tuscany are football, horse racing and speed cycling, which culminates in the Grand Tour of Italy. All important events are watched avidly on television.

In Florence, there is a racecourse in the Cascine park:
Ippodromo le Cascine, tel: 055-360598.

Shopping

What to Buy

The quality of goods in Italy is very high and prices generally reasonable – especially when the currency exchange rates work in your favour. See also *Tuscan Craftsmanship* on pages 118–19.

Some suggested purchases are as follows:

Fashions: dresses, hats, linen, gloves, silk ties and shirts, knitwear, boutique goods (including classic fashion from top designers) and jewellery.

Leather goods: prices are not necessarily rock bottom but the quality is often excellent and the designs appealing. Shoes and handbags are particularly good buys, but you can also choose from everything from boxes and belts to luggage, briefcases and wallets.

Cloth: silk, linen, wool and cotton.

Handicrafts: lace and table-cloths; pottery and ceramics; gold and silver ware; alabaster and marble objects; woodwork; straw and raffia goods; glass and crystal work; art books and reproductions; marbled paper; rustic household goods; prints; antiques; reproduction furniture; Tuscan impressionist and modern paintings.

Alcohol: regional red wines (especially Chianti), and Italian spirits, liqueurs and aperitifs such as Grappa or Liquore Strega.

Food: olive oil, herbs, locally-made pasta, cheese, bottled vegetables, truffles, dried mushrooms ... you name it!

Duty-Free and Duty-Paid Allowances

For EU citizens, provided goods obtained in the EU are for your personal use, no further tax needs to be paid. EU law sets out recommended guide levels; anyone who brings in more than the sanctioned amounts must be able to show that the goods are for personal use only.

The guide levels for **duty-paid** goods are:
• 800 cigarettes **or** 200 cigars **or** 1 kg tobacco.
• 10 litres spirits **and** 20 litres intermediate products (such as port and sherry) **and** 90 litres wine (of which not more than 60 litres can be sparkling) **and** 110 litres beer.
• gifts up to £71.

The guide levels for **duty-free** goods are:
• 200 cigarettes **or** 100 cigarillos **or** 50 cigars **or** 250 g tobacco.
• 2 litres still table wine **and** 1 litre spirits.
• 60 ml perfume and 250 ml toilet water.
• gifts up to £71.

For citizens outside the EU, the duty-free allowances remain as follows:
• 200 cigarettes **or** 50 cigars **or** 250 g of smoking tobacco.
• 1 litre of alcohol **or** 2 litres of fortified or sparkling wine.
• gifts worth up to £136.

Duty-Free Goods

Certain items (e.g. alcohol, tobacco, perfume) are limited as to the amount you may take in or out of the country, and these amounts vary for those coming from within the EU, from other European countries or from outside Europe. There is even more variation according to whether the goods were bought duty-paid (i.e. in Italy) or duty-free (i.e. at the airport). *See the box above.*

If planning to import or export large quantities of goods, or goods of very high value, you should contact the Italian Consulate and your own customs authorities beforehand to check on any special regulations which may apply. Note that different regulations apply to all types of commercial import and export.

For the exportation of antiques and modern art objects, an application must be presented to the Export Department of the Italian Ministry of Education. If the request is granted, a tax in accordance with the value of the items must be paid.

Shopping Hours

These have changed somewhat over the past few years, with shops tending to stay open a little later than in the past. Food stores and general shops open 8.30am–1pm and 4 or 5pm–7.30pm. They stay open a little later in the summer. Many of the bigger supermarkets now stay open through lunch and close at around 8.30pm.

Department stores and other shops in bigger cities will stay open all day (9.30am–7.30/8pm), and there is now limited Sunday opening in such places.

Food shops are usually closed on Wednesday afternoons in Tuscany, but this changes in the summer months, when early closing is usually on Saturday afternoon. Many clothing shops are closed on Monday mornings.

Where to Shop

Chain stores such as Upim and Standa can be found in most towns in Tuscany. Foreign languages are spoken in most shops in cities, large towns and tourist resorts.

Open-air markets are held usually once or twice a week in almost all tourist resorts.

Supermarkets are found in most of the resorts and in all towns. Baby food can be bought everywhere at chemists (*farmacie*), supermarkets and grocers.

Tobacconist's shops (called *tabacchi*) are licensed to sell postage stamps, *schede* (telephone cards), salt and candles, besides cigarettes and tobacco.

Shopping in Florence

Despite tourism, consumerism and high labour costs, Florence still has a reputation as a city with high standards of craftsmanship in many spheres, from silver jewellery to marbled paper.

If you wish to visit craftsmen at work, consult the tourist office and ask for their booklets on crafts, e.g. *Tra Artigianato ed Arte* (*From Craftsmanship to Art*). Although a bit out of date, this lists the main craftsmen still practising in the city. For example, the **Santa Croce leather school**, on Piazza Santa Croce, is a popular place for visitors to watch skilled Florentine leather-workers.

BOOKS

After Dark, Via de' Ginori 47r.
Feltrinelli International, Via Cavour 12/20, tel: 055-219524. This is the most comprehensive and respected bookshop in Florence.
Seeber, Via de' Tornabuoni 70r, tel: 055-215697. The shop has a good selection of books in English and Italian.
The Paperback Exchange, Via Fiesolana 31r, north of the Santa Croce district, is no ordinary bookshop. For a start, it stocks just about every book ever written on Florence still in print, and many that are no longer published. In addition, it operates a system whereby you get a credit based on a percentage of the original price of any book you trade in, which can be

used to buy books from their vast stock of quality second-hand English and American paperbacks. The shop is run by enthusiasts who know everything there is to know about Florence and books.

BOUTIQUES

Florence is a high-spot for fashion, and the centre is full of top designer boutiques. The most elegant street is the Via de' Tornabuoni where Versace, Valentino and other big names in fashion have their outlets.

Other exclusive streets are the Via Calzaiuoli and Via Roma (both have a stunning range of leather goods), Via della Vigna Nuova and Via del Parione.

The top designer shops are:
Giorgio Armani, Via della Vigna Nuova 51r, tel: 055-219041. For a more affordable Armani, although quality is not always guaranteed, visit Emporio Armani, Piazza Strozzi 14–16r, tel: 055-284315.
Brioni, Via Calimala 22, tel: 055-210646. Classic men's style; exquisitely made clothes. Brioni has dressed James Bond in his latest films.
Enrico Coveri, Via de' Tornabuoni 81, tel: 055-211263.
Ferragamo, Palazzo Spini-Feroni, Via de' Tornabuoni 2, tel: 055-292123. These famous Florentine shoemakers have now branched out into accessories and clothes.
Gucci, Via de' Tornabuoni 73, tel: 055-264011. This international Florentine firm has developed a tighter, more sophisticated range in recent years but the belts and handbags are still their trademark.
Emilio Pucci, Via de' Pucci 6, tel: 055-283061/2 and at Via della Vigna Nuova 97.
Raspini, Via Roma 25–29, tel: 055-213077.
Valentino, Via della Vigna Nuova 47r, tel: 055-282485.
Gianni Versace, Via de' Tornabuoni 13, tel: 055-296167.

Clothes & Shoes Size Guides

Women's Dresses/Suits

US	Italy	UK
6	38/34N	8/30
8	40/36N	10/32
10	42/38N	12/34
12	44/40N	14/36
14	46/42N	16/38
16	48/44N	18/40

Women's Shoes

US	Italy	UK
4½	36	3
5½	37	4
6½	38	5
7½	39	6
8½	40	7
9½	41	8
10½	42	9

Men's Suits

US	Italy	UK
34	44	34
—	46	36
38	48	38
—	50	40
42	52	42
—	54	44
46	56	46

Men's Shirts

US	Italy	UK
14	36	14
14½	37	14½
15	38	15
15½	39	15½
16	40	16
16½	41	16½
17	42	17

Men's Shoes

US	Italy	UK
6½	—	6
7½	40	7
8½	41	8
9½	42	9
10½	43	10
11½	44	11

CERAMICS
Sbigoli, Via Sant'Egidio 4r, tel: 055-2479713. Has a good choice of hand-painted ceramics, both traditional and contemporary designs.

FABRICS

Antico Setificio, Via L. Bartolini 4, tel: 055-213861. This wonderful shop specialises in fabrics produced along traditional lines, above all silk, which is still woven on 18th-century looms *(see pages 118–19)*. **Casa dei Tessuti**, Via de' Pecori, 20–24, tel: 055-215961. Fine silks, linens and woollens.

GLOVES

Madova, Via Guicciardini 1r. Every kind of glove you could imagine and all of them beautifully made.

JEWELLERY

The Ponte Vecchio is the main place visitors first encounter Florentine jewellery. Although the setting is atmospheric, most of the craftsmen work in very different conditions. There is still a flourishing jewellery trade in Florence (particularly in Oltrarno, on the south side of the river), although most gold jewellery is in fact made in Arezzo nowadays.

However, the following traditional goldsmiths and silversmiths remain:

Giovanni Barone, Piazza Duomo 36r. Goldsmith.

Brandimarte, Via Bartolini 18/r, tel: 055-239381. Handcrafted silver goods and jewellery in a large store. This is where all the Florentine signoras go to buy wedding presents. Good prices.

Marzio Casprini, Via dei Serragli 56. Silversmith.

Gatto Bianco, Borgo SS Apostoli 12r. Goldsmith. Contemporary designs in gold and silver.

Exclusive Jewellery: if you can afford to push the boat out, these two Florentine establishments are well worth adding to your itinerary:

Buccellati, Via de' Tornabuoni 71r, tel: 055-239 6579.

Torrini, Piazza del Duomo 10r, tel: 055-2302401.

LEATHER

Leather goods are, of course, the best buy in the city. Quality ranges from the beautifully tooled creations of local artisans to shoddy goods aimed at undiscerning tourists. For top of the range quality (and prices), you should start with the designer boutiques in the Via de' Tornabuoni or shops in streets around the Piazza della Repubblica.

Try the following outlets:

Raspini, Via Roma 25–29. Sells superb leather bags and coats as well as high quality fashions.

Il Bisonte, Via del Parione 31r. This internationally famous name started life in this very street. Bags, luggage and other leather goods at high prices.

Furla, Via Tosinghi 5r. Bags and accessories in contemporary designs. There is also a branch in Siena in Via di Città.

For more down-to-earth prices, head for the **San Lorenzo market** northwest of the Duomo (see *Markets*), where numerous street stalls sell shoes, bags, belts, wallets and the Santa Croce area.

MARBLED PAPER

Marbled paper is very closely associated with Florence and many of the designs echo ancient themes or Medici crests. You should attempt to visit at least one of the following:

Giulio Giannini e Figlio, Piazza Pitti 37r. This is Florence's longest established marbled paper shop.

Il Papiro, Via Cavour. These marbled paper designs are on display in Il Papiro's three Florentine branches.

Il Torchio, Via de' Bardi 17. Cheaper than some other shops and with interesting designs. You also see the artisans at work here. They sell to Liberty, where prices are sky high.

MARKETS

Straw Market (Mercato del Porcellino): hand-embroidered work, Florentine straw, leather goods, wooden objects and flowers.

Flea Market (Mercato delle Pulci, Piazza dei Ciompi): objects from the past – basically junk, but great fun.

Sant'Ambrogio (Piazza Ghiberti): vegetables, fruit, food, flowers and clothes.

San Lorenzo Market (Mercato di San Lorenzo, Piazza San Lorenzo): the covered market sells vegetables, fruit, meat and cheeses etc., while the surrounding streets are filled with stalls that sell clothes, shoes, leather goods and jewellery.

Cascine Market (Mercato delle Cascine, Tuesdays mornings only): produce, household goods and clothing. This market is popular with Florentines.

PHARMACY

Officina Profumo Farmaceutica di Santa Maria Novella, Via della Scala 16. Housed in a frescoed chapel, this fascinating shop was founded by monks in the 16th century. It sells herbal remedies, but more tempting is the range of beautifully packaged perfumes, shampoos, lotions and room scents.

SHOES

Cresti, Via Roma 9r. There are beautifully crafted shoes on sale here, and available at much lower prices than at Ferragamo.

Ferragamo, Via de' Tornabuoni 16. Italy's most prestigious shoemaker, providing hand-tooled shoes of all descriptions and beautifully crafted ready-to-wear collections. Ferragamo boasts that once one has worn its shoes, nothing else feels good enough.

Francesco, Via di Santo Spirito 62r. This is the place to have unpretentious hand-made shoes tooled in classic designs by a traditional craftsman.

SUPERMARKETS

Esselunga, Via Masaccio 274 and Via Pisana 130.
Consorzio Agrario, Piazza San Firenze 5r.
Standa, Via Pietrapiana 42/44.
Coop, Via Nazionale 32r.
Conad, Via L. Alamanni 2r.

Shopping in Siena

Food and Wine

Siena is known for its **confectionery**, particularly a type of bread, known as *panforte*, which is made from a sweet dough, flavoured with vanilla and full of candied citrus fruits. The most famous maker of such specialities is **Nannini** at Piazza Matteotti 21, Piazza del Monte 95/99 and **Bar Pasticceria Nannini** at Via Banchi di Sopra 24. (The owner's daughter is, by the way, one of Italy's best-known female rock singer.)

Pan co' Santi is another Sienese cake made with raisins and nuts, traditionally eaten on All Saints' Day. *Cavallucci* are small biscuits with chopped nuts and *Copate* are biscuits made of soft nougat with wafers on each side.

Siena Province produces a variety of good **wines** including Chianti, Brunello di Montalcino, and Nobile di Montepulciano. The Permanent Italian Wine Exhibition in Fortezza Medicea, tel: 0577-288497, was set up for the display and sale of regional wines. Visitors can discover and appreciate a wide variety of Italian wines. Wine traders may purchase and export their selections.

Crafts

Local production of wrought-iron and copper, ceramics, crystal and stained glass provide a wide choice for visitors. **Giogi Leonardo & Co**, at Antica Siena, Piazza del Campo 28, tel: 0577-46496, sells beautiful blue and yellow porcelain.

Children

Children's Activities

At first sight, Tuscany appears to be a paradise for adults but not an immediate choice for kids: Renaissance art does not have obvious appeal to easily-bored youngsters. However, Tuscany has much to offer children of all ages, from medieval castles to ice creams galore and plenty of child-friendly restaurants. In addition, there are several good parks, nature reserves and numerous opportunities for horse-riding, cycling and swimming. Much of the coast of Tuscany, particularly the well-equipped resorts near Viareggio and the sandy beaches on islands such as Elba, is also great for children.

There are also traditional children's attractions such as zoos and wildlife parks, including one based on Pinocchio in Collodi. Most cities have permanent or visiting fun fairs, known as **Luna Parks**.

Most Tuscan festivals are fun for children too, especially the Lenten carnivals, the horse races, the jousting, boat pageants, and all the tiny food festivals (*see Diary of Events on page 349*). Depending on the time of year that you visit, you may find a travelling circus or children's theatre, especially around Florence and Prato.

Teenagers may well be interested in a study holiday focusing on crafts, sports, cooking or languages (*see below*).

To find out what's on, above all in summer, check the newspaper listings in *La Repubblica* or *La Nazione* as well as *Events*, the Florence-based magazine. If you read Italian, buy *Firenze Spettacolo*, which has a good children's section: *Città & Ragazzi*.

Some of the suitable places in Tuscany for children are:
The Boboli Gardens (*Giardini di Boboli*), situated around the Pitti Palace in Florence, are fun for children to clamber around. There is an amphitheatre, strange statues and grottoes, as well as a handy café.

The Cascine, Florence's other main park, is popular with local families and at weekends is full of children, many of whom come to visit the tiny zoo.

Giardino dei Tarocchi, near Capalbio, is a bizarre garden inspired by tarot cards.

Ludoteca Centrale, Piazza SS Annunziata 13, Florence, tel: 055-247 8386. Open 9am–1pm, 3–6.45pm; closed on Wednesday and Saturday afternoon. This is a fun children's centre with games, music and audiovisual equipment for the under-sixes.

The Maremma is a good place for walks and wildlife spotting.

Pinocchio Park (*Parco di Pinocchio*) at Collodi, near Pisa, is an obvious choice for children, tel: 0572-429364. Open 8.30am–sunset.

Pistoia Zoo, Via Pieve a Celle, Pistoia, tel: 0573-911219. A compact zoo but one of the best in the region.

Zoo Fauna Europa, just south of the town of Poppi, tel: 0575-529079. A conservation centre for such breeds as the lynx and the Apennine wolf.

Canadian Island, Via Gioberti 15, Florence, tel: 055-677567. You can leave your children here if you (or they) are fed up with dragging around the sights. They can play with Italian children in an English-speaking environment. Charges are about L.40,000 for an afternoon. Open Monday–Friday afternoons only and Saturday morning.

Language

Language Tips

In Tuscany, the Italian language is supplemented by regional dialects. In large cities and tourist centres you will find many people who speak English, French or German. In fact, due to the massive emigration over the last 100 years, you may encounter fluent speakers of foreign languages. Do not be surprised if you are addressed in a New York, Melbourne or Bavarian accent: the speaker may have spent time working abroad.

It is well worth buying a good phrase book or dictionary, but the following will help you get started. Since this glossary is aimed at non-linguists, we have opted for the simplest options rather than the most elegant Italian.

Basic Communication

Yes *Sì*
No *No*
Thank you *Grazie*
Many thanks *Mille grazie/tante grazie/molte grazie*
You're welcome *Prego*
Alright/Okay/That's fine *Va bene*
Please *Per favore or per cortesia*
Excuse me (to get attention) *Scusi* (singular), *Scusate* (plural)
Excuse me (to get through a crowd) *Permesso*
Excuse me (to attract attention, e.g. of a waiter) *Senta!*
Excuse me (sorry) *Mi scusi*
Wait a minute! *Aspetta!*
Could you help me? (formal) *Potrebbe aiutarmi?*

Certainly *Ma, certo*
Can I help you? (formal) *Posso aiutarLa?*
Can you show me...? *Può indicarmi...?*
Can you help me? *Può aiutarmi, per cortesia?*
I need ... *Ho bisogno di ...*
I'm lost *Mi sono perso*
I'm sorry *Mi dispiace*
I don't know *Non lo so*
I don't understand *Non capisco*
Do you speak English/French/German? *Parla inglese/francese/tedesco?*
Could you speak more slowly, please? *Può parlare piu lentamente, per favore?*
Could you repeat that please? *Può ripetere, per piacere?*
slowly/quietly *piano*
here/there *qui/la*
What? *Quale/come?*
When/why/where? *Quando/perchè/dove?*
Where is the lavatory? *Dov'è il bagno?*

Greetings

Hello (Good day) *Buon giorno*
Good afternoon/evening *Buona sera*
Good night *Buona notte*
Goodbye *Arrivederci*
Hello/Hi/Goodbye (familiar) *Ciao*
Mr/Mrs/Miss *Signor/Signora/Signorina*
Pleased to meet you (formal) *Piacere di conoscerLa*
I am English/American *Sono inglese/americano*
Irish/Scottish/Welsh *irlandese/scozzese/gallese*
Canadian/Australian *canadese/australiano*
Do you speak English? *Parla inglese?*
I'm here on holiday *Sono qui in vacanze*
Is it your first trip to Milan/Rome? *E il Suo primo viaggio a Milano/Roma?*
Do you like it here? (formal) *Si trova bene qui?*
How are you (formal/informal)? *Come sta/come stai?*
Fine thanks *Bene, grazie*

See you later *A più tardi*
See you soon *A presto*
Take care *Sta bene*

New acquaintances are likely to ask you:
Do you like Italy/Florence/Siena/my city? *Le piace Italia/Firenze/Siena/la mia città?*
I like it a lot (is the correct answer) *Mi piace moltissimo*
It's wonderful (an alternative answer) *E meravigliosa/favolosa*
(Both responses can be applied to food, beaches, the view, etc.)

Telephone Calls

the area code *il prefisso telefonico*
I'd like to make a reverse charges call *Vorrei fare una telefonata a carico del destinatorio*
May I use your telephone, please? *Posso usare il telefono?*
Hello (on the telephone) *Pronto*
My name's *Mi chiamo/Sono*
Could I speak to...? *Posso parlare con...?*
Sorry, he/she isn't in *Mi dispiace, è fuori*
Can he call you back? *Può richiamarLa?*
I'll try again later *Riproverò più tardi*
Can I leave a message? *Posso lasciare un messaggio?*
Please tell him I called *Gli dica, per favore, che ho telefonato*
Hold on *Un attimo, per favore*
A local call *una telefonata locale*
Can you speak up please? *Può parlare più forte, per favore?*

In the Hotel

Do you have any vacant rooms? *Avete camere libere?*
I have a reservation *Ho fatto una prenotazione*
I'd like... *Vorrei...*
a room with twin beds *una camera a due letti*
a single/double room (with a

In the Hotel contd

double bed) *una camera singola/doppia (con letto matrimoniale)*
a room with a bath/shower *una camera con bagno/doccia*
for one night *per una notte*
for two nights *per due notti*
We have one with a double bed *Ne abbiamo una matrimoniale*
Could you show me another room please? *Potrebbe mostrarmi un'altra camera?*
How much is it? *Quanto costa?*
on the first floor *al primo piano*
Is breakfast included? *E compresa la prima colazione?*
Is everything included? *E tutto compreso?*
half/full board *mezza pensione/pensione completa*
It's expensive *E caro*
Do you have a room with a balcony/view of the sea? *C'è una camera con balcone/con una vista del mare?*
a room overlooking the park/the street/the back *una camera con vista sul parco/che da sulla strada/sul retro*
Is it a quiet room? *E una stanza tranquilla?*
The room is too hot/cold/noisy/small *La camera è troppo calda/fredda/rumorosa/piccola*
Can I see the room? *Posso vedere la camera?*
What time does the hotel

close? *A che ora chiude l'albergo?*
I'll take it *La prendo*
big/small *grande/piccola*
What time is breakfast? *A che ora è la prima colazione?*
Please give me a call at... *Mi può chiamare alle...*
Come in! *Avanti!*
Can I have the bill, please? *Posso avere il conto, per favore?*
Can you call me a taxi please? *Può chiamarmi un tassì, per favore?*
dining room *la sala da pranzo*
key *la chiave*
lift *l'ascensore*
towel *l'asciugamano*
toilet paper *la carta igienica*
pull/push *tirare/spingere*

Eating Out

Bar snacks and drinks

I'd like... *Vorrei...*
coffee *un caffè (espresso:* small, strong and black)
un cappuccino (with hot, frothy milk)
un caffelatte (like *café au lait* in France)
un caffè lungo (weak, served in a tall glass)
un corretto (laced with alcohol, probably brandy or grappa)
tea *un tè*
lemon tea *un tè al limone*
herbal tea *una tisana*
hot chocolate *una cioccolata*

calda
orange/lemon juice (bottled) *un succo d'arancia/di limone*
fresh orange/lemon juice *una spremuta di arancia/di limone*
orangeade *un'aranciata*
water (mineral) *acqua (minerale)*
fizzy/still mineral water *acqua minerale gasata/naturale*
a glass of mineral water *un bicchiere di minerale*
with/without ice *con/senza ghiaccio*
red/white wine *vino rosso/bianco*
beer (draught) *una birra (alla spina)*
a gin and tonic *un gin tonic*
a bitter (Vermouth, etc.) *un amaro*
milk *latte*
a (half) litre *un (mezzo) litro*
bottle *una bottiglia*
ice cream *un gelato*
cone *un cono*
pastry *una pasta*
sandwich *un tramezzino*
roll *un panino*
Anything else? *Desidera qualcos'altro?*
Cheers *Salute*
Let me pay *Offro io*
That's very kind of you *Grazie, molto gentile*

In a restaurant

I'd like to book a table *Vorrei riservare una tavola*
Have you got a table for...?

Pronunciation and Grammar Tips

Italian speakers claim that pronunciation is straight forward: you pronounce it as it is written. This is approximately true but there are a couple of important rules for English speakers to bear in mind: *c* before *e* or *i* is pronounced "ch", e.g. *ciao, mi dispiace, la coincidenza.* *Ch* before *i* or *e* is pronounced as "k", e.g. *la chiesa.* Likewise, *sci* or *sce* are pronounced as in "sheep" or "shed" respectively. *Gn* in Italian is rather like the sound in "onion", while *gl* is

softened to resemble the sound in "bullion".

Nouns are either masculine (*il*, plural *i*) or feminine (*la*, plural *le*). Plurals of nouns are most often formed by changing an *o* to an *i* and an *a* to an *e*, e.g. *il panino, i panini; la chiesa, le chiese.*

Words are stressed on the penultimate syllable unless an accent indicates otherwise.

Like many languages, Italian has formal and informal words for "You". In the singular, *Tu* is

informal while *Lei* is more polite. Confusingly, in some parts of Italy or in some circumstances, you will also hear *Voi* used as a singular polite form. (In general, *Voi* is reserved for "You" plural.) For visitors, it is simplest and most respectful to use the formal form unless invited to do otherwise.

There is, of course, rather more to the language than that, but you can get a surprisingly long way towards making friends with a few phrases.

Avete una tavola per ...?
I have a reservation *Ho fatto una prenotazione*
lunch/supper *il pranzo/la cena*
We do not want a full meal *Non desideriamo un pasto completo*
Could we have another table? *Potremmo spostarci?*
I'm a vegetarian *Sono vegetariano/a*
Is there a vegetarian dish? *C'è un piatto vegetariano?*
May we have the menu? *Ci dia la carta?*
wine list *la lista dei vini*
What would you like? *Che cosa prende?*
What would you recommend? *Che cosa ci raccomanda?*
home-made *fatto in casa*
What would you like as a main course/dessert? *Che cosa prende di secondo/di dolce?*
What would you like to drink? *Che cosa desidera da bere?*
a carafe of red/white wine *una caraffa di vino rosso/bianco*
fixed price menu *il menu a prezzo fisso*
the dish of the day *il piatto del giorno*
VAT (sales tax) *IVA*
cover charge *il coperto/pane e coperto*
That's enough; no more, thanks *Basta (così)*
The bill, please *Il conto per favore*
Is service included? *Il servizio è*

Bar Notices

• *Prezzo a tavola/in terrazza* **Price at a table/terrace** (often double what you pay standing at the bar)
• *Si paga alla cassa* **Pay at the cash desk**
• *Si prende lo scontrino alla cassa*
• **Pay at the cash desk**, then take the receipt (*lo scontrino*) to the bar to be served; this is common procedure
• *Signori/Uomini* **Gentlemen** (lavatories)
• *Signore/Donne* **Ladies** (lavatories)

incluso?
Where is the lavatory? *Dovè il bagno?*
Keep the change *Va bene così*
I've enjoyed the meal *Mi è piaciuto molto*

Menu Decoder

Antipasti (hors d'oeuvres)
antipasto misto **mixed hors d'oeuvres** (including cold cuts, possibly cheeses and roast vegetables– ask, however)
buffet freddo **cold buffet** (often excellent)
caponata **mixed aubergine, olives and tomatoes**
insalata caprese **tomato and mozzarella salad**
insalata di mare **seafood salad**
insalata mista/verde **mixed/green salad**
melanzane alla parmigiana **fried or baked aubergine** (with parmesan cheese and tomato)
mortadella/salame **salami**
pancetta **bacon**
peperonata **grilled peppers** (drenched in olive oil)

Primi (first courses)
Typical first courses include soup, *risotto*, *gnocchi* or numerous varieties of pasta in a wide range of sauces. In the North, *risotto* and *gnocchi* are more common than pasta but the reverse is true in Central Italy.
il brodetto **fish soup**
il brodo **consommé**
i crespolini **savoury pancakes**
gli gnocchi **dumplings**
la minestra **soup**
il minestrone **thick vegetable soup**
pasta e fagioli **pasta and bean soup**
il prosciutto (cotto/crudo) **ham** (cooked/cured)
i suppli **rice croquettes**
i tartufi **truffles**
la zuppa **soup**

Secondi (main courses)
Typical main courses are fish-, seafood- or meat-based, with accompaniments *(contorni)* that vary greatly from region to region.

La carne (meat)
allo spiedo **on the spit**
arrosto **roast meat**
al ferro **grilled without oil**
al forno **baked**
al girarrosto **spit-roasted**
alla griglia **grilled**
involtini **skewered veal, ham, etc.**
stagionato **hung, well-aged**
stufato **braised, stewed**
ben cotto **well-done** (steak, etc.)
al puntino **medium** (steak, etc.)
al sangue **rare** (steak, etc.)
l'agnello **lamb**
il bresaolo **dried salted beef**
la bistecca **steak**
il capriolo/cervo **venison**
il carpaccio **lean beef fillet**
il cinghiale **wild boar**
il coniglio **rabbit**
il controfiletto **sirloin steak**
le cotolette **cutlets**
il maiale **pork**
il fagiano **pheasant**
il fegato **liver**
il fileto **fillet**
il lepre **hare**
il maiale **pork**
il manzo **beef**
l'ossobuco **shin of veal**
la porchetta **roast suckling pig**
il pollo **chicken**
le polpette **meatballs**
il polpettone **meat loaf**
la salsiccia **sausage**
saltimbocca (alla romana) **veal escalopes with ham**
le scaloppine **escalopes**
lo stufato **stew**
il sugo **sauce**
il tacchino **turkey**
la trippa **tripe**
il vitello **veal**

Frutti di mare (seafood)
Beware the word "*surgelati*", meaning frozen rather than fresh.

affumicato **smoked**
alle brace **charcoal grilled/barbecued**
alla griglia **grilled**
fritto **fried**
ripieno **stuffed**
al vapore **steamed**
le acciughe **anchovies**
l'anguilla **eel**

Pasta Dishes

Common pasta shapes
cannelloni (stuffed tubes of pasta); *farfalle* (butterfly-shaped pasta); *tagliatelle* (flat noodles, similar to *fettucine*); *tortellini* and *ravioli* (different types of stuffed pasta packets); *penne* (quill-shaped tubes, smaller than *rigatoni*).

Typical pasta sauces
pomodoro (tomato); *pesto* (with basil and pine nuts); *matriciana* (ham and tomato); *arrabbiata* (spicy tomato); *panna* (cream); *ragù* (meat sauce); *aglio e olio* (garlic and olive oil); *burro e salvia* (butter and sage).

Frutti di mare (seafood) contd

l'aragosto **lobster**
il baccalà **dried salted cod**
i bianchetti **whitebait**
il branzino **sea bass**
i calamari **squid**
i calamaretti **baby squid**
la carpa **carp**
i crostacei **shellfish**
le cozze **mussels**
il fritto misto **mixed fried fish**
i gamberi **prawns**
i gamberetti **shrimps**
il granchio **crab**
il merluzzo **cod**
le molecche **soft-shelled crabs**
le ostriche **oysters**
il pesce **fish**
il pescespada **swordfish**
il polipo **octopus**
il risotto di mare **seafood risotto**
le sarde **sardines**
la sogliola **sole**
le seppie **cuttlefish**
la triglia **red mullet**
la trota **trout**
il tonno **tuna**
le vongole **clams**

I legumi/la verdura (vegetables)

a scelta **of your choice**
i contorni **accompaniments**
ripieno **stuffed**
gli asparagi **asparagus**

la bietola **similar to spinach**
il carciofo **artichoke**
le carote **carrots**
i carciofini **artichoke hearts**
il cavolo **cabbage**
la cicoria **chicory**
la cipolla **onion**
i funghi **mushrooms**
i fagioli **beans**
i fagiolini **French (green) beans**
le fave **broad beans**
il finocchio **fennel**
l'indivia **endive/chicory**
l'insalata mista **mixed salad**
l'insalata verde **green salad**
la melanzana **aubergine**
le patate **potatoes**
le patatine fritte **chips/French fries**
i peperoni **peppers**
i piselli **peas**
i pomodori **tomatoes**
le primizie **spring vegetables**
il radicchio **red, slightly bitter lettuce**
la rughetta **rocket**
i ravanelli **radishes**
gli spinaci **spinach**
la verdura **green vegetables**
la zucca **pumpkin/squash**
gli zucchini **courgettes**

I dolci (desserts)

al carrello **(desserts) from the trolley**
un semifreddo **semi-frozen dessert (many types)**
la bavarese **mousse**
la cassata **Sicilian ice cream with candied peel**
le fritelle **fritters**
un gelato (di lampone/limone) **(raspberry/lemon) ice cream**
una granita **water ice**
una macedonia di frutta **fruit salad**
il tartufo (nero) **(chocolate) ice cream dessert**
il tiramisù **cold, creamy rum and coffee dessert**
la torta **cake/tart**
lo zabaglione **sweet dessert made with eggs and Marsala wine**
lo zuccotto **ice cream liqueur**
la zuppa inglese **trifle**

La frutta (fruit)

le albicocche **apricots**
le arance **oranges**
le banane **bananas**
il cocomero **watermelon**
le ciliege **cherries**
i fichi **figs**
le fragole **strawberries**
i frutti di bosco **fruits of the forest**
i lamponi **raspberries**
la mela **apple**
il melone **melon**
la pesca **peach**
la pera **pear**
il pompelmo **grapefruit**
le uve **grapes**

Basic foods

l'aceto **vinegar**
l'aglio **garlic**
il burro **butter**
il formaggio **cheese**
la focaccia **oven-baked snack**
la frittata **omelette**
la grana **parmesan cheese**
i grissini **bread sticks**
l'olio **oil**
la marmellata **jam**
il pane **bread**
il pane integrale **wholemeal bread**
il parmegiano **parmesan cheese**
il pepe **pepper**
il riso **rice**
il sale **salt**
la senape **mustard**
le uova **eggs**
lo yogurt **yoghurt**
lo zucchero **sugar**

Sightseeing

Si può visitare? **Can one visit?**
il custode **custodian**
il sacristano **sacristan**
Suonare il campanello **ring the bell**
aperto/a **open**
chiuso/a **closed**
chiuso per la festa **closed for the festival**
chiuso per ferie **closed for the holidays**
chiuso per restauro **closed for restoration**
Is it possible to see the church? *E possibile visitare la chiesa?*

Entrata/uscita **Entrance/exit**
Where can I find the custodian/sacristan/key? *Dove posso trovare il custode/ il sacristano/la chiave?*
We have come a long way just to see ... *Siamo venuti da lontano proprio per visitare ...*
It is really a pity it is closed *E veramente peccato che sia chiuso*
(The last two should be tried in desperation – pleas for sympathy open some doors.)

At the Shops

What time do you open/close? *A che ora apre/chiude?*
Closed for the holidays (typical sign) *Chiuso per ferie*
Pull/push (sign on doors) *Tirare/spingere*
Entrance/exit *Entrata/uscita*
Can I help you? (formal) *Posso aiutarLa?*
What would you like? *Che cosa desidera?*
I'm just looking *Sto soltanto guardando*
How much does it cost? *Quant'è, per favore?*
How much is this? *Quanto viene?*
Do you take credit cards? *Accettate carte di credito?*
I'd like... *Vorrei...*
this one/that one *questo/quello*
I'd like that one, please *Vorrei quello lì, per cortesia*
Have you got ...? *Avete ...?*
We haven't got (any) ... *Non (ne) abbiamo...*
Can I try it on? *Posso provare?*
the size (for clothes) *la taglia*
What size do you take? *Qual'è Sua taglia?*
the size (for shoes) *il numero*
Is there/do you have ...? *C'è ...?*
Yes, of course *Sì, certo*
No, we don't (there isn't) *No, non c'è*
That's too expensive *E troppo caro*
Please write it down for me *Me lo scriva, per favore*
cheap *economico*
Don't you have anything cheaper? *Ha niente che costa di meno?*
It's too small/big *E troppo piccolo/grande*
brown/blue/black *marrone/blu/nero*
green/red/white/yellow *verde/rosso/bianco/giallo*
pink/grey/gold/silver *rosa/grigio/oro/argento*
No thank you, I don't like it *Grazie, ma non è di mio gusto*
I (don't) **like it** *(Non) mi piace*
I'll take it/I'll leave it *Lo prendo/Lo lascio*
It's a rip-off (impolite) *Sono prezzi da strozzini*
This is faulty. Can I have a replacement/refund? *C'è un difetto. Me lo potrebbe cambiare/rimborsare?*

Tourist Signs

Most regions in Italy have handy signs indicating the key tourist sights in any given area:

Abbazia (Badia) **Abbey**
Basilica **Church**
Belvedere **Viewpoint**
Biblioteca **Library**
Castello **Castle**
Centro storico **Old town/ historic centre**
Chiesa **Church**
Duomo/Cattedrale **Cathedral**
Fiume **River**
Giardino **Garden**
Lago **Lake**
Mercato **Market**
Monastero **Monastery**
Monumenti **Monuments**
Museo **Museum**
Parco **Park**
Pinacoteca **Art gallery**
Ponte **Bridge**
Ruderi **Ruins**
Scavi **Excavations/ archaeological site**
Spiaggia **Beach**
Tempio **Temple**
Torre **Tower**
Ufficio turistico **Tourist office**

Conversion Charts

Metric–Imperial:
1 centimetre = 0.4 inch
1 metre = 3 ft 3 ins
1 kilometre = 0.62 mile
1 gram = 0.04 ounce
1 kilogram = 2.2 pounds
1 litre = 1.76 UK pints

Imperial–Metric:
1 inch = 2.54 centimetres
1 foot = 30 centimetres
1 ounce = 28 grams
1 pound = 0.45 kilogram
1 pint = 0.57 litre
1 UK gallon = 4.55 litres
1 US gallon = 3.78 litres

Anything else? *Altro?*
The cash desk is over there *Si accomodi alla cassa*
Give me some of those *Mi dia alcuni di quelli lì*
a (half) kilo *un (mezzo) chilo*
100 grams *un etto*
200 grams *due etti*
more/less *più/meno*
with/without *con/senza*
a little *un pocchino*
That's enough/No more *Basta così*

Types of shops
antique dealer *l'antiquario*
bakery/cake shop *la panetteria/pasticceria*
bank *la banca*
bookshop *la libreria*
boutique/clothes shop *il negozio di moda*
bureau de change *il cambio*
butcher's *la macelleria*
chemist's *la farmacia*
delicatessen *la salumeria*
department store *il grande magazzino*
dry cleaner's *la tintoria*
fishmonger's *la pescheria*
food shop *l'alimentari*
florist *il fioraio*
grocer's *l'alimentari*
greengrocer's *l'ortolano/il fruttivendolo*
hairdresser's (women) *il parucchiere*
ice cream parlour *la gelateria*
jeweller's *il gioielliere*

Types of Shops contd
leather shop *la pelletteria*
market *il mercato*
news-stand *l'edicola*
post office *l'ufficio postale*
shoe shop *il negozio di scarpe*
stationer's *la cartoleria*
supermarket *il supermercato*
tobacconist *il tabaccaio* (also usually sells travel tickets, stamps, phone cards)
travel agency *l'agenzia di viaggi* (also usually books domestic and international train tickets).

Travelling

Transport
airport *l'aeroporto*
arrivals/departures *arrivi/partenze*
boat *la barca*
bus *l'autobus/il pullman*
bus station *l'autostazione*
car *la macchina*
connection *la coincidenza*
ferry *il traghetto*
ferry terminal *la stazione marittima*
first/second class *la prima/seconda classe*
flight *il volo*
left luggage office *il deposito bagagli*
motorway *l'autostrada*
no smoking *vietato fumare*
platform *il binario*
porter *il facchino*
railway station *la stazione (ferroviaria)*
return ticket *un biglietto di andata e ritorno*
single ticket *un biglietto di*
andata sola
sleeping car *la carrozza letti/il vagone letto*
smokers/non-smokers *fumatori/non-fumatori*
stop *la fermata*
taxi *il tassì*
ticket office *la biglietteria*
train *il treno*
WC *il gabinetto*

At the airport
Where's the office of BA/Alitalia? *Dov'è l'ufficio della British Airways/dell'Alitalia?*
I'd like to book a flight to Venice *Vorrei prenotare un volo per Venezia*
When is the next flight to ...? *Quando parte il prossimo aereo per...?*
Are there any seats available? *Ci sono ancora posti liberi?*
Have you got any hand luggage? *Ha bagagli a mano?*
I'll take this hand luggage with me *Questo lo tengo come bagaglio a mano*
My suitcase has got lost *La mia valigia è andata persa*
My suitcase has been damaged *La mia valigia è rovinata*
The flight has been delayed *Il volo è rimandato*
The flight has been cancelled *Il volo è stato cancellato*
I can put you on the waiting list *Posso metterLa sulla lista d'attesa*

At the station
Can you help me please? *Mi può aiutare, per favore?*

Days & Dates

morning/afternoon/evening *la mattina, il pomeriggio, la sera*
yesterday/today/tomorrow *ieri/oggi/domani*
the day after tomorrow *dopodomani*
now/early/late *adesso/presto/ritardo*
a minute *un minuto*
an hour *un'ora*
half an hour *un mezz'ora*
a day *un giorno*
a week *una settimana*
Monday *lunedì*
Tuesday *martedì*
Wednesday *mercoledì*
Thursday *giovedì*
Friday *venerdì*
Saturday *sabato*
Sunday *domenica*
first *il primo/la prima*
second *il secondo/la seconda*
third *il terzo/la terza*

Where can I buy tickets? *Dove posso fare i biglietti?*
at the ticket office/at the counter *alla biglietteria/allo sportello*
What time does the train leave? *A che ora parte il treno?*
What time does the train arrive? *A che ora arriva il treno?*
Can I book a seat? *Posso prenotare un posto?*
Are there any seats available? *Ci sono ancora posti liberi?*
Is this seat free/taken? *È libero/occupato questo posto?*

Numbers

1	*Uno*	**13**	*Tredici*	**70**	*Settanta*
2	*Due*	**14**	*Quattordici*	**80**	*Ottanta*
3	*Tre*	**15**	*Quindici*	**90**	*Novanta*
4	*Quattro*	**16**	*Sedici*	**100**	*Cento*
5	*Cinque*	**17**	*Diciassette*	**200**	*Duecento*
6	*Sei*	**18**	*Diciotto*	**500**	*Cinquecento*
7	*Sette*	**19**	*Diciannove*	**1,000**	*Mille*
8	*Otto*	**20**	*Venti*	**2,000**	*Duemila*
9	*Nove*	**30**	*Trenta*	**5,000**	*Cinquemila*
10	*Dieci*	**40**	*Quaranta*	**50,000**	*Cinquantamila*
11	*Undici*	**50**	*Cinquanta*	**1 Million**	*Un milione*
12	*Dodici*	**60**	*Sessanta*		

I'm afraid this is my seat *E il mio posto, mi dispiace*
You'll have to pay a supplement *Deve pagare un supplemento*
Do I have to change? *Devo cambiare?*
Where does it stop? *Dove si ferma?*
You need to change in Rome *Bisogna cambiare a Roma*
Which platform does the train leave from? *Da quale binario parte il treno?*
The train leaves from platform one *Il treno parte dal binario uno*
When is the next train/bus/ ferry for Naples? *Quando parte il prossimo treno/pullman/ traghetto per Napoli?*
How long does the crossing take? *Quanto dura la traversata?*
What time does the bus leave for Siena? *Quando parte l'autobus per Siena?*
How long will it take to get there? *Quanto tempo ci vuole per arrivare?*
Will we arrive on time? *Arriveremo puntuali?*
Next stop please *La prossima fermata per favore*
Is this the right stop? *E la fermata giusta?*
The train is late *Il treno è in ritardo*
Can you tell me where to get off? *Mi può dire dove devo scendere?*

Directions
right/left *a destra/a sinistra*
first left/second right *la prima a sinistra/la seconda a destra*
Turn to the right/left *Gira a destra/sinistra*
Go straight on *Va sempre diritto*
Go straight on until the traffic lights *Va sempre diritto fino al semaforo*
Is it far away/nearby? *E lontano/vicino?*
It's five minutes' walk *Cinque minuti a piedi*
It's 10 minutes by car *Dieci minuti con la macchina*
You can't miss it *Non può non vederlo*
opposite/next to *di fronte/ accanto a*
up/down *su/gìu*
traffic lights *il semaforo*
junction *l'incrocio, il bivio*
building *il palazzo*
Where is ...? *Dov'è ...?*
Where are ...? *Dove sono ...?*
Where is the nearest bank/ petrol station/bus stop/ hotel/garage? *Dov'è la banca/il benzinaio/la fermata di autobus/l'albergo/l'officina più vicino/a?*
How do I get there? *Come si può andare?* (or: *Come faccio per arrivare a ...?*)
How long does it take to get to ...? *Quanto tempo ci vuole per andare a ...?*
Can you show me where I am on the map? *Può indicarmi sulla cartina dove mi trovo?*
You're on the wrong road *Lei è sulla strada sbagliata*

On the Road
Where can I rent a car? *Dove posso noleggiare una macchina?*
Is comprehensive insurance included? *E completamente assicurata?*
Is it insured for another driver? *E assicurata per un altro guidatore?*
By what time must I return it? *A che ora devo consegnarla?*
underground car park *il garage sotterraneo*
driving licence *la patente (di guida)*
petrol *la benzina*
petrol station/garage *la stazione servizio*
oil *l'olio*
Fill it up please *Faccia il pieno, per favore*
lead free/unleaded/diesel *senza piombo/benzina verde/diesel*
My car won't start *La mia macchina non s'accende*

Road Signs

Accendere le luci in galleria **Lights on in tunnel**
Alt **Stop**
Autostrada **Motorway**
Attenzione **Caution**
Avanti **Go/walk**
Caduta massi **Danger of falling rocks**
Casello **Toll gate**
Dare la precedenza **Give way**
Deviazione **Diversion**
Divieto di campeggio **No camping allowed**
Divieto di sosta/Sosta vietata **No parking**
Divieto di passaggio/Senso vietato **No entry**
Dogana **Customs**

Entrata **Entrance**
Galleria **Tunnel**
Guasto **Out of order** (e.g. phone box)
Incrocio **Crossroads**
Limite di velocità **Speed limit**
Non toccare **Don't touch**
Passaggio a livello **Railway crossing**
Parcheggio **Parking**
Pedaggio **Toll road**
Pericolo **Danger**
Pronto Soccorso **First aid**
Rallentare **Slow down**
Rimozione forzata **Parked cars will be towed away**
Semaforo **Traffic lights**
Senso unico **One way street**

Sentiero **Footpath**
Solo uscita **No entry**
Strada interrotta **Road blocked**
Strada chiusa **Road closed**
Strada senza uscita/Vicolo cieco **Dead end**
Tangenziale **Ring road/bypass**
Tenersi in corsa **Keep in lane**
Traffico di transito **Through traffic**
Uscita **Exit**
Uscita (autocarri) **Exit for lorries**
Vietato il sorpasso **No overtaking**
Vietato il transito **No thoroughfare**

My car has broken down *La macchina è guasta*
How long will it take to repair? *Quanto tempo ci vorrà per la riparazione?*
The engine is overheating *Il motore si scalda*
Can you check the ...? *Può controllare ...?*
There's something wrong (with/in the) ... *C'è un difetto (nel/nella/nei/nelle) ...*
... **accelerator** *l'acceleratore*
... **brakes** *i freni*
... **engine** *il motore*
... **exhaust** *lo scarico/ scappamento*
... **fanbelt** *la cinghia del ventilatore*
... **gearbox** *la scattola del cambio*
... **headlights** *le luci*
... **radiator** *il radiatore*
... **sparking plugs** *le candele*
... **tyre(s)** *la gomma (le gomme)*
... **windscreen** *il parabrezza*

Health

Is there a chemist's nearby? *C'è una farmacia qui vicino?*
Which chemist is open at night? *Quale farmacia fa il turno di notte?*
I don't feel well *Non mi sento bene*
I feel ill *Sto male/Mi sento male*
Where does it hurt? *Dove Le fa male?*
It hurts here *Ho dolore qui*
I suffer from ... *Soffro di ...*
I have a headache *Ho mal di testa*
I have a sore throat *Ho mal di gola*
I have a stomach ache *Ho mal di pancia*
Have you got something for air sickness? *Ha/Avete qualcosa contro il mal d'aria?*
Have you got something for sea sickness? *Ha/Avete qualcosa contro il mal di mare?*
antiseptic cream *la crema antisettica*
sunburn *lo scottato del sole*
sunburn cream *la crema antisolare*

sticking plaster *il cerotto*
tissues *i fazzoletti di carta*
toothpaste *il dentifricio*
upset stomach pills *le pillole anti-coliche*
insect repellent *l'insettifugo*
mosquitoes *le zanzare*
wasps *le vespe*

Emergencies

Help! *Aiuto!*
Stop! *Fermate!*
I've had an accident *Ho avuto un incidente*
Watch out! *Attenzione!*
Call a doctor *Per favore, chiama un medico*
Call an ambulance *Chiama un'ambulanza*
Call the police *Chiama la Polizia/i Carabinieri*
Call the fire brigade *Chiama i pompieri*
Where is the telephone? *Dov'è il telefono?*
Where is the nearest hospital? *Dov'è l'ospedale più vicino?*
I would like to report a theft *Voglio denunciare un furto*
Thank you very much for your help *Grazie dell'aiuto*

Further Reading

General

For general information about Italy, you should consult the Italian State Tourist Office's *Italy Traveller's Handbook*, which is updated yearly.

Italian Touring Club regional guides and maps are available from **Stanfords**, Long Acre, London WC2E 9LP, tel: 0171-836 1321. An excellent selection of books and maps on Italy is available from **The Travel Bookshop** at 13 Blenheim Crescent, London W11 2EE, tel: 0171-229 5260. Both of these shops can handle orders placed over the phone.

Art and History

The Architecture of the Italian Renaissance, by Peter Murray. Thames and Hudson.
Autobiography, by Benvenuto Cellini. Penguin Classics.
A Concise Encyclopedia of the Italian Renaissance, edited by J.R. Hale. Thames and Hudson.
The Civilization of the Renaissance in Italy, by Jacob Burckhardt. Phaidon Press.
Etruscan Places, by D.H. Lawrence. Olive Press.
The Florentine Renaissance and *The Flowering of the Renaissance* by Vincent Cronin. Fontana.
The High Renaissance and *The Late Renaissance and Mannerism*, by Linda Murray. Thames and Hudson.
The Italian Painters of the Renaissance, by Bernard Berenson. Phaidon Press.
The Italian World, by John Julius Norwich. Thames and Hudson.
Lives of the Artists, vols. 1 & 2, by Giorgio Vasari. Penguin Classics.

Machiavelli, by Anglo Sydney. Paladin.
The Merchant of Prato, by Iris Origo. Penguin.
Painter's Florence, by Barbara Whelpton Johnson.
The Rise and Fall of the House of Medici, by Christopher Hibbert. Penguin.
Siena: A City and its History, by Judith Hook. Hamish Hamilton.

Travel Companions

A Room with a View, by E.M. Forster. Penguin.
D.H. Lawrence and Italy, by D.H. Lawrence. Penguin.
Italians, by David Willey. BBC Publications.
The Italians, by Luigi Barzini. Hamish Hamilton.
Italian Hours, by Henry James. Century Hutchinson.
Love and War in the Apennines, by Eric Newby. Picador.
The Love of Italy, by Jonathan Keates. Octopus.
Pictures from Italy, by Charles Dickens. Granville Publishing.
The Stones of Florence, by Mary McCarthy. Penguin.

Specifically on Tuscany
Companion Guide to Tuscany, by Archibald Lyall. Collins.
Florence Explored, by Rupert Scott. The Bodley Head.

A Guide to Tuscany, by James Bentley. Penguin.
Traveller's Guide to Elba, by Christopher Serpell and Jane Serpell. Jonathan Cape.
Tuscany, an Anthology, by Laura Raison. Cadogan Books.
The Villas of Tuscany, by Harold Acton. Thames and Hudson.

The following are in Italian:
Domenica Dove (itineraries in Tuscany), by Giorgo Battini. Bonechi Editore.
Guerra in Val d'Orcia (an account of the war in Tuscany), by Iris Origo. Bompiani.
Le Più Belle Passeggiate nella Nostra Terra (walks in Tuscany), by *La Nazione.*

Other Insight Guides

Apa Publications has a comprehensive selection of books covering Italy.

Insight Guides to *Italy, Florence, Rome, Bay of Naples, Venice,*

Umbria, South Tyrol, Sardinia and *Sicily*
Thoroughly updated and expanded, the best-selling *Insight Guide: Rome* lifts the lid on Italy's capital.

Insight Pocket Guides to *Tuscany, Florence, Milan, Rome, Venice, Sardinia* and *Sicily.*

Insight Pocket Guide: Florence provides tailor-made tours of Italy's art capital. Perfect for a short break. Includes a full-size pull-out map.

Insight Compact Guide Venice is excellent for practical on-the-spot information.

ART & PHOTO CREDITS

Maps Polyglott Kartographie
Berndtson & Berndtson Publications
Cartographic Editor **Zoë Goodwin**
Production **Stuart A. Everitt**
Design Consultants
Klaus Geisler, Graham Mitchener
Picture Research **Hilary Genin**

Index

Numbers in italics refer to photographs

n

o

p

The World of Insight Guides

400 books in three complementary series cover every major destination in every continent.

The Insight Approach

The book you are holding is part of the world's largest range of guidebooks. Its purpose is to help you have the most valuable travel experience possible, and we try to achieve this by providing not only information about countries, regions and cities but also genuine insight into their history, culture, institutions and people.

Since the first Insight Guide – to Bali – was published in 1970, the series has been dedicated to the proposition that, with insight into a country's people and culture, visitors can both enhance their own experience and be accepted more easily by their hosts. Now, in a world where ethnic hostilities and nationalist conflicts are all too common, such attempts to increase understanding between peoples are more important than ever.

Insight Guides:
Essentials for understanding
Because a nation's past holds the key to its present, each Insight Guide kicks off with lively history chapters. These are followed by magazine-style essays on culture and daily life. This essential background information gives readers the necessary context for using the main Places section, with its comprehensive run-down on things worth seeing and doing.

Finally, a listings section contains all the information you'll need on travel, hotels, restaurants and opening times.

As far as possible, we rely on local writers and specialists to ensure that information is authoritative. The pictures, for which Insight Guides have become so celebrated, are just as important. Our photojournalistic approach aims not only to illustrate a destination but also to communicate visually and directly to readers life as it is lived by the locals. The series has grown to almost 200 titles.

Compact Guides:
The "great little guides"
As invaluable as such background information is, it isn't always fun to carry an Insight Guide through a crowded souk or up a church tower. Could we, readers asked, distil the key reference material into a slim volume for on-the-spot use?

Our response was to design Compact Guides as an entirely new series, with original text carefully cross-referenced to detailed maps and more than 200 photographs. In essence, they're miniature encyclopedias, concise and comprehensive, displaying reliable and up-to-date information in an accessible way. There are almost 100 titles.

Pocket Guides:
A local host in book form
However wide-ranging the information in a book, human beings still value the personal touch. Our editors are often asked the same questions. Where do *you* go to eat? What do *you* think is the best beach? What would *you* recommend if I have only three days? We invited our local correspondents to act as "substitute hosts" by revealing their preferred walks and trips, listing the restaurants they go to and structuring a visit into a series of timed itineraries.

The result: our Pocket Guides, complete with full-size fold-out maps. These 100-plus titles help readers plan a trip precisely, particularly if their time is short.

Exploring with Insight:
A valuable travel experience
In conjunction with co-publishers all over the world, we print in up to 10 languages, from German to Chinese, from Danish to Russian. But our aim remains simple: to enhance your travel experience by combining our expertise in guidebook publishing with the on-the-spot knowledge of our correspondents.

" I was first drawn to the Insight Guides by the excellent "Nepal" volume. I can think of no book which so effectively captures the essence of a country. Out of these pages leaped the Nepal I know – the captivating charm of a people and their culture. I've since discovered and enjoyed the entire Insight Guide series. Each volume deals with a country in the same sensitive depth, which is nowhere more evident than in the superb photography. "

Sir Edmund Hillary

zi

...........by Michel-
...........18) (**A**); Tabernacle by da
...ttignano (1416) (**B**); *Annunciation* by
Filippo Lippi (c.1440) (**D**); Pulpits by
Donatello with frieze of the Passion
(c.1460) (**E/F**); Reading Room,
designed largely by Michelangelo (**H**).
Tombs & Memorials: memorial slab to
Cosimo the Elder; Donatello's tomb
below (**C**); tomb of Piero and Giovanni
de' Medici by Verrocchio (1469–72)
(**G**); tombs of Giuliano and Lorenzo de'
Medici (**I**); monument to Lorenzo and
Giuliano de' Medici, inc. *Madonna and
Child* by Michelangelo (**J**).

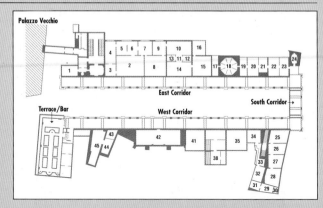

Palazzo Vecchio

East Corridor

South Corridor →

Terrace/Bar

West Corridor

Duomo (Santa Maria del Fiore)

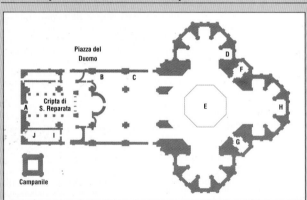

Piazza del
Duomo

Cripta di
S. Reparata

Campanile

Frescoes/Works of Art: astronomical
clock, with face painted by Paolo
Uccello (1443) (**A**); *Dante Explains the
Divine Comedy* by di Michelino (1465)
(**C**); *Pietà* by Michelangelo (not the
original) (**D**); best view of the *Last
Judgement* fresco in cupola by Giorgio
Vasari (1570s) (**E**); lunettes by Luca
della Robbia (**F /G**); main altar with
bronze shrine by Lorenzo Ghiberti
(1432–42) (**H**).
Memorials: memorial to soldier of
fortune (*condottiere*) John Hawkwood
by Paolo Uccello (1436) (**B**); bust of
Giotto (1490) (**I**); bust of Brunelleschi
by Andrea Cavalcanti (1447) (**J**).

Church of San Lorenzo

Highlights of the Uffizi (listed by
room no.): *Maestàs* by Cimabue,
Giotto & Duccio (**2**); *Annunciation*
by Simone Martini, 1333 (**3**);
Federico da Montefeltro by Piero
della Francesca, c.1460 (**7**); *Battle
of San Romano* by Paolo Uccello,
1456 (**7**); works by Botticelli,
including *Primavera* and *Birth of
Venus* (**10–14**); *Adoration of the
Magi* by Leonardo da Vinci, 1481
(**15**); *Doni Tondo* by Michelangelo
(**25**); *Madonna of the Goldfinch*
and *Portrait of Leo X* by Raphael
(**26**); *Venus of Urbino* by Titian
(**28**); *Madonna of the Long Neck*,
c.1535 by Parmigianino (**29**);
Young Bacchus by Caravaggio (**43**).

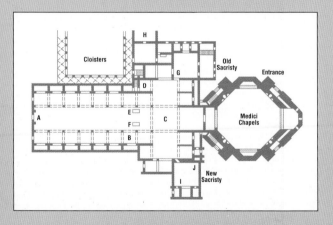

Cloisters

Old
Sacristy

Entrance

Medici
Chapels

New
Sacristy